THE HEART AND THE ABYSS

Preventing Abortion

Ward Biemans SJ

Connor Court Publishing

Published in 2016 by Connor Court Publishing Pty Ltd

Copyright © Ward Biemans S.J.

All rights reserved. No part of this book may be reproduced or transmitted in any form or by any means, electronic or mechanical, including photocopying, recording or by any information storage and retrieval system, without prior permission in writing from the publisher.

Connor Court Publishing Pty Ltd
PO Box 224W
Ballarat VIC 3350
sales@connorcourt.com
www.connorcourt.com

ISBN: 978-1-925138-96-2

Front cover photo: Christianne Chin A Paw

Cover design by Maria Giordano

Printed in Australia

Imprimatur: 10 December 2015
Mgr. Dr. Jozef Marianus Punt, Bishop of Haarlem-Amsterdam

"If you gaze for long into an abyss, the abyss gazes back into you."

Friedrich Nietzsche – *Beyond Good and Evil*

CONTENTS

Abbreviations 9
Acknowledgements 10
Preface 11
Introduction 13

Chapter 1: The abortion legislation in the United Kingdom and the Netherlands 29
1.1 The British Abortion Act 30
1.1.1 The history of the Abortion Act 30
1.1.2 Political attempts to change the abortion legislation
1.2 The Dutch Termination of Pregnancy Act 34
1.2.1 Objective 1: "Guaranteeing a decision-making process with all due care, as well as prevention by means of education and aftercare" 41
1.2.2 Objective 2: "Guaranteeing the quality of the medical intervention" 45
1.2.3 Objective 3: "The prevention of commercial practices" 48
1.3 A comparison between the abortion legislation in the U.K. and the Netherlands 49
1.4 Consequences of the legal abortion praxis in the U.K. and the Netherlands 50
1.4.1 Statistical data on abortion in the U.K. 51
1.4.1.1 England and Wales 52
1.4.1.2 Scotland 52
1.4.1.3 Northern Ireland 53
1.4.1.4 Some characteristics of abortion clients in the U.K. 53
1.4.2 Statistical data on abortion in the Netherlands 56
1.4.2.1 Some characteristics of abortion clients in the Netherlands 57
1.4.3 Evaluation of the differences in abortion numbers in the United Kingdom and the Netherlands 60
1.4.3.1 Demographical developments in the U.K. and the Netherlands 65
1.4.3.2 Abortion and ethnicity 67
1.4.3.3 The legalization of abortion has contributed to an increased demand 68
1.5 Inconsistencies between legal prescriptions and current abortion praxis U.K. and the Netherlands 71
1.5.1 The grounds for abortion in the U.K. 71
1.5.2 Inconsistencies in the Dutch implementation of the Termination of Pregnancy Act 74
1.6 The medicalization of abortion 79

Chapter 2: Human autonomy and procured abortion 83
2.1 Pleading for women's autonomy: abortion and the three feminist waves in the U.K. and the Netherlands 83
2.1.1 The first feminist wave 84
2.1.2 Between the Wars 85
2.1.3 The second feminist wave 85
2.1.4 The U.K.: a shift in the public opinion regarding abortion 87

2.1.5 The Netherlands: a shift in the way of looking at early human life........................89
2.1.6 The third feminist wave..90
2.2 The argument of a woman's autonomy in relation to abortion................................93
2.2.1 Philosophical views on human autonomy..94
2.2.2 The autonomy principle according to Kant..94
2.2.3 Applying Kantian ethics to the issue of abortion..97
2.2.4 The capabilities approach, abortion and human dignity: Martha Nussbaum.........99
2.2.5 Voluntary and involuntary abortion...102
2.2.6 Abortion and the problem of empiricism...105
2.2.7 A woman's autonomy used as an argument for legalizing abortion....................107
2.3 Human conscience and human autonomy..109
2.3.1 Human conscience and the sources of morality...111
2.3.2 Abortion and conscientious objections..113

Chapter 3: Mental and physical risks and effects of induced abortion on women 115
3.1 Psychological risks and effects after abortion...116
3.1.1 Methodological issues...117
3.1.2 Positive psychological effects of abortion..120
3.1.3 Negative psychological effects of abortion..124
3.1.3.1 Quantitative studies..125
3.1.3.2 Qualitative studies..131
3.1.3.3 Qualitative long-term studies...134
3.1.4 Risk factors for women's mental health...136
3.1.5 Mental health effects on men after abortion..137
3.1.6 Recommendations for future research...139
3.2 Physical risks and effects of induced abortion on women.....................................140
3.2.1 Abortion and subsequent preterm birth...140
3.2.2 The association between abortion and breast cancer...144
3.2.3 The association between abortion and subsequent maternal mortality...............151
3.2.4 Complications after induced abortion..153
3.3 Pregnancy or abortion? Psychological and relational factors................................153
3.3.1 The reasons women give for requesting an abortion..154
3.3.1.1 The results of the evaluation of the Dutch abortion practice reviewed............155
3.3.1.2 Doubting the decision to abort..160
3.3.2 Pregnancy or abortion: relational factors...162
3.3.2.1 Maternal-foetal attachment...162
3.3.2.2 Ambivalence because of memories of the woman's own childhood................163
3.3.2.3 Ambivalence in the relationship with the partner..166
3.3.2.4 Pregnancy and domestic violence...171
3.3.3 The quality of the relationship after abortion...172
3.4 The abortion legislation in the U.K. and the Netherlands does not guarantee women's autonomy..174

Chapter 4: The human embryo, its rights and its dignity..................177
4.1 Embryonic and foetal development..................180
4.2 The right to life and the dignity of the unborn child in international documents and in European jurisprudence..................187
4.2.1 The European Convention of Human Rights..................189
4.2.2 The right to life in the case of Vo versus France..................194
4.2.3 The legal recognition of the dignity of the human embryo within the European context..................197
4.3 The status of the human embryo..................199
4.3.1 The status of the early human embryo..................200
4.3.1.1 Monozygotic twinning..................203
4.3.1.2 Ensoulment: delayed or immediately at fertilisation?..................205
4.3.1.3 Spontaneous abortions..................209
4.3.2 The personhood of the embryo..................210
4.3.2.1 The active, specifiable potentiality of the human embryo..................212
4.3.2.2 The difference between 'something' and 'someone'..................215

Chapter 5: Towards an authentic and responsible reproductive decision making process..................217
5.1 Various philosophical views on reproductive decision making..................218
5.1.1 The ethical intention in relation to others: Paul Ricoeur..................219
5.1.2 Rational choice theory on fertility..................226
5.1.3 Consequentialism and abortion..................228
5.1.4 The future of value argument..................228
5.1.5 A bioethical view on human dignity..................231
5.1.6 Contemporary liberal philosophy and abortion: John Rawls..................233
5.1.7 The principle of respect for every basic value in every act..................237
5.1.8 The principle of acts with double effect in relation to abortion..................238
5.2 The medicalization of pregnancy: prenatal diagnosis, foetal treatment and perinatal palliative care..................239
5.3 Parental dilemmas after a diagnosis of a serious impairment of the foetus..................245
5.4 An ethical conclusion on procured abortion..................249

Chapter 6: A historical search for a universalization of the ethics of abortion 253
6.1 Abortion in the teaching of the Catholic Church..................256
6.1.1 Sacred Scripture, early Christianity and the Middle Ages..................257
6.1.1.1 The Old Testament..................257
6.1.1.2 Early Christianity..................262
6.1.1.3 The Middle Ages..................268
6.1.3 The twentieth and twenty-first century..................273
6.1.3.1 The rise and decline of youth care, the care for unmarried mothers and their children in Catholic institutions in the twentieth century..................274
6.1.3.2 The Second Vatican Council and beyond..................276
6.1.4 The Magisterium's reaction to prenatal diagnosis..................286

6.1.5 Abortion in relation to the Magisterial teaching of family values and virtues......288
6.1.6 Abortion and canon law..291
6.2 The Christian interpretation of human conscience throughout the centuries...........294

Chapter 7: Abortion prevention, sex education, counselling and pastoral care..299
7.1 Alternatives to abortion in the U.K. and the Netherlands..300
7.1.1 Personal assistance and financial support after an unintended pregnancy in the U.K..300
7.1.2 Personal assistance and financial support after an unintended pregnancy in the Netherlands..302
7.1.3 Adoption and foster care...304
7.2 Sex and Relationships Education (SRE) in the U.K. and the Netherlands..............306
7.3 Counselling and pastoral care in case of unintended pregnancy..............................310
7.3.1 Preventive counselling..311
7.3.2 Informational aspects of guidance..313
7.3.3 Emotional aspects of guidance...314
7.3.4 Spiritual aspects of guidance..315
7.3.5 Several cases..316
7.4 Counselling after prenatal diagnosis..318
7.5 Spiritual and pastoral care after prenatal diagnosis...321
7.6 Abortion, counselling and virtue ethics...325
7.7 Abortion prevention and the proof of fatherhood..329
7.8 Counselling and pastoral care after abortion...330

Chapter 8: Preventing abortion..337

Summary in Dutch - Samenvatting in het Nederlands......................................342
Bibliography..357
Index...385

Abbreviations

AAS	Acta Apostolica Sedis
ALRA	Abortion Law Reform Association
APA TFMHA	American Psychological Association, Task Force on Mental Health and Abortion
BMJ	British Medical Journal
CCC	Catechism of the Catholic Church
CSSR	Congregation of the Most Holy Redeemer
DPP	Director of Public Prosecutions
DSM	Diagnostic and Statistical Manual of Mental Disorders
EPIC	European Prospective Investigation into Cancer and nutrition
EPICure	Population based studies of survival and later health status in extremely premature infants
Eurostat	European Union Institute for Statistical research
FSE	Franciscan Sisters of the Eucharist
GP	General Practitioner
MD	Medical Doctor
MP	Member of Parliament
NGvA	Dutch Association of Abortion Specialists
NHS	National Health Service
OFM	Order of Friars Minor (Franciscans)
OP	Order of Preachers (Dominicans)
OSA	Order of Saint Augustine
OSB	Order of Saint Benedict
PTSD	Post-Traumatic Stress Disorder
RCOG	Royal College of Obstetricians and Gynaecologists
RIVM	National Institute for Public Health and the Environment
RU486	Mifepristone, abortion pill
SDB	Salesians of Don Bosco
SJ	Society of Jesus (Jesuits)
SRE	Sex and Relationships Education
ST	Summa Theologica
STI	Sexually Transmitted Infection
UNICEF	United Nations Children's Fund
VBOK	Association for the Protection of the Unborn Child
WAZ	Termination of Pregnancy Act
WPF	World Population Foundation

Acknowledgements

Several persons have helped me with the realization of this book. I want to express my gratitude to David Paton from the Nottingham University Business School, Josephine Quintavalle from the 'One of us' Federation, Helen Watt from the Anscombe Bioethics Centre, Mechteld Visser from the University of Amsterdam and Bea Zonneveld from Siriz. I thank the editors of the *Manual of Catholic Medical Ethics, Responsible Healthcare from a Catholic Perspective* (Ballarat, 2014), Willem Cardinal Eijk, Lambert Hendriks, Janthony Raymakers and John Fleming, for which I contributed a brief chapter on procured abortion.

A special word of thanks to Anne Criado, for reading the entire manuscript and suggesting many corrections. Thanks to Rick Ganz SJ, Steven van der Grinten SJ and Charlie Moutenot SJ for their encouragement. Finally, I want to thank Mariéle Wulf from the Tilburg School of Catholic Theology in the Netherlands, for giving many valuable commentaries for this work.

Preface

At the heart of the abortion debate is a seemingly simple proposition: given the basic biology that the fertilised human egg is scientifically speaking a living human being the orthodox Catholic understanding that the ethical rule against killing should apply before as well as after birth seems self-evident. Understandably, however, the abortion debate in practice becomes far more complex. Legalising abortion has implications far beyond the unborn baby: for the mother who have to face the agonising choice of whether or not to terminate the life of her developing baby, for the father who may have no legal role in the decision but whose influence, for good or ill, is hard to ignore, for doctors who face pressure to collaborate in the taking of life itself and for a society which increasingly sees abortion as a necessary consequence of the desire to separate the sexual act from reproduction.

Given this complexity, it is not enough for those who wish to promote the Gospel of Life within the Church to restrict themselves to ethics or moral theology. Rather, it is necessary to take seriously the insights provided by medicine and the broad range of social sciences. Examples of such an integrated approach are all too rare and this is precisely why I was so pleased to read Ward Biemans' work presented in this volume. Biemans' text is particularly welcome given how successfully he has drawn together so many different academic perspectives.

The context for Biemans' work is the development of law and practice on abortion in the United Kingdom and The Netherlands. The choice of these two countries is apposite. The UK (with the exception of Northern Ireland) was one of the earliest western countries to legalise abortion and the UK law provided a template for many other countries with similar legal frameworks, most particularly across the Commonwealth. Whether or not the reality matches the theory, the Netherlands has come to be seen as the ultimate liberal country in which abortion is (relatively) rare but almost always legal. Thankfully, the Western European context provides a basis for a much more complete discussion of the issues and arguments surrounding abortion which will be of immense value right across the world.

Biemans draws together insights from the fields of medicine, economics, psychology, politics, law, theology and ethics. He engages effectively with the most recent empirical work on the practical impact of abortion law and uses this to provide fresh insight into the key ethical debates. Integrating such disparate fields is no easy task and it is to his great credit that he has managed to find a balance between rigor and accessibility which will enable this work to be of use to a broad range of users. The importance of caring for both the mother and baby have been understood and put into practice by the pro-life movement for many years, as has the recognition that women need care and reconciliation rather than condemnation after abortion. This understanding is central to Biemans' work, as is his conclusion that rights and needs of the mother and the unborn baby are not only of paramount importance but complementary to each other rather than in opposition.

Given Biemans' understanding of theology and Church history, this volume will surely become a standard source of reference within Catholic institutions. However, I am confident its reach will be much greater than that. The approach is balanced and scholarly, but it is hard for the reader to avoid the conclusion that the right to life of the unborn, the rights of women and the social consequences of abortion should not be seen as standing in opposition to each other and requiring of compromise. Rather, laws which protect the vulnerable unborn, also protect mothers and society as a whole. Of course this has been the wisdom of the Catholic Church for centuries, but it is wonderful to see such a clear-sighted presentation of the logic and evidence in their entirety.

Professor David Paton
Chair of Industrial Economics
Nottingham University Business School
Jubilee Campus
Nottingham NG8 1BB
United Kingdom
David.Paton@nottingham.ac.uk
October 2015

Introduction

In this research, the focus is on two case studies: the legislation and practice regarding procured – or, in medical terms, induced – abortion in the United Kingdom (U.K.) and the Netherlands.[1] Between 1970 and 2013, the number of procured abortions among British women in their fertile age has more than doubled.[2] According to the Royal College of Obstetricians and Gynaecologists (RCOG), at least one third of British women will have one or more procured abortions during their years of fertility.[3] In the Netherlands, legalisation only took place in 1981, after lengthy political debates, but especially between 1990 and 2013 the number of abortions has also risen considerably.[4] About one fourth of Dutch women decides to have an abortion at some stage during their fertile years.[5] The increase in abortion numbers is a lamentable situation, as would be agreed upon by all parties in the abortion debate. At the same time, psychological and epidemiological research shows that circa 20% of all women who have had a procured abortion, suffer from long-term negative mental health problems.[6] This figure entails some 42,000 British women and 6,000 Dutch women each year.

At the time of the legalization of abortion in the Western world, only a few methodologically sound studies on the psychological risks and effects of abortion had appeared.[7] Since then, much psychological and epidemiological research has been undertaken in relation to the consequences of procured abortion for women's mental and physical health. The structure of this study is based on a moral philosophical framework developed by Paul

---

[1] The official Latin medical terminology for legalised procured abortion is *abortus provocatus lege artis*.
[2] Cf. part 1.4.1.
[3] Royal College of Obstetricians and Gynaecologists (RCOG), *The Care of Women Requesting Induced Abortion. Evidence-based Clinical Guideline Number 7*, London, 2011, p. 1.
[4] Cf. part 1.4.2.
[5] M.R.M. Visser, A.J.G.M. Janssen, M. Enschedé, A.F.M.N. Willems, Th.A.M. te Braake, K. Harmsen, E.M.A. Smets, J.C.J.M. de Haes and J.K.M. Gevers, as commissioned by ZonMw Consultancy: *Evaluatie Wet afbreking zwangerschap*. Amsterdam, 2005, p. 59.
[6] Cf. chapter 3.
[7] Germain Grisez, *Abortion. The Myths, the Realities and the Arguments*. New York and Cleveland, 1970, p. 84.

Ricoeur, which makes it possible to integrate empirical, social-scientific data with ethical and theological presuppositions. In his essay "The problem of the foundation of moral philosophy", Paul Ricoeur offered a philosophical analysis, which will be helpful for such an integration.[8] His theoretical model has made it possible to establish passageways between historical theology and the social and human sciences.[9] It also serves as a framework from which recommendations can be made for the counselling and pastoral care of women - and if possible, their partners - after the discovery of an unintended pregnancy.

Paul Ricoeur's research has been recognised as a demonstration of the fruitful relation between philosophy and theology, between faith and culture.[10] Towards the end of his long academic career, Ricoeur has written several essays on ethics in general and on medical ethics in particular. His book *Oneself as another* offers an extended discussion on the moral and ethical dimension of selfhood and personal identity.[11] As a starting point for this discussion, he defines an "ethical intention" as "aiming at the 'good life' with and for others, in just institutions".[12] From the outset of his work, he suggests that the selfhood of oneself implies otherness to such an intimate degree that one cannot be thought of without the other.[13] In the course of this study it will be elaborated what this viewpoint implies for the decision-making process after the discovery of an unintended pregnancy. The legislators in the U.K. and the Netherlands have created a legal possibility

---

8 Paul Ricoeur, "The problem of the foundation of moral philosophy" Originally published as *Le problème du fondement de la morale,* in: *Sapienza. Rivista internazionale di filosofia e di teologia,* 1975, 28, 3, pp. 313-337, translated into English by David Pellauer, in: *Philosophy Today,* 1978, 22, 3, pp. 175-192; translated into Dutch by Hendrik Opdebeeck, *Het probleem van de grondslagen van de moraal.* Kampen, 1995.

9 Cf. Anne Fortin-Melkevik, "Methods in Theology: Interdisciplinary Thought in Theology", *Concilium,* 1994, 6, pp. 101-111, here p. 107.

10 In 2003, Paul Ricoeur received the 'International Paul VI Award' from Pope John Paul II, conferred every five years to a personality or institution distinguished in a significant way in the field of the culture of religious inspiration. Cf. John Paul II, *Address to the participants of the International Paul VI Award ceremony.* Vatican, 2003.

11 Paul Ricoeur, *Oneself as another.* Originally published as *Soi-même comme un autre* [1990]; translated by Kathleen Blamey, Chicago, 1992, in particular the chapters 7, 8 and 9, pp. 140-296.

12 Ibid., p. 172.

13 Ibid., p. 3.

of procured abortion, an act in which the life of another human being is always directly at stake.[14]

A few years after *Oneself as another*, Ricoeur shows his interests in applied ethics, with an essay on medical practice.[15] In this essay, he mentions three precepts of "practical wisdom" in relation to medical judgment. The first precept regards singularity, which implies that one person cannot be substituted for another.[16] Each person must be treated as a unique individual. As regards this precept, immediately the question needs to be asked whether procured abortion is a medical act which is essentially different from most other medical interventions, because it does not only involve the life and health of a woman, but it involves the life of another unique human being in its embryonic stage.

Ricoeur's second precept for prudent medical judgment underscores the indivisibility of each person.[17] This precept is opposed to a fragmentation of the biological, psychological and the social dimension of each person's existence. Often within the abortion praxis, there is the risk that psychological and social dimensions of the woman's existence disappear from the physician's focus of attention, as a result of a medicalization of abortion and of pregnancy as such. Medicalization has been described by Peter Conrad as the "process by which nonmedical problems become defined and treated as medical problems, usually in terms of illnesses or disorders".[18] An abortion clinic or hospital may adopt a medical and procedural approach in the encounter with a woman who has an unintended pregnancy, while little attention is paid to underlying problems, which are often of a relational or psychological nature.[19] In this study, research to relationship problems before and after abortion and psychological research will receive much attention. It will be shown that often, relationship problems are the most important underlying reason for women to choose for an abortion.

---

14 Ricoeur speaks of the issue of abortion in *Oneself as another* (pp. 270-271). His view will be discussed in chapter 5.
15 Paul Ricoeur, The Three Levels of Medical Judgment. In: Idem, *Reflections on The Just*. [2001] Translated by David Pellauer, Chicago, 2007, pp. 198-212.
16 Ibid., p. 202.
17 Ibid.
18 Peter Conrad, "Medicalization and Social Control", *Annual Review of Sociology*, 1992, 18, pp. 209-232.
19 Cf. chapter 3.

At first, however, it is necessary to point out what according to Ricoeur seems to constitute an ethical intention as such. Therefore, a more detailed discussion of his essay on the foundation of moral philosophy will follow, thus providing the philosophical framework for this study.

Ricoeur starts his inquiry by exploring the notion of freedom as the principle source of ethics. Freedom, however, is always limited because human existence is an embodied existence. Our personal freedom is limited because of an inevitable difference between our ideals and desires and the realization of these ideals and desires in real life.

This limitation of personal freedom can be clearly encountered in decision making processes after the discovery of an unintended pregnancy. Such a decision making process is both delicate and complex. It is delicate because it involves the most intimate level of decision making, a decision which will always have irrevocable consequences. It is complex because the decision the woman makes is always embedded in a context with other people, her partner first of all, but also her doctor and his or her assistants, the family, other advisers and politicians who have passed legislation. Before she makes a choice, the decision is already situated in certain circumstances, motivated by certain reasons and grounded by certain explicit or implicit presumptions of what is actually happening inside her: the growth of another human being.

Ricoeur's thought on the idea of freedom shows similarities with the thinking of Immanuel Kant: according to Kant, the objective reality of freedom cannot be proven in any way on the basis of natural laws, nor in any possible experience.[20] From this, the question arises how freedom can be objectified. For Ricoeur, the whole problem of ethics arises from the question: what does it mean for someone to attest to his - or her - freedom? Freedom can only be shown in works in which freedom is objectified. As such, freedom can only attest to itself in its works.[21]

---

20 Immanuel Kant, Grundlegung zur Metaphysik der Sitten, [1785], in: Wilhelm Weischedel, (Ed.), *Immanuel Kant, Werke in sechs Banden*, 2005, IV, BA 114, 115.
21 Ricoeur, P., 1978, op. cit., p. 176.

Human autonomy

In many Western countries, freedom in reproductive choices means that after the discovery of an unintended pregnancy a woman may autonomously choose to legally undergo an abortion or to bring her pregnancy to term. In chapter 1, it will be analysed to what extent the implementation of the abortion legislation in the U.K. and the Netherlands is consistent with the legislator's original intentions in both countries. This will be done by analysing empirical data on the legalised abortion practice and the abortion statistics of the U.K. and the Netherlands. It will be argued that the abortion legislation itself has resulted in a rise in abortion numbers, both in the U.K. and the Netherlands.[22] Besides discussing the existing social scientific evidence, a reconsideration will take place of the ethical aspects of procured abortion. It will be shown that both the British and the Dutch abortion legislation and praxis show various inconsistencies.

Further, the medicalization of pregnancy as such has become apparent as a result of the increasing possibilities of prenatal diagnosis during the past decades. Parents are confronted with moral decisions regarding the life or death of their initially wanted child, when a certain foetal anomaly has been detected. In this regard, it will be critically examined whether or not it could be reasonably expected from parents to take such radical decisions.

As a third precept for prudent medical judgment, Ricoeur mentions the notion of self-esteem, which has to do with the recognition of one's own value.[23] In chapter 2, it will be elaborated in what sense the idea of human autonomy could contribute to a woman's self-esteem as regards reproductive decisions. At the same time, it will be pointed out what problems can result from a too one-sided focus on human autonomy. Procured abortion is a typical example of an action which can cause serious tension between human autonomy and human conscience, because care for a new human life can be considered as a matter of ultimate concern.

In order to get more clarity with regard to the tension between autonomy and conscience, the historical roots in feminist thought regarding women's autonomy in reproductive matters will be investigated in chapter 2. It will be shown that for authors who are considered representative for the first

---

22 Cf. part 1.4.3.3.
23 Ricoeur, P., 2007, op. cit., p. 202.

feminist wave in the U.K. and the Netherlands, legal abortion was far from obvious. During the third feminist wave, several authors elaborated a concept of relational autonomy, rather than interpreting autonomy in a strictly individualistic manner. Other contemporary philosophers such as David Velleman and Jennifer Denbow seek to apply Kantian ethics in their approach to human autonomy and its limitations in choices regarding life or death.[24] Denbow argues that a woman's autonomy could be at risk because the available option of legal abortion weakens her negotiating position compared to her partner. The question will be raised how ethical theories as have been developed by Immanuel Kant, Martha Nussbaum and Judith Jarvis Thompson are doing justice to finding the balance between autonomous choice and respect for unborn human life. Often the presupposed autonomy of a woman with an unintended pregnancy is at threat because of underlying relationship problems.

In chapter 3 it will be analysed with the help of social scientific and epidemiological research what evidence has been presented which points at negative consequences of induced abortion for women's mental and physical health.[25] Scientific evidence as well as controversies within the international fields of empirical research published between 1985 and 2015 on the physical and mental consequences of induced abortion will be reviewed. Recent research outcomes within these fields evoke new questions about induced abortion. By analysing these outcomes, we will get a clearer picture of the short term and long term consequences of the abortion praxis for women and indirectly for men and for their mutual relationships, as well as on the methodological difficulties in this area of research.

---

24 J. David Velleman, "Against the Right to Die", originally published in: *Journal of Medicine & Philosophy*, 1992, 17, 6, pp. 665-681, revised in 2004; Jennifer Denbow, "Abortion: When Choice and Autonomy Conflict", *Berkeley Journal of Gender, Law and Justice*, 2005, pp. 216-228.

25 The term 'induced abortion' is often used in medical and psychological literature, in order to distinguish this from spontaneous abortion. Theologians often speak of 'procured abortion'. In this study I will use both terms, induced and procured abortion, for any abortion that is planned and executed.

The other

As a second step in his construction of an ethical theory, Ricoeur introduces the idea of the second person as well as the idea of freedom which is in this second person.[26] One really enters into the problem of morality if one posits freedom in this second person as an acknowledgment that *my* freedom is to want the freedom of the other. If one would doubt one's own freedom, because one feels forced to take a decision because of all kinds of circumstances, then it would also become difficult to believe in the freedom of the other person and to help him or her to become free. Ricoeur dwells on Edmund Husserl's *Fifth Cartesian Meditation*, which states that if I do not know what it means to be an "I", an "*ego*", the problem of a second person, an "*alter ego*", could not be understood.[27] Husserl himself expresses it like this: "In any case then, within myself, within the limits of my transcendentally reduced pure conscious life, I *experience* the world (including others) – and, according to its experiential sense, not as (so to speak) my *private* synthetic formation but as other than mine alone [*mir fremde*], as an *intersubjective* world, actually there for everyone, accessible in respect of its objects to everyone."[28] According to Ricoeur, ethics in general arises from the redoubled task of making the freedom of the other person come to pass as similar as my own, because the other is like me (*mon semblable*).[29]

The third step in Ricoeur's approach to the problem of the foundations of morality concerns the mediation by means of what he calls "institution".[30] After the affirmation of the freedom of the first and second person, with this term institution the notion of "ought" is introduced as an anonymous third person, "one", in the sense that "one ought". At the origin of what one expresses in terms of values, norms and laws, something neutral arises, which one encounters as the problem of objectivity in theoretical philosophy. This problem concerns the impossibility of proving that values or virtues have the status of entities. Therefore, every form of freedom

---

26 Ricoeur, P., 1978, op. cit., pp. 178-179.
27 Ibid., p. 178.
28 Edmund Husserl, *Cartesian Meditations. An introduction to phenomenology*. Translated by Dorion Cairns. The Hague, 1960, p. 91.
29 Ricoeur, P., 1978, op. cit., pp. 178-179.
30 Ibid., pp. 179-182.

needs to be mediated in certain institutions, either relational institutions such as the family, or juridical, economic, social and political institutions. This makes it possible to take into account notions as value, norm, law and indeed natural law.[31] These terms need successive clarification in relation to the abortion dilemma.

As soon as one considers procured abortion, several values are at stake. It is obvious that the value of the unborn human life is directly at threat, besides the value of freedom of the persons who are involved in the decision making process. Ricoeur further mentions the value of justice, the institutional instrument which makes it possible that different forms of freedom can coexist. He concludes that, in the end, justice means the affirmation "that you may be free".[32] However, the first possibility for a human being is to exist. According to Mariéle Wulf, in these existential decisions the criterion for ethical behaviour should be the greater possibility.[33] Empirically, it is impossible to demonstrate that a human embryo is not a human being.[34] Therefore, if ethics takes the greater possibility as its starting point, then it should consider the human embryo or foetus as the person it will become in the future: a child, a teenager, an adult.[35] In the course of this study, it will be shown that the recognition of the future value of the embryo is indeed a crucial step in the decision making process after the discovery of an unintended pregnancy.

After the notion of value, Ricoeur introduces the notion of a norm.[36] The idea of a norm introduces an element of division, because it could happen in life that a person's wish is in contradiction with what is generally considered to have more value than this person's wish.

The essential function of norms is to shelter what we have called values from the arbitrariness of each individual human being.[37] Here, Ricoeur

---

31 Ibid., p. 182.
32 Ibid., p. 183.
33 Mariéle Wulf, *Morele denkpatronen. Wetten, waarheid, waardigheid. Handboek moraaltheologie, deel 2. Geschiedenis en methoden van de moraaltheologie.* Almere, 2013 (b), pp. 252-253, 335 and 368; cf. part 6.1.3.2.
34 Cf. part 4.1.
35 Normally, the medical profession speaks of a foetus when the embryo is more than ten weeks old.
36 Ricoeur, P., 1978, op. cit., pp. 184-185.
37 Ibid., p. 185.

affiliates with Georg W.F. Hegel who points out the element of universality in relation to a person's rational will. According to Hegel, freedom is to will something determinate, yet in this determinacy to be by oneself and to revert once more to the universal.[38] Ricoeur distinguishes the term "ethics" as the aim of an accomplished life, from the term "morality" as the articulation of this aim in norms.[39]

The idea of imperative, next in Ricoeur's hermeneutical analysis of the problem of the foundation of morality, adds the element of command to the notion of a norm, either in the form of a command given by a person to oneself or a command given by a certain authority. In the first form the idea of imperative has been recognised throughout the centuries with regard to one's personal conscience. Regarding the second form, the formal system of authority has for instance been described by Max Weber in his sociological theory of motivation, giving examples of authority in the family, in business relations, or in structures of Church and State.[40]

In the previous century, processes of democratisation, emancipation and secularisation have contributed to a much smaller role of authorities in reproductive decision making, be it the authority within the family, the school or the role of State and Church authorities.[41] For instance, Francis Fukuyama describes how in virtually all modernizing societies, the role of the family has diminished in importance, which could not only be seen in the decline in fertility rates, but also in the decline of marriage rates, the increase of divorce rates and the steady growth of the percentage of out-of-wedlock births.[42] Although the process of individualization has led to an increased participation of women on the labour market, a drawback of this development is the increased pressure many young women experience with regard to their reproductive choices.

Following Ricoeur's line of reasoning, in chapters 4 and 5 a transition will be made from values to relevant norms. In chapter 4 the focus of

---

38 Georg W.F. Hegel, "Grundlinien der Philosophie des Rechts", [1821], in: Idem, *Werke 7*. Frankfurt am Main, 1970, § 7, *Zusatz*, p. 57.
39 Ricoeur, P., 1992, op. cit., p. 170.
40 Max Weber, *Wirtschaft und Gesellschaft. Grundrisse der verstehende Soziologie*. Tübingen, 1976.
41 Francis Fukuyama, *The Great Disruption. Human Nature and the Reconstitution of Social Order*. New York, 1999, pp. 36-47; Alexander E.M. van der Does de Willebois, *Het vaderloze tijdperk*. Brugge, 1984, p. 24.
42 Fukuyama, F., op. cit. pp. 36-47.

attention is on the human embryo. First, normal embryonic and foetal development will be sketched. After that, an analysis will be made of the lack of recognition of the right to life of the human embryo in international documents and treaties and in European jurisprudence. Further in this chapter, the main bioethical and moral theological arguments regarding the status of the human embryo will be investigated. The bioethical discussion focuses on the question of whether the embryo needs to be considered as a person with a right to life, and if so, at what moment of its development. Closely related to this discussion is the metaphysical question regarding the ensoulment of the human embryo. Recent theories about monozygotic twinning will be discussed, because these theories try to give an answer to the question of the immediate ensoulment of the embryo at conception.

In chapter 5, philosophical backgrounds will be analysed with regard to the reproductive decision making process. It will be argued that the future value of the embryonic life should be included in this process. In this regard, the term human dignity will be introduced and explained. On the other hand, it will be shown that the rational choice theory on fertility and the utilitarian and consequentialist decision making models are problematic in relation to procured abortion.

As an illustrious example of contemporary liberal philosophy, John Rawls' theory of justice will be discussed. It will be shown that his deliberate avoidance of the use of a metaphysical concept of the human person has direct implications for his ethical view on abortion and embryonic rights. Paul Ricoeur's phenomenological approach will then be applied to the abortion dilemma, because with this approach it is recognised that autonomy cannot go without the solicitude for others. After these philosophical considerations, conclusions are drawn regarding the morality of abortion.

Universality

After having dealt with the notions of value, norm and imperative, Ricoeur then arrives at the idea of law, which adds to the other notions of value, norm and imperative a requirement for universality, a potential universalization.[43] Laws have the scope of universality in order to protect certain values. Similarly to Kant in his theory of maxims, Ricoeur introduces

---

43 Ricoeur, P., 1978, op. cit., pp. 187-189.

two simple questions which could function as a criterion for universality in decision making processes: "Would I want everyone else to do the same?" and "Could my desire serve as a universal law?"[44]

At this point, Ricoeur mentions that an analogy to a law of nature could be justified.[45] He argues that as rational human beings, we want to resolve the division we discover within ourselves as a result of the opposition between on the one hand our desires and values and on the other hand societal norms or universal laws. "We cannot have concepts of action simply juxtaposed to concepts implied by the knowledge of nature. We want to reconcile these two forms of rationality."[46] Therefore, he proposes reflecting on the sort of analogy that may exist between imperatives submitted to a criterion of universality and what we call assertive laws. Ricoeur points out the possibility of whether the idea of a natural law could be used as a limit concept, "the concept where the rational order in which we can place action may receive its model from the order of nature".[47]

Within the areas of philosophy of law and moral philosophy, the various interpretations of the concept of natural law are heavily contested, especially within the Anglo-Saxon tradition.[48] However, in recent years the areas of natural law theory and philosophy of law have had a particularly fruitful encounter in the work of Germain Grisez and John Finnis.[49] For instance, Finnis' theory has been described as "remarkably and distinctively modern, post-Kantian in its individualistic stress on obligation as self-undertaken commitment."[50] According to Grisez, the first principle in natural law, "the good is to be done and pursued; the bad is to be avoided", is in no

---

[44] Ibid., p. 187.
[45] Ibid. The French original speaks of *"la loi de la nature"*. Cf. Paul Ricoeur, "Le problème du fondement de la morale.", *Sapienza. Rivista internazionale di filosofia e di teologia*, 1975, 28, 3, pp. 313-337, here p. 329.
[46] Ricoeur, P., 1978, op. cit., p. 187.
[47] Ibid, p. 188.
[48] Jean-Pierre Wils, "Naturrecht", in: Jean-Pierre Wils and Christoph Hübenthal, *Lexikon der Ethik*, Paderborn, 2006, pp. 273-275.
[49] Knud Haakonssen, "Natural Law", in: Lawrence C. Becker and Charlotte B. Becker (eds.), *Encyclopedia of Ethics*. Second edition, Vol. II, New York and London, 2001, pp. 1205-1212; John Finnis, *Natural Law and Natural Rights*. Second Edition. Oxford, 2011; Germain Grisez, *The Way of the Lord Jesus*, Vol. I, *Christian Moral Principles*, Quincy, Ill., 1983. Cf. parts 5.1.2, 5.1.7 and 5.1.8.
[50] Haakonssen, K., op. cit., p. 1210.

way opposed to human freedom.[51] On the contrary, principles of natural law could serve as a source of a more fundamental valorisation for ethics against voluntarism of the State; historically it has functioned as such.[52]

As a final step in his attempt to offer a foundation for morality, Ricoeur inserts the evangelical perspective in the ethical order.[53] He stresses that the strategic level where the evangelical morality operates is precisely that of the ethical intention, understood in the three modalities of freedom, the freedom of the second person and the mediation through institutions. It could be argued that his approach shows some similarity with a natural law theory as has been developed by Germain Grisez; the two approaches differ, however, in the explicit definition of basic human goods and therefore in the importance given to the object as a source of morality.[54] The decisive character of the object of the human act for moral judgment has also been stressed by Pope John Paul II in his encyclical *Veritatis Splendor*.[55]

Within moral theology, there is a vast amount of literature on procured abortion. Recent publications frequently come from the United States, where abortion has been hotly debated ever since legalization took place. In Europe however the flow of literature on abortion has diminished significantly, more so within moral theology than within moral philosophy. An explanation for this might be that both the moral theological and the societal positions concerning procured abortion seem to have been fixed by the Magisterium of the Church on the one hand and by the democratic majorities in almost all European countries on the other. There seems to be a divide that is barely bridgeable. However, this does not imply that the problem has been resolved, either on a societal or a personal level. If people on both sides of the divide would be willing to face the underlying human tragedies, then possibly the two positions could be gradually reconciled.

Chapter 6 provides a historical overview of the moral theological thinking on procured abortion throughout the ages. I have chosen to mainly limit myself to an analysis of theological developments within the

---

[51] Grisez, G., 1983, op. cit., pp. 41-72 and pp. 173-204, in particular pp. 178-180.
[52] Cf. Ricoeur, P., 1978, op. cit., p. 189. Ricoeur gives the historical example of protests against slavery in the name of natural law.
[53] Ricoeur, P., 1978, op. cit., pp. 189-191.
[54] Grisez, G., 1983, op. cit., pp. 121-125; cf. parts 2.3.1 and 5.1.7.
[55] John Paul II, Encyclical *Veritatis Splendor*, Vatican, 1993, n. 79; cf. part 6.2.3.2.

Roman Catholic Church. A reason for such a limitation has been given by John Finnis, who argues that in our civilization, the principal bearer of an explicit theory about natural law happens to have been the Roman Catholic Church.[56] As a more personal occasion for this research, I recall that in 2008, in a speech to the members of the General Congregation n. 35 of the Society of Jesus, Pope Benedict XVI asked for an exploration and illumination of certain themes, which are continuously discussed and called into question in today's secular culture, such as "the salvation of all humanity in Christ, of sexual morality, of marriage and the family".[57] In her response to Pope Benedict's address, the General Congregation asks of every Jesuit "to examine his own way of living and working at 'the new frontiers of our time', an examination which includes the themes mentioned by the Pope".[58] This appeal can be seen as an enormous challenge and at the same time a continuing source of inspiration, which it certainly has been for me in the course of writing this book.

Speaking of the role of the Church with regard to the defence of the human dignity of unborn children, Pope Francis recently acknowledged that "we have done little to adequately accompany women in very difficult situations, where abortion appears as a quick solution to their profound anguish..."[59] This remark is notwithstanding the efforts made by pro-life organisations in some parts of the world, which are often Church-based, like in the United States, Canada and several European countries.[60] Therefore, in this research both the developments in moral theology regarding abortion and their practical implications will be reconsidered.

The call of the Second Vatican Council for an openness to the world has resulted in a broadening of the subject areas available to contemporary theological analysis, because of a growing interest in human experience

---

[56] Finnis, J., op. cit., p. 124.
[57] Benedict XVI, "Address to the Fathers of the General Congregation of the Society of Jesus", 21 February 2008.
[58] General Congregation n. 35 of the Society of Jesus, decree 1, "With renewed vigor and zeal. The Society of Jesus responds to the invitation of the Holy Father", Rome, 2008, n. 15.
[59] Francis, Apostolic Exhortation *Evangelii Gaudium*, Vatican, 2013, n. 214.
[60] Chapter 7 will focus more in detail on the existing pro-life initiatives in the U.K. and the Netherlands.

and practice.⁶¹ More specifically, the opening up of the object of practice initially led to a move within theological research to the social and human sciences. According to Anne Fortin-Melkevik and others, the adoption of these sciences has made "practices" not only the privileged object of theological research but, even more importantly, its new foundation.⁶² Thus, the interdisciplinary method and openness to the world have allowed theology to be open to itself and to take account of its functioning and its presuppositions. By doing so, the role of theology has been modified internally, having been confronted with a new public space which comprises the university, society and the believing community.⁶³

Christian ethics aims at a protection of basic values according to Revelation, such as life, truth, love and friendship.⁶⁴ Moral theology as a science shows that the lack of respect for these basic values call upon existential questions which often are not answered in a satisfactory way in social ethics. In late modern times, basic values often have been threatened by the abuse of freedom.⁶⁵ It is considered a task for moral theologians to safeguard genuine freedom, sometimes by safeguarding the limits of this freedom. At the same time, moral theology ought to look for creative solutions which respect freedom, in the name of a new creation.⁶⁶

Developments in moral theology and more specifically in the thinking of the Magisterium of the Catholic Church on abortion, autonomy and sexual morality will be reviewed in chapter 7. At the end of this chapter, the perspective will be widened again, when possibilities for education, counselling, prevention and aftercare will be elaborated. The counselling

---

61 Second Vatican Council, Pastoral Constitution on the Church and the Modern World *Gaudium et Spes*, Vatican, 1965, n. 2; Cf. Fortin-Melkevik, A., op. cit., pp. 101-111.
62 Fortin-Melkevik, A., op. cit., p. 103. An example of contemporary practical theology is the work of Dutch theologian Johannes van der Ven. Cf. Johannes A. van der Ven, *Practical Theology: An Empirical Approach*, Kampen, 1993, pp. 112-156. Chris Hermans shows that Van der Ven uses the hermeneutics of Paul Ricoeur as a theoretical basis for his empirical-theological cycle. Cf. Chris A.M. Hermans, "When theology goes 'practical'. From applied to empirical theology", in: Chris A.M. Hermans, and Mary E. Moore, (Eds.), *Hermeneutics and empirical research in practical theology. The Contribution of Empirical Theology by Johannes A. van der Ven*. Leiden/Boston, 2004, pp. 21-51.
63 Fortin-Melkevik, A., op. cit., p. 105.
64 Cf. Wulf, C.M., 2013 (b), op. cit., p. 439; cf. Finnis, J., op. cit., p. 158.
65 Cf. chapter 6.
66 Cf. Wulf, C.M., 2013 (b), op. cit., pp. 340-342.

practices and pastoral care after the discovery of an unintended pregnancy and after the prenatal diagnosis of a certain abnormality of the embryo will be reviewed. Finally, in chapter 8 ways to stimulate the prevention of procured abortion will be investigated.

Chapter 1

The abortion legislation in the United Kingdom and the Netherlands

The scientific and political debate on abortion in the U.K. and the Netherlands is multidisciplinary in its nature, with contributions coming from jurists, sociologists, medical doctors, epidemiologists, psychologists, philosophers and theologians. The scientific debate is highly specialised, the issue of abortion is mainly discussed by scientists within their own discipline. An interdisciplinary approach to this issue is hardly practiced.

In the political arena, defenders and opponents of legal abortion are often fiercely divided. In the U.K., this division is across party lines. For instance, Members of Parliament (MP's) of both Houses in the U.K. have formed an all-party pro-life group and an all-party group on sexual and reproductive health (also known as all-party pro-choice group).[67] In the Netherlands, this phenomenon does not exist. In this country, a majority of the political parties did not want to make fundamental changes to the abortion legislation after the 2005 evaluation of the Termination of Pregnancy Act.[68]

The legalization of abortion in the U.K. and the Netherlands has taken place in the context of similar international developments. In the latter half of the twentieth century, procured abortion was legalised in many Western countries. For example, in the United States legalization took place in 1973, after the well-known decision of the Supreme Court in *Roe vs. Wade*. France legalised abortion in 1975, West Germany in 1976, Italy in 1978, the

---

67 At 30 July 2015, the registered chair of the All-Party Parliamentary Pro-Life Group is Ms. Fiona Bruce MP (Cons.). In July 2015, the All-Party Parliamentary Group on Sexual and Reproductive Health is chaired by Baroness Gould of Potternewton (Lab.).
68 Visser, M.R.M. et al., op. cit.

Netherlands in 1981 and Belgium in 1990.[69] The Abortion Act in England, Wales and Scotland has passed Parliament in 1967.

First, the British and Dutch Abortion Acts will be schematised. (1.1 and 1.2) A comparison will be made between the legislation and praxis in both countries (1.3). By means of statistical research, the consequences of the legal abortion praxis can be shown. (1.4) These data call into question the degree of consistency between the legal prescriptions and the current abortion praxis in the U.K. and the Netherlands. (1.5) Finally, part 1.6 deals with the phenomenon of medicalization of abortion, which has had a great influence on the implementation of the legislator's intentions.

1.1 The British Abortion Act

The British Abortion Act, which has passed Parliament in 1967, has had a long previous history. The U.K. abortion law is based on earlier Acts of Parliament of 1861 and 1929, which have not been abolished by the Abortion Act 1967. Secondly, after the enforcement of the Abortion Act several attempts have been made by British MP's to change the abortion legislation. Only once, in 1990 this has resulted in a revision of the Abortion Act.

1.1.1 The history of the Abortion Act

In 1861, Parliament accepted the Offences Against the Person Act, which only applied in England and Wales. Under this Act it was prohibited to use any "poison or other noxious thing", to "unlawfully" procure an abortion either for oneself or for another person or to unlawfully supply means for that end. The prescribed punishment was imprisonment. Originally, this Act was interpreted as prohibiting all abortions, except those performed on the grounds of necessity, in order to save the life of the pregnant woman.

In 1929 followed the Infant Life (Preservation) Act, which also only applied to England and Wales. This Act makes it an offence to "destroy the life of a child capable of being born alive", but it is also defending

---

[69] Mary Ann Glendon, *Abortion and Divorce in Western Law: American Failures, European Challenges.* Cambridge (Ma.), 1987, p. 14; For Belgium: United Nations Department of Economic and Social Affairs, Population Division: *Abortion Policies. A Global Review. Volume I, Afghanistan to France; Volume II, Gabon to Norway and Volume III, Oman to Zimbabwe.* New York, 2002, Vol. 1, p. 55.

termination of a pregnancy "in good faith for the purpose [...] of preserving the life of the mother". For instance, if the woman suffered from nephritis, tuberculosis, cardiac disease, cancer, insanity or epilepsy, these were considered acceptable conditions for the termination of pregnancy.[70] But if a woman had been pregnant for a period of twenty-eight weeks or more, that "shall be prima facie proof that she was at that time pregnant of a child capable of being born alive".[71]

In *Rex v. Bourne*, a 1938 case brought before the House of Lords, the Court interpreted the Offences Against the Person Act to permit a fourteen-year-old girl who had become pregnant as a result of rape to have an abortion. Since *Rex v. Bourne* provided only a defence for someone who had been prosecuted for an abortion, the burden was on a defendant to show that the abortion had been necessary to protect a woman's physical or mental health.[72]

In 1967, the U.K. Parliament accepted the Abortion Act, which applies to England, Scotland and Wales but not to Northern Ireland, where the 1861 Act and the Criminal Justice (Northern Ireland) Act of 1945 are the defining principles. In 1990, with the acceptance of the Human Fertilisation and Embryology Act, some amendments to the Abortion Act were made. The most significant of these amendments was the reduction of the upper time limit on the vast majority of abortions from 28 weeks of gestation to 24 weeks, taking "into account the advances in neo-natal and post-natal care".[73] Third trimester abortion are executed if there is a risk to the life of the pregnant woman, a risk of grave permanent injury, or if a serious handicap of the child has been discovered.[74] It has to be noted that in most

---

70 Stephen Brooke, "Abortion Law Reform 1929 – 1968", in: Michael D. Kandiah and Gillian Staerck (eds.), *The Abortion Act 1967*: Institute of Contemporary British History Witness Seminar, London, 2002, pp. 15-20. 22-5.
71 Section 1(1 and 2) of the Infant Life (Preservation) Act 1929.
72 *Rex v. Bourne*, 1939, 1 K.B. 687, 694; 1938 All E.R. 617, 619. Cf. Laura Katzive and Anika Rahman, *Central and Eastern Europe: an examination of abortion laws in the global context*. Presented by K.H. Martinez at the Schweitzer Conference on Improving Quality of Reproductive Health Services: Focus on Abortion Care, Prague, January 24-26, 2001, note 8.
73 Lord Bishop of Bradford, Abortion (Amendment) Bill, House of Lords debate 14 December 1989, vol. 513, c. 1469.
74 If the abortion takes place under one of the grounds A, B, E, F or G in the Abortion Act, as will be explained below.

other European countries the abortion legislation is stricter. For instance, in Germany, France and Belgium the gestation limit is 12 weeks of pregnancy. In the Republic of Ireland, the legalization of abortion in 2013 regards cases in which the woman's life is at risk.[75]

The Abortion Act of 1967 creates a series of conditions in relation to abortion "when a pregnancy is terminated by a registered medical practitioner if two registered medical practitioners are of the opinion, formed in good faith," - except in an emergency - that one of the stipulated grounds is met. These grounds were originally given a letter, A to G, to which medical practitioners still refer. Accordingly, in the U.K. the grounds for abortion are:

- A) the continuance of the pregnancy would involve risk to the life of the pregnant woman greater than if the pregnancy were terminated;

- B) the termination is necessary to prevent grave permanent injury to the physical or mental health of the pregnant woman;

- C) the pregnancy has not exceeded its twenty-fourth week and the continuance of the pregnancy would involve risk, greater than if the pregnancy were terminated, of injury to the physical or mental health of the pregnant woman;

- D) the pregnancy has not exceeded its twenty-fourth week and the continuance of the pregnancy would involve risk, greater than if the pregnancy were terminated, of injury to the physical or mental health of any existing children of the family of the pregnant woman; or

- E) there is a substantial risk that if the child were born it would suffer from such physical or mental abnormalities as to be seriously handicapped;

Or in emergency, certified by the operating practitioner as immediately necessary:

- F) to save the life of the pregnant woman; or

- G) to prevent grave permanent injury to the physical or mental health

---

75 In 2013, the Protection of Life During Pregnancy Act has been enforced, allowing termination of pregnancy in cases when two doctors have certified a risk of loss of life from a physical illness, in cases where one doctor has certified a risk of loss of life from a physical illness in emergency, or when three doctors have certified a risk of loss of life from suicide. Cf. Government of Ireland, "Protection of Life During Pregnancy Act", in: *Irish Statute Book*, nr. 35 of 2013.

of the pregnant woman.[76]

According to the Department of Health, in 2013 the vast majority (97%) of abortions were undertaken under ground C. In assessing the risk to the health of the woman and earlier children, physicians may take into account the woman's actual or reasonably foreseeable environment The vast majority (99.84%) of ground C only terminations were reported as being performed because of a risk to the woman's mental health.[77]

In 2013, 34% of abortions were performed in hospitals of the National Health Service (NHS) and 64% in clinics under NHS contract, run for instance by the British Pregnancy Advisory Service (BPAS). This makes a total of 98% of abortions funded by the NHS. The remaining 2% were privately funded.[78] Usually a woman who considers an abortion, will go to her local G.P. first, where she can receive a pregnancy test. If she is referred to a hospital or clinic, she will see a consultant or a senior doctor and then be admitted for the operation. There is no official waiting period. Every abortion needs the approval of two doctors.

The Abortion Act has a conscientious objection clause which permits doctors or nurses to refuse to participate in abortions. According to the RCOG Guideline, these objections do not apply in emergency situations, when the life of the woman is at risk. Doctors who have a conscientious objection to abortion must tell a woman of her right to see another doctor.[79]

As regards adult women requesting an abortion, their consent must be given voluntarily. Other criteria for valid consent, summarised by the General Medical Council, are the following:

- the woman must have sufficient capacity to understand the procedure and its alternatives;

- the decision must be based on sufficient and accurate information.

Legally, the father of the child has no rights to demand or refuse an abortion. In individual cases male partners brought unsuccessful legal

---

[76] Cf. Government of the U.K., Abortion Act 1967, c. 87, section 1. This section has been slightly amended in the Human Fertilisation and Embryology Act 1990, c. 37, section, 37.
[77] Department of Health, *Abortion Statistics, England and Wales: 2013*, London, 2014, p. 12.
[78] Ibid., p. 11.
[79] RCOG, op. cit., p. 20.

actions in attempts to prevent women obtaining abortions.[80] In these cases, of which Paton versus the U.K. is the most well-known, it is assumed that there is no direct risk of the woman's life involved.[81] If this were the case, then a different moral situation arises.[82]

In the U.K., competent young women under 18 are legally entitled to consent to an abortion. However, often the family is involved in decision making, unless the young woman specifically wishes to exclude them. When the young woman is under 16 and considered competent to give consent, doctors have an obligation to encourage her to involve her parents, but generally they should not override her view. When minors are non-competent, only a holder of parental responsibility, or the court, can give consent to treatment.[83]

1.1.2 Political attempts to change the abortion legislation

During the second reading of the Abortion Bill in the House of Lords in 1965, Thomas Shaw pointed at the relevance of the doctrine of double effect in relation to procured abortion.[84] This doctrine has its origin in natural law and is still part of English law.[85] According to the moral principle of double effect, an act which has both a good and a bad effect can be morally justified if four conditions are fulfilled simultaneously: 1) The act as such must be good or indifferent, but not intrinsically evil; 2) The good effect may not be realised by the negative side-effect; 3) The agent's intention must be good; 4) There must be a proportionately grave reason to allow the

---

80 Ibid., p. 26.
81 Cf. part 4.2.1.
82 Cf. part 5.1.8.
83 RCOG, 2011, pp. 24-25.
84 House of Lords debate 30 November 1965, Abortion Bill, *vol. 270 cc. 1139-241*. Thomas Shaw is quoted as Lord Craigmyle.
85 The doctrine of double effect also plays an important role in the current discussion on euthanasia and palliative sedation. Cf. Richard Huxtable, "Get out of jail free? The doctrine of double effect in English law", in: *Palliative Medicine*, 2004, 18, pp. 62-68.

justification of negative side-effects.[86]

Thomas Shaw reminded the Lords of the fact that Members of Parliament, when they accepted the Offences Against the Person Act in 1861 repeatedly used the word "unlawful" in relation to abortion, thus indicating that also lawful abortions exist, if they are performed in order to save the life of the mother. With the same intention, the Infant Life (Preservation) Act had been accepted in 1929. An example of a lawful abortion would be when a surgeon performs a hysterectomy (a removal of the uterus) in the case of a pregnant woman with an advanced cancer of the womb.[87] In this case all four conditions of the principle of double effect are fulfilled simultaneously.

The problem of the abortion praxis which, according to Shaw, would result from the 1965 Abortion Bill, is that "in the case of an ordinary abortion where, although the motive of the surgeon may be above suspicion, none of the other three conditions is fulfilled."[88] He predicted that the acceptance of the Abortion Bill would lead to an enormous increase in the number of abortions, as had been the case in Russia, the Scandinavian countries, Hungary and Japan.[89] In the next chapter, it will be pointed out that his prediction became true.

Since 1967, members of Parliament have introduced a number of private member's bills to change the abortion law. Four resulted in substantial debates (in 1975, 1977, 1979 and 1987) but all failed. In 1974, the Lane Committee investigated the workings of the Act and declared its support.

The Abortion Act was revised in 1990. Then, Parliament decided that the upper gestational limit for legally performing an abortion should be brought

---

86 W.J. Eijk, "The Fundamental Assumptions of Medical Ethics", in: Eijk, W.J., Hendriks, L.M., Raymakers, J.A. and Fleming, J.I. (eds.), *Manual of Catholic Manual Ethics. Responsible Healthcare from a Catholic Perspective,* Ballarat, 2014, pp. 46-135, here pp. 113-114; Grisez, G., 1970, op. cit., p. 329. The origin of the principle of double effect goes back to St. Thomas Aquinas in his treatment of the case of legitimate self-defense of one's own life against a present and otherwise unavoidable attack. Cf. Thomas Aquinas, *Summa Theologica (S.T.),* II-II, q. 64, a. 7, c. Edition in Latin, Ottawa, 1953, or in the English translation, Benziger Bros. edition, 1947, translated by Fathers of the English Dominican Province.
87 The example is mentioned by Thomas Shaw, Lord Craigmyle, during the House of Lords debate of 30 November 1965 on the Abortion Bill, *vol. 270,* col. 1224.
88 Ibid.
89 Ibid., cc. 1227-1228.

back from 28 weeks to 24 weeks. For this, evidence had been presented that the chance of survival of very premature neonates had increased because of medical progress.

In 2007 the House of Commons Science and Technology Committee evaluated scientific developments in relation to abortion. An important limitation of their inquiry was that the Committee decided beforehand not to look at the ethical and moral dimensions of abortion. Defining themselves as a "Committee that examines scientific and technological issues… we decided to focus on scientific and medical evidence relating to abortion and explicitly ruled out ethical or moral issues in the published terms of reference."[90] Up to 2008, pro-life organisations have frequently argued that the moral dimension of abortion should be taken into account in the political discussion. However, this did not come about, despite a recommendation of the House of Commons Science and Technology Committee in 2005 to form a joint committee of both Houses.[91] The chairman of the Science and Technology Committee, MP Phil Willis (Lib. Dem.), had his proposal to form a joint committee refused by the Leader of the House.[92] The idea to consider both ethical and scientific aspects in the debate was therefore rejected, when the Science and Technology Committee decided to look at the issue themselves.

The issue of procured abortion was planned to be re-discussed in the British parliament in 2008, in the slipstream of the Human Fertility and Embryology Bill (HFEB). The HFEB deals with the issues of infertility treatment, embryonic research and stem cell research. However, the debate on abortion did not take place, because of the many complexities of the HFEB which the Government wanted to be discussed first.[93]

In 2008, when the Second Reading of the Human Fertility and Embryology Bill took place in the House of Commons, MPs voted to retain the current legal limit of 24 weeks for having an abortion. As a preparation for the Parliamentary debate, the House of Commons Science and

---

90 House of Commons, Science and Technology Committee, *Scientific Developments Relating to the Abortion Act 1967. Twelfth Report of Session 2006/2007, Volume I*, London, 2007, p. 5.
91 Ibid.
92 House of Commons, Hansard Debates for 3 July 2006, col. 536.
93 I will not enter into the fierce discussion this Bill has caused in the U.K., because this goes beyond the focus of this research.

Technology Committee took up the task of evaluating the latest scientific developments in relation to abortion.[94] In their report the Committee treats the available scientific evidence regarding:

- survival rates of foetuses who were born at 22-26 weeks of gestation;
- the ability of foetuses to consciously experience pain below the gestational limit of 24 weeks.

To the Committee, evidence has been presented of survival rates of extremely preterm babies (after 22-26 weeks of gestation), in the period between 1995 and 2006. This evidence suggests an increase to a survival rate of 40% of neonatal intensive care admissions at 24 weeks, but little improvement in neonatal survival rates at gestations of 22 or 23 weeks.[95] A part of the improvement of the survival rate at 24 weeks could be explained out of changes in neonatal practice, for example the improved access to tertiary neonatal intensive care units and to postnatal transfer services in England since 2003. At the same time, the lack of improvement of neonatal survival rates at gestations of 22 or 23 weeks could be explained out of a higher risk of complications because of the survival of babies who would previously have died.[96]

However, when the Committee debated their findings, a minority report had been presented by two Committee members in which they made reference to evidence coming from the U.S. showing that survival rates depend very much on clinical decisions and the quality of care available

---

94 House of Commons, Science and Technology Committee: *Scientific Developments Relating to the Abortion Act 1967. Twelfth Report of Session 2006/2007*. London, 2007 (a). This Committee consists of eleven Members of Parliament, six of them belonging to the Labour Party, three to the Conservative Party and two to the Liberal Democratic Party.

95 Ibid., p. 17. Cf. Kate L. Costeloe, Enid M. Hennessy, Sadia Haider, Fiona Stacey, Neil Marlow and Elizabeth S. Draper, "Short term outcomes after extreme preterm birth in England: comparison of two birth cohorts in 1995 and 2006 (the EPICure studies)", *BMJ* 2012; 345: e7976 doi: 10.1136/bmj.e7976.

96 Cf. Costeloe, K.L. et al., op. cit., p. 5 of 14.

in the hospital or centre at which the mother presents.[97] As regards the foetal ability to experience pain, the Committee concludes that, "while the evidence suggests that foetuses have physiological reactions to noxious stimuli, it does not indicate that pain is consciously felt, especially not below the current upper gestational limit of abortion."[98] But again, in the minority report, evidence by Anand et al. has been put forward, who state that foetuses feel pain using different neural mechanisms than adults and that these mechanisms are present at earlier than 20 weeks gestation.[99]

In the Parliamentary debate which followed the Committee's inquiry, amendments proposing reductions to 22 weeks and 20 weeks were defeated by 304 to 233 votes and 332 to 190 votes respectively.[100] Finally, during the Third Reading, amendments were presented to:
- remove the legal requirement for two doctors' signatures to authorise abortions;
- to allow trained nurses and other health care practitioners to carry out abortions;
- to extend the locations where abortions can take place to primary care level;
- to remove conscientious objection in respect to providing emergency contraception provision and
- to extend the 1967 Abortion Act to Northern Ireland.

---

[97] The American study is of Hoekstra et al., which shows higher neonatal survival rates at a tertiary centre in Minneapolis, Minnesota, in comparison to the EPICure study: for the years 1986-2000 survival-to-discharge rates at 23, 24, 25 and 26 weeks were 66% (number of patients = 53), 81% (n = 97), 85% (n = 115) and 93% (n = 117). Cf. R.E. Hoekstra, T.B. Ferrara, R.J. Couser, N.R. Payne, and J.E. Connett, "Survival and Long-Term Neurodevelopmental Outcome of Extremely Premature Infants Born at 23–26 Weeks' Gestational Age at a Tertiary Centre", *Pediatrics*, 2004, 113, pp. e1–e6, here e3. Cf. House of Commons Science and Technology Committee, 2007 (a), op. cit., p. 74. The two MP's who drew up the minority report were Mrs. Nadine Dorries and Dr. Bob Spink (Cons.)

[98] House of Commons Science and Technology Committee, 2007 (a), op. cit., p. 25.

[99] Ibid., p. 74. Reference has been made to: Curtis L. Lowery, Mary P. Hardman, Nirvana Manning, Barbara Clancy, R. Whit Hall, and K.J.S. Anand, "Neurodevelopmental Changes of Fetal Pain", *Seminars in Perinatology*, 2007, 31, pp. 275-282.

[100] House of Lords debate of 20 May 2008, col. 222-282.

None of these amendments were heard because of a programme motion put forward by the Health Minister at the time, Dawn Primarolo, setting a time limit for further debate, which was accepted by the House of Commons.[101]

In 2011, an amendment to the Health and Social Care Bill was rejected by the House of Commons which would have given women with unintended pregnancies the option to receive independent information, advice and counselling, independently of the organizations providing abortion services such as the British Pregnancy Advisory Service and Marie Stopes International.[102]

One year later, MP Nadine Dorries (Con.) pleaded in vain for a reduction of the limit for legal abortion from 24 to 20 weeks, pointing at the inconsistency of the present situation in British hospitals: "In one room in a hospital, there might be a premature poorly baby born at 22 or 23 weeks at whom the NHS will throw everything it has to help it survive. In another room in the same hospital, a healthy baby will be aborted at 24 weeks."[103] In her reaction, Parliamentary Under-Secretary of State for Health Anna Soubry (Con.) stated that the Government did not have plans to review the Abortion Act 1967.[104]

---

[101] House of Commons debate of 22 October 2008, col. 324-335.
[102] The amendment was introduced by MP Nadine Dorries (Con.) during the House of Commons debate of 7 September 2011, col. 362-391.
[103] Cf. Parliamentary debate, 31 October 2012, Westminster Hall, Column 72WH. Ms. Dorries' view is supported by Dr. Max Pemberton, who writes that "many doctors are uncomfortable with the current cut-off point. It is not something we openly discuss, because we know it is a highly emotive area. But privately, many doctors will express discomfort that the current legislation is inherently illogical and inconsistent. Any doctor who has found themselves in the neonatal intensive care unit of a hospital will be acutely aware of it. In the same hospital where doctors are trying to save a premature baby born at, say, 23 weeks, a woman down the corridor is legally allowed to undergo a late-stage abortion on a foetus of the same gestation. So on the one hand we throw considerable money and resources to try to save a baby's life, while on the other we sanction its destruction." In: *Daily Telegraph*, 14 October 2012.
[104] Parliamentary debate, 31 October 2012, Column 91WH.

1.2 The Dutch Termination of Pregnancy Act

The Termination of Pregnancy Act forms part of the Dutch Criminal Code.[105] Only a doctor who is authorised by the State can legally carry out an abortion. The bill for the Termination of Pregnancy Act was accepted in 1980 by Parliament (76 versus 74 votes) and in 1981 by the Senate (38 versus 37 votes).[106]

In 2006, 25 years after the enforcement of the Act, the Dutch Parliament should have evaluated its implementation. For the evaluation of the Dutch abortion legislation and praxis an extensive investigation had been completed by Mechteld Visser et al.[107] But on the day the Parliamentary discussion was planned, the Cabinet fell.[108]

In 2007, a new Government was formed, a coalition of Christian-democrats, moderate socialists and a small protestant party. In the final coalition agreement some initiatives relating to alternatives to abortion were proposed, such as adoption, accompaniment and support for pregnant women and young mothers.[109] In 2008, for the first time in their history, a Dutch pro-life organisation received state support for their housing project for young mothers.[110] Still, the evaluation of the Termination of Pregnancy Act did not lead to fundamental changes in the abortion legislation. Let us therefore look at the principles of the Act as they came into being in 1981.

The Termination of Pregnancy Act has two principles:
- the juridical protection of unborn human life and
- the woman's right to assistance in case of an unwanted pregnancy.[111]

---

[105] Termination of Pregnancy Act (*Wet Afbreking Zwangerschap* (WAZ)), Criminal Code, or '*Wetboek van Strafrecht*', 1981, nr. 257.
[106] The bill was proposed by Ministers De Ruiter (CDA, Christian Democrats) and Ginjaar (VVD, Liberals). Cf. VBOK, *Omzien in verwachting*, Amersfoort, 1996, p. 35.
[107] Visser, M.R.M. et al., op. cit..
[108] On 29 June 2006, cf. Parliamentary document nr. 30371, nr. 4.
[109] 'Coalitieakkoord tussen de Tweede Kamerfracties van CDA, PvdA en ChristenUnie', 7 February 2007, p. 42.
[110] As will be shown in more detail in part 7.1.1.
[111] Parliamentary Document, Kamerstukken II, 1978/1979, 15475, nr. 3, p. 24.

During the Parliamentary discussion of the bill in 1979, the lawmaker has tried to clarify these two principles as follows: "The bill presupposes, that aid should be given to women, who as a result of an unwanted pregnancy, find themselves in an emergency situation. We consider termination of unborn human life as such a serious and radical intervention, that this can only be accepted if the woman's emergency makes the intervention inescapable. This principle brings with it that the doctor, the woman and those who might be involved in the preparation of a decision about abortion, each for his or her own part, should act with the greatest possible care, realizing the big responsibility for the unborn human life and for the consequences for the woman and her relatives."[112]

It is clear that in the case of abortion there is an intrinsic tension between these two principles. The lawmaker tried to resolve this tension by formulating three main objectives of the Act, which are the following:

1) guaranteeing a decision-making process with all due care, as well as prevention by means of education and aftercare.

2) guaranteeing the quality of the medical intervention.

3) prevention of commercial practices.[113]

First, the way in which the Dutch Government has tried to fill in these three objectives will be evaluated. After that, the two underlying principles from the Act will be addressed.

1.2.1 Objective 1: "Guaranteeing a decision-making process with all due care, as well as prevention by means of education and aftercare"

In Article 82A of the Dutch Criminal Code it is stated that depriving a child from its life, when it is reasonably to be expected that it would be viable outside the mother's womb, is to be considered as manslaughter. In 1979, the Dutch legislature has defined a limit of 24 weeks gestation for the viability of the foetus outside the womb. After this limit, a woman who has an abortion is liable to punishment. In 2014, Don Ceder has criticized the tenability of the 24-weeks limit, given the advances in neonatology.[114]

---

112 Ibid., nr. 1-4, p. 9.
113 Ibid., nr. 6, p. 31.
114 Don Ceder, "De grens van het leven", *Pro Vita Humana*, 2014, 21 (2), p. 1. On the criterion of foetal viability, see part 4.1.

Most first-trimester abortions (week 1-12) are performed in specialised abortion clinics, whereas second-trimester abortions (week 13-24) are more often performed in a hospital. Abortions after prenatal diagnosis usually take place in the hospital where the diagnosis was made. If, in cases of children with extremely severe defects, a doctor decides to perform a third trimester abortion then this decision must be reviewed by a special commission.[115]

The Act prescribes as a first step in the decision-making process a consultation between the pregnant woman, one or more medical assistants and maybe the begetter (the father) or the woman's parents. During this consultation, alternatives to abortion ought to be discussed.[116]

The presence of the begetter and the parents is not obligatory. Only when the woman is younger than 16, parental consent is needed. The explanatory memorandum of the Termination of Pregnancy Act states in this regard that normally "an institutionalised procedure" for the consultation of third persons apart from the woman and the consultant is not adequate and could even harm the decision-making process.[117]

For the same reason the legislature did not want to fill in the term "emergency situation", which is mentioned in article 5 of the Act. This article states that every decision to abort has to be taken with all due care and can only be executed when the emergency situation has been proven inevitable. During the Parliamentary debate in 1979 the term "emergency situation" was described as "a situation of mental emergency in which a woman finds herself because of her unwanted pregnancy, also when there is no direct danger of physical or psychological damage."[118] So the legislator has confirmed clearly that it is the woman's judgment of her own situation which is decisive in the case of a possible abortion, without giving objective criteria of what an emergency situation should entail. In 2010 and 2011, Members of Parliament asked the Government if they would be willing to formulate criteria to determine what is meant by an emergency situation, or

---

115 Parliamentary Document, Tweede Kamer der Staten Generaal 2005–2006, 30 300 XVI, nr. 90, p. 6. The commission consists of a chairman, three doctors and an ethicist. Their task is to inform the College of Procurators-General on the reports in these cases.
116 Termination of Pregnancy Act, 1981, Art. 5, part 2a.
117 Parliamentary Document, Kamerstukken II, 1978/1979, 15475, nr. 1-4, pp. 16-17; Kamerstukken I, 1980/1981, 15475, nr. 59b, pp. 12-15.
118 Parliamentary Document, Kamerstukken II, 1979/1980, 15475, nr. 6, p. 41.

to do research in order to find ways of preventing abortions by supporting women who find themselves in emergency situations. But in both cases, the Government neither formulated criteria nor commissioned further research.[119]

In 2013, 24,832 first trimester abortions and 5,769 second trimester abortions have been carried out in Dutch abortion clinics.[120] One year earlier, in 2012 Dutch abortion clinics received € 13,2 million as subsidies for these interventions.[121]

If a woman thinks that carrying her pregnancy to term would not be an adequate solution for her situation, then the doctor could decide for an abortion. So in every case the law prescribes that two autonomous decisions are to be made, one by the woman who wants the abortion and the other by the doctor who grants her request or not. A doctor or nurse cannot be obliged to perform or to take part in an abortion, if there are conscientious objections.[122] Important in this regard is that the doctor should investigate if the woman has been put under social pressure to undergo the abortion. If this would be the case, the doctor should reject the woman's request for an abortion.[123]

---

119 In April 2010, Secretary of State Mrs. J. Bussemaker stated that "the judgment to determine what is an emergency situation can only be given by the woman, often in dialogue with her partner and in every case with her doctor…For an outsider and also for me, it is impossible to determine what is an emergency situation." Cf. Parliamentary Document, Tweede Kamer der Staten Generaal, 2009-2010, 32123XVI, nr. 122, p. 16. In April 2011, Minister of Health, Welfare and Sport, Mrs. E. Schippers, answered to the question "if the Government was willing to do research in order to connect the policy to reduce the number of abortions to the causes, if the Government did not have insight in the background for the enormous increase of abortions in the last 20 years." She replied that she "did not see a reason for further research." Cf. Parliamentary Document, Tweede Kamer der Staten Generaal, 2010-2011, 30371, nr. 20, p. 7.
120 Healthcare Inspectorate, 2014, p. 7.
121 College voor Zorgverzekeringen, *Financieel verslag uitvoeringstaken CVZ 2012*, Diemen, 2013, p. 8.
122 WAZ, 1981, art. 20. It is common practice, that a health care institution takes measures to ensure that conscientious objections of nurses or caregivers are respected. In practice, this means that in cases of abortion or euthanasia, they can hand over to a colleague the care for the patient who is involved. Cf. Verpleegkundigen en Verzorgenden Nederland (V&VN), Commissie Ethiek, "Omgaan met gewetensbezwaren, wie moet de gevolgen dragen?", 2008, p. 5.
123 Cf. Nederlands Genootschap van Abortusartsen, *Beroepscode Abortusartsen*, Utrecht, 2012, n. 2.1.1.

It is remarkable that in the abortion legislation the woman's autonomous decision is so dominant. The father's role in the decision making process has been minimised to the doctor's obligation to check that no social pressure has been used by the father to opt for an abortion. But in reality, a man can show many other attitudes that could be of influence on the woman's decision, for instance attitudes of ignoring one's responsibility, of indifference or of escapism or of violence.[124] In other cases, the incidence of domestic violence may cause a pregnant woman not wanting to reveal to her doctor the social pressure put on her.[125]

The Dutch law prescribes that a five-day term for reflection must be observed before an abortion can take place. During this term the woman could consult another specialist, such as a social worker, a psychologist or a spiritual guide (for instance, a pastor or imam). Also the doctor or medical assistant could ask for further advice in case of doubt or conflict situations. Within this five-day term the doctor may decide not to treat or to refer the woman. In that case, he needs to give the woman written notice which includes the date which the woman first came to him for advice concerning her pregnancy.[126]

Often, care after an abortion involves a medical check by the G.P. in which methods of contraceptives might be discussed. Circa 40% of the women have been told in the clinic or hospital that psychosocial aftercare is available to them.[127] One of the arguments which have been often mentioned to support the legalization of abortion is that clinics are able to promote prevention by means of sex education. It is argued, for instance by Benagiano and Pera, that contraception and sex education have resulted in a low abortion number in the Netherlands and elsewhere, in comparison with other countries.[128] Still, as will be shown in the next chapter, the introduction of sex education did not prevent the increase of abortion numbers, neither in the Netherlands nor in the U.K., after the legalization of abortion. In this regard, Ketting and Visser conclude that despite the increased avoidance

---

124 Cf. parts 3.3.2.3.
125 Cf. part 3.3.2.4.
126 WAZ, 1981, art. 3, part 5.
127 Visser, M.J.M. et al., op. cit., p. 89.
128 Giuseppe Benagiano and Alessandra Pera, "Decreasing the need for abortion: challenges and constraints", *International Journal of Gynecology and Obstetrics*, 70 (2000), pp. 35-48.

of unwanted pregnancies in the Netherlands in the previous century, due to the large scale introduction of methods of family planning, women and couples have been increasingly apt to choose abortion if an unwanted pregnancy nevertheless occurs.[129]

1.2.2 Objective 2: "Guaranteeing the quality of the medical intervention"

Until the 1960s the method that was mostly used to cause an illegal abortion was by means of injection of some toxic fluid into the uterus. There was also a less frequent practice of abortions for therapeutic reasons, in order to save the life of the mother. These were mainly done by curettage. Abortions of the first category in particular were not without danger for the mother's life. Illegal abortions could also lead to permanent infertility and other complications.[130] Because of the illegality of abortion, doctors and all kinds of other people secretly offered their services in "life matters" or "period disturbances" with advertisements under pseudonyms. Since 1967, multidisciplinary abortion teams were founded in Dutch hospitals and clinics.[131] Although it has been well-known that these abortion teams did not only perform abortion on strictly medical indications, during the 1960s the Public Prosecution Service less and less prosecuted doctors who performed illegal abortions.[132]

During the 1970s, the number of abortions among Dutch women was estimated between 15,000 and 20,000 per year.[133] Still, many abortion requests were refused by G.P.'s and gynaecologists.[134] During these years, there was considerable traffic of Dutch women going to the United Kingdom to have an abortion there, while on the other hand many West German women

---

129 E. Ketting, and A.P. Visser, "Contraception in the Netherlands: the low abortion rate explained", *Patient Education and Counseling*, 1994, 23, pp. 161-171.
130 Stichting Samenwerkende Abortusklinieken/ Centra voor Seksuele Gezondheid Nederland (StiSAN), C. Rijneveld (red.) '*Als het moet, doe het goed*', Heemstede, 2002., p. 2.
131 Jan de Bruijn, *Geschiedenis van de abortus in Nederland. Een analyse van opvattingen en discussies 1600-1979*. Amsterdam, 1979, pp. 50-56, 106-107 and 183-184.
132 Visser, M.R.M. et al., op. cit., p. 25.
133 Parliamentary Documents, Kamerstukken II, 1978-1979, 15 475, nr. 3, *Regelen met betrekking tot het afbreken van zwangerschap (Wet afbreking zwangerschap)*, Memorie van Toelichting, p. 13.
134 Parliamentary Documents, Kamerstukken II, 1971-1972, 10 719, nr. 7, *Bijlage bij de Memorie van Antwoord*, p. 1.

came to the Netherlands because of the availability of abortion clinics.[135] In 1979, the Dutch Government remarked in this regard that "the letter of the law and the reality were in complete disagreement".[136]

When abortion was legalised in 1981, the legislature formulated the requirements that clinics and hospitals must meet, both on a material and professional level, to obtain an authorization. Authorised clinics and hospitals have the obligation to provide adequate aftercare to all women, prevent infections and provide sex education. The clinics are regularly inspected by Government officials who have to control the medical quality of the practice, as well as the correct application of other abovementioned legal aspects.

Nowadays, the method that is mostly used for abortion up to thirteen weeks is aspiration, by which the woman's uterus is emptied by means of suction for which an electric pump is used. For second trimester abortions the method of dilatation and evacuation is used, which consists of opening the cervix of the uterus and emptying it using surgical instruments. Regarding these methods, in an euphemistic way Visser et al. speak of "removing the fruit instrumentally by means of dilatation and evacuation".[137] Phillip Stubblefield, MD describes how for second trimester abortions foetal parts are extracted slowly and carefully, rotating the instrument within the uterus.[138] In this description, it is not mentioned that before its extraction from the uterus, the foetus has been literally torn into pieces. After the abortion, the surgeon "carefully examines the fetal parts to be sure all have been evacuated".[139]

In hospitals and clinics, for first trimester abortions often the abortion

---

[135] Van Eeden mentions that some 1,600 Dutch women have been aborted in the U.K. between 1968 and 1972. He notices that real numbers probably have been higher, since doubts exist if all foreign women have been registered. Cf. R. van Eeden, *Abortus in Engeland*, Den Haag, 1975, p. 13. Visser et al. notice that in 1980, so one year before legalization, 26,200 women came from Western Germany for an abortion in the Netherlands. Cf. Visser, M.R.M. et al., op. cit., p. 59.
[136] Parliamentary Documents, Kamerstukken II, 1978-1979, 15 475, nr. 3, p. 13.
[137] Visser, M.R.M. et al., op. cit., p. 56.
[138] Phillip G. Stubblefield, "First and Second Trimester Abortion", in: David H. Nichols and Daniel L. Clarke-Pearson, (Eds.), *Gynecologic, Obstetric, and Related Surgery*. Second Edition, St. Louis, 2000, pp. 1033-1048, here pp. 1042-43.
[139] Ibid., p. 1043.

pill RU486 is used.[140] After the introduction of RU486 in France in 1988, other EU countries also allowed its use. The abortion pill can induce abortion in women up to nine weeks pregnant, without intervention of a medical doctor. RU486 interferes with the normal function of the hormone progesterone, that stimulates the nutrition of the uterine lining, and can also prevent a normal implantation of the embryo in the uterus. Research in the U.S. shows that 2% of the women who used RU486 before 49 days of pregnancy and 4% of the women who used RU486 between 50 and 63 days of pregnancy had severe bleeding (haemorrhaged) afterwards ($P = 0.008$).[141] Research in France and the Netherlands shows an 'effectiveness' of RU486 of 95-97%.[142]

When the abortion pill was introduced into the Netherlands, the Minister of Health answered questions from two Members of Parliament by stating that the Termination of Pregnancy Act is equally applicable with this new method.[143] In the U.K., midwives, health visitors or nurses may administer RU486, provided a medical practitioner has prepared and signed a local protocol or individual prescription.[144] In the Netherlands only licensed abortion clinics and hospitals are authorised to supply RU486 to women.[145]

There are both juridical and medical arguments for avoiding clandestine abortions by means of legalization. From a juridical point of view, it has been argued that in the past, before the legalization, the prevention of clandestine abortions had proven to be very difficult.[146] The medical

---

140 RU486 is also known by its generic name, mifepristone, and by Mifegyne, the name under which RU486 is marketed in Europe.
141 Irving M. Spitz, Wayne Bardin, Lauri Benton and Ann Robbins, "Early pregnancy termination with mifepristone and misoprostol in the United States", *New England Journal of Medicine*, 1998, 338, pp. 1241-1247, here p. 1243.
142 E. Koster, J. Rademakers, A.C. Jansen-Van Hees and F. Willems, *Medicamenteuze abortus als alternatief voor de zuigcurettage: eerste ervaringen met de abortuspil in Nederland*. Utrecht, 2001, p. 36.
143 Parliamentary Documents: Aanhangsel Handelingen II 1997-1998, p. 1593; Aanhangsel Handelingen II 1998-1999, p. 1851.
144 Royal College of Obstetricians and Gynaecologists, 2011, p. 70.
145 Visser, M.R.M. et al., op. cit., p. 31
146 For an historical account of the ineffectiveness of combatting clandestine abortions in the Netherlands in the first half of the 20th century, see Bruijn, J. de, op. cit., pp. 95-112.

argument that is often used is that clandestine abortions cause more risks to the health and even the life of the woman than abortions in licensed clinics and hospitals. This might indeed be true, because of the application of unsafe methods and a lack of aftercare.

But the substitution of clandestine practices by licensed clinics has taken its toll. The free and confidential service that is offered in abortion clinics in the Netherlands and in the U.K. has resulted in a steady increase in the total number of abortions in both countries in the last decades.[147]

1.2.3 Objective 3: "The prevention of commercial practices"

In order to prevent commercial practices, abortion is offered free of charge to women who have Dutch citizenship. In principle other women need to pay for the intervention. Clinics and hospitals have to work on a non-profit basis. With this system the legislature aims to prevent commercial and clandestine activities.

As part of their evaluation study, Visser et al. did research among 21 organisations who are involved in the abortion policy and law making, either as a professional association or as a pressure group. Many of these organisations mentioned the risks of RU486 becoming available via the internet. In the U.K. and the Netherlands, sale of RU486 in a pharmacy or online is illegal. In 2011, the British Daily Mail investigated the online sale of RU486, discovering that pills were widely available from online pharmacies.[148] When RU486 is used in a home situation, the following risks apply: no assistance of a medical professional in the decision making process before the abortion; no guarantee of professional help in case of medical complications; no attention to prevention and aftercare.[149]

All these risks are a serious threat to the objectives of the abortion legislation. Illegal online sale of RU486 also endangers the reliability of the abortion registration. According to the law, all hospitals and clinics licensed to perform abortions are required to report relevant information to the Inspectorate quarterly. However, without any insight into the size of the online sale of RU486, it is unlikely that the Inspectorate has a complete

---

147 Cf. parts 1.4.1 and 1.4.2.
148 Sophie Borland, "'Backstreet abortion' pills being illegally sold on the internet for just £15", on: *Mail Online*, 5 March 2011.
149 Visser, M.R.M. et al., op. cit., p. 150.

overview of all abortions that have taken place in the Netherlands.

In 2014, an opinion poll among 2,055 British adults, representative of the British population, found out that 89% of all adults agreed with the statement that a woman requesting an abortion should always be seen in person by a qualified doctor.[150]

1.3 A comparison between the abortion legislation in the U.K. and the Netherlands

The abortion legislation in the Netherlands is based on principles that are similar to those recognised in the U.K. as in many other Western countries. For instance, in both countries, the role of the man is not legally recognised, although in practice the man will often be involved in the decision making process. The absence of a legal recognition of the man in a decision to abort, could lead to situations in which a man's willingness to take upon himself the responsibility for his actions, is completely ignored. In the current juridical framework in the U.K. and the Netherlands, a woman could one-sidedly decide for an abortion, even without having consulted her partner. In some 10% of the decisions to abort, Dutch women did not tell anyone that they were pregnant, besides their doctor. In these cases, the man's informed consent is being neglected during the whole decision making process.[151] Even in the case of a married couple, the woman's husband is powerless in these situations from a juridical point of view.[152]

One difference between the legal requirements in the two countries is that in the U.K. a young woman under 16, who is considered competent to give consent, can legally ask for an abortion without her parents' consent. In the Netherlands, this is not allowed.

As regards the obligatory five-day term in the Netherlands, Visser et al. have found that most healthcare workers find this term useful.[153] It can prevent impulsive decisions and it might also have a positive psychological influence on coping with an abortion. An inquiry in the U.K. among some 1,500 men and women in 2006 found that 77% would support a compulsory cooling-off period between diagnosis of pregnancy in a clinic or hospital

---

150 ComRes, "Christian Institute Abortion Poll", London, 2014.
151 Cf. part 3.3.2.2, Cf. Visser, M.R.M. et al., op. cit., p. 86.
152 Cf. part 1.2.1.
153 Visser, M.R.M. et al., op. cit., p. 108.

and any abortion.[154]

In the same questionnaire respondents were asked whether they would support doctors having a legal duty to provide access to advice both from abortion providers and from organisations offering alternatives such as adoption. This has the support of 89% of the British respondents.[155] In the Netherlands this legal obligation already exists, but often alternative scenarios are not discussed during counselling before a decision is made.[156]

Unlike in many other European countries, both in the U.K. and the Netherlands third trimester treatments (after 24 weeks) are executed. Both in the U.K. and in the Netherlands, a doctor or nurse who has a conscientious objection to performing or taking part in an abortion, has the right to express this objection. In the U.K., the General Medical Council advises as "good medical practice" that doctors explain their conscientious objections to a woman who wants an abortion and also mention their right to see another doctor.[157]

1.4 Consequences of the legal abortion praxis in the U.K. and the Netherlands

Since procured abortion has been legalised in the U.K. and the Netherlands, the incidence of abortion has steadily increased. Since legalization took place in the U.K. in 1967, the number of abortions has more than doubled. Also in the Netherlands an substantial increase of the number of abortion has taken place since legalization in 1981.

Therefore, the question needs to be raised whether the abortion legislation in the U.K. and the Netherlands has resulted in a tendency among pregnant women to increasingly decide in favour of an abortion. Statistical data on abortion in the U.K. and the Netherlands, as well as some characteristics of British and Dutch women who have undergone an abortion provide a clear picture of the consequences of the abortion legislation in both countries. (1.4.1 and 1.4.2) In particular, the increase of the number of abortions after

---

[154] CommunicateResearch, "Choose Life Poll", London, 2006, p. 39.
[155] Ibid., p. 43.
[156] Cf. part 1.5.
[157] Cf. House of Commons Science and Technology Committee, *Scientific Developments Relating to the Abortion Act 1967. Twelfth Report of Session 2006/2007, List of Evidence*, submission from the Department of Health, 2007, p. 2.

prenatal diagnosis is a reason for concern. The developments in abortion numbers in the two countries are evaluated, including a consideration some relevant demographical and sociological data. (1.4.3) Demographical research shows that changes have taken place in the fertility rate in both countries and that a relation exists between abortion numbers and ethnicity. Sociological research points out that the legalization of abortion itself has led to an increased demand.

1.4.1 Statistical data on abortion in the U.K.

In the U.K., as in many other Western countries, the occurrence of abortion is expressed in an age-standardised abortion rate, that expresses the number of abortions per thousand women between 15 and 44 years of age (see figure 1).

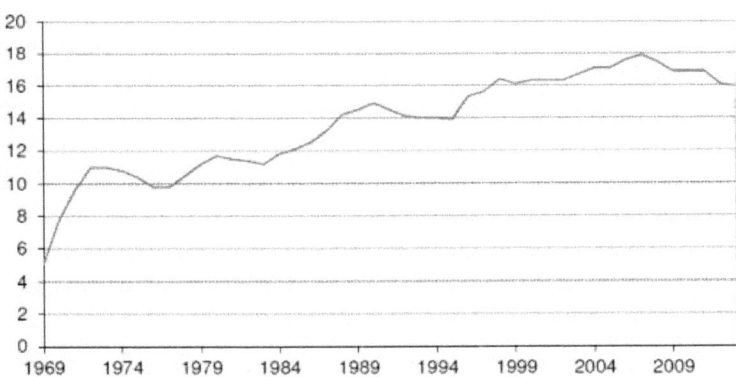

Figure 1: Age-standardised abortion rate per 1,000 women aged 15-44, England and Wales, 1969-2013

Source: Department of Health, *Abortion Statistics, England and Wales: 2013. Summary information from the abortion notification forms returned to the Chief Medical Officers of England and Wales*. London 2014, p. 9.

Although the general trend until 2007 is one of a fairly constant rise, there are some periods in which the rise is stronger than in other years. During the first years after legalization the number of abortions increased rapidly. As an explanation for the sudden increase in 1977 and in 1995, Colin

Francome points out that the mentioning of potential negative side effects of the birth control pill in the British media may have caused a decrease in the use of the pill, followed by a rise in the abortion rate.[158] The decrease in the abortion rate since 2007 comes together with a slight increase in the birth rate in the U.K. in the same period. Still, the abortion rate contributes significantly to the fact that total birth rates of British women are well below the rate needed for population replacement.[159]

1.4.1.1 England and Wales

In 2013, the total number of abortions in England and Wales was 185,331. This was 2.1% more than in 2003 (181,582). Only 5,469 of these were abortions for non-residents.[160] By comparison, the number of live births in England and Wales was 698,512 births in 2013.[161] This means that of all pregnancies 21% ends with an abortion.

1.4.1.2 Scotland

11,777 abortions were performed in Scotland in 2013, compared to 13,902 in 2008. After a sustained increase in the abortion numbers between 1968 and 2008, there has been a substantial decrease in the last five years. However, in that same period, the birth rate in Scotland also fell. The vast majority of abortions were undertaken under ground C of the Abortion Act. The Scottish abortion rate has always been lower than that of England and Wales.[162] In 2013, the abortion rate for Scottish women aged 15-44 was 11.2 for every 1000 women. The Information Services Division Scotland states that the rate of abortions continues to show a clear link with the level of deprivation. In areas of high deprivation the rate is 14.4 per 1000 compared to 8.2 per 1000 for the least deprived areas of Scotland.[163]

---

158 Colin Francome, *Abortion in the USA and the UK*. Hants, 2004, p. 33.
159 Cf. part 1.4.3.1.
160 Department of Health, 2014, op. cit., p. 5.
161 Office for National Statistics, Parents' Country of Birth, England and Wales, 2013.
162 Francome, C., op. cit. p. 39.
163 Information Services Division Scotland, *Abortion Statistics 2013*, Edinburgh, 2014, p. 3 and table 1.

1.4.1.3 Northern Ireland

The 1967 Abortion Act does not apply to Northern Ireland. In England and Wales, in 2013 there were 5,469 abortions to residents of other countries, principally Northern Ireland (14.7%) and the Irish Republic (67.3%). In Northern Ireland, between 30 and 60 terminations of pregnancy are performed legally each year, for medically approved conditions.[164] In 2015, the High Court of Justice in Northern Ireland has granted leave to the Northern Ireland Human Rights Commission for a judicial review of the current abortion legislation.[165]

1.4.1.4 Some characteristics of abortion clients in the U.K.

In this part the following characteristics of abortion clients in the U.K. will be pointed out: gestation, age, family type and marital status, ethnic background and the incidence of abortion after prenatal diagnosis.

Gestation

Most abortions in the U.K. are performed before 13 weeks gestation. Some 9% of all abortions in 2013 were carried out at 13 or more weeks gestation, a percentage that has slightly decreased during the last decade.[166]

Age

From the age of thirteen onwards, the abortion rates quickly rise to a peak at the age of twenty-two, where a rate of 30 women per 1000 is reached. In 2013 in England and Wales, there were 773 abortions to women under the age of fifteen.[167] Looking more closely at pregnancies under the age of eighteen, it gets clear that the relationship between social deprivation and the number of abortions shows a different picture than can be seen in the overall abortion numbers. Lee et al. found that the Inner London region shows the highest proportion of under-18 abortions, whereas mining, manufacturing and industrial regions show the lowest proportion of under-

---

164 Department of Health, 2014, op. cit., p. 52; Family Planning Association, *Factsheet Abortion Practice and Provision in Northern Ireland*, Belfast, 2014, p. 3
165 Alan Erwin, "Northern Ireland abortion law can be challenged, court rules.", *Irish Times*, 2 February 2015.
166 Department of Health, 2014, op. cit., p. 5.
167 Ibid, 2014, p. 10.

18 abortions.[168]

A study by Clifford Hill of over 2,000 young people in England aged 13–15 found that, in families headed by a married couple, 13% of the children were sexually active. The percentage doubled (26%) for young people living in one-parent families. The figure was 24% for the children of cohabiting couples, 26% where the parents were separated, 23% where children divided their time between two parents living apart, 24% where the parents were divorced, and 35% where children did not live with either parent.[169]

Family type and marital status

The percentage of lone parent families in relation to all families with children in England and Wales shows an increasing trend, from 25% in 2000 to 29% in 2011.[170] This figure is relevant for the number of abortions, since 81% of abortions in 2013 in England and Wales were carried out on single women.[171] This latter percentage has risen slowly from 71% since 1996.[172] Abortion rates of single women can be compared with the percentage of all women in their fertile years (15 – 44 years of age) who are either single, married or divorced and not remarried. In 2009, these percentages were respectively 60%, 34% and 6%.[173] It is therefore clear to see that the incidence of abortions among married women is substantially lower than among other women.

Looking further back, a very clear trend can be seen in the marriage rates among women, especially among teenagers in the U.K. During the 1960s the marriage rate among teenage women increased steadily, but it declined

---

168 Ellie Lee, Steve Clements, Roger Ingham, and Nicole Stone, *A matter of choice. Explaining national variation in teenage abortion and motherhood.* Southampton, 2004, pp. 11-12.
169 Clifford Hill, *Sex under sixteen? Young People Comment on the Social and Educational Influences on Their Behaviour.* London, 2000, p. 58; Cf. Joost van Loon, *Deconstructing the Dutch Utopia. Sex education and teenage pregnancy in the Netherlands.* London, 2003, p. 55.
170 Office for National Statistics, *2011 Census Analysis: How do Living Arrangements, Family Type and Family Size Vary in England and Wales?* London, 2014, p. 5, chart.
171 Department of Health, 2014, p. 15. As regards Scotland, the Information Services Division Edinburgh does not provide data regarding women's marital status in their 2013 publication on abortion statistics.
172 Department of Health, *Abortion Statistics England and Wales: 2006*, London 2007, p. 12.
173 United Nations Statistics Division, Demographic Statistics, "Population by marital status, age, sex and urban/rural residence", cf. UNdata, accessed 15 December 2015.

dramatically thereafter, from 67 married teenage women per 1000 in 1970 to 9 per 1000 in 1994. According to Kaye Wellings and Roslyn Kane, the reason for this decrease is that women were increasingly avoiding unwanted pregnancies and the consequent need to legitimise births in wedlock.[174] The crude marriage rate (per 1,000 inhabitants) in the U.K. has decreased from 8.5 in 1970 to 4.5 in 2011.[175] Besides the decreasing number of marriages, it is undoubtedly true that women were not only increasingly avoiding unwanted pregnancies, but also unwanted births through abortion.

Ethnicity

Of women whose ethnic background was recorded in hospitals and clinics in 2013, 76% were reported as White, 9% as Black or Black British and 9% as Asian or Asian British. This differs from the ethnicity population estimates based on the 2011 census where 86% are reported as White, 7.5% as Asian or Asian British and 3.3% as Black or Black British.[176] So, the percentage of abortions is highest among Black or Black British women, followed by Asian or Asian British women and then by White women.

Abortion after prenatal diagnosis

Among the total number of abortions, the abortions performed on medical grounds after prenatal diagnosis (ground E) form a particular category. The number of ground E abortions in England and Wales has increased steadily from 2,036 in 2006 to 2,732 in 2013. With regard to the ground E cases, the most commonly reported anomalies were of the nervous system (24%) and the musculoskeletal system (8%); Down's syndrome (22%) was the most commonly reported chromosomal abnormality.[177]

In 2010 in Scotland, 142 abortions were carried out under ground E of which 47 were for chromosomal conditions such as Down's syndrome, 37 for anomalies of the nervous system, with the remaining 58 being for other

---

174 Kaye Wellings and Roslyn Kane, "Trends in teenage pregnancy in England and Wales: how can we explain them?", *Journal of the Royal Society of Medicine*, 1999, 92, pp. 277-282.
175 European Commission, "Marriage and divorce statistics", cf. Eurostat, accessed 15 December 2015.
176 Department of Health, 2014, op cit., p. 10.
177 Ibid., p. 27; Department of Health, 2006, op cit., Table 7b.

conditions.[178]

Mike Wyldes and Ann Tonks conclude that the increase in terminations of pregnancy for foetal anomaly, which they measured in the West Midlands between 1995 and 2004, is likely to be due to the increasing sensitivity of screening programmes.[179] In the U.K., the abortion rate is estimated to be 92% of all women who were confronted with a diagnosis of Down's syndrome.[180]

1.4.2 Statistical data on abortion in the Netherlands

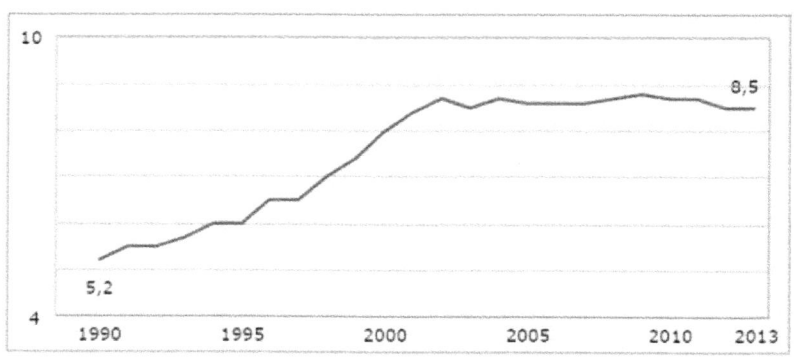

Figure 2: The abortion rate per 1,000 women aged 15-44 in the Netherlands between 1990 and 2013

Source: Inspectie voor de Gezondheidszorg (Health Care Inspectorate), *Jaarrapportage 2013 van de Wet Afbreking Zwangerschap*. Utrecht, 2014, p. 17.

The numbers given in figure 2 include all abortions, also those before 44 days of amenorrhoea (absence of menstruation). Since 2006, abortions before 44 days (better known as overtime treatments or early abortions) are included in the abortion law and therefore also in the abortion

---

[178] Information Services Division Scotland, 2014, Table 1.
[179] M.P. Wyldes and A.M. Tonks, "Termination of pregnancy for fetal anomaly: a population-based study 1995 to 2004", *British Journal of Obstetrics and Gynaecology*, 2007, 114, pp. 639-642.
[180] T. Tymstra, J. Bosboom and K. Bouman, "Prenatal diagnosis of Down's Syndrome: Experiences of women who decided to continue with the pregnancy", *International Journal of Risk & Safety in Medicine*, 2004, 16, pp. 91-96.

registration.

During the 1980s, the first years after legalization, the number of abortions decreased some 10%. Probably this has to do with the strong decrease in the birth rate during the 1970s. As shown in figure 2, from 1990 onwards there has been a rise in the abortion rate in the Netherlands of 60%. From 2002 onwards there seems to be a degree of stabilization. In 2013 there were 30,601 terminations of pregnancy, this is 24 more than in 2012.[181] Again by comparison, the number of live births in the Netherlands in 2013 was 171,341. This means that some 15% of all pregnancies end in an abortion.[182]

1.4.2.1 Some characteristics of abortion clients in the Netherlands

In order to make a comparison between abortion clients in the U.K. and in the Netherlands, the same characteristics of part 1.4.1.4 will now be pointed out: gestation, age, family type and marital status, ethnic background and the incidence of abortion after prenatal diagnosis.

Gestation

In the Netherlands, half of the women who had an intervention in a clinic were given an abortion during the first five weeks of pregnancy. Some 5% of the women had an abortion during the second trimester (between the 13th and 24th week). This latter percentage has risen since 1990 because of the more frequent application of prenatal diagnosis. According to several experts, no abortions on social indication are executed between 22 and 24 weeks of gestation.[183]

Age

Most abortions take place in the age group 20-24 (25%). Between 1990

---

181 Inspectie voor de Gezondheidszorg, 2014, p. 14.
182 Looking at the previous century, one can see that up to the 1940s the abortion percentage among women rose from 7,3% in 1883 until 23,5% in 1948, then decreased to 19% in 1963 and less than 10% in the 1970'ies. After that abortion percentages rose again. Cf. Bruijn, J. de, op. cit., pp. 101 and 201.
183 Ministerie van Volksgezondheid, Welzijn en Sport, *Verslag 'Behandelgrens pasgeborenen en grens abortushulpverlening'*, bijlage bij Kamerstuk 30371, nr. 21, Den Haag, 2011.

and 2004, the abortion rate among teenagers rose significantly. This rise (160%) was bigger than the rise of 67% seen for women of all ages. Also the number of teenage pregnancies rose during this period. After 2002, the number of terminations of pregnancy among teenagers is declining.[184]

Family type and marital status

The percentage of lone parent families in relation to all families with children in the Netherlands has increased from 16% in 2001 to 21% in 2014.[185] In 2004, 41% of all women who had an abortion lived alone, 20% were married, 18% were living together, 17% were staying with their parents. In 1994, these percentages were 43%, 26%, 20% and 11% respectively.[186] So, the percentage of married women having an abortion has decreased, whereas especially the percentage of women having an abortion while staying with their parents, has increased during this period.

The abortion rates of single women can be compared with the percentage of all Dutch women in their fertile years (15 – 44 years of age) who are either single, married or divorced and not remarried. In 2004, these percentages were respectively 52%, 42% and 6%.[187] The incidence of abortions among married women is thus much lower than among other women.

During the last decades in the Netherlands the percentage of men and women who choose to leave the parental home in order to live alone or with others who are not a family, has risen substantially to more than half of all men and women. At the same time, the group of men and women returning to their parents after having lived on their own, is increasing steadily. Of these women, one third mentions the end of a relationship as the main reason to return to their parents.[188] Finally, the crude marriage rate (per 1,000 inhabitants) in the Netherlands has decreased from 9.5 in 1970 to 3.8 in 2013.[189]

---

184 Inspectie voor de Gezondheidszorg, 2014, p. 20; Visser, M.R.M. et al., op. cit., pp. 68-69.
185 Centraal Bureau voor de Statistiek (CBS), Statline, 2014.
186 Visser, M.R.M. et al., op. cit., p. 62.
187 Cf. United Nations Statistics Division, Demographic Statistics, "Population by marital status, age, sex and urban/rural residence", cf. UNdata, accessed 15 December 2015.
188 Centraal Bureau voor de Statistiek, *Relatie en gezin aan het begin van van de 21ste eeuw.* Den Haag/Heerlen, 2009, pp. 21-22.
189 European Commission, "Marriage and divorce statistics", cf. Eurostat, accessed 15 December 2015.

Ethnicity

As regards ethnic background, 36.4% of abortion clients are of Dutch origin, 9.9% are from Surinam, a former Dutch colony, 5.8% originate from the Dutch Antilles islands, 3.5% are Turkish, 5.5% are Moroccan, 24% are from other countries. 14.8% of abortion clients are registered as "ethic background unknown".[190]

Based on data from clients of Dutch abortion clinics, NGO Rutgers WPF estimated the abortion rate per 1000 women according to the land of origin (2011). The differences are big: the Netherlands 4.3, Surinam 31.2, Dutch Antilles 43.1, Turkey 8.7 and Morocco 17.0.[191] The application of sex education might be one reason to explain these differences, as is mentioned by Visser et al.[192] However, a connected problem, as Angela van den Broek et al. of the Netherlands Institute for Social Research point out, is that the existing provision of parenting support services does not always meet the needs and wishes of non-Western migrants, and professionals are often inadequately equipped to provide the right parenting support.[193]

Abortion after prenatal diagnosis

In the previous decade, there has been a substantial rise in the number of abortions performed on medical grounds after prenatal diagnosis. Since 2000, the number of second trimester abortions executed in hospitals has more than quadrupled from 184 to 842 in 2013. Especially in the last couple of years, there is a strong increase in the number of abortions executed in hospitals after 20 weeks gestation. Data from the national Health Care Inspectorate show an increase from 140 abortions executed in hospitals between 20 and 24 weeks in 2005 to 377 in 2013. The Health Care Inspectorate confirms that this increase in hospital abortions is related to

---

190 Maaike Goenee, Charles Picavet and Ciel Wijsen, *Factsheet Landelijke abortus registratie 2011*, Rutgers WPF, Utrecht, 2013, p. 6. WPF stands for World Population Foundation.
191 Ibid., p. 6.
192 Visser, M.R.M. et al., op. cit., p. 65.
193 Angela van den Broek, Ellen Kleijnen and Saskia Keuzenkamp, *Naar Hollands gebruik? Verschillen in gebruik van hulp bij opvoeding, onderwijs en gezondheid tussen autochtonen en migranten*. Sociaal en Cultureel Planbureau, Den Haag, 2010, p. 123.

the 20 week ultrasound scan.[194]

In 1998 in the Netherlands, the abortion rate after the detection of Down's syndrome was 95% in the group of women of 36 years of age and older and 82% among other women.[195] In 2009, Mohangoo and Buitendijk reported that in the period 2005-2007 there was a significant increase in the number of stillborn babies who had spina bifida or hydrocephaly.[196] The researchers did not distinguish between stillborn babies after abortion or after a natural cause of death. For Down's syndrome or other chromosomal anomalies, the number of stillborn babies has increased significantly in the period 2005-2007, compared to the period 1997-2004.[197]

A clear increase in the number of stillborn babies with spina bifida or hydrocephaly at 21, 22 and 23 weeks gestation has been measured between 2005 and 2007. For anencephaly and cleft lip or cleft palate no significant increase has been measured in this period.[198]

1.4.3 Evaluation of the differences in abortion numbers in the United Kingdom and the Netherlands

In figure 3, a comparison has been made between the number of abortions in England and Wales and in the Netherlands between 1990 and 2010.

---

194 Inspectie voor de Gezondheidszorg, 2014, p. 25; cf. A.D. Mohangoo and S.E. Buitendijk, *Aangeboren afwijkingen in Nederland 1997-2007. Gebaseerd op de landelijke verloskunde en neonatologie registraties*. TNO KvL/P&Z 2009/112, Leiden, 2009, pp. 72-73.
195 Tymstra, T. et al., op. cit., p. 91.
196 Mohangoo, A.D. and Buitendijk, S.E., op. cit., pp. 60-63.
197 Ibid., p. 68.
198 Mohangoo A.D. and Buitendijk, S.E., op. cit., pp. 70-71.

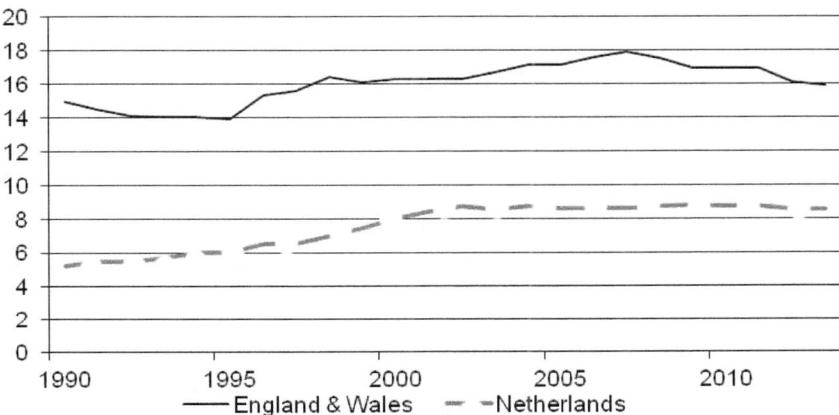

Figure 3: Abortion rate per 1,000 women aged 15-44 in England & Wales and in the Netherlands, 1990-2013

Source: Department of Health, 2014, p. 18; Inspectie voor de Gezondheidszorg, 2014, p. 39.

One can see that during this period, in England and Wales the abortion rate is substantially higher than in the Netherlands and also shows more fluctuations. In both countries there has been an increasing number of abortions, the increase has been relatively stronger in the Netherlands.

The Dutch abortion rate is comparable to Belgium (9.3 in 2011) and higher than in Germany (5.6 in 2013). The British abortion rate is lower than in Sweden (20.7 in 2012) or the Russian Federation (34.9 in 2011), and equal to the United States (15.9 in 2013).[199] The fact that abortion numbers in the U.K. and the Netherlands are lower than for instance in Sweden or the Russian Federation, is no reason for complacency. On the contrary, a critical self-evaluation seems to be appropriate, given the increasing numbers in the last decades.

Reflecting on the difference between the abortion number in the U.K. and the Netherlands, one explanation could be a difference in expected well-being of children in the two countries. As an indicator for child well-being, a composite measure has been developed by the United Nations Children's

---

199 Inspectie voor de Gezondheidszorg, 2014, p. 18.

Fund (UNICEF).²⁰⁰ This overall child well-being ranking distinguishes between six broad dimensions of well-being: material well-being, health and safety, educational well-being, family and peer relationships, behaviours and risks and subjective well-being. The ranking shows that among 21 European countries and the United States, the average child well-being ranking of the Netherlands is lowest, which implies the best score. On the other hand, the U.K. occupies the twenty-first position with the highest average, despite relative high spending on cash benefits and tax concessions for families.²⁰¹ The UNICEF report concludes that there is no obvious relationship between levels of child well-being and measures of economic prosperity such as the Gross Domestic Product (GDP) per capita.²⁰² Reproductive decisions made by parents depend on much more than financial perspectives.

It is shown in figure 4 that from the age of 13 to 19, the number of abortions climbs rapidly, more so in the U.K. than in the Netherlands.

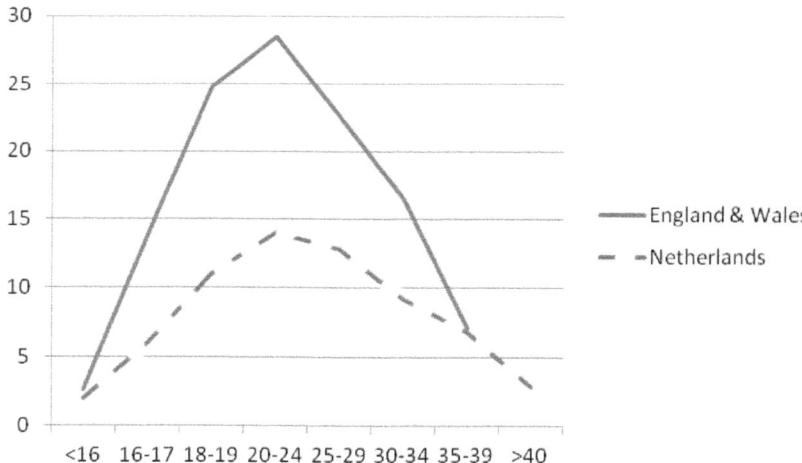

Figure 4: Crude abortion rates per 1,000 women per age group in 2013
Source: Department of Health, 2014, p. 21; Goenee, M. et al, Rutgers WPF, 2013, p. 2-3.

---

200 UNICEF, *An overview of child well-being in rich countries. A comprehensive assessment of the lives and well-being of children and adolescents in the economically advanced nations.* Report card 7. Florence, 2007, p. 2.
201 Peter Saunders, "Income Support for Families and the Living Standards for Children", in: Sheila Kamerman, Shelley Phipps and Asher Ben-Arieh, (eds.), *From Child Welfare to Child Well-Being. An International Perspective on Knowledge in the Service of Policy Making.* Dordrecht, etc. 2010, pp. 275-292, esp. pp. 281 and 286.
202 UNICEF, op. cit., p. 3.

The first reason for the difference between the two countries is the higher number of teenage pregnancies in the U.K., as compared to the Netherlands.[203] Wellings and Kane explain the high teenage birth and abortion rates in the U.K. by the sharp increase in teenage sexual activity in the period between 1930 and 1970, while in the period thereafter the marriage rate showed a dramatic decline.[204] In the years from 1969 to 1996, the number of teenage births has decreased by about 40%, whereas the number of teenage abortions has quadrupled.[205]

In 1999 the British Government launched the Teenage Pregnancy Strategy, in order to reduce the rate of teenage conceptions in England over a period of ten years.[206] Scotland, Wales and Northern Ireland decided their initiatives independently. Part of the underlying motivation for the Government's action to reduce the number of teenage conceptions, was the relatively poor health and socioeconomic status of teenage mothers and their children. An important element in this strategy was a media awareness campaign. The main messages of this campaign were the promotion of resistance to peer pressure to engage in early sexual activity and the encouragement of the use of contraception if sexually active. Advice on sex and relationships via a telephone helpline and a supporting website was also offered. A further goal was to try to improve the proportion of teenage parents who are in education, training or employment.

Sourafel Girma and David Paton have investigated the effectiveness of the promotion of long acting reversible forms of contraception (LARCs) based on the implementation of the English Teenage Pregnancy Strategy between 2004 and 2012.[207] They did not find statistically significant evidence that LARCs or other birth control variables are associated with fewer teenage pregnancies. These results are consistent with earlier studies

---

[203] The under-18 conception rate in England and Wales in 2012 is 27.9 conceptions per thousand women. Cf. Office for National Statistics, 2014. In the Netherlands, the under-20 conception rate in 2012 is 13 conceptions per thousand women. Cf. Charles Picavet and Ineke van der Vlugt, *Factsheet Tienerzwangerschappen in Nederland*, Rutgers WPF, Utrecht, 2014, p. 1.
[204] Cf. part 1.4.1.4.
[205] Wellings, K. and Kane, R., op. cit., pp. 279-280.
[206] Department for Children, Schools and Families and Department of Health, *Teenage Pregnancy Strategy: Beyond 2010*, London 2010, p. 12.
[207] Sourafel Girma and David Paton, "Is education the best contraception: the case of teenage pregnancy in England?", *Social Science & Medicine*, 2015, 131, pp. 1-9

on the access to family planning services in the U.K.[208] In contrast, they did find a significant negative association between teenage pregnancies and educational performance during secondary education. Further, increases in the non-white proportion in the population are also associated with significantly fewer teenage pregnancies.[209]

A relevant question is whether the efforts to reduce the number of teenage pregnancies would also have an effect on the number of teenage abortions. According to a British cohort study by Paul Wilkinson et al., the number of teenage abortions rose by 7.5% during the first five years of the national teenage pregnancy strategy.[210] However, between 2003 and 2013, the abortion rate among teenagers in England and Wales has indeed diminished significantly, whereas the total number of abortions has increased.[211] Reflecting on the content of the British National Health Service media campaign focusing on sex and young people, one of the strategic elements, it is remarkable how little attention is given to sustainability of relationships, or more concretely, on the link between the possibility of abstinence and marriage preparation. The main issues are sexuality, contraception and health including the risk of infections.[212]

Besides the relatively high number of teenage pregnancies in the U.K. as compared to the Netherlands, a second reason for the higher abortion rate is the absence of a legal requirement for parental consent for teenage women. According to Hans-Christian Raabe, evidence from across the world and especially from the analysis of parental involvement laws in the U.S. shows that parental involvement laws do not increase teenage pregnancies. The introduction of parental notification reduces teenage abortion rates by 10-20%.[213]

As regards marital status, there are no big differences between the two

---

208 David Paton, "Random behaviour or rational choice? Family planning, teenage pregnancy and sexually transmitted infections", *Sex Education*, 2007, 6, (3), pp. 281-308, here p. 283; David Paton, "The economics of family planning and underage conceptions", *Journal of Health Economics*, 2002, 21, pp. 207–225.
209 Girma, S. and Paton, D., op. cit., p. 5.
210 Paul Wilkinson, Rebecca French, Roslyn Kane, Kate Lachowycz, Judith Stephenson and Chris Grundy, "Teenage conceptions, abortions, and births in England, 1994-2003, and the national teenage pregnancy strategy", *The Lancet*, 2006, 25, pp. 1879-1886.
211 Department of Health, 2014, op. cit., p. 5.
212 On the NHS-website 'Sex and young people', accessed 8 December 2015.
213 Hans-Christian Raabe, in: House of Commons Science and Technology Committee, op. cit., p. 164.

countries, where around 20% of all abortions are carried out on married women. The percentage of married women having an abortion is slowly decreasing in both countries, whereas the number of single women is increasing. In both countries, the total number of marriages has decreased steadily during the last four decades. Little attention has been given to this development in health policy or educational guidelines.[214]

Finally, in the U.K. in recent years there has been a strong increase in the use of the abortifacient drug RU486 (also known as mifepristone). Medical abortion accounted for about 49% of total abortions in the U.K. in 2013.[215] In the Netherlands the increase of medical abortions has been less strong.[216]

1.4.3.1 Demographical developments in the U.K. and the Netherlands

Looking at the historical development in the average number of children that a Dutch woman received, a sharp decline can be seen between 1850 and 2010. In 1875 women had four children on average.[217] One of the reasons for the decline in the birth rate after 1880 is the campaign for birth control that was initiated by the Neo-Malthusian movement.[218] After a peak in the birth rate during the 1940s, the average number of children decreased below two, with a remarkably strong decline after 1965, influenced by a strong focus on family planning with contraceptive means. The Dutch Ministry of Foreign Affairs mentions four reasons for this focus on family planning: concerns about the prospect of overpopulation; a campaign for new family planning legislation by the influential Dutch Society for Sexual Reform (Nederlandse Vereniging voor Sexuele Hervorming, NVSH) and the women's movement during the 1960s; the recognition of family planning as an important aspect of general practice by the Dutch College of General Medical Practitioners (NHG) at the end of the 1960s and the availability of contraceptives under

---

214 Cf. part 7.2 as regards the U.K.
215 Department of Health, 2014, op. cit., p. 14.
216 In 2013, 69.8% of all procured abortions have were instrumental abortions; 18.5% were medical abortions and 11.6% were executed by a combined method. Cf. Inspectie voor de Gezondheidszorg, 2014, p. 27.
217 Dutch Interdisciplinary Demographical Institute (NIDI), 2005.
218 Bruijn, J. de, op. cit., pp. 41-148.

the national health insurance scheme since 1971.[219] Similarly, in the U.K. the pill was first prescribed in clinics of the Family Planning Association (FPA) in 1961. Within ten years the pill had been prescribed to over a million women. In 1974, the FPA network of over 1,000 clinics was handed over to the National Health Service (NHS). Also other factors, such as the desire for a career contributed to women deciding to delay becoming mothers.

Figure 5 shows the number of live births per 1,000 population in the U.K. and the Netherlands between 1960 and 2010.

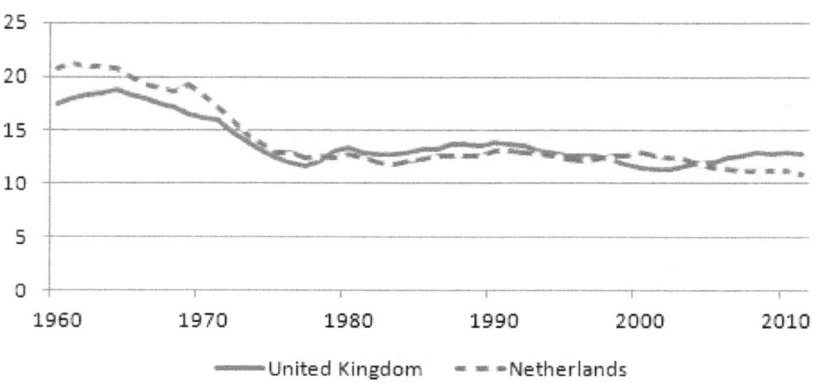

Figure 5: Crude birth rate (live births per 1,000 population in the U.K. and the Netherlands, 1960-2010

Sources: Office for National Statistics, National Records of Scotland, Northern Ireland Statistics and Research Agency, 2013; Centraal Bureau voor de Statistiek, 2012.

In the early seventies both in the Netherlands and in the U.K. the birth rate decreased sharply. From then the average birth rate per woman is below the so-called replacement level of 2.1, which is the number of children needed to replace the whole generation of men and women. In recent years, in the U.K. there has been a slight recovery of the birth rate. In the Netherlands the birth rate has decreased further in the first decade of the 21st century.

The European Union Institute for Statistical research (Eurostat) compares the fertility rates of all the member states. It needs to be noted

---

219 Ministry of Foreign Affairs, *Q&A Abortion in the Netherlands*, The Hague, 2011, p. 7.

that the fertility rate is an estimated number, computed by adding the fertility rates by age for women in a given year. In 2013, the total fertility rate in the 28 member states is about 1.55.[220] This means that in the nearby future the European population will age, and probably will even decrease, if the fertility rate is not compensated by migration.

1.4.3.2 Abortion and ethnicity

The phenomenon of migration has had major consequences for the practice and prevention of abortion, as is shown in figure 6.

Ethnic group	Population in 2011 (x 1.000.000)	Percentage of total population in 2011 (%)	Legal abortions according to ethnicity in 2013 (%)	Percentage of women who had one or more previous abortions by ethnic group (2013) (%)
White	48	86	76	36
Asian or Asian British	4.4	7.5	9	33
Black or Black British	1.9	3.3	9	49
Chinese or other ethnic Group	0.6	1.0	2	31
Mixed	1.3	2.2	3	45
Total	56.2	100	100	37

Figure 6: Abortions among ethnic groups in England and Wales, 2013

Source: Office for National Statistics, *Ethnicity and National Identity in England and Wales 2011*, Titchfield, 2012, p. 3-4; Department of Health, 2014, p. 10-11.

If the various ethnic groups in the U.K. are compared, it becomes clear that the percentage of abortions is much higher among women belonging to the Black or Black British ethnic group, the percentage of the

---

220 European Commission, "Total fertility rate", Eurostat, accessed 21 December 2015.

total number of abortions (9%) being almost three times as much as the percentage of Black or Black British women in the total population (3.3%). The Asian or Asian British, the Chinese, Other and Mixed ethnic group also have relatively higher abortion rates. These data indicate that the current prevention measures do not suffice for these ethnic groups of women in the U.K. Research by the Dutch G.P. Nizaar Makdoembaks on abortion, the prevention of sexually transmitted infections (STI's), child abuse and human trafficking in Amsterdam South-East also points at a lack of care and control for the various ethnic groups living in that part of the city.[221]

1.4.3.3 The legalization of abortion has contributed to an increased demand

Visser et al. mention three causes for the increased number of abortions in the Netherlands: the increased number of requests for abortion by foreign clients, the diminished use of contraceptives among both Dutch and migrant inhabitants, and a higher incidence of sexually transmittable diseases, with inherent risks for the embryo.[222] These explanations are relevant on a short and medium term, but are not sufficient to provide a long term analysis of what has been changed in the British and Dutch societies.

In this part it is investigated if the mere existence of professional abortion clinics and the fact that abortions are offered free of charge has caused an increased demand for abortions. Visser et al. do not mention this explanation in their evaluation of the Dutch abortion practice. They do notice that more than 90% of the women expressed satisfaction with the overall treatment - not with the abortion itself - in the clinic, before, during and shortly after the intervention.[223] It is likely that the impression of satisfaction is passed on to other women who are thinking of having an abortion.

Evidence can be found for the hypothesis that the existence of abortion clinics and the free treatments have caused an increased demand for abortions by reversing the question: Would more restrictive abortion laws or more costly treatments result in a lower abortion number? The social

---
221 Nizaar Makdoembaks, *Geheime abortus maskeert kindermisbruik. Hoge embryosterfte door falend soa-beleid.* Amsterdam, 2008.
222 Visser, M.R.M. et al., op. cit., p. 58.
223 Ibid., p. 91.

scientific study by Mark Levels clearly shows that restrictive abortion laws affect reproductive behaviour.[224] He has compared the abortion legislation in 34 European countries between 1960 and 2010 and has then made a selection of 39,321 women in 13 countries in order to measure the effect of restrictive abortion laws on reproductive behaviour. He concludes that "compared to when abortion was legal only to save a woman's life, women were more likely to terminate a pregnancy if abortion was legal for reasons of physical (b= 1.050), even more likely if abortion were legal for reasons of mental health (b= 1.376), more likely still when abortion for socioeconomic reasons were permitted (b= 1.472), and most probable if abortion was available on request (b= 1.548)."[225] Levels has also found that Dutch women are more likely to choose to have an abortion if the availability of abortion providers increases (b= 0.195; $p < 0.01$).[226] If the U.K. and the Netherlands would introduce more restrictive abortion laws, Levels' theoretical model predicts that this would result in fewer abortions, if other individual characteristics and other laws and circumstances were held constant.[227]

Research in the U.S. had been conducted from a different angle. Marshall Medoff has looked at the real price of an abortion.[228] After 1976, several states in the U.S. have banned the use of their public funds to pay for Medicaid abortions for indigent women. He found that increases in the real price of an abortion caused a statistically and numerically significant decline in the pregnancy rate of all women of childbearing age and teens (ages 15-19). Similarly, a parental involvement law (similarly to the condition for an abortion in the Dutch Termination of Pregnancy Act for teenagers up to the age of 16) induces a decline in the pregnancy rate of all women of childbearing age and an even numerically larger decrease in the teen pregnancy rate. Phillip Levine has shown that in the U.S., where parental involvement laws were enforced in 33 states since 1979, these laws did

---

224 Mark Levels, *Abortion laws in Europe between 1960 and 2010. Legislative developments and their consequences for women's reproductive decision-making*. Dissertation, Nijmegen, 2011.
225 Ibid., pp. 193-194. The reported relationships are all significant ($p < 0.05$); the effects are controlled for underreporting sensitivity.
226 Ibid., p. 225.
227 Ibid., pp. 167-204, here p. 193.
228 Marshall H. Medoff, "Abortion costs, sexual behavior, and pregnancy rates", *The Social Science Journal*, 2008, 45, pp. 156-172.

not only result in fewer abortions, but in fewer teen pregnancies overall.[229] There has been no significant impact from parental involvement laws on the number of births.

Looking at the last 50 years, one can see an evolution from the legal acceptance of abortion in exceptional cases, via the acceptance of abortion up to 24 weeks if certain grounds are met, to the acceptance of late abortions (in the U.K. as of 1967, in the Netherlands as of 2007).

In summary, a first observation which can be made from the statistical and legal data over the last five decades, is that with the current policy in the U.K. and the Netherlands the demand for abortions has increased significantly. Despite all the efforts in the area of prevention, the number of abortions among ethnic minorities remains relatively high in both countries. In-depth research has shown that besides socio-economic differences and language problems also deeper lying cultural differences and sometimes a relation with sexual abuse play a role.

In the U.K., the number of abortions among teenagers is significantly higher than in the Netherlands, partly due to the absence of a legal requirement of parental consent below the age of 16. There is also a higher number of teenage pregnancies in the U.K. Both in the U.K. and in the Netherlands, the percentage of abortions among ethnic minorities is substantially higher than among native citizens. In both countries the number of single people has strongly increased in the last decades. It is clear that the percentage of abortions among married women in both countries is much lower than among other categories of women.

Between 2005 and 2015, in the Netherlands the number of abortions of handicapped children has increased considerably. This increase is connected to the introduction of the standard ultrasound (SEO). Research in the U.K. revealed that almost 30% of geneticists make use of a directive counselling style towards termination of pregnancy.[230]

As a result of these developments and because of the powerful cultural, economic and political currents which encourage the idea of efficiency in society, it is not unrealistic to suppose that social pressure has increased

---

229 Phillip B. Levine, "Parental involvement laws and fertility behavior", *Journal of Health Economics*, 2003, 22, pp. 861-878.
230 Cf. part 7.4.

to such an extent that parents who expect a handicapped baby feel almost obliged to let their initially wanted child be aborted.

For the reasons mentioned above, the objective of the abortion legislation to protect the unborn human life has proven to be insufficiently maintained. Although the intention of the lawmakers had been to keep the abortion number low, it has been shown that by liberalizing the abortion legislations, the British and Dutch Governments contributed to the increase in the abortion number in both countries.

It is very likely that by legalising abortion, the number of clandestine abortions has been reduced. But the claim that legalization prevents abortion in general, cannot be maintained, given the overall increase in the abortion number in the U.K. and the Netherlands in the years following legalization.

1.5 Inconsistencies between legal prescriptions and current abortion praxis in the U.K. and the Netherlands

In 1966, when the British Parliament was debating the Bill for the Abortion Act, MP David Steel declared that: "[It is] not the intention of the promoters of the Bill to leave a wide open door for abortion on request."[231] Similarly, in the late 1970s the Dutch Ministers Leendert Ginjaar and Job de Ruiter stated in their explanatory memorandum to the Members of Parliament that not only information about alternatives for abortion should be offered by the doctor, but also that the doctor should make certain that "the emergency of the woman could not be ended in another way than by terminating the pregnancy".[232]

The increasing abortion numbers in both countries give rise to investigate the consistency of the current implementation of the abortion legislation in the U.K. and the Netherlands with these original intentions.

1.5.1 The grounds for abortion in the U.K.

It has been shown that in the U.K., the vast majority (97%) of all induced abortions is performed under ground C and that almost all of these abortions are performed, presuming that the continuance of pregnancy would involve a greater risk of injury to the mental health of the woman. When in 2007

---

231 Northern Ireland Assembly, Official Report, 20 June 2000, 2.00 pm.
232 Parliamentary Documents, Kamerstukken II, 1978-1979, 15 475, nr. 3, p. 27.

the House of Commons Science and Technology Committee wrote their report on the scientific developments relating to the Abortion Act 1967, a long list of organisations submitted comments on their findings. This very high percentage of 97% has led to indignation and criticism on the part of several pro-life organizations. For instance, the ProLife Alliance writes that it is "absolutely impossible to accept that such a large number of abortions under ground C conform to the terms of the Abortion Act."[233] Ellie Lee makes the point that in fact, the Abortion Act empowers doctors and labels women seeking abortion as weak and vulnerable.[234] Josephine Quintavalle, co-foundress of Corethics, argues that medical and psychological health represent two very different categories of health care and therefore should be separated under the conditions of the Abortion Act.[235]

Some 1% of abortions are currently performed under ground D of the Act which permits abortion to avoid "injury to physical or mental health of any existing children or family". With the current available data it is unclear in what cases and for what reasons this ground D has been indicated.[236]

In 2013, MP David Alton (House of Lords, crossbencher) asked the British Government what action they intended given the assertions that doctors routinely notify abortions on the grounds of a threat to the mental health of the mother when no evidence of any such threat exists.[237] In his reaction, Parliamentary Under-Secretary of State Earl Howe replied that "[a]llegations of terminations carried out outside the Abortion Act are taken extremely seriously and doctors, or other health professionals, failing to adhere to the Abortion Act will be referred to the police."[238]

---

233 Submission of the ProLife Alliance, in: House of Commons Science and Development Committee, *Twelfth Report, List of written evidence on the Scientific Developments Relating to the Abortion Act 1967*, 2007, pp. 36-46, here p. 45. The Guild of Catholic Doctors also states that "forms are quite often lacking proper reasons for the abortion to be performed and the law is being broken all the time". In: Ibid., pp. 70-72.

234 Ellie Lee, "Tensions in the Regulation of Abortion in Britain", *Journal of Law and Society*, 2003, 30, 4, pp. 532-553, here p. 535.

235 Submission from Comment on Reproductive Ethics (Corethics), in: House of Commons Science and Technology Committee, op. cit., pp. 47-52.

236 Ibid, p. 51.

237 House of Lords, written answers 25 February 2013, Column WA183. Lord Alton based his question on the BBC '*Panorama*' broadcast of 4 February 2013, which investigated the incidence of selective abortion based on gender.

238 Ibid., Column WA184.

Within the context of global migration, recent evidence shows significant differences in sex ratios of children born to Indian immigrants in England and Wales, pointing at the incidence of sex-selective abortion in the U.K.[239] A 2012 undercover investigation of the *Daily Telegraph* showing a doctor in Manchester offering to abort a female foetus because of her gender caused a fierce public debate and a lawsuit against the two doctors involved.[240] In normal circumstances, sex-selective abortions are considered illegal in the U.K.[241] In the Parliamentary debate following the investigation, MP David Burrowes (Con.) argued that the Abortion Act needed clarification because of a lack of transparent information and no real safeguards.[242] However, an amendment, introduced by MP Fiona Bruce (Con.) in 2015 to clarify the Abortion Act with regard to the prohibition of sex-selective abortions was rejected. Instead, Parliament decided in favour of an assessment of the evidence regarding sex-selective abortions in England, Wales and Scotland. If the evidence would be confirmed, then the Secretary of State will "determine and publish a strategic plan to tackle substantiated concerns".[243]

The reality shows that the application of the categories for the grounds on which physicians permit an abortion, do not give precise indications for emergency situations. The United Nations report on abortion policies therefore concludes that in the United Kingdom "abortions are available virtually on request".[244] Moreover, an abortion is available free of charge through the National Health Service and the consent of the spouse is not a prerequisite of the termination of pregnancy.

---

239 Sylvie Dubuc and David Coleman, "An increase in the sex ratio of births to India-born mothers in England and Wales: Evidence for sex-selective abortion", *Population and Development Review*, 2007, 33, pp. 383–400. In England and Wales, the average sex ratio at birth (male / female births) is 105,6. The authors call abortion of female foetuses "the most plausible explanation". Cf. ibid., pp. 387 and 392.
240 Cf. Holly Watt and Claire Newell, "Law 'does not prohibit' sex-selection abortions, DPP warns", *Daily Telegraph*, 7 October 2013; Trevor Grundy, "Gender-Based Abortions Spark Outrage In England As Sex Selection Becomes An Option", *The Huffington Post*, 10 October 2013.
241 Cf. British Medical Association, *The law and ethics of abortion*. London, 2007, p. 4.
242 House of Commons, debate 9 October 2013, Westminster Hall, col. 92WH.
243 House of Commons, debate 23 February 2015, col. 150.
244 United Nations Department of Economic and Social Affairs, Population Division: *Abortion Policies. A Global Review. Volume III, Oman to Zimbabwe*. New York, 2002, p. 157.

In the U.K. there are less legal requirements than in the Netherlands before an abortion can be executed. There is no obligatory parental consent for young women under 16, no compulsory cooling-off period between diagnosis of pregnancy and an abortion, no legal duty on doctors to provide access to advice from organisations offering alternatives to abortion, and finally there are more grounds on which a third trimester abortion is allowed.[245]

Still, public opinion in the U.K. is in favour of a legal duty on doctors to provide access to advice from organisations offering alternatives to abortion and is also supportive of a cooling-off period before a final decision is taken.[246] A fully informed consent is a first prerequisite for an abortion praxis that is more in conformity with the original intentions of the lawmakers, which are summarised by initiator David Steel as "not to leave a wide open door for abortion on request".[247]

1.5.2 Inconsistencies in the Dutch implementation of the Termination of Pregnancy Act

Several serious lacunae can be traced in the implementation of the Dutch Termination of Pregnancy Act, as well as in the recognition of the ethical, psychological and social problems that are directly linked with the abortion praxis. The following four prescriptions from the Termination of Pregnancy Act will now be treated, in order to evaluate the degree of consistency between these prescriptions and the current praxis:

1) With every decision-making process before an abortion takes place, it needs to be verified if there is an emergency situation;[248]

2) Alternatives to abortion ought to be discussed;[249]

3) It needs to be verified that the request to have an abortion has been made free of external pressure, after careful consideration, recognizing the responsibility for unborn life and in awareness of the consequences for the woman herself and for her relatives;[250]

---

245 Cf. part 1.1.
246 Cf. part 1.3.
247 Cf. footnote 231.
248 Termination of Pregnancy Act, 1981, Art. 5, part 1.
249 Ibid., Art. 5, part 2a.
250 Ibid., Art. 5, part 2b.

4) A physician will only perform an abortion if, according to his findings, he thinks this is justified.²⁵¹

Ad 1) In the Netherlands, already during the Parliamentary debate on the introduction of the Termination of Pregnancy Act it has become clear that because of legal objections the legislature did not want to define what situations can be considered as emergencies.²⁵² Also in the "Guideline for counselling women considering termination of pregnancy" of the Dutch Association of Abortion Specialists (NGvA), there are no fixed criteria of what is to be called an emergency situation.²⁵³ According to staff members of abortion clinics it would even be an undesirable situation if the legislature would modify the Act in this way, because of the "subjective" character of the term "emergency situation".²⁵⁴ At the time of the evaluation, one clinic has pleaded for a legal prohibition of sex-selective abortions.²⁵⁵

In this regard, Imber remarks that the absence of debate about how physicians in abortion clinics actually make their decisions, makes it look as if they are merely the instruments of others' decisions, whether those others are women or state legislatures. Given the legally protected confidentiality of the physician-patient relation, the only way to interfere with the abortion decision would be by outlawing the diagnostic tests themselves.²⁵⁶

Ad 2) During the consultation in an abortion clinic or hospital, the medical assistant has an obligation to inform or discuss the possibility of alternatives, such as adoption, financial support from the Government or intensified care from the surroundings or professional agencies.²⁵⁷ However, the extended evaluation of the Dutch abortion practice showed that in a majority of consultations (57% in the clinics and in 64% in the hospitals) a scenario of bringing the pregnancy to term has not been discussed.²⁵⁸ As to why this issue so often is not discussed, medical assistants and directors of

---

251 Ibid., Art. 5, part 2c.
252 Cf. part 1.2.1.
253 Nederlands Genootschap van Abortusartsen, *Guideline for counselling women considering termination of pregnancy*. Translated by Joop Hoekstra. Original title: Richtlijn begeleiding van vrouwen die een zwangerschapsafbreking overwegen. Utrecht, 2011, pp. 55-57.
254 Visser, M.R.M. et al., op. cit., p. 121.
255 Ibid.
256 J.B. Imber, "Abortion Policy and Medical Practice", *Society*, 1990, 28, :27-34.
257 These alternatives are not defined in the Act. They will be discussed later in part 7.1.
258 Visser, M.R.M. et al., op. cit., p. 85.

the abortion clinics answered that this would only be the case if the woman herself initiated a discussion on alternatives or when the assistant thinks that an alternative solution is possible (in case of doubts, conscientious objections or a long gestation).[259]

The practice of discussing possible alternatives only if the woman wishes to do so has been integrated in the NGvA-guideline.[260] As a motivation for this approach, the NGvA states that "[d]iscussing alternatives is especially needed with women who have not yet made a choice."[261] However, this statement is contradicted by several authors, such as Monica O'Reilly, an American family nurse practitioner who has undertaken an extensive literature review on option counselling of women with unintended pregnancies.[262] She argues that "the practice of non-directive, comprehensive options counselling is paramount and should be standard practice for all clinicians".[263] Comprehensive options counselling includes discussing parenthood, adoption or foster care.

Discussing these various options after the discovery of an unintended pregnancy is indeed crucial, also because unintended pregnancy is associated with risks such as tobacco and alcohol use during pregnancy, low birth weight, infant mortality, child abuse or physical abuse, depression and insufficient resources for child development.[264] As will be pointed out in the final chapters of this book, appropriate counselling and guidance strategies are needed in order to reduce these risks.

In the evaluation of the Dutch abortion legislation, consultants also were asked if they would speak about alternatives to abortion in the specific case of a foetal anomaly detected with prenatal diagnosis. The reasons they gave not to do so, are very diverse: in two cases prenatal diagnosis had indicated severely handicapped twins and a child with Down's syndrome. In other

---

259 Ibid., pp. 108 and 122.
260 Nederlands Genootschap van Abortusartsen, 2011, op. cit., p. 63.
261 Ibid., p. 58.
262 Monica O'Reilly, "Careful counsel: Management of unintended pregnancy", *Journal of the American Academy of Nurse Practitioners*, 2009, 21, pp. 596–602; Katherine E. Simmonds and Frances E. Likis, "Providing Options Counseling for Women With Unintended Pregnancies", *Journal of Obstetric, Gynecologic, and Neonatal Nursing*, 2005, 34 (3), pp. 373-379, here 375.
263 O'Reilly, M., op. cit., p. 601.
264 Simmonds, K.E. and Likis, F.E., op. cit., p. 374.

cases the woman did not show any doubts, or it was a very early pregnancy, or the woman did not want to talk about alternatives.[265] However, in most of these cases when a foetal anomaly has been detected, the pregnancy was initially wanted. For this reason, encouraging careful reflection in a non-directive way and providing education materials on possible treatment, future perspectives and care facilities seems even more necessary.[266]

Ad 3) The Termination of Pregnancy Act prescribes that the request to have an abortion needs to be made after careful consideration. Further, according to the Medical Treatment Contracts Act, counsellors must inform their patients about the expected effects and related risks of the treatment.[267] Unfortunately, this important aspect of the obligation to inform about possible physical and mental health risks has not been investigated during the evaluation of the abortion practice in the Netherlands.[268] Neither has this obligation to inform been addressed at the regulatory inspection of abortion clinics by the Health Care Inspectorate in 2012.[269] In the next chapter it will be shown that both physical and mental health risks are at stake when procured abortion is considered.

The evaluation further shows that doctors and medical assistants are inclined to follow the woman in her desire to have the abortion. For example, the directors of abortion clinics all say that in the end it is the woman who decides. Their main concern is that the decision is taken carefully and in freedom.[270] This line of thinking is indeed in accord with the intention of the Termination of Pregnancy Act. But here one has to ask if there is not an ambiguity in the Act itself. Because, in order to avoid subjectivity, the Act prescribes that two autonomous decisions need to be made, one by the woman, one by the doctor. In reality, the main criterion for the medical staff seems to be a procedural one, and not a criterion concerning content.[271] In

---

265 Visser, M.R.M. et al., op. cit., p. 106.
266 Cf. parts 3.1.3 and 7.4.
267 Medical Treatment Contracts Act (in Dutch: Wet Geneeskundige Behandelovereenkomst (WGBO), Art. 448.
268 Other aspects of the decision making have been evaluated, such as the obligation to discuss alternatives. Cf. Visser, M.R.M. et al., op. cit., pp. 82-88.
269 Inspectie voor de Gezondheidszorg, *Verantwoorde zorg in abortusklinieken, met ruimte voor verbetering*. Utrecht, 2013.
270 Visser, M.R.M. et al., op. cit., p. 121.
271 As is admitted by Visser et al. on p. 102.

this way, the abortion praxis leaves all responsibility – and all remorse, if the decision is regretted afterwards – to the woman.

Ad 4) According to the NGvA guideline, the counsellor must give the woman the opportunity to express and explain her reasons for a termination of pregnancy. He must also make certain that the decision is taken with due care.[272] However, as has been pointed out above, within the current praxis the counsellor is not required to assess the degree of emergency in the situation, nor is it a standard procedure to discuss alternatives.

About two-thirds of Dutch women who come to an abortion clinic or hospital has been referred by a G.P.[273] The way in which general practitioners (G.P.'s) gather and process information about a woman and her specific situation when she requests an abortion has been empirically investigated by Tirza van Laar-Jochemsen et al.[274] Van Laar-Jochemsen et al. conclude that the information given by G.P.'s on consequences, risks and alternatives to abortion is provided only when women ask for it, which is in a limited number of cases.[275] An exchange of ethical opinions between the G.P. and the woman is even rarer. This situation can impede the prospect that a decision is based on fully-informed consent of the woman, but similarly, the G.P. might also lack essential information of the woman's situation and her state of mind.

In the second part of their study, van Laar-Jochemsen et al. investigate is how G.P.'s contribute to the prevention and treatment of psychosocial consequences among women after an abortion, and how this care can be improved.[276] They suggest that more attention be given to aftercare, as regards emotional stability and coming to terms with the loss of the unborn. Instructions for G.P.'s could help improve both prevention and aftercare.

---

272 Nederlands Genootschap van Abortusartsen, 2011, op. cit., p. 57.
273 Visser, M.R.M. et al., op. cit., p. 56.
274 T.W. van Laar-Jochemsen, C.E. Zijp-Zuidema and H. Jochemsen, *Psychische problematiek bij vrouwen na abortus provocatus en de rol van de huisarts*, Prof. dr. G.A. Lindeboom Instituut, Ede, 2006. A G.P. is called 'huisarts' in Dutch.
275 Laar-Jochemsen, T.W. van et al., op. cit., pp. 99-100.
276 Ibid., pp. 66-102.

1.6 The medicalization of abortion

Since the 1960s, the phenomenon of medicalization in the Western world has attracted the interest of sociologists.[277] It has to be reminded that the problem of abortion is first of all an ethical issue, because it deals with moral conduct regarding life and death. The relevant questions which people ask themselves when they think of abortion, are much broader than the world of medicine. Pregnant women and their partners will ask themselves questions about the possible future of their child, about his or her quality of life, about their capabilities to raise the child. Lawmakers will think of the criteria according to which abortion should be legal or should be forbidden, whereas ethicists study the moral grounds for these criteria.

But since the latter half of the previous century, the ethical problem of abortion is treated more and more as a medical issue, a development which Ellie Lee calls the "de-moralization" of abortion.[278] As a consequence, the legal aim has shifted from the protection of the innocent towards the reduction of suffering. A first clear indication for the medicalization of abortion is the frequent use of the term "patients" in official documents for women who consider an abortion. Calling pregnant women "patients" suggests that they have a certain illness of which they can be cured by a doctor. For instance, Visser et al. in their report speak 14 times of "patients", meaning women who have been clients of an abortion clinic.[279] Also the Dutch Termination of Pregnancy Act law speaks 5 times of "patients" in this regard. The U.K. Abortion Act does not use the term "patient", but consequently speaks of (pregnant) women.

In the political discourse, one could also encounter the phenomenon of medicalization of abortion. Formally, both for the British and the Dutch law, abortion remains a criminal offense. But the reasons why an abortion can be considered legally justifiable have been defined in medical terms. This has precisely been the intention of one of the initiators of the British

---

[277] A thorough study on how medicalization has influenced the decision-making process regarding abortion in the U.S. and the U.K. has been conducted by Ellie Lee: *Abortion, Motherhood and Mental Health. Medicalizing Reproduction in the United States and Great Britain.* New York, 2003. She argues that motherhood itself has been medicalised with the growing attention for the problem of postnatal depression. Cf. Lee, E., 2003 (a), op. cit., pp. 181-220.
[278] Lee, E., 2003 (a), op. cit., pp. 81-114.
[279] Visser, M.R.M. et al, op. cit..

Abortion Act, Steel, which can be illustrated by his intervention at the start of the parliamentary debate in 1967, when the assessment of the risk of a continuance of a woman's pregnancy for her life or health was at stake: "[On the contrary,] we are leaving to the medical profession what members of that profession consider and have represented to us that they, and they alone, have every right and qualification to determine and that it is not for Parliament to tie their hands."[280]

As we have seen in the previous section, in almost all cases in the U.K., the legal ground on which abortion is permitted is ground C, presuming that the continuance of the pregnancy would involve risk of injury to the mental health of the pregnant woman. In the Dutch abortion law formal grounds are lacking, but also here the doctor has to tell the woman if he is willing to execute the abortion or not.

There is evidence that, from the first years after the enactment of the Abortion Act, a majority of British G.P.'s, consultant psychiatrists and consultant gynaecologists would, generally speaking, recommend or perform abortion if a request had been made by for instance an unmarried university student in her final year, before ten weeks of pregnancy and if serious consideration had been given to alternatives.[281] The questionnaires did not mention a risk to the health of the woman. John Keown concludes that these studies lend support to the view that apparently, a significant number of abortions has been performed for social reasons.[282]

This discrepancy between the medical criteria of the Abortion Act and the reality that abortions are performed for social reasons has been analysed from a socio-political view by Fran Amery.[283] She argues that the medicalization of abortion was "a fraught and incomplete process involving fundamental tensions over doctors' responsibilities".[284] One the one hand, the Abortion Act facilitated doctors by granting them authority in women's

---

[280] D. Steel, MP, during the House of Commons debate of June 1967, vol. 749 cc. 895-1102 (Medical termination of Pregnancy Bill), here col. 900.

[281] John Keown, *Abortion, doctors and the law. Some aspects of the legal regulation of abortion in England from 1803 to 1982*. Cambridge, 1988, pp. 120-128.

[282] Ibid., p. 137.

[283] Fran Amery, "Social Questions, Medical Answers. Contesting British Abortion Law", *Social Politics*, 2014, 21 (1), pp. 26-49.

[284] Ibid., p. 26.

reproductive decision-making processes. On the other hand, this medical model of care has been criticised by feminist writers who challenged precisely this dominance of the medical profession in relation to women's reproductive choices.

Therefore, in the next chapter it will be investigated to what extent the value of human autonomy, advocated so often by feminist writers, has truly been safeguarded by the current legislation of abortion in the U.K. and the Netherlands.

Chapter 2

Human autonomy and procured abortion

The abortion legislation which became current practice in the U.K. after 1967 and in the Netherlands since 1981 seeks to protect women's autonomy in the individual decision making process regarding an unintended pregnancy. The striving for this objective has a long history. During the 19th and 20th centuries in the U.K. and the Netherlands, several women who were considered as representing the feminist movement first attempted to introduce exceptions on the prohibition of abortion and later sought to legalise abortion, pleading for the possibility of an autonomous choice in reproductive matters. In the third feminist wave however, several authors pointed out the limitations of this autonomy principle. (2.1)

By many philosophers after the age of Enlightenment, the principle of autonomous choice has been valued as a starting point for individual decision making. The autonomy principle has been elaborated in various ways, by philosophers such as Immanuel Kant and Martha Nussbaum and it has been applied to the abortion dilemma by Judith Jarvis Thompson. (2.2) Finally, the relation between the historical and present understanding of human conscience and human autonomy will be dealt with. (2.3)

2.1 Pleading for women's autonomy: abortion and the three feminist waves in the U.K. and the Netherlands

The main issues for representatives of the first, second and third feminist waves are women's autonomy, emancipation and sexual liberation. (2.1.1., 2.1.3 and 2.1.6) Dealing with these issues, feminist writers also wrote about abortion. Initially, during the 1930s in the U.K., a plea to legalise certain abortion methods did not receive much attention. (2.1.2) But during the second feminist wave, the public opinion in the U.K. regarding abortion shifted. (2.1.4) Also in the 1960s, a change took place in the Netherlands in the opinion of psychiatrists and other medical specialists with regard to the legalization of abortion. (2.1.5) Finally, with the third feminist wave, critics have been raised at the overestimation of autonomous choice in the late modern era. (2.1.6) For this reason, a critical philosophical reflection will be made. (2.1.7)

2.1.1 The first feminist wave

During the nineteenth and the early twentieth centuries, in the Western world the first feminist wave was aimed at expanding women's possibilities for education, improving employment possibilities and for women's suffrage. Influential feminist writers like Marie Stopes (1880-1958) in Britain or Aletta Jacobs (1854-1929) in the Netherlands strove for more social and moral equality between men and women. However, neither of these women favoured abortion. Marie Stopes pleaded for education regarding conjugal love and parenthood, as well as for knowledge of the prevention of conception, rather than for a legal right to abortion.[285] Aletta Jacobs, who as a doctor had been among the first Dutch women to provide information on contraception, was convinced that sex-education would lower the number of illegal abortions. For her, abortion had to remain an exceptional medical intervention which was not capable of contributing to the emancipation of women.[286]

A long time before the acceptance by the U.K. Parliament of the Abortion Act 1967, abortion was permitted only in exceptional cases, for severe physical or mental health reasons on the part of the woman. Still, in the U.K. there has been a long history of resistance against the classification of abortion as a criminal offence, which was based on the Offences Against the Person Act of 1861. The Abortion Law Reform Association (ALRA)

---

[285] She writes: "Further, alas, it is true that even in our most civilized cities there are many to whom abortion by some means or other is the only method known by which they can limit the size of their families." In: M.C. Stopes, *Contraception (Birth control), its theory, history and practice. A Manual for the Medical and Legal Professions*. London, 1927, p. 5; Marie Stopes is the author of *Married Love* (London, 1918, Dutch translation: *Hij en zij in het huwelijk. Nieuwe bijdrage tot de oplossing van het sexueele vraagstuk*. Amsterdam, 1931) and *Radiant Motherhood* (London, 1920, Dutch translation: *Hij en zij en hun kind. Een boek voor jonge echtgenooten en voor allen, die de toekomst moeten maken*, Amsterdam, 1925). See also Aylmer Maude, *Marie Stopes: Her Work and Play*. London, 1933, pp. 149-153; Olive Banks, *Becoming a Feminist. The Social Origins of 'First Wave' Feminism*. Sussex, 1986, pp. 26 and 69-70.

[286] Bruijn, J. de, op. cit., pp. 73, 78 and 188.

had already been founded in the 1930s with the aim of lifting all restrictions on abortion. ALRA wanted abortion legalised in circumstances where a woman's physical health was threatened, but also in the light of social, economic and psychological criteria. Its members believed that women, rather than the state or the medical profession should be the ultimate judges of whether a pregnancy should continue or be terminated.[287]

2.1.2 Between the Wars

In the period between the two World wars, the plea for autonomy in relation to abortion in Britain was motivated by considerations of the marked class divisions. Many testimonies showed that working-class women in particular paid a heavy physical price for multiple pregnancies. In this period of high unemployment, many women and men tried to find ways to avoid large families, in order to combat poverty. Feminists and working-class activists within the Labour Party launched a campaign for wider access to birth control and information on contraception. Regarding abortion methods, the British historian Stephen Brooke shows historical evidence for a clear class divide between the availability of curettage, which was more affordable for upper and middle-class women and the more dangerous use of abortifacient pills, nonsurgical implements such as crochet hooks and knitting needles, and folk remedies such as slippery elm bark, still in use among working-class women in the 1930s.[288] But until this time, the extra-parliamentary strategy used by ALRA in order to instigate legalization had failed.

2.1.3 The second feminist wave

The second wave of feminism peaked in the 1960s and 1970s and touched on every area of women's experience, including family, sexuality and work. For example, Simone de Beauvoir's *The Second Sex*, in the English translation of 1953, and Betty Friedan's *The Feminine Mystique* of 1963, became influential in Western Europe and the United States. In relation to the problem of abortion, it is clear that De Beauvoir focussed on what she saw as the discriminated position of women in a male dominated society.

---

287 Brooke, S., op. cit., pp. 15-20.
288 Brooke, S., 2002, op. cit., p. 16.

Likewise, Friedan explained a widespread feeling of unhappiness among American women as coming from a struggle with their identity, which they experienced as depending of their husband and family. Being involved in the women's movement, De Beauvoir actively campaigned for the liberalisation of abortion and contraception in France.[289] Friedan founded the National Association for the Repeal of Abortion Laws, renamed National Abortion Rights Action League after the U.S. Supreme Court legalised abortion in 1973.

In the Netherlands the article *"Het onbehagen bij de vrouw"* ("The woman's discomfort") of 1967 by Joke Smit is generally considered as marking the beginning of the second wave of feminism. She pleaded for equality for men and women on the labour market and she saw motherhood rather as a disadvantage for women than as something which could be fulfilling as well.[290] Abortion rights were thus launched as an instrument for emancipation.[291]

Still, Smit argued that abortion should be an "escape route that would die out because of the teaching of an effective contraceptive mentality."[292] A contraceptive mentality supports the idea that sexual reproduction can be technologically controlled. Smit thought that teaching contraceptive behaviour to the young generation would result in a decline in the abortion number and she was not alone in this presumption. Two years later, a commission of Dutch psychiatrists formulated the same conviction in their report on the abortion question.[293]

In the 1970s, Dutch politicians discussed the issue of providing alternatives for abortion to women who did not have sufficient means to bring an unintended pregnancy to term. The discussion was characterised

---

289 Alison T. Holland, *Simone de Beauvoir and the Women's Movement,* Northumbria, 2002.
290 Joke Smit, "Het onbehagen bij de vrouw", *De Gids,* 130, nr. 9-10, 1967, pp. 267-281, for example p. 20, where she describes motherhood as "their second coincidence, after the first, which was their marriage."
291 Ibid., p. 29: "If somewhere we need an over-simplified feminism then it is here. Because if somewhere we can speak of class injustice on a large scale, of systematic discrimination towards a specific section of the population, if somewhere women are considered as voiceless, then it is in the area of abortion legislation."
292 Ibid., p. 30.
293 Aart A. Fischer et al., "Rapport Abortus-vraagstuk van Commissie van de Nederlandse Vereniging voor Psychiatrie en Neurologie", *Medisch Contact,* 1970, 25, p. 152.

by little political will to provide material support to these women. This stance was supported by sociological research, for instance by Ruut Veenhoven who claimed that material support given to pregnant women could only be a solution in isolated cases.[294] He maintained that stimulating this would be too expensive and that it would be impossible to determine if a pregnancy is unwanted or not. Further he argued that in many cases material circumstances do not play a role when a pregnancy is unwanted and that these are seldom the most important consideration for women.

At the same time, attitudes towards sexual permissiveness and promiscuity in the Netherlands shifted, like in other Western countries. Sociological research by Gerbert Kraaykamp shows that attitudes towards pre-marital sex have become substantially more liberal between 1965 and 1995.[295] The same cannot be said for extra-marital sex, for which prevailing attitudes initially liberalised until the mid-1970s, but then reversed to more traditional values. Kraaykamp notes that attitudes towards permissiveness tend to be more conservative among Dutch women (although differences with men are decreasing), elderly people, married couples and those practising religion.

2.1.4 The U.K.: a shift in the public opinion regarding abortion

During the 1960s in the U.K. and elsewhere a shift took place in the public opinion regarding the permissiveness of abortion, partly due to some tragic incidents. In 1961, reports came up of seriously deformed children born to mothers who had taken the sedative drug Thalidomide prescribed to alleviate morning sickness. Pictures of deformed children were spread quickly by the ever growing media. The same year, the dangers associated with using this drug during pregnancy became clear and it was taken from the market, after having affected more than 300 children.[296]

Secondly, in 1966 the British Ministry of Health reported that the two main causes of maternal deaths in England and Wales were pulmonary embolism and abortion. On radio and television there were programmes on

---

[294] Ruut Veenhoven, "Alternatieven voor abortus", in: *Politiek Perspectief*, 1 nr. 5, Sept./Okt. 1972, pp. 27-31.
[295] Gerbert Kraaykamp, "Trends and Countertrends in Sexual Permissiveness: Three Decades of Attitude Change in The Netherlands 1965–1995", *Journal of Marriage and Family*, 2002, 64, pp. 225–239, here pp. 230-232.
[296] Brooke, S., 2002, op. cit., p. 16.

"the horror of backstreet abortions." Undoubtedly, both tragic phenomena contributed to the change in public opinion in favour of legal abortion.[297]

One of the architects of the Bill which became the Abortion Act 1967 was the MP David Steel (Lib.). In an interview, held in 1997 on the occasion of the thirtieth anniversary of the Abortion Act, he mentions the tragic deaths of women from criminal abortion: "The number of deaths of women from criminal abortion showed up in the Home Office statistics each year as somewhere between 30 and 50 and that was only the tip of the iceberg. The public wards of every hospital had cases of either self-induced or botched abortion sufferers. It seemed to me a genuine social problem."[298]

Steel refers to a report produced by the Church of England in 1965, in which a justification is sought for a new law on abortion, in order to deal with the problem of illegal abortions.[299] The report speaks of the criterion of necessity, a well-known term in common law. In fact, any surgical operation is made lawful if it is done by necessity, thus removing it from the category of mutilation. According to authors of the report, the criterion of necessity is based on two conditions: "it is required that the evil averted by the operation must be greater than the evil performed; and that no more evil may be done than is reasonably necessary to avert the greater evil."[300]

It is hard to see how these two conditions could be established. The authors of the report indicate that they "would extend the justification of necessity to cover a real threat to the physical or mental health of the mother, that is, to her psycho-physical well-being..."[301] Therefore, there may be cases in which the general right of the foetus to live and develop "may be offset by other conflicting rights".[302] The authors speak of cases in which

---

[297] Stephen Brooke, "A New World for Women? Abortion Law Reform in Britain during the 1930s", *American Historical Review*, 106, 2001, pp. 431-459.

[298] The Rt. Hon Lord Steel of Aikwood, MP (Liberal, Liberal Democrat) between 1966 and 1997, in: Ann Furedi and Michael Hume, (eds.), *Abortion Law Reformers. Pioneers of Change*. Stratford-upon-Avon, 2007, originally published in 1997, p. 50.

[299] Church Assembly Board for Social Responsibility, Church of England, *Abortion. An Ethical Discussion*. Oxford, 1965, p. 7. The Committee who wrote the report was chaired by Rev. Canon I.T. Ramsey.

[300] Ibid., p. 33.

[301] Ibid., p. 34.

[302] Ibid., p. 32.

"there would arise a balance of interest between the foetus on the one side and the mother and family on the other."[303]

The possibility of an abortion is thus described as a woman's right, a turning point in the history of the British abortion legislation.[304] The basic value of human life has been subordinated to the value of psycho-physical well-being. In the political discussions which followed the Church of England's report, the opinion that a woman has a right to autonomy after the discovery of an unwanted pregnancy was adopted by a majority of the members of the British Parliament in 1967.

2.1.5 The Netherlands: a shift in the way of looking at early human life

In the late 1960s in the Netherlands another important shift took place in the discussion from the strictly medical definition of abortion as the taking away of embryonic life, towards a subjective definition of human life. This is clearly illustrated in the already mentioned report of the commission of Dutch psychiatrists, appearing in 1969, which explicitly states that "the moment, at which one is about to speak of a human life, is subjectively determined."[305] Psychiatrist Aart Fischer and his co-authors give as advice to their colleagues in the medical profession who principally reject procured abortion to "accept the woman's autonomous feelings and values as primarily given". Such a doctor "respects the woman's values, if he shows her that his point of view is subjective; that he rejects her request not because her convictions are wrong or bad, but because he, as a human being and not as an expert, values her early pregnancy differently". As a motivation for a "yes, unless" attitude towards abortion is mentioned the "more and more accepted values, that each human being has the right to self-fulfilment and that the community has the task to create the opportunities for this."[306]

The report implied the abandoning of the until then strictly legal protection of the human embryo. At the same time, multidisciplinary teams of gynaecologists, psychologists and social workers were formed at academic centres, aimed at changing the rejecting attitude towards abortion

---

303 Ibid., pp. 40-41.
304 Cf. part 1.1.
305 Fischer, A.A. et al., op. cit., p. 149.
306 Fischer, A.A. et al., op. cit., pp. 148-149.

and at "providing help as much as possible".³⁰⁷ These teams, tolerated by national and local governments, could be considered as precursors of the current abortion clinics. During the seventies and eighties, many women who came to a Dutch abortion clinic were from neighbouring countries in Europe, mainly from Western Germany, where the abortion legislation had been more strictly upheld.³⁰⁸

Although these multidisciplinary teams were functioning in the Netherlands from the beginning of the 1970s, it would take until 1981 when the Dutch Parliament legalised abortion. As has been shown, this legalization lead to a further increase of the number of abortions in the next decades. These and other developments, similar in large parts of the Western world, challenged some representatives of the third feminist wave to rethink their position on abortion and choice, as will be discussed in the next part.

2.1.6 The third feminist wave

The term "third wave" feminism has been popularised by the American author and activist Rebecca Walker in 1992.³⁰⁹ In the article she reacts against the claim that America has entered an era of postfeminism, pleading once more for equality of women, a "fight which is far from over", as long as men do not "prioritize our freedom to control our bodies and our lives".³¹⁰ According to Heywood, third-wave feminism has never had a single-issue agenda that distinguishes it from other movements for social justice. The emphasis on gender has been part of a much larger agenda for environmental, economic and social justice in a globalised context. Another characteristic for this inclusive approach is that "third wave also seeks to create a feminism that includes men and looks at gender as something that men have as well as women".³¹¹

As regards the issue of procured abortion, Ami Lynch states that "for

---

307 Ibid., p. 153.
308 Bruijn, J. de, op. cit., p. 291, footnote 59; Visser, M.R.M. et al., op. cit., p. 59.
309 Rebecca Walker, "Becoming the Third Wave", in: Leslie L. Heywood (ed.), *The Women's Movement Today. An Encyclopedia of Third-Wave Feminism*, Westport (CT.) and London, 2006, Vol. 2, pp. 3-5.
310 Ibid.
311 Heywood, L.L., op. cit., Vol. 1, p. XX.

feminists of all 'waves', it is seen as a cornerstone to women's rights".[312] However, it has been shown above that for first wave feminists like Mary Stopes or Aletta Jacobs such a statement is untenable.[313] Even for second wave feminists such as Joke Smit, legal abortion is not considered as a goal as such, but as a means for women's emancipation.[314]

A difference between second and third-wave feminists and their view on abortion is that for second-wave feminists, abortion is considered as an issue of choice, whereas many third-wave feminists note that there may be "financial, geographical, cultural, and/or familial hindrances on that choice".[315] Although most third-wave feminists want to maintain the possibility of safe and legal abortions, they acknowledge that abortion is not always a free choice.[316]

Some feminist authors such as Natasha Walters point at the widespread phenomenon of "hyper-sexualisation" in Western society, which could lead to different forms of abuse of sexuality and which could make victims in the form of teenagers or adult women becoming pregnant against their will.[317] This hyper-sexualisation could thus become a real threat for women's autonomy.

According to Shelley Budgeon, a critical analysis of autonomy in general has been at the core of feminist critiques of Western metaphysics.[318] Treating third-wave feminism, Budgeon mentions several authors who have criticised accounts of late modernity, because of the overestimation of the extent to which choice is available to individuals. The focus on freedom of choice has led to an "unjustified prominence being granted to agency and personal autonomy."[319] For instance, Lorraine Code has maintained that "a 'hyperbolized' version of autonomy, associated with self-mastery and self-

---

312 A. Lynch, "Abortion", in: Heywood, L.L., op. cit., Vol. 1, pp. 1-4.
313 In part 2.1.1.
314 Smit, J., op. cit., p. 29.
315 Lynch, A., op. cit., p. 3.
316 Ibid.
317 Anna Abram, "Sexual and Relationship Education in Great Britain: Problems and Opportunities for Faith Schools with Special Reference to the Roman Catholic Context." In: Konrad Glombik (ed.), *Wychowanie Seksualne w Rodzinie i w Szkole*. Opole, 2010, pp. 11-24. She refers to Natasha Walters' *Living Dolls: The Return of Sexism*, London, 2010.
318 Shelley Budgeon, *Third-Wave Feminism and the Politics of Gender in Late Modernity*. New York, 2011, p. 131.
319 Ibid., p. 133.

reliance, dominates the social imaginary of white Western societies and thus promotes a form of unbridled individualism, which is at odds with feminist ideals".[320]

The one-sided focus on autonomy can be illustrated by qualitative sociological research by Julia Brannen and Ann Nilsen among British and Norwegian university students.[321] Asked about their future perspectives, the female Norwegian students indicated that:

[T]hey expected to try out different types of jobs before they settled down, and were adamant that they did not want to get stuck in 'boring jobs'. For these young women, the future brought challenges which they felt confident they could master. They were expectant rather than apprehensive, and they believed that it was 'up to them' what they made of the future. They perceived few constraints arising from their status as women. However, in discussing when they intended to have children, young women were concerned about their biological clocks ticking away and were acutely aware they could not defer childbirth indefinitely. ... In the male groups generally, there was a singular lack of concern about any problems they might encounter as fathers. In contrast to Norway, we noted that the British students were more concerned about the insecurity of the labour market (in the late 1990s). They also subscribed to notions of 'individual choice' in ways of managing their employment and family careers, if and when they became parents.[322]

Brannen and Nilsen's research illustrates the importance of career perspectives for both male and female students. Having children seems to become of secondary importance, although this kind of prioritizing especially worries the young women. On the other hand, there is the rather unrealistic and egocentric idea of young men to their 'individual choice' in becoming parents. This idea sounds unrealistic, because parenthood is of course not a choice made individually. However, male students put their female partners under time pressure by making such a statement, particularly if these young women have a desire to become a mother. This might in turn cause psychological pressure on both sides, which then threatens their relationship itself.

Therefore, third wave feminists have made efforts to retrieve the concept

---

320 Ibid., p. 138.
321 Julia Brannen and Ann Nilsen, "Individualisation, choice and structure: a discussion of current trends in sociological analysis", *The Sociological Review*, 2005, 53, 3, pp. 412-428.
322 Ibid., p. 420.

of autonomy by reworking it as a relational concept.³²³ These theories presuppose that autonomy is a capacity that is socially conditioned and thus challenge the position that autonomy necessarily requires independence and separation from others. If one supports such a relational view on autonomy, consideration needs to be given to the possible consequences for young couples if after the discovery of an unintended pregnancy one partner is in favour of abortion, but the other partner expresses serious doubts with regard to this option. In the course of this study, this kind of dilemmas will receive further attention.

Closely related to these considerations regarding reproductive decisions is the bioethical question regarding the moment from which we are to speak of the coming into existence of a new human being. It has been shown that under the influence of a subjective definition of human life, formulated by Dutch psychiatrists in the late 1960s, the discussion regarding legalisation of abortion gained a new impulse. Later in this study, it will be made clear that this subjective definition has since been contradicted by numerous embryologists and other scientists, by showing evidence that new human life starts at the moment of fertilisation, with the formation of a zygote.³²⁴

Firstly, the argument of autonomous choice in relation to abortion will be more closely analysed.

2.2 The argument of a woman's autonomy in relation to abortion

The starting point for the abortion legislation in the U.K., the Netherlands and many other Western countries is the fact that a woman's personal autonomy is more highly valued than the protection of unborn human life, in circumstances indicated by the woman and by her doctor(s). In recent literature, self-determination or self-governance is seen as the defining

---

323 See for instance: Marilyn Friedman, *Autonomy, Gender, Politics*. Oxford, 2003 or C. Mackenzie and N. Stoljar (eds.) *Relational Autonomy: Feminist Perspectives on Autonomy, Agency and the Social Self*. Oxford, 2000. Cf. Budgeon, S., op. cit., pp. 146-150.
324 In part 4.3.1. Some standard works in the area of embryology are for instance: William J. Larsen, *Human Embryology*, 3rd ed., Philadelphia, 2001, here p. 1; Keith L. Moore and T.V.N. Persaud, *The Developing Human. Clinically oriented embryology*. 7th ed., Philadelphia, 2003, here p. 16; cf. Patrick Lee, *Abortion & Unborn Human Life*, 2nd ed., Washington DC, 2010, pp. 71-72.

feature of autonomy.[325] In his overview of the idea of autonomy of moral agents, Thomas Hill states that, despite the very different interpretations of the idea of autonomy within philosophy, all authors see autonomous agents as self-governing or self-determining.[326]

The focus of attention in this part is the precarious balance between an autonomous decision and respect for the unborn human life. It will be discussed to what extent ethical theories as have been developed by Immanuel Kant, Martha Nussbaum and Judith Jarvis-Thompson manage to find this balance.

2.2.1 Philosophical views on human autonomy

Although ancient Greek writers used the term *autonomia* when describing a political concept for city-states, the concept of autonomy with regard to persons only received attention since the age of Enlightenment and most particularly by Immanuel Kant. Therefore, the Kantian view of autonomy will be discussed (2.2.2) and then applied to the abortion dilemma. (2.2.3) For some contemporary philosophers of the Anglophone world, the autonomously choosing individual has received a central place. In particular, the philosophical work of Martha Nussbaum and Rosalind Dixon will be critically analysed in relation to the abortion issue. (2.2.4) Finally the way in which the autonomy principle has been used as an argument for legalizing abortion, for instance by Judith Jarvis Thompson, will be discussed. (2.2.5)

2.2.2 The autonomy principle according to Kant

The formula of autonomy is stated by Kant as: "Act according to the maxim, which at the same time can make itself to a universal law".[327] This formula is closely linked to two other formulas. The first is Kant's general categorical imperative: "Act only according to that maxim whereby you can at the same time will that it should become a universal law". The second is

---

325 Andrews Reath, "Autonomy, ethical", in: Edward Craig (Ed.), *Routledge Encyclopedia of Philosophy*, vol. I, London, 1998, pp. 586-592.
326 Thomas Hill, "Autonomy of moral agents", in: Becker, L.C. and Becker, C.B., op. cit., Vol. I, pp. 111-115.
327 Kant, I., [1785], 2005, op. cit., IV, BA 81; cf. Mariéle Wulf, *Een antropologie van de christelijke ethiek. Beschuldigd, bevrijd, bemind. Handboek Moraaltheologie, deel 1. Inleiding in de moraaltheologie.* Almere, 2013 (a), p. 135.

the so-called "means-end formula", which, according to Kant, is subjectively binding for every person who acts in a rational way: "Act in such a way that you treat humanity, whether in your own person or in the person of another, always at the same time as an end, and never just as a means".[328]

In Kant's anthropology, these three formulas form the essential characteristics of the moral law.[329] They are not just formal principles, they also set contents, by presuming the capacity of the human person to recognise dignity and freedom both in themselves and to respect them in other persons, as far as they are an end.[330] For Kant, autonomy is the foundation of the dignity of every human and rational nature.[331] An autonomous person 'gives' a universal law to himself in the sense that he acts because he recognises that there is a law of reason, a normative requirement, that requires him to do a certain action. This makes that autonomy, understood in this way, is contrary to arbitrariness because it is an orientation to the most inner law.[332] A person acts in an autonomous way if he acts from the recognition of a law of reason, also if his inclination is perhaps not to act according to this particular, universal law.[333]

Kant contrasts the freedom of the will, manifest in autonomy, with the dependence of the will on external or heteronomous causes and interests.[334] For Kant, heteronomy of the will is the "source of all improper moral principles".[335] The immanent moral law must be the only guiding principle for the autonomous person. According to Kant, this moral law cannot be deduced from whatever object, nor from another person or the community, nor from a rewarding or punishing God, who compels a certain ethical

---

328 Kant, I., [1785], 2005, op. cit., IV, BA 84 and BA 67; cf. Howard Caygill, *A Kant Dictionary*, Oxford, 1995, pp. 100-101.
329 Wulf, C.M., 2013 (a), op. cit., p. 135.
330 Cf. Claudia Mariéle Wulf, *Was ist gut? Eidetische Phänomenologie als Impuls zur moraltheologischen Erkenntnistheorie*. Vallendar, 2010, pp. 153-164, in particular p. 157.
331 Kant, I., [1785], 2005, op. cit., IV, BA 79.
332 Wulf, C.M., 2013 (1), op. cit., p. 136; cf. part 2.3 on human conscience and human autonomy.
333 Cf. John Skorupski, "Autonomy and impartiality", in: Jens Timmermann (ed.), *Kant's Groundwork of the Metaphysics of Morals. A Critical Guide*. Cambridge, 2009, p. 164.
334 Caygill, H., op. cit., p. 223.
335 Kant, I., [1785], 1911, op. cit., p. 441.

behaviour.³³⁶

In the critical reception of Kant, this stress on the autonomously thinking and willing individual has met with theological, philosophical and anthropological objections. As an Enlightenment philosopher, Kant excludes in his writings a meaningful relation between a creature and his Creator, between freedom and God-given dignity.³³⁷ Secondly, according to the Italian philosopher Giuseppe Abbà, the interpretation by Kant of the morality of the person departs from a hermeneutics based on a dualistic approach of subjects: on the one hand, by approaching the subject as a phenomenon, influenced by external circumstances, while on the other hand using a so-called transcendental notion of the free subject, independent of the experience of the action and which would not be marked by acts which have an external object.³³⁸ In addition, Martin Rhonheimer states that "personal autonomy is present, rather, when someone does something because he has recognized it as good – and thus that it 'ought' to be done."³³⁹ He shows that Thomas Aquinas already argued in a similar way, saying that the person who avoids evil because it is evil, is free, but he who acts being moved by another does not act freely.³⁴⁰

Thirdly, postmodern criticism accuses Kant that he asks too much of men with his insistence on autonomy. In this regard, Jean-Pierre Wils remarks that dependence and passivity are just as much anthropological data, as is the striving for sovereignty and autonomy.³⁴¹

---

336 Cf. Wulf, C.M., 2010, op. cit., p. 96; Martin Rhonheimer, *Natural Law and Practical Reason. A Thomist View of Moral Autonomy.* Translated from the German by Gerald Malsbary. New York, 2000, pp. 213-214.
337 Cf. Wulf, C.M., 2010, op. cit., p. 159.
338 Giuseppe Abbà, *Quale impostazione per la filosofia morale? Ricerche di filosofia morale – 1.* Rome, 1996, pp. 96-102. According to Kant, the free will of the person is the same as the practical reason in its purest form. Its freedom is not a freedom of choice or of arbitrariness, but the freedom of spontaneity of the will, in the sense that its determination comes from reason itself and not from inclinations of a sensible nature. Ibid., pp. 98-99.
339 Rhonheimer, M., op. cit., p. 214.
340 Thomas Aquinas, *Super secundam epistolam S. Pauli ad Corinthios Lectura,* c. III, lect. 3, n. 112; Translated into French by Jean-Éric Stroobant de Saint-Éloy O.S.B., *Commentaire de la deuxième épître aux Corinthiens.* Paris, 2005, p. 113.
341 Jean-Pierre Wils, *Versuche über Ethik. Studien zur theologischen Ethik.* Freiburg, 2005, p. 105.

2.2.3 Applying Kantian ethics to the issue of abortion

Despite the above mentioned criticism, one could wonder to what extent Kantian ethics can be helpful in relation to decision-making processes regarding an unintended pregnancy. This can be illustrated by applying Kantian ethics to the abortion dilemma in the imaginary story of a teenage girl called Laura. She has become pregnant against her will, due to incautious sexual intercourse with a young man she does not really love. After having discovered that she is pregnant, she has this thought: "I do not want children to be born when it is expected that they will live in great misery for a long time." She has attempted to formulate a universal law with regard to unintended pregnancies. She then considers the following maxim based on this universal law: "I will not let my child be born, because of the great misery which is to be expected for him or her for a long time".

Reflecting on Laura's maxim, the first striking observation that it seems obvious to her that she is indeed considering the life or death of her unborn child. If she would act according to the maxim she has formulated, it would mean the unborn child's death. Now it might occur to her that actively wanting the death of the unborn child would imply a grave injustice towards the unborn child. The child would be made victim of her and her partner's incautious behaviour. On the other hand, she might consider the circumstances in which the child would be born, if it were to be born. She asks herself if she could raise the child alone, if their relationship would come to an end and she also wonders what would be the situation if they would continue their relationship and become parents. These thoughts makes her feel very ambiguous and leave her inconclusive.

If we follow Laura's strain of thoughts, it is remarkable that on the one hand, if she would act according to her maxim and chooses to have an abortion, it would certainly result in the unborn child's death. If on the other hand, she would bring her pregnancy to term, it would confront her with many uncertainties, such as her own capabilities to raise the child, her partner's capabilities, the implications for their relationship and above all the uncertainty of what would become of the child. Continuing the pregnancy would not give one clear perspective, but would in fact give room for many scenarios, including the possibilities of placing the child in foster care or putting the child up for adoption. After pondering a long time on these scenarios, it suddenly comes to her mind that maybe she should look at the unborn child not as a means of which she can dispose, but rather as an end. This thought radically changes her way of looking at the whole situation, by finally making her able to accept the certainty that her life from now on will contain many uncertainties.

Some contemporary philosophers argue that Kantian ethics could be helpful in relation to decision-making processes regarding an unintended pregnancy. One of these authors, David Velleman, has pointed out that the autonomy principle as it is used in Kantian moral theory, could be interpreted in two very different ways.[342] On the one hand, a person's autonomy could be seen as the person's *capacity* for self-determination. If Kant's categorical imperative would be obeyed, then a person ought to decline from acting for reasons that cannot be proposed as valid for all rational beings, including those who are affected by our action. On the other hand, personal autonomy could be seen as adopting maximizing one's options as the goal, thus valuing one's *opportunities* for self-determination.[343] This latter interpretation is far removed from the Kantian understanding of human autonomy. Kant formulated the principle of autonomy as follows: "Always choose in such a way that in the same volition the maxims of the choice are at the same time present as a universal law".[344] Humanity as such needs to be the aim of making moral choices and not having as much options as possible.

However, autonomy is often considered by people in today's society as having as many options as possible.[345] Velleman shows that a person who has more options is placed in a weaker tactical position in her negotiations than a person who is bound by just one option.[346] This is illustrated by Jennifer Denbow in another case of a pregnant, indigent woman who is in an abusive relationship with a man on whom she is financially dependent.[347] She wants to bring the pregnancy to term and raise the child, but her partner

---

342 Velleman, J.D., op. cit.
343 Ibid., p. 3.
344 Kant, I., [1785], 2005, op. cit., IV, BA 87. English translation of the autonomy principle in: Caygill, H., op. cit., p. 88.
345 Denbow, J., op. cit., pp. 216-228.
346 Velleman, J.D., op. cit., pp. 6-9.
347 Denbow, J., op. cit., pp. 220-224.

disagrees. Thus, the woman is put into a vulnerable position. Denbow states that if this woman were constrained by the lack of an option to abort, this would make her position stronger. But with the possibility of a legal abortion, she may feel pressured if she thinks that she cannot care for the child or if she fears that she or the child may be subjected to a violent father. If she has feelings or doubts of this kind, it is likely that she will not reveal them during the intake consultation at the abortion clinic because she may well be aware that the clinic might refuse her request assuming she is acting under social pressure and instead refer her for further counselling.[348]

Contrary to the feelings of the pregnant woman, it happens that the male begetter thinks he has less responsibility to care for both the woman and the child when the woman has freely chosen not to have an abortion.[349] As a result, some men react with an attitude of indifference to the woman's choice to bring her pregnancy to term.[350] Denbow concludes that the negotiating position of a man who wants his partner to abort is thus strengthened because of the existence of a choice and places additional pressure upon the woman to terminate her pregnancy.[351] It has thus been shown that for a woman to have more opportunities does not automatically mean that her autonomy increases as well. A Kantian understanding of autonomy implies an orientation to values. In this understanding, the highest value is the human person and his will to act morally, because the human person is considered as an end in itself.[352]

2.2.4 The capabilities approach, abortion and human dignity: Martha Nussbaum

Other attempts have been made to integrate Kantian ethics in a contemporary view on human capabilities, human dignity and abortion. Starting with the Kantian maxim to treat each person as an end rather than

---

348 In part 3.3.1.2 it will be shown that about a quarter of Dutch women report doubts before and during the consultation and that in comparable qualitative research found percentages are even higher.
349 George A. Akerlof, Janet L. Yellen and Michael L. Katz, "An Analysis of Out-of-Wedlock Childbearing in the United States", *Quarterly Journal of Economics*, 1996, 111, pp. 277-317; here p. 311.
350 Cf. part 3.3.2.3.
351 Denbow, J., op. cit., p. 222.
352 Kant, I., [1785], 2005, op. cit., IV, BA 20; cf. Wulf, C.M., 2013 (a), op. cit., p 136.

as a means, Martha Nussbaum and Rosalind Dixon applied a capabilities approach to the abortion dilemma.[353] Originally, this theoretical approach, developed by Nussbaum, served as an alternative to economic theories in the context of global development, with the objective to broaden the focus on economic growth of a nation or region to an assessment of women's quality of life. A second objective of the capabilities approach is to address questions of social justice, since in many parts of the world women lag behind as regards access to food, health care, education, etc.[354]

The key question of the capabilities approach is: "What is each person able to do and to be?" According to this approach, each and every person is entitled to a minimum threshold level of ten central capabilities or opportunities, of which life itself is the first.[355] Human dignity is not only based on rationality, but is understood inclusively: it is inherent in sentience, emotion, affection, physical health, and appetite as well as in rationality.[356]

A strong point of the capabilities approach is that it sees human beings with severe cognitive disabilities as full equals in dignity. The capabilities approach also recognises that the foetus to a certain extent possesses human dignity, because it is at least potentially sentient and an agent. But, according to Dixon and Nussbaum, this dignity is to be distinguished from that of human beings after birth, because of the foetus' "dependent and

---

[353] Rosalind Dixon and Martha C. Nussbaum, "Abortion, Dignity and a Capabilities Approach", *Chicago Public Law and Legal Theory Working Paper*, No. 345, Chicago 2011, pp. 1-17.

[354] Martha C. Nussbaum, *Women and Human Development: The Capabilities Approach*. Cambridge, U.K., 2000, p. 1.

[355] "Being able to live to the end of a human life of normal length; not dying prematurely, or before one's life is so reduced as to be not worth living." The other nine capabilities include bodily health; bodily integrity; senses, imagination and thought; emotions; practical reason; affiliation; other species; play and control over one's environment. Cf. Dixon, R. and Nussbaum, M.C., op. cit., pp. 16-17.

[356] Ibid., p. 5. Nussbaum and Dixon state that it is for this reason, that the capabilities approach (CA) has a more inclusive understanding of human dignity than Kant's ethics. But this interpretation of Kant's conception of human dignity is too limited. It is true that according to Kant, true virtue is purely based on principles. But, so he states, "these principles are not just speculative rules, but the awareness of a feeling which lives in every human heart and which extends much further than the special grounds of pity or favour. I believe, I summarize everything, if I say: it is the feeling of beauty and the dignity of human nature." Cf. Immanuel Kant, *Beobachtungen über das Gefühl des Schönen und Erhabenen*. [1764], Leipzig, ca. 1913, part 2, p. 18, translation is mine.

merely potential status".³⁵⁷

There are several objections to make against this stance. The fact that, before viability, a foetus is dependant of one single person does not necessarily make a difference for his or her moral status. One could think of other situations in which a person is completely dependent on one other person. In his book on the ethics of abortion, Christopher Kaczor mentions the hypothetical example of a hospital, deprived of all of its personnel because of a tyrant's order to serve injured military personnel elsewhere. Only one doctor remains hidden in order to save the patients. The question now is whether the moral status of the patient has changed, following the evacuation of the hospital staff. Or, whether the moral status of the patient would change again if several more doctors were to arrive at the hospital. Indeed, moral status has nothing to do with whether a vulnerable human being is dependent upon many other people or only a single other person.³⁵⁸

However, the question of whether foetuses have a full or only a potential moral status is more complicated. It is possible by means of a reappraisal of Aristotelian metaphysics and in particular by applying his idea of active potentiality, to consider the human embryo as a human being with the capacity for full personhood.³⁵⁹ Here, a critical note needs to be made to the argument made by Dixon and Nussbaum that "any demand a woman makes to access an abortion on therapeutic grounds is based on claims with the same type of normative force as those made on behalf of the foetus".³⁶⁰ The fundamental difference is that after an abortion the foetus is dead and therefore any claim regarding his or her health has become irrelevant. Therefore, it needs to be concluded that the normative force of women's claims for therapeutic interventions is not of the same type as claims made on behalf of the foetus in the case of an abortion.

It makes much sense to compare women who demand an abortion and women who want to bring their pregnancy to term. Any woman who wants to bring a pregnancy to term at the cost of possible serious psychological or

---

357 Dixon, R. and Nussbaum, M.C., op. cit., p. 6.
358 Cf. Christopher Kaczor, *The Ethics of Abortion. Women's Rights, Human Life, and the Question of Justice*. New York and London, 2011, p. 99.
359 Cf. part 4.3.1.2.
360 Dixon, R. and Nussbaum, M.C., op. cit., p. 8, underscore is theirs.

psycho-social difficulties could indeed make a justified claim for necessary therapeutic assistance. Precisely in these cases, a capabilities approach could be a great help already during the pregnancy, in order to investigate how a woman's capabilities could be supported with professional means, so as to encourage her and possibly her partner as well in their preparations for the future.

2.2.5 Voluntary and involuntary abortion

In building up his philosophy on selfhood in relation to the other, Paul Ricoeur takes recourse to Aristotle in his distinction between voluntary and involuntary actions.[361] Aristotle calls a certain action voluntary, when "the origin of his moving the instrumental parts is in himself, and if the origin of something is in himself, it depends on himself whether he does that thing or not."[362] On the other hand, involuntary actions are characterised by compulsion or ignorance: "That is compulsory of which the moving principle is outside, being a principle in which nothing is contributed by the person who is acting or feeling the passion".[363]

The distinction between voluntary and involuntary actions and the grey area which could be found in-between these two poles could be made more concrete in the decision-making processes regarding unintended pregnancy. Often, the distinction then becomes more subtle. For instance, if a young pregnant woman desires to bring her pregnancy to term, this desire might be suppressed if she fears that becoming a mother would cause a delay to her career perspectives. This fear might be reinforced by shame, for instance if she has been financially supported by her parents in her studies. In other situations, fear might be mixed with uncertainty about the relationship, especially when this relationship has been short-lived.

Thus, it could happen that the real motives for a young woman considering an abortion could be, rather than a free choice, a desire to avoid a conflict with her boyfriend, or to avoid a negative reaction on the part of her parents, or to avoid her own feelings of shame during the rest of her gestational period. These motives might then be reinforced by her boyfriend's attitude, if he makes explicit objections to becoming a father,

---

361 Ricoeur, P., 1992, op. cit., pp. 88-112.
362 Aristotle, *Nicomachean Ethics*. Translation, introduction and commentary by Sarah Broadie and Christopher Rowe, Oxford, 2002, Book III, n. 1110a15, p. 123.
363 Ibid.

or if he implicitly shows that he is unwilling to take up his responsibility, in situations where communication between the two begetters is poor or absent.

In such cases, apart from a life-threatening situation for the fœtus, also the relationship itself might be put under pressure. The man's attitude creates a certain dependency on the part of the woman, especially when it comes to future perspectives and career planning. The woman's career would most likely be delayed if she chooses to continue her pregnancy, but the man's career would be unlikely to be delayed if he were to refuse to take on the role of being a father. According to the law, a mother has a right to the father's financial contribution for raising the child. But if a pregnant woman insists on bringing the pregnancy to term against his will and thus holding him liable for begetting the child, the chances are high that tensions in their relationship will increase. If she wants to save their relationship, the temptation to terminate the pregnancy against her will, could then become very real. In those cases, one could hardly speak of a voluntary termination of pregnancy.

In these situations, it could become life-saving if efforts are being made to increase the capabilities of both begetters by means of professional counselling.[364] At the same time, the importance of a more informal dialogue, such as between a young pregnant woman, her friend and her parents should not be underestimated. In many cases, after the discovery of an unintended pregnancy, the issue of responsibility for the unborn child will be part of a familial conversation.

Here, the notion of responsibility for one another brings forth the question of imputation of a certain action to someone. In Aristotelian terms, the term "imputation" can be used to designate the act of holding an agent responsible for actions which in themselves are considered to be permissible or not permissible. For Aristotle, criteria of voluntary or involuntary actions are from the start criteria of moral and even juridical imputation, of praise and blame: "if the voluntary deserves praise and blame, the involuntary calls for pardon and pity".[365]

If Aristotle's line of reasoning is followed, dismissibility could

---

364 Cf. chapter 7.
365 Ricoeur, P., 1992, op. cit., p. 99.

become a criterion to ascribe an action to an agent.[366] In the case of a familial dialogue where the daughter has decided to speak openly of her pregnancy, dismissibility could become relevant on the part of the parents. If their pregnant daughter has a desire to bring the pregnancy to term, but foresees problems with her partner or with her career perspectives, her parents could first of all dismiss her from blame, for she has had the courage to tell them not only what has happened, but also about her desire to care for her child. They could also anticipate on dismissing her friend, by showing their willingness to discuss future arrangements with them. Pardon and pity would indeed be required if parents showed willingness to make a constructive contribution to their daughter's and possibly also to their grandchild's future.

In more general terms, Ricoeur adds a question mark to the notion of attribution of a certain series of events to a particular agent. He objects to the idea of preferential choice as is used by Aristotle, which is expressed in terms of causal efficiency as regards the power to act. Here, Ricoeur asks himself what is meant by the "power to act".[367] He refers to Immanuel Kant, who points out the necessary dialectical character of the notion of power of acting. Kant states that besides causality in accordance with the laws of nature, it is necessary to assume that there is another causality, that of freedom.[368] Ricoeur basically agrees with Kant's analysis, but points out the difficulties of attributing a determined series of events to a particular agent, because of the way the actions of each of us are intertwined with the actions of everyone else.[369]

The difficulty of attributing a determined series of events to a particular agent is relevant in situations where two lovers have voluntarily chosen to have sexual intercourse, without having communicated to one another if they would want a child. In those situations, it could happen that the woman would actually want to bring her pregnancy to term, but her partner explicitly or implicitly disagrees. The series of events which have led to the woman's pregnancy can of course not be attributed to her alone, not even

---

366 Ibid., p. 100.
367 Ibid., pp. 101-112.
368 Cf. Immanuel Kant, *Critique of Pure Reason*. Translated and edited by Paul Guyer and Allen W. Wood, Cambridge, 1998, p. 484; cf. Ricoeur, P., 1992, op. cit., p. 102.
369 Ricoeur, P., 1992, op. cit., p. 107.

if her partner had declared before the conception took place, that he did not consider himself ready to become a father. Such a statement does not dismiss him from his moral responsibility. This moral responsibility could later be transformed into a legal responsibility, if the woman decides to bring her pregnancy to term.

In these situations, only the two lovers could recall what conversations they had had before deciding to spend the night together, whether they had discussed certain precautionary measures, if and how they have put them into practice and what sort of emotions, passions and expressed or unexpressed desires played a part on both sides during that night. Any imputation of culpability by a third person, for instance by the couple's parents, followed by an advice to have the embryo aborted, would be a bad example of 'efficient causality' thinking, possibly with fatal consequences.

2.2.6 Abortion and the problem of empiricism

'Efficient causality' thinking could be summarised by stating that "a woman has a problem of an unintended pregnancy; she can resolve this problem by having her pregnancy terminated in a clinic, in a hospital or even at home". At first sight, one could think that a woman's autonomy is served by this type of thinking. However, on a deeper level, in situations which have been described in the previous part, existential questions a pregnant woman might ask herself are not seriously looked at. For instance, she might ask herself how she would function as a mother of her child or, how she and her partner would function as parents, how their future would look like.

In more general, philosophical terms, an attitude of 'resolving the problem of an unintended pregnancy' could be described as an empiricist approach. Such an approach is widespread in our Western societies. According to Bernard Lonergan, empiricism is based on the assumption that knowing is like looking, that the real is what can be seen, heard, touched, tasted, smelt, felt. What is left out in this type of reasoning is meaning.[370] Such an empiricist approach has implications for all three human beings who are involved in a decision making process regarding an unintended pregnancy: first of all for the foetus, whose earthly life will abruptly end as

---

370 Bernard Lonergan, *Method in Theology*, Toronto, 1972, p. 238.

a result of the abortion.

The empiricist approach could also work out very negatively for the pregnant woman in case she decides to have an abortion. Most women will be aware of the intrinsic worth of the developing foetal life. However, in situations as have been described in the previous part, this intrinsic worth is not acknowledged by the male begetter or by the woman's parents. If the idea of the intrinsic worth of the unborn human life does not receive any attention, then it could become apparent a long time after an abortion has taken place, but then in the form of remorse or of other psychological complications.[371]

As is often forgotten, an empiricist approach could also have negative implications for the male begetter. There might be situations in which a man has made a statement that he does not consider himself ready to become a father. The actual meaning of such a statement might in some cases be laid in a certain emotional blockade, influenced by negative experiences in his own childhood. In other situations a man might feel pressured because of financial concerns, or because of possible negative consequences for his career or study. Sometimes experienced pressure could change into aggressive behaviour.[372] On the other hand, if a man were to have a tacit desire to become a father, it could be lifesaving to express this desire to his partner and to discuss future arrangements, possibly with the help of a counsellor, or his employer, or with other persons in their families or peer group.

One could speak of an autonomous choice for instance if a man follows his most inner law of reason and seeks to resolve obstacles which are contrary to this most inner law. For instance, if a man would accept the woman's decision to bring her pregnancy to term, even if he feels himself that he is not yet ready to become a father, then this choice respects both the woman's autonomy and the life of the foetus. In doing so, his self-esteem could be left unaffected by taking up responsibility for his actions.

According to moral theologian Franz Böckle, the empirical way as such does not extend to an acknowledgment of the essence of what it is to be

---

371 Cf. part 3.1.
372 Cf. part 3.3.2.4 on domestic violence.

human.[373] Or, to put it in other words: a closed anthropological view of the human person, which states that we could fully determine in a philosophical or even empirical way what it is to be human, deprives man from the mystery of what it is to be human. Anthropology needs to remain open in an hermeneutical way, because a fully detailed definition of what it is to be human cannot be grasped.[374] Therefore, the anthropological principle of the open question is at the basis of every anthropology. This openness is in itself an ethical requirement, because it is constitutive for any discourse on humanity.[375]

In the empiricist approach, then, the relevance of hidden desires and emotions, the potential of human relationships and the yet unknown capacities of the unborn do not receive the attention they deserve. Still, in our Western society this empiricist approach has often been at the root of the common use of the argument of favouring a woman's autonomy from the beginning of the process of legalizing abortion up to the present time.

2.2.7 A woman's autonomy used as an argument for legalizing abortion

In the 1970s, the autonomy argument was used by some theologians and philosophers in order to defend a woman's right to free choice in relation to abortion. For instance, Daniel Callahan claims that abortion decisions should be left, finally, up to the women themselves. Society, he argues, does not have the right decisively to interpose itself between a woman and the abortion she wants, since there is no clear and present danger to the common good.[376] For Callahan, the right to respect the unborn human life does not weigh up against the woman's right to decide for an abortion if she has serious reasons to do so. In the same line of thinking Judith Jarvis Thomson argues that abortion ought to be permissible in some cases.[377]

Focussing on a woman's autonomy, many thinkers arguing in this direction

---

373 Franz Böckle, *Grundbegriffe der Moral. Gewissen und Gewissensbildung.* Würzburg, 1966, p. 50.
374 Cf. Klaus Demmer, *Deuten und handeln. Grundlagen und Grundfragen der Fundamentalmoral.* Freiburg im Breisgau, 1985, p. 25.
375 Cf. Wulf, C.M., 2013 (b), op. cit., p. 244.
376 Daniel Callahan, *Abortion: Law, Choice and Morality,* London, 1970, p. 493.
377 Judith Jarvis Thomson, "A Defense of Abortion", *Philosophy & Public Affairs,* Vol. 1, n. 1, 1971, pp. 47-66.

are not equally considering the role of the two other human beings directly involved in the woman's pregnancy: the foetus and the male begetter. They might view the foetus as a human being with an unequal status, compared to the civil rights of the mother. Other current philosophers stress that the foetus cannot be considered a person with a right to live, as will be discussed later.[378]

First, the usage of the autonomy argument in relation to a supposed right for a legal abortion will be considered. It is questionable whether it is right to speak of securing women's autonomy, if this autonomy is threatened by a lack of support from significant others, from the male begetter in the first place, but also from possible caregivers, parents, friends, family members, neighbours, (local) authorities or other financial supporters. If the male begetter is not willing to take his responsibility, then this will directly influence the woman's autonomous decision. Similarly, if the search for alternatives for abortion is not taken seriously by health care workers in their dialogue with the pregnant woman, again this will influence the woman's autonomy.

Seen from a philosophical point of view, it is impossible to decide for another human being, if living or not living would be the better option. We cannot make visible the value of not-living. In its non-being, life can never show its value.[379] So, the argument to plead for an abortion because the future life of this particular unborn human being would not have any value, is philosophically unsound.

The autonomy argument in relation to abortion has been defended by many writers because a woman's rights with regard to her own body are involved. For instance, Thomson has used the analogy of a burglar. If a burglar manages to climb into a house because a window has been left open, then he still has no right to enter the house.[380] In the same way, the foetus has not been given a right to enter a woman's body and therefore she can legitimately remove an unwanted foetus from within her body. The fact that she knows that burglars exist and that she has voluntarily left open the window, does not make her even partly responsible. If she has taken

---

378 Cf. chapter 4.
379 Claudia Mariéle Wulf, *Der Mensch – ein Phänomen. Eine phänomenologische, theologische und ethische Anthropologie*. Vallendar, 2011, p. 418.
380 Jarvis Thomson, J., op. cit., pp. 58-59 and 65.

precautionary measures to prevent the burglar from entering the house, it would be even more legitimate to expel him.

A first difference is that the woman's action of leaving the window open does not directly cause the burglar to enter the house, whereas a man and a woman conceiving a child cause the child to be where it is, even if they tried to prevent it.[381] Similarly, Patrick Lee argues that parents have a special responsibility to their children.[382] They know that all methods of family planning have a certain rate of failure. Liability is a generally accepted principle if we cause certain damage to others. "Thus, contrary to Thomson's argument, we *are* responsible for the natural and foreseen results of our actions even if we try to avoid them."[383]

Secondly, a burglar enters a person's house under his own power, whereas a foetus cannot be held accountable for what it does.[384] So, if there is agreement on the foetus' innocence with regard to his or her existence, it must be the parents who are responsible for the foetus' life. They then have to ask themselves what, according to their informed conscience, can morally be expected from them after the discovery of an unintended pregnancy.

2.3 Human conscience and human autonomy

According to the British and Dutch legislation, the decision to have an abortion has been mainly left to a woman's conscience. Therefore, in this part the notion of conscience will be more closely considered. The *Encyclopedia of Ethics* gives as definition of human conscience: "Conscience" primarily stands for the consciousness human individuals sometimes have that a specific action they either have done or propose to do is morally required or forbidden; and secondarily, for their disposition (*habitus*) to be thus conscious.[385]

---

381 Cf. Kaczor, C., op. cit., p. 162.
382 Lee, P., op. cit., p. 118.
383 Ibid.
384 Kaczor, C., op. cit., pp. 164-165.
385 Alan Donagan, "Conscience", in: Becker, L.C. and Becker, C.B., (Eds.), op. cit., Vol. I., pp. 297-299. The term 'conscience' cannot be equated with the psychoanalytical term 'superego', because in psychoanalytic personality theory, the activity of the superego is often unconscious, and further because its directives may actually be at odds with the person's conscious values. Cf. R. Harré and R. Lamb (Eds.), "Superego", in: Ibid., *The Encyclopedic Dictionary of Psychology*. Oxford, 1983, pp. 619-620.

This definition shows a twofold orientation of human conscience: on the one hand, moral decisions are based on the application of human conscience in a concrete situation. On the other hand, people develop a more fundamental disposition to take decisions based on their conscience.

Within modern moral theology, the distinction between conscience (in Greek: *syneidesis*) and *synderesis* (or *Urgewissen* in German) has been maintained.[386] In this distinction, conscience is considered as the practical judgment regarding our actions. *Synderesis* is defined as "the inborn knowledge of the primary principles of moral action".[387] Human conscience is formed by the knowledge of these primary principles and fundamental values, taking into consideration the circumstances that are present.

According to a contemporary phenomenological understanding of conscience, this distinction concretely takes the form of an inner dialogue, which is constitutive for human freedom.[388] This dialogue has been characterised as inevitable, because it is only by becoming conscious of our thoughts and feelings, that this inner dialogue can take place. Everything which does not belong to the content of this dialogue (such as subconscious feelings or diffuse contents), might influence the person's thoughts, but is not accessible as long as he is not conscious of it. The working of human conscience is also twofold: it makes the person able to reflect on his own deeds and thoughts and to judge these thoughts and deeds as good or evil according to a pre-given moral norm.[389] Because conscience is the fulfilment of practical reason, following our conscience does not mean following a subjective, but an objective norm, insofar as this norm is known to us as objective.[390]

Particularly relevant for making moral choices is the link between human conscience and human autonomy. Human conscience is the centre of autonomous morality. This autonomy is not only a "freedom of" (autos),

---

[386] Wulf, C.M., 2009, op. cit., pp. 81-83; cf. Böckle, F., op. cit., p. 68, Würzburg, 1966, p. 68 or Demmer, K., 1985, op. cit., p. 40. Cf. part 6.2 for the Christian interpretation of human conscience.
[387] Cf. *Merriam-Webster Dictionary*, Springfield, Mass., 2005.
[388] Wulf, C.M., 2009, op. cit., p. 83.
[389] Ibid., pp. 84-85.
[390] Cf. Ludger Honnefelder, "Praktische Vernunft und Gewissen", in: Anselm Hertz et al., *Handbuch der Christlichen Ethik*, Bd. 3, Freiburg, 1982, p. 37.

but also a "freedom for" (nomos).³⁹¹ The above mentioned distinction between *synderesis* and conscience makes it clear that someone who knows the basic ethical norm, could nevertheless make a mistake. The situational conscience should always be related to the *synderesis*, the innate knowledge of moral principles and fundamental values. Thus, human conscience is characterised by a twofold orientation, internally towards the immanent moral law and externally towards the needs of others. Human conscience remains free, decisions remain autonomous if someone takes his or her decisions based on this twofold orientation.³⁹²

According to moral theologian Mariéle Wulf, within the modern discussion on autonomy, an objective, twofold orientation on the immanent moral law and the needs of other persons is often lacking.³⁹³ If this is the case, autonomy becomes arbitrariness, a form of self-determination without responsibility for one's choice. Autonomy could also become a radical form of emancipation, which asks too much of the individual, for instance when the other party in a decision-making process avoids to take any stance whatsoever, or when the other's opinion is simply ignored. In such situations, one is unable to oversee the consequences of a decision.³⁹⁴

2.3.1 Human conscience and the sources of morality

In their overview on the foundations of Christian morality, Livio Melina et al. describe how in the course of the 18th and 19th century, the interpretation of the functioning of the human conscience has been influenced by Enlightenment philosophy and later by idealism.³⁹⁵ At that time, a movement developed which tended to affirm a radical autonomy of human conscience, without any reference to external or objective moral norms. Philosophers such as Rousseau or Fichte reject the possibility of

---

391 Wulf, C.M., 2013 (b), op. cit., pp. 212-213.
392 Ibid., p. 133.
393 Wulf, C.M., 2013 (a), op. cit., p. 136.
394 Wulf, C.M., 2010, op. cit., p. 4; cf. part 5.1.3 on consequentialism.
395 Livio Melina, José Noriega and Juan José Pérez-Soba, *Camminare nella Luce dell'Amor. I fondamenti della morale cristiana*. Siena, 2008, p. 602.

there being an erroneous conscience.³⁹⁶ By rejecting this possibility, human conscience becomes an infallible instance, exalted above all criticism. In this way, in an mentality which dominates our modern times, the Christian idea that "acting against conscience is always sinful" (cf. Rom. 14, 23) has been transformed in a reductionist way to: "the only possible way to sin is to act against conscience".

According to Augustine, it is in human interiority that man discovers the truth which dwells there. This presence is at the same time transcendent.³⁹⁷ The question which immediately arises from this insight, and which is very relevant for moral theology and thus for our question regarding the abortion dilemma, is: if the transcendental truth dwells in man, can an erroneous conscience be possible? This theme already emerges in the debate between Peter Abelard and Bernard of Clairvaux in the twelfth century.³⁹⁸ Abelard sees the decisive point regarding human conscience in the novelty of Christianity and he deduces from this novelty every moral reference, confirming that there cannot be sin if not in matters which go against human conscience.³⁹⁹ Bernard sees as a risk in this position that it would lead to the unbearable situation of man making himself a law by preferring his own will to the universal and eternal law.⁴⁰⁰ A second objection to Abelard's opinion is that he leaves out both the object of our acts and the given circumstances in the here and now as sources for morality, stating that it is only our consent which is decisive for moral behaviour.

In the contemporary teaching of the Catholic Church, three sources of morality are distinguished: the object of our acting, the person's intentions

---

396 Jean-Jacques Rousseau, *Émile, ou, de l'éducation*. Translated in Dutch by Anneke Brassinga, Meppel, 1980, Bk. IV, p. 278; Johann G. Fichte, "System der Sittenlehre", in: J.G. Fichte, *Johann Gottlieb Fichte's Nachgelassene Werke*, vol. III, Bonn, 1835, p. 90: "Das Gewissen irrt nie, und kann nicht irren; denn es ist dat unmittelbare Bewusstsein des Begriffs, über welches kein anderes Bewusstsein hinausgeht."

397 "In interiore homine habitat veritas. Et si tuam naturam mutabilem inveneris, transcende et te ipsum." Cf. Augustine, *De vera religione*, XXXIX, 72. Translated in German by Josef Lössl, Augustinus, Die wahre Religion, in Ibid., *Opera – Werke*, Paderborn, 2007, Vol. 68, pp. 200-201.

398 Cf. Melina, L. et al., op. cit., pp. 602 and 605.

399 Petrus Abelard, *Scito te ipsum seu Ethica*, XIV. In the German translation by Philipp Steger, *Erkenne dich selbst*, Hamburg, 2006, pp. 29-31.

400 Bernard of Clairvaux, *De diligendo Deo*, translated in German by Gerhard B. Winkler, *Bernhard von Clairvaux. Sämtliche Werke lateinisch/deutsch*, Innsbruck 1990, I, XIII, pp. 136-137.

and the given circumstances of the action.[401] If conscience is considered as infallible, then two of these sources are being neglected and the person's intentions become decisive in judging the morality of the act. In this way, the objective significance of our actions (*finis operis*) gets lost, because it is absorbed in the subjective moment of decision (*finis operantis*).[402] Therefore, although the Church acknowledges the binding character of a person's conscience, its dignity is derived from the universal and objective norms of morality, or, in other words, from the truth about moral good and evil.[403]

2.3.2 Abortion and conscientious objections

Particularly relevant in the juridical domain, besides the conscience of the woman who is requesting an abortion, are the judgments of conscience and possible conscientious objections of the doctor or nurse who is requested to execute one or more abortions. In this regard, jurist Ben Vermeulen concludes that as a result of the increased secularisation, a strong tendency has been evolved to reject the idea that conscience could be deduced from an objective, normative moral system, based on religion or philosophy.[404]

In a recent attempt to bring back an objective element in a further subjective description of conscience, Anders Schinkel considers conscience as "a concerned awareness of the moral quality of our own contribution to the process of reality, including our own being".[405] Referring to Paul Tillich, he argues that matters of ultimate concern and not just any concern are specific to judgments of conscience.[406] According to Tillich, all people have an ultimate concern, articulated or less articulated, religious or not. Often, when a person is grasped by ultimate concern, it has to do with truth, beauty or goodness.[407]

---

401 Catechism of the Catholic Church, 1997, n. 1750.
402 Melina, L. et al., op. cit., p. 606.
403 John Paul II, 1993, n. 60; cf. part 6.2 on the historical interpretation of conscience within Christianity.
404 Ben P. Vermeulen, *De vrijheid van geweten, een fundamenteel rechtsprobleem*, Arnhem, 1989, p. 311. See also M.A.J.M. Buijssen, "De rechtspositie van gewetensbezwaarden in de gezondheidszorg", in: *Pro Vita Humana*, 2003, nr.3-4, pp. 98-101.
405 Anders Schinkel, *Conscience and Conscious Objections*. Dissertation, Faculty of Philosophy, Free University of Amsterdam, 2006, p. 349.
406 The work Schinkel is referring to is: Paul Tillich, *Dynamics of faith*, London, 1957, p. 1.
407 Schinkel, A., op. cit., p. 368; cf. Tillich, P., op. cit., pp. 105-108.

In a way comparable to Schinkel and applying the right of conscientious objections in abortion legislation, Christopher Kaczor stresses that judgments of conscience are made at the conclusion of a process of moral deliberation from fundamental moral principles about what is right and wrong when all things are considered (*ultima facie*) and that conscience ought not to be seen as "a *prima facie* value, which can and should be overridden in the interest of other moral obligations that outweigh it in a given circumstance".[408] What is at stake here, is a supposed duty of physicians or other health care professionals to refer women who ask for an abortion to other providers if they feel that they cannot in conscience comply with the woman's request. As we have already seen, according to the RCOG guideline British doctors must inform a woman about her right to see another doctor if they have conscientious objections regarding the requested abortion.

It is obvious that in the case a pregnant woman would act against her conscience by choosing to have an abortion, this could lead to severe psychological problems afterwards. Therefore, it needs to be investigated what evidence has been gathered of possible negative effects of procured abortion on women's mental health.

---

408 Kaczor, C., op. cit., pp. 191-192; He is commenting on an opinion of the American College of Obstetricians and Gynecologists (ACOG), Committee on Ethics, *The Limits of Conscientious Refusal in Reproductive Medicine: Opinion 385*. Washington 2007, reaffirmed 2010, p. 3.

Chapter 3

Mental and physical risks and effects of induced abortion on women

According to Paul Ricoeur, values, norms, and laws could play a mediating role along the trajectory of the realization of freedom in intersubjectivity.[409] In the two coming chapters the focus of attention will be on individual values related to the abortion dilemma. This chapter deals with the values of life and health of the woman, in particular after having made a choice for an induced abortion. In chapter 4, the value of the unborn human life will be central.[410] In chapters 4 and 5 the transition from values to relevant moral norms and laws regarding abortion will be made.

Scientific evidence has been gathered of empirical research in medicine and the human sciences published between 1985 and 2015 regarding the short and long term physical and mental health risks and effects of induced abortion on women. If necessary, methodological problems regarding these types of research will be discussed. (3.1 and 3.2)

Women (and men) give various reasons for choosing to terminate a pregnancy. (3.3) These reasons will be looked at by means of a critical analysis of results coming from epidemiological, psychological and social psychological research. Empirical research discussed in this chapter is not restricted to the U.K. and the Netherlands, but also contains research results from countries which are culturally comparable, such as other Western European countries, the U.S., Australia and New Zealand. This way of comparison is common practice in medical and psychological (meta)studies. Obviously, medical, epidemiological and psychological research needs to meet certain methodological conditions, which will be explicitly considered in the relevant parts of this chapter.

---

409 Ricoeur, P., 1978, op. cit., pp. 180 and following.
410 In his book on natural law and natural rights, John Finnis calls life, including health, a first basic value. Cf. Finnis, J., op. cit., p. 86; cf. Grisez, G., 1970, op. cit., pp. 307-321; cf. part 5.1.7.

3.1 Psychological risks and effects after abortion

Psychological effects after procured abortion could either occur shortly after the intervention or many years afterwards. The scientific literature further distinguishes several risk factors for psychological disturbance in the aftermath of abortion. Before analysing these risks and effects, it is necessary to discuss methodological difficulties regarding post-abortion psychological research. (3.1.1) Several reviews have been published regarding the literature on psychosocial effects of induced abortion. Carlo Bellieni and Giuseppe Buonocore reviewed research papers on abortion and subsequent mental health published between 1995 and 2011.[411] In the U.K., the National Collaborating Centre for Mental Health developed a review of the mental health outcomes of induced abortion.[412] A third major study is the 2008 report of the Task Force on Mental Health and Abortion by the American Psychological Association (APA TFMHA), chaired by Brenda Major.[413] Earlier, John Thorp et al. made an overview of studies coming from the U.S. and Europe which focussed on the evidence of long-term physical and psychological health consequences of induced abortion.[414] Finally, two literature studies into post-abortion psychological effects have been conducted in the Netherlands.[415]

In the international literature, both positive and negative psychological reactions after abortion are reported, acknowledging that often psychological reactions after abortion have an ambivalent nature of both positive and negative thoughts and feelings. (3.1.2 and 3.1.3) Critically reviewing the scientific data, a distinction has been made between quantitative and qualitative studies published between 1985 and 2015. Among the risk

---

411 Carlo V. Bellieni, and Giuseppe Buonocore, "Abortion and subsequent mental health: Review of the literature", *Psychiatry and Clinical Neurosciences*, 2013, 67, pp. 301–310.
412 National Collaborating Centre for Mental Health, *Induced Abortion and Mental Health. A systematic review of the mental health outcomes of induced abortion, including their prevalence and associated factors.* London, 2011.
413 American Psychological Association, Task Force on Mental Health and Abortion. *Report of the Task Force on Mental Health and Abortion,* Washington DC, 2008.
414 John M. Thorp, Katherine E. Hartmann and Elisabeth Shadigian, "Long-Term Physical and Psychological Health Consequences of Induced Abortion: Review of the Evidence", *Obstetrical and Gynecological Survey,* 2002, 58, 1, pp. 67-79.
415 T.W. van Laar – Jochemsen et al., op cit. and Maartje van Kooten, Willy van Berloo and Ine Vanwesenbeeck, *Psychosociale gevolgen van abortus. Een overzicht van de literatuur,* RutgersNissogroep, Delft, 2004.

factors for negative mental health effects on women (3.1.4), one is the man's attitude towards her pregnancy, although the literature on men and abortion is rather scarce. (3.1.5)

3.1.1 Methodological issues

A lot of research has been done in order to get more clarity on the psychological effects of procured abortion. However, there are a number of methodological problems with the existing research material. Therefore, several remarks need to be made before presenting and analysing the scientific results. The following issues are distinguished: 1) ethical limitations; 2) sample size; 3) geographical limitations; 4) controlling for confounding factors 5) the initial consent to participate; 6) the attrition rate; 7) social desirability, which leads to under-reporting; 8) the dissonance hypothesis, which might lead to underestimating negative effects; 9) the use of different measurement instruments; 10) the independence of the researcher and 11) the ideology of the researcher.

1) Ethical limitations: In the first place there is an ethical objection to an experimental set-up in relation to abortion. The APA TFMHA rightly states that a randomised clinical trial is even impossible in this regard, because "it is neither desirable nor ethical to randomly assign women who have unwanted pregnancies to an abortion versus delivery versus adoption group."[415] It is therefore difficult to speak of causality in relation to abortion and negative mental health effects, as long as other possible confounding factors, such as a low socio-economic status or an earlier history of depression, are not properly excluded.

2) Sample size: Many studies are conducted with small samples, so that results are not always representative. This is certainly not to deny the value of in-depth studies. Practically speaking, this type of research can only be done with small samples. On the other hand, quantitative studies require a certain sample size in order to obtain statistically valid results. In this regard, Priscilla Coleman et al. recommend a minimum sample size of 300 persons for quantitative studies.[417] As will be shown, a number of large-

---

416 American Psychological Association, op. cit., p. 8.
417 Priscilla K. Coleman, David C. Reardon, Thomas W. Strahan and Jesse R. Cougle, "The psychology of abortion: A review and suggestions for future research", *Psychology & Health*, 2005, 20, 2, pp. 237-271, here p. 249.

scale record-based studies using medical claims data in the U.S., Finland and Canada, a New Zealand cohort study and a Swedish multi-centre study have successfully avoided many of the methodological limitations of other post-abortion research.

3) Geographical limitations: A third limitation of post-abortion psychological research has to do with the geographical area chosen. Studies conducted in an area with a very different cultural, sociological or legal climate can generate very different results. Therefore, psychological studies coming from African or Asian countries are excluded in this research, because of the focus on the effects of abortion in the U.K. and the Netherlands. However, some results from European, American, Australian and New-Zealand studies are included. The criterion to include these studies is that research and control groups did not show great cultural, socio-economical or ethnical differences with the situation in the U.K. and the Netherlands.[418] Finally, as regards epidemiological research, some Asian studies are included, since these studies focus on the physical consequences of induced abortion. As will be shown, the results of these studies can be interpreted transculturally.

4) Controlling for confounding factors. Crucial for the determination of a link between abortion and negative mental health effects is a proper control for confounding factors. Negative mental health effects might not be necessarily an effect of an abortion history, but the consequence of socio-economic circumstances, an earlier history of depression, differences in the cultural background or other variables. Therefore the control group has to be characterised by similar life circumstances as the sample of women with an abortion history.

5) A fifth possible limitation of psychological research regards the initial consent to participate. In some studies the initial consent is as low as 60%. This leaves open the question of why so many women (in these cases up to 40%) did not want to participate.

6) Attrition during the course of an investigation takes place because people do not want to participate anymore or fall out because of other circumstances. Some long term studies report a reasonably high initial

---

[418] Reviews by Thorp et al., Van Laar-Jochemsen et al., Van Kooten et al. and by the APA TFMHA all make this kind of international comparisons.

consent, but suffer from an attrition rate as high as 60%.[419] Of course this makes it hard to draw reliable conclusions.

7) The phenomenon of social desirability can also play a role in abortion research. When the social context reinforces the repression of negative feelings, then it is likely that these repressed feelings will not be reported either in an interview or questionnaire. Denial and avoidance of negative reactions after an abortion has been demonstrated in several studies.[420] In some quantitative studies, a woman's abortion status was verifiable, when data were collected from medical records. In other studies however, the abortion history was established based on self-report. In these cases, underreporting can be a problem, which is demonstrated in several studies in the U.S.[421]

8) As a further possible bias in post-abortion psychological research Van Laar-Jochemsen et al. mention the so-called dissonance hypothesis.[422] A dissonance between the abortion itself and an actual negative attitude towards abortion could result in a positive adaptation of the women's attitude to their behaviour. This makes them report less negative emotions than they actually experience to justify the choice for themselves.

9) Another problem is that the various studies often use different measuring instruments and systems of classification. From the 1960'ies onwards, many studies were conducted with non-standardised psychiatric measurement instruments.[423] The APA TFMHA therefore pleads for a clinically relevant measure as the minimum standard for measuring impact.[424] This is not to say that all research of post-abortion psychological effects has to make use of standardised quantitative methods. It is especially difficult in quantitative research to measure the deeper layers of consciousness regarding the moral judgment and the coping of women after they have had an abortion. Applying the method of in-depth interviews adds to the knowledge of psychological effects of abortion. In qualitative research, specifically certain relationship and contextual factors that are influencing

---

419 Coleman, P.K. et al., 2005, op. cit., p. 249.
420 Cf. G. Zolese and C.V.R. Blacker, "The psychological consequences of therapeutic abortion", *British Journal of Psychiatry*, 1992, 160, pp. 742-749, here p. 748; Laar-Jochemsen, T.W. van et al., op. cit., p. 22.
421 American Psychological Association, op. cit., p. 17.
422 Laar-Jochemsen, T.W. van et al., op. cit., p. 21; cf. Kooten, M. van et al., op. cit., p. 72.
423 Zolese G. and Blacker, C.V.R., op. cit., p. 742.
424 American Psychological Association, op. cit., p. 18.

post-abortion mental health can come to the surface.

10) The independence of the researcher. Some major studies on the effects of the current abortion legislation, such as the Dutch evaluation report, are written under Government orders as regards the length of time when results have to be submitted. As an implication of this, questions regarding long term effects of abortion on the mental health of women or their partners, or the effects on their relationship are not included in the study design.

Another important factor regarding the independence of the researcher is the long term strategy of the institutions who are financing the research team. For instance, the British report on induced abortion and mental health by the National Collaborating Centre for Mental Health has been funded by the Department of Health. A strong financial dependence from national Governments could imply that controversial issues such as long term negative mental health effects of abortion, which often come to the surface in small scale, qualitative research, do not get the attention they deserve.

11) Finally, a phenomenon that could heavily influence the interpretation of results coming from abortion research is the ideology of the researcher. Especially in the United States during the eighties and beyond there has been a strong polarization of the abortion discussion ('pro-lifers' vs. 'pro-choicers'). This is probably related to the irreversibility of an abortion: either the embryo dies or stays alive. It is therefore essential for everyone who does research in this area to keep striving towards objectivity, in the search for scientific evidence and transparency, in the sense that interests are declared.

3.1.2 Positive psychological effects of abortion

Maartje van Kooten et al. state that most studies conclude that a majority of the women do not report problems after an abortion.[425] Their study quotes various authors who have found positive reactions among women who have had an abortion. They mention as positive psychological reactions: relief, satisfaction, improvement of self-esteem/self-identity and improvement of the relationship with the partner. Most of these findings regard short-term reactions.[426]

---

425 Kooten, M. van et al., op. cit., p. 77.
426 Laar-Jochemsen, T.W. van et al., op. cit, p. 27.

In this regard, Priscilla Coleman et al. comment that "relief" after an abortion is generally undefined. "Women who state they felt relief following an abortion may variously mean that they were relieved that they would not have the responsibility of a child to care for, relief that they had made it beyond the stressful day of the abortion, relief that they were no longer being pressured by others, relief that there was no longer a risk of their parents or their partner discovering the pregnancy, relief that the physical symptoms of pregnancy were over, ... or other forms of relief."[427] So, there can be stress factors directly having to do with the abortion, or other stress factors more having to do with the relationship of the woman with her partner and with significant others.

Research material coming from Western Europe on the feeling of relief after abortion is limited.[428] Anne Nordal Broen et al. have interviewed 40 Norwegian women who experienced miscarriages and 80 women who underwent abortions.[429] These women were asked to rate their feelings of relief, grief, loss, guilt, shame and anger in a scale ranging from 1 (not at all) to 5 (very much). Women who had had an induced abortion rated significantly more relief at all interviews (at 10 days, 6 months, 2 years and 5 years after the abortion). However, the feelings themselves were not defined nor described by the women who filled in the questionnaire. Methodological weaknesses are the small sample sizes and the statistically significant differences in marital status (women with miscarriage are more often married or cohabitant than women with induced abortion) and what is called "vocational activity" (women with miscarriage were less often in education and more often in a regular employment than women with induced abortion). Therefore, these results cannot be generalised to a larger population of women.

In the international literature, the American study by Brenda Major et

---

427 Coleman, P.K. et al., 2005, op. cit. pp. 258-259.
428 T.W. van Laar-Jochemsen et al. mention only one Norwegian study, of Anne N. Broen, Torbjørn Moum, Anne S. Bødtker and Øivind Ekeberg, "Psychological Impact on Women of Miscarriage Versus Induced Abortion: A 2-Year Follow-up Study", *Psychosomatic Medicine*, 2004, 66, pp. 265-271. In the following, I will use the 5-year study Broen et al. published one year later.
429 Anne N. Broen, Torbjørn Moum, Anne S. Bødtker, and Øivind Ekeberg, "The course of mental health after miscarriage and induced abortion: a longitudinal, five-year follow-up study", *BMC Medicine*, 2005, 3, 18.

al. deals in an adequate way with the methodological problems described above.[430] The sample size is considerably larger (442 women who had a first-trimester abortion in 1993). Demographic characteristics such as marital status are comparable to national, U.S. averages. One remarkable result regarding the feeling of relief is that the intensity of this feeling diminished significantly within two years, similar to other, positive emotions but contrary to negative emotions.[431] However, the lack of a control group of women who did not choose to have an abortion makes it difficult to make a comparison of the reported emotions with other groups of women.

In two studies in the U.K. and the Netherlands, "satisfaction" is measured after an abortion. Pauline Slade et al. use the "Satisfaction with Care Scale", to assess satisfaction with hospital care. Their intention is to compare medical and surgical abortions. They conclude that there is no significant difference in satisfaction with care between the two groups.[432] Likewise, Mechteld Visser et al. measure women's satisfaction with the overall treatment in the clinic or hospital. Their conclusion is that the satisfaction with care is high.[433] But these results do not imply that these women were satisfied with the fact that they had the abortion as such.

As regards the increase of self-esteem, this is not confirmed by Richard Henshaw et al., who conducted a prospective study among 363 abortion patients in Aberdeen, Scotland.[434] They concluded that there was a significant negative correlation between abortion and self-esteem scores. A limitation of this study is that they only measured the psychological effects at 16 days after the abortion. In the same way, also the Dutch evaluation study did only ask women to give their reactions two weeks after the abortion had taken

---

430 Brenda Major, Catherine Cozzarelli, M. Lynne Cooper, Josephine Zubek, Caroline Richards, Michael Wilhite and Richard H. Gramzow, "Psychological Responses of Women After First-Trimester Abortion", *Archives of General Psychiatry*, 2000, 57, pp. 777-784.
431 Ibid., p. 781.
432 P. Slade, S. Heke, J. Fletcher and P. Stewart, "A comparison of medical and surgical termination of pregnancy: choice, emotional impact and satisfaction with care", *British Journal of Obstetrics and Gynaecology*, 1998, 105, pp. 1288-1295.
433 Visser, M.R.M. et al., op. cit., p. 92.
434 Richard Henshaw, Simon Naji, Ian Russell and Allan Templeton, "Psychological responses following medical abortion (using mifepristone and gemeprost) and surgical vacuum aspiration. A patient-centered, partially randomised prospective study", *Acta Obstetrica et Gynecologica Scandinavica*, 1994, 73, pp. 812-818.

place. Visser et al. did not do any research on the long-term psychological effects of the intervention.[435]

Scientific evidence shows that often men and women have ambivalent thoughts and feelings before an abortion.[436] It is significant, that this ambivalence remains after the abortion has taken place. For instance, Anneli Kero and Ann Lalos interviewed 57 women and 26 men in Umeå, Sweden, one year after an abortion.[437] Although the sample size is small, the chosen method of interviewing gives some insight into the mixture of feeling among men and women after abortion. The people interviewed came from different life-situations: some were married, others were cohabiting, some were in relationship but not cohabiting and others were single. The group contained both students and the employed, people who had children and those who did not. One question was to express one's current feelings and experiences in connection with the abortion performed one year previously. The most frequently chosen words among the women were "responsibility", "maturity", "relief", "grief", "release" and "injustice". Among men the most frequently chosen words were "responsibility", "maturity", "grief", "relief" and "powerlessness". 52% of the women and 64% of the men had experienced a conflict with their conscience before the abortion. 59% of the women and 55% of the men had ethical reflections one year after the abortion, using words such as "guilt" and "injustice" to characterise these feelings.

Summarizing the search for positive psychological effects of abortion so far, Coleman's conclusion that "well-designed research specifically documenting how the procedure enhances women's quality of life is generally absent from the professional literature", needs to be confirmed.[438] As will be shown in the next part, David Fergusson et al. similarly state that in general, there is no evidence in the literature on abortion and mental health that suggests that abortion reduces the mental health risks of unwanted or mistimed pregnancy.[439]

---

435 Visser, M.R.M. et al., op. cit., p. 72.
436 Cf. parts 3.3.1.2. and 3.3.2.
437 Anneli Kero and Ann Lalos, "Ambivalence – a logical response to legal abortion: a prospective study among women and men", *Journal of Psychosomatic Obstetrics and Gynecology*, 2000, 21, pp. 81-91.
438 Coleman, P.K. et al., 2006, op. cit. p. 259.
439 D.M. Fergusson, L.J. Horwood and J.M. Boden, "Does abortion reduce the mental health risks or unwanted or unintended pregnancy? A reappraisal of the evidence", *Australian and New Zealand Journal of Psychiatry*, 2013, 47 (9), pp. 819-827.

3.1.3 Negative psychological effects of abortion

Much research has been done to the negative psychological effects of abortion on women, often occurring on a longer term. Among the negative reactions after induced abortion, the following five reactions are reported as the most frequently prevalent: depression, guilt, fear, sadness and regret.[440]

Psychologists and psychiatrists speak of depression when a variety of symptoms are present on an almost daily basis, such as: a long lasting depressive mood, a lack of interest or joy in daily activities, a clear loss or increase of weight, insomnia or hypersomnia, psychomotor agitation or restraint, tiredness or lack of energy, feelings of worthlessness or excessive guilt, decreased ability to concentrate, to think or decide, repetitious thoughts on death or suicide.

As regards feelings of guilt, in most cases these are related to the unborn child. Motives of self-interest to choose an abortion may sometimes lead to feelings of guilt.[441] Adolescents often feel guilty about their impulsive sexual behaviour and its consequences. Some women also experience guilt because of their religious convictions.[442]

Fear and sadness are often experienced shortly before and after the abortion. Fear usually diminishes with time. Sadness can be caused either by the choice to have an abortion or by the abortion itself. Finally some women report feelings of regret after the abortion.

As regards emotional responses after abortion, Pauline Slade et al. did not find differences between women who had medical or surgical abortions.[443]

---

440 Laar-Jochemsen, T.W. van et al., op. cit., pp. 27-43.
441 Marijke J. Korenromp, *Parental adaptation to termination of pregnancy for fetal anomalies*. Doctoral thesis, Utrecht University, 2006, p. 127.
442 For instance, Ellen Wiebe et al. found that among 53 Canadian Muslim women who presented for abortion at a clinic, 49% expressed their guilt because of Islam. However, among these women, answers were so diverse that they could not be generalised. Cf. Ellen Wiebe, Roya Najafi, Naghma Soheil and Alya Kamani, "Muslim women having abortions in Canada. Attitudes, beliefs, and experiences", *Canadian Family Physician*, 2011, 57, April, e134-e138.
443 P. Slade et al., op. cit., pp. 1288-1295.

3.1.3.1 Quantitative studies

Several studies show an association between abortion and Post-Traumatic Stress Disorder (PTSD).[444] For instance, in 2008 results were presented of prospective research among 140 Dutch speaking women by Arnold van Emmerik et al.[445] This study pointed out that approximately two months after their abortion experience, participants reported moderately elevated levels of re-experiencing and avoidance (mean Impact of Event Scale (IES) = 22.67, Standard Deviation (SD) = 18.49). A considerable proportion reported scores that exceeded even the more stringent clinical cut-off points.[446] Re-experiencing (in dreams or flashbacks, for example) and avoidance (for instance efforts to avoid feelings or thoughts associated with the abortion) are among the behavioural symptoms that accompany PTSD according to the DSM-5 diagnostic clusters.[447] Van Emmerik et al. conclude that "[e]ven at moderate levels...post-traumatic stress after elective abortion likely represents a significant problem considering the large number of elective abortions worldwide."[448]

Similar findings are reported by Lydia Hamama et al., who examined the impact of elective and spontaneous abortion on mental health during subsequent pregnancy.[449] Their results show that of the 405 women who were interviewed, 32.6% ranked the elective or spontaneous abortion as their worst or second worst trauma exposure. The women's appraisal that the elective or spontaneous abortion has been traumatic for them was significantly associated with both PTSD and depression.[450]

---

444 Maureen Curley and Celeste Johnston, "The Characteristics and Severity of Psychological Distress After Abortion Among University Students", *Journal of Behavioral Health Services & Research*, 2013, pp. 279–293, here p. 289.
445 Arnold A.P. van Emmerik, Jan H. Kamphuis and Paul Emmelkamp, "Prevalence and Prediction of Re-Experiencing and Avoidance after Elective Surgical Abortion: A Prospective Study", *Clinical Psychology and Psychotherapy*, 2008, 15, pp. 378-385.
446 Ibid., p. 382.
447 American Psychiatric Association, "Factsheet on Posttraumatic Stress Disorder", Washington, 2013; Laar-Jochemsen, T.W. van et al., op. cit., p. 30.
448 A.A.P. van Emmerik et al., op. cit., p. 383.
449 Lydia Hamama, Sheila A.M. Rauch, Mickey Sperlich, Erin Defever and Julia S. Seng, "Previous experience of spontaneous or elective abortion and risk for posttraumatic stress and depression during subsequent pregnancy", *Depression and Anxiety*, 2010, August 27(8), pp. 699–707.
450 Ibid., p. 704.

A Swedish multi-centre study by Inger Wallin Lundell et al. found that of the 1,470 women who had requested an induced abortion and who had filled in a questionnaire in the clinic or hospital, 4% had a point prevalence of PTSD and 23% of Post-Traumatic Stress Symptoms (PTSS).[451] They also discovered that women who reported high levels of anxiety or depression at the time of the induced abortion were more likely to fulfill criteria for ongoing PTSD or PTSS. Further, PTSS was significantly associated with a low educational level. Wallin Lundell et al. recommend that women who have had trauma experiences in the past and/or have had symptoms of mental distress need more consideration and alertness from the medical personnel when they are counselled in a clinic or hospital.[452]

It is clear that persistent avoidance of stimuli associated with the abortion experience can make effective treatment of mental health problems much more difficult. In this regard, Rosanna Hess has found in interviews with women years after an abortion took place, that almost all women used various avoidance strategies to cope with the memory of the abortion. It is therefore possible that women who have a diagnosed depression, do not acknowledge that this depression has something to do with the abortion.[453]

The Dutch obstetrician Marijke Korenromp has investigated psychological consequences of abortion after the discovery of a certain foetal anomaly.[454] Between 2 and 7 years after the abortion of a foetus with an anomaly, some 15% of the women suffer from features of post-traumatic stress syndrome at a pathological level; some 11% suffer from depression at a pathological level. For men the numbers are lower, but still

---

[451] Inger Wallin Lundell, Inger Sundström Poromaa, Örjan Frans, Lotti Helström, Ulf Högberg, Lena Moby, Sigrid Nyberg, Gunilla Sydsjö, Susanne Georgsson Öhman, Ingrid Östlund and Agneta Skoog Svanberg, "The prevalence of posttraumatic stress among women requesting induced abortion", *The European Journal of Contraception and Reproductive Health Care,* 2013, 18, pp. 480–488.

[452] Ibid., pp. 485-487.

[453] Rosanna Hess, "Dimensions of Women's Long-Term Post-abortion Experience", *The American Journal of Maternal/Child Nursing,* 2004, 29, 3, pp. 193-198.

[454] Marijke J. Korenromp, Godelieve C.M.L. Page-Christiaens, J. van den Bout, Eduard J.H. Mulder, Joke Hunfeld and Caterina M. Bilardo, "Psychological consequences of termination of pregnancy for fetal anomaly: similarities and differences between partners", *Prenatal Diagnosis,* 2005, 25, pp. 1226-1233.

8% scored pathological levels of depression.[455]

Carlo Bellieni and Giuseppe Buonocore reviewed seven studies which compared abortion and unplanned pregnancies that ended in delivery. Of these studies, four showed a higher risk for loss of self-esteem, anxiety disorders, depression, suicide ideation, and substance abuse disorder or substance abuse rate in the abortion groups, two studies showed no difference and in one case, results were indicative of a prevalence of depression in the case of abortion only among married women.[456] One of the studies which showed no difference is a British study by Anne Gilchrist et al. Her study did show that self-harm is more common in women with induced abortion (Relative Risk (RR) 1.7 (95% Confidence Interval (CI) 1.1-2.6)), although rates of total reported psychiatric disorder were no higher after abortion.[457] The study by Gilchrist et al. uses as a comparison group women who did not request an abortion but whose pregnancy was "unplanned".[458] A weakness of this study is that a whole group of women who 'planned' their pregnancy is left out in the study design. Therefore results cannot be generalised to the whole of society. Given the ambivalence many women experience when they discover that they are pregnant, 'unwantedness' is an unclear criterion which might also change during a pregnancy. Usually, this change is in the direction of an increasing maternal-foetal attachment [459]

Bellieni and Buonocore have also compared studies measuring a risk of mental disorder in the groups of women who had had an abortion versus those who gave birth. Thirteen studies support the presence of risk of abortion versus childbirth, whereas five studies show no risk in the abortion group.[460] For instance, David Reardon et al. (2003) point out an increase in the number of cases of depression in women who have had an

---

455 Ibid., p. 1228.
456 Bellieni, C.V. and Buonocore, G., op. cit., p. 302-306.
457 A.C. Gilchrist, P.C. Hannaford, P. Frank and C.R. Kay, "Termination of pregnancy and psychiatric morbidity", *British Journal of Psychiatry*, 1995, 167, pp. 243-248.
458 Ibid., p. 243.
459 Cf. part 3.3.2.1.
460 Bellieni, C.V. and Buonocore, G., op. cit., p. 302.

abortion.[461] Their investigation took place in California among more than 15,000 women who took part in the Medicaid program and who had an abortion. The control group was formed of more than 41,000 women who also took part in the Medicaid program, and who had decided to bring to term their unintended pregnancy. The research was done retrospectively at six different moments (after 90 and 180 days, and after 1, 2, 3 and 4 years). The researchers found that women who had had an abortion visited a psychiatrist more frequently than women in a control group, with a significant difference (an odds ratio varying from 1.5 to 2.6, with a 95% confidence interval).[462] The most prevalent psychiatric diagnosis was "single-episode depressive psychosis".[463]

Still, some methodological problems remain, as Reardon himself admits. Although he has checked the possibility of other intervening variables, such as socioeconomic status and age, the marriage status was not taken into account as a result of a lack of available data. Also the previous psychiatric admissions and pregnancies more than one year before the abortion were unknown because of a lack of a complete medical history. Yet, this omission could very likely have diluted the observed differences, because the women who were in the control group might also have had a history of previous abortion(s).[464]

In reaction to the continuing debate on the relation between induced abortion and mental health problems, David Fergusson et al. reversed the question: Does abortion reduce the mental health risks of unwanted or unintended pregnancy?[465] In a review of eight earlier studies performed in the last two decades, they conclude that there is consistent evidence to show that abortion is not associated with a reduction in rates of mental health problems ($p > 0.75$). Abortion is associated with small to moderate increases in risks of anxiety (Adjusted Odds Ratio (AOR) 1.28, 95% Confidence

---

[461] David C. Reardon, Jesse R. Cougle, Vincent M. Rue, Martha W. Shuping, Priscilla K. Coleman and Philip G. Ney, "Psychiatric admissions of low-income women following abortion and childbirth", *Canadian Medical Association Journal,* 2003, 168 (10), pp. 1253-1256.
[462] The odds ratio is a measure for the relative probability that a certain effect occurs (f.i. preterm birth) if a certain event (f.i. an induced abortion) has or has not taken place.
[463] Reardon, D.C. et al., 2003, op. cit., p. 1255.
[464] Ibid., p. 1256.
[465] Fergusson, D.M. et al., 2013(a), op. cit., pp. 819-827.

Interval (CI) 0.97-1.70; p<0.08), alcohol misuse (AOR 2.34, 95% CI 1.05-5.21; p<0.05, illicit drug use/misuse (AOR 3.91, 95% CI 1.13-13.55; p<0.05) and suicidal behaviour (AOR 1.69, 95% CI 1.12-2.54; p<0.01).

Earlier, Fergusson et al. reported from an analysis of data from a 30-year longitudinal study in which they sought to examine the extent to which variations in pregnancy outcomes, including induced abortion, live birth and pregnancy loss are associated with increased (or decreased) risks of a range of common mental health problems (major depression, anxiety disorders, suicidal ideation, alcohol dependence and illicit drug dependence).[466] One strength of this analysis is that it makes use of a combination of both prospective and retrospective reports. In particular, they report about a birth cohort of 534 young women in the Christchurch urban region in New Zealand, studied to the age of 30. The abortion legislation in New Zealand does not differ very much from the U.K. and the Netherlands. In order to obtain a legal abortion in New Zealand, a woman must obtain the approval of two specialist consultants, the consultants must agree that either (1) the pregnancy would seriously harm the life or the physical or mental health of the woman, (2) the pregnancy is the result of incest, (3) the woman is severely mentally handicapped, or (4) a foetal abnormality exists. An abortion will also be considered on the basis of the pregnant woman's young age or when the pregnancy is the result of rape.[467]

Fergusson et al. also looked at several potential sources of confounding factors relating to pre-abortion background. These include: socio-economic factors; childhood and family factors; mental health and personality factors.[468] Not surprisingly given the evidence summarised by Thorp et al., also Fergusson et al. find that those becoming pregnant and seeking abortions had significantly (Probability (P)<0.5) higher rates of disorder than the "not pregnant group" and, with the exception of anxiety disorder significantly higher rates of disorder than the "pregnant no abortion group". Also after control for confounders these results remained statistically significant.

---

466 D.M. Fergusson, L.J. Horwood and J.M. Boden, "Abortion and mental health disorders: evidence from a 30-year longitudinal study", *British Journal of Psychiatry*, 2008, 193, pp. 444-451.
467 American Psychological Association, op. cit., pp. 44-45.
468 Fergusson, D.M. et al., 2008, op. cit., p. 448; David M. Fergusson, L. John Horwood and Elizabeth M. Ridder, "Abortion in young women and subsequent mental health", *Journal of Child Psychology and Psychiatry*, 2006, 47 (1), pp. 16-24.

The concurrent data suggested that after adjustment for confounding those women exposed to abortion had rates of mental health problems that were 1.37 (95% CI 1.16-1.62) times higher than for those who had not become pregnant ($P<0.001$). As adverse mental health outcomes, illicit drug dependence was measured most often, besides alcohol dependence and anxiety disorder.

In their analysis of 2008, Fergusson et al. also distinguished between a live birth that was associated with an unwanted or adverse reaction to pregnancy and a live birth with no reported adverse reactions. Their earlier results of 2006 did not make this distinction, as has been criticised by the APA TFMHA.[469] They found that for both models, having a live birth, whether with or without an unwanted/adverse reaction, there was no association with significant increases in mental health outcomes after adjustment for confounding variables.[470] This latter finding demonstrates that the criterion of the pregnancy being unwanted or not is not a decisive criterion for the association with mental health problems. The limitation the APA TFMHA chooses for defining a comparable control group is therefore not supported by the results of Fergusson et al. This limitation can be considered an example of selection bias and can therefore do harm when reviewing the evidence for the association between abortion and mental health problems.

Fergusson et al. conclude that their findings are consistent with the view that experiencing a procured abortion has a small causal effect (here: a higher risk of about 30%) on the mental health of women. They state that their conclusions have important implications for the legal status of abortion in societies such as New Zealand and the U.K., where over 90% of abortions are authorised on the grounds that proceeding with the pregnancy would pose a serious threat to the woman's mental health.[471] The primary reasons that women seek an abortion are personal and social, rather than relating to mental health concerns.[472]

Finally, Julia Steinberg and Nancy Russo have shown in a retrospective study among American women that after controlling for pre-pregnancy

---

469 American Psychological Association, op. cit., p. 52.
470 Fergusson, D.M. et al., 2008, op. cit., p. 448.
471 Ibid., p. 450.
472 Cf. part 3.3.1.1.

anxiety symptoms, rape experience and other covariates, abortion was no longer found to be associated with increased risk for anxiety symptoms.[473] Pre-pregnancy anxiety symptoms may be caused by intimate partner violence or other forms of violence.[474] However, they do conclude that "women who terminate a first pregnancy have significantly higher rates of experiencing anxiety symptoms (EAS) compared to women who deliver a first pregnancy."[475] Therefore, their study confirms the relevance of addressing the possibility of intimate partner violence during counselling after the discovery of an unintended pregnancy.[476]

3.1.3.2 Qualitative studies

By means of qualitative research it is possible to gain a deeper insight in the struggles some women go through after an abortion. Anneli Kero, Ulf Högberg and Ann Lalos have investigated the psychological effects of abortion by means of a qualitative study among Swedish women.[477] At four months after the abortion, the women were asked retrospectively about their immediate post-abortion reactions. Although many women showed ambivalent reactions, describing both positive and painful feelings, 21% mentioned they had gone through a period of severe emotional distress. For this latter group, the decision to have an abortion had been made with difficulty and entailed much conflict. For example, three clearly stated that they wanted to give birth and another five were ambivalent. Furthermore, nine had experienced having an abortion as causing a conflict of conscience. Two stated their religion had made the decision even more difficult. This group of women described their reactions directly post-abortion in terms of a mourning process, a crisis and/or depression.

---

473 Julia R. Steinberg and Nancy F. Russo, "Abortion and anxiety: what's the relationship?", *Social Science and Medicine*, 2008, 67, pp. 238-252.
474 For instance, Ann Coker found that intimate partner violence was associated with abortion in 6 of 8 studies that addressed this association. Two studies also noted an association between abortion and both physical and sexual abuse. Cf. Ann L. Coker, "Does physical intimate partner violence affect sexual health? A systematic review", *Trauma, Violence, & Abuse*, 2007, 8(2), pp. 149–177.
475 Steinberg, J.R. and Russo, N.F., op. cit., p. 243.
476 Cf. part 3.3.2.4.
477 Anneli Kero, Ulf Högberg and Ann Lalos, "Wellbeing and mental growth – long-term effects of legal abortion", *Social Science & Medicine*, 2004, 58, pp. 2559-2569.

One year after the abortion, the researchers interviewed the women again. Figure 7 shows some examples of reasons and statements of women with severe emotional distress directly post-abortion:

Reason for abortion at the time of abortion	Statements 4 months later	Statements 1 year later
"I really wanted to give birth to the child but our finances would not allow it..." (Victoria*)	"... considered if I did right or wrong...afraid of sterility...have been alone in all this...a friend is pregnant...I am reminded all the time...I don't think so much anymore...try to forget it..." (Victoria)	"...it is not possible to undo it, could not have done otherwise, have no anxiety...but I am so afraid of being pregnant, have no desire for sex and I get tense because of it...my husband does not understand it...I had maternal feelings when I understood that I was pregnant...I try to convince myself ...that I do not want to have children...a defence when you have had an abortion though I did not want it..." (Victoria)
"...financial and emotional insecurity, insecure future... enormous responsibility... you have to think of the good of the child." (Frieda)	"...felt like a murderer... abortion is completely wrong... I have been depressed since the abortion, suffered anguish and sleeping problems... isolated myself... a week ago I asked the child and God to forgive me and now I have started to talk to my partner...it has been better and this last week I have felt much better..." (Frieda)	"The abortion has been very hard... it has been a hard and painful year... the decision feels wrong and I regret it...the first four months were terrible and I thought I would never feel good again... thought I acted ethically wrongly... but I can live with it...I do not feel ashamed anymore for having had an abortion... regarded the abortion as a paradox...great pain, release and relief..." (Frieda)
"have no stable partner relationship, poor finances ...it is for the good of the child..." (Alice)	"suffered very much mentally... I have been against abortion... he did not want me to keep the child... (Alice)	"...before I thought that abortion was something awful... I do not think that today... I do not feel ashamed of having had an abortion...it is good to have abortion as an alternative... have a new partner... managed the abortion much better than I expected..." (Alice)
"...I have two children who are just leaving the small child stage... now I want to do things for myself, educate myself..." (Julia)	"...the first week it was very hard...I cried and thought a lot of the child...worked it through and talked a lot... then it has diminished...I do not think so much about it now..." (Julia)	"...the right decision in the situation I was in... mourn the child, got pregnant again...felt ashamed of the new child because of the abortion...the pregnancy was not planned...thought of abortion but I could not manage to have another one... it is right to have this child..." (Julia)

"a doubtful relationship... time of crisis..." (Agnes)	"...I got into a crisis...felt regret, thought I had made the wrong decision... worked through the crisis in therapy for some months... now it is alright... I am pregnant in 8-9 weeks..." (Agnes)	"...what I did is not possible to undo... but I will always regret it...abortion is wrong for me...I am so much stronger and happier now since I got a child... now I would manage her alone..." (Agnes)

Figure 7: Examples of reasons for abortion and typical statements concerning experiences of the abortion process in women with severe emotional distress directly post-abortion (n=12)

Source: Kero, A., Högberg U. and Lalos, A., 2004, op. cit., p. 2566. *: names are pseudonyms

In order to cope effectively with psychological distress after abortion, it's inevitable to develop an awareness of death. Regarding these types of experiences, German psychiatrist Peter Petersen distinguishes four different levels of experience.[478] First, he mentions normal psychological experience, with feelings of guilt, reproach, stability and/or indifference. The women cited above, especially Victoria, Frieda and Agnes clearly show feelings of guilt and reproach. If the dominant reaction is one of indifference or stability, then often at this stage a deeper awareness is suppressed with the aid of forms of defence such as positivism or empiricism, by saying for example that the embryo has been nothing more than a lump of cells and that the aborted embryo is gone by now. Death, seen as a strictly natural scientific process, is considered an absolute ending of life. Petersen: "This kind of anthropology condemns us to passivity. As a motionless rabbit we stare at the snake's open mouth, of death, - there is no more human life after death. The immutability of our inflexible thinking celebrates its final triumph..."[479] If one holds such an anthropological view, an attitude of indifference or even relief after an abortion could be psychologically explained as consequent. But, by limiting oneself to the methods of natural science in order to formulate an answer to the existential question of human

---

[478] Peter Petersen, "Awareness of death and interpersonal relations after induced abortion", *Zeitschrift für Geburtshilfe und Perinatologie*, 1987, 191, 2, pp. 47-54. Petersen worked for more than 30 years as psychiatrist and professor for psychotherapy in Germany.

[479] Peter Petersen, *Schwangerschaftsabbruch – unser Bewußtsein vom Tod im Leben. Tiefenpsychologische und anthropologische Aspekte der Verarbeitung.* Stuttgart, 1986, p. 291.

life, one develops a reductionist view of reality.[480]

Secondly, a breakthrough of destructive deep awareness takes place, with chaos and panic, revulsion and hate. Frieda describes her feelings of depression that causes anguish and isolation. In Alice's situation, the relationship breaks down. Thirdly, acceptance of existential reality comes in, experiencing guilt at having been party to killing a member of the human species, genetically related to his or her parents. One can see that at this stage, reactions differ greatly. Frieda and Agnes still regret their decision after one year, whereas Alice seems to have changed her opinion of abortion. Fourthly, responsibility and a feeling of guilt toward the dead child develop; it is here that the interhuman relationship is fulfilled, because the mental image of the child becomes like an independent being. Only at this point full awareness of death occurs. The absence of shame after one year, while still admitting that the decision has been wrong, indicates that Frieda has gone through the whole coping process of developing an awareness of the death of her child, of accepting her responsibility, of grief and of reconciliation.

3.1.3.3 Qualitative long-term studies

Few recent investigations have empirically verified the long-term psychological effects of the abortion experience with in-depth interviews. Rosanna Hess has interviewed women in the U.S. who had an elective abortion more than 5 years and up to 31 years before the interview.[481] Almost each woman was interviewed twice. Although the sample size is very small (n=17), this phenomenological, narrative study reveals some important aspects of the long-term post-abortion experience. Hess distinguished five themes from the women's narratives: making the decision, coping with the memories, gaining perspective, seeking help and recognizing its worth. For instance, there is the aspect of secrecy, problematic in order to cope with the memories. Patty (names are pseudonyms) reveals that she wanted the abortion, but kept it a secret for fear of hurting her parents: "I've had

---

[480] Or in the words of Bernard Lonergan: "Reductionists extend the methods of natural science to the study of man. Their results, accordingly, are valid only in so far as a man resembles a robot or a rat and, while such resemblance does exist, exclusive attention to it gives a grossly mutilated and distorted view." Cf. Lonergan, B., op. cit., p. 248.

[481] Hess, R.F., op. cit., pp. 193-198.

this hidden for 21 years. There's not a day that goes by that I don't think about this. And I feel bad that I could never tell my parents."[482] Several women rode an "emotional roller coaster" for decades. Angela, 23 years post-abortion, described it as trying to hold a beach ball under the waves. "When those feelings would come up I would do everything to stuff it back down again. I was constantly pushing it down, trying to forget about it."[483]

The in-depth interviews also revealed some elements of the spiritual dimension in the women's lives after the abortion. Frances said her self-image was transformed after her conversion to Christ: "I remember the walls coming down that I had built up; all these things that I'd pushed way deep down and denied. Looking back now I didn't realize how ashamed I was. I think a lot of it had to do with the abortions."[484]

Several of the women who described a predominantly negative aftermath sought help and healing. Rosalie believed that helping others would help her: "I decided to help myself. My bishop always told me, 'When you're doing the best to help somebody else, you're doing the best to help yourself.'"[485] She volunteered her time at a pregnancy care centre. Others sought help in post-abortion support groups. Noreen said, "We could all share our experiences. I can't go up to somebody, even just, even a friend. I think being able to talk with women who have had the similar or same experience, and just being able to say, 'Yes this is what I felt. Oh, you felt that way too?' was healing."[486] As part of the steps to healing learned in the support group some women personalised the aborted foetus or visualised the experience. Frances, who had three abortions, said, "I finally named them. I named every single one of them."[487]

As an example of coming to recognise the foetus' worth, I quote Gwen, who worked for a pro-life organization: "So that has been important in my life, to want to give women their options, to educate them, and let them know there are other options out there than abortion."[488]

---

482 Ibid., p. 195.
483 Ibid.
484 Ibid., p. 196.
485 Ibid.
486 Ibid.
487 Ibid.
488 Ibid.

Abortion can not only have a negative psychological impact on women who undergo the procedure, but also on nurses working in abortion care. Alysson Lipp and Anne Fothergill, who did individual open-ended interviews with nurses working in abortion care in the NHS in Wales, conclude that the effect of abortion care on nurses should not be underestimated. Working in abortion care is stressful because of the level of emotional labour required.[489]

Looking at the methodological aspects of qualitative studies like the one of Hess or of Lipp and Fothergill, one has to note the very small sample size and the lack of comparison group. Therefore, Hess' and similar studies are not included in the evaluation of the APA TFMHA. Often with this type of research, it is not possible to show a causal link between a history of abortion and the incidence of depression, PTSD or other disorders. But on the other hand, it has been shown that in-depth interviews reveal other information on the women's lives and in particular regarding the spiritual dimension, than does quantitative research. It requires that the interviewer not only asks about the effects of the abortion on the woman's life, but also about the meaning of the abortion experience in the woman's present life. If women reveal a long-lasting, negative influence of a past abortion on their current state of mind, then possibly new ways could be opened up for healing or reconciliation.[490] A further advantage of qualitative research is that it includes the possibility to ask additional probing questions to clarify comments made by the participants in the interview.[491]

3.1.4 Risk factors for women's mental health

Several studies make mention of possible risk factors for negative psychological consequences after abortion. Brenda Major et al. found out that a pre-pregnancy history of depression consistently predicted poorer post-abortion mental health and more negative abortion-related emotions

---

[489] Allyson Lipp and Anne Fothergill, "Nurses in abortion care: Identifying and managing stress", *Contemporary Nurse*, 2009, 31, pp. 108-120. Similarly, Hanna in her phenomenological study found three types of moral distress among nurses working in abortion care, which she identified as "shocked", "muted" and "suppressed" distress. In: D.R. Hanna, "The Lived Experience of Moral Distress: Nurses Who Assisted With Elective Abortions", *Research and Theory for Nursing Practice*, 2005, 19, 1, pp. 95-124.
[490] Cf. part 7.8.
[491] As Hess has done in her interviews, cf. Hess, R.F., op. cit., p. 194.

and evaluations. In addition, younger women evaluated their abortion more negatively, as did women who already had children at the time of the abortion.[492]

Hanna Söderberg et al. indicate the following risk factors associated with emotional distress up to one year after abortion: living alone, poor emotional support from family and friends, an adverse post-abortion change in the relationship with the partner, an underlying ambivalence or adverse attitude to abortion and being actively religious.[493] Regarding the latter 'risk factor': it is indeed supported by evidence that women who have had an abortion and who tended to believe that foetuses are human, scored lower on well-being variables than women who have had an abortion and who were of the opinion that foetuses are not human.[494] It would be interesting to see to what extent women's beliefs about the nature of the foetus are founded on scientific data, since biologists are unanimously of the opinion that foetuses are human[495], or that their opinions are more the result of a strategy to cope with the loss caused by the abortion.

Finally, Hess found that women who express feelings of coercion about termination by partners or parents are at an increased risk of post-abortion dysphoria (negative moods).[496] This brings us to the important role men can have in the decision-making process and to the impact abortion can have on men.

3.1.5 Mental health effects on men after abortion

Not only women can suffer from negative mental health effects after abortion, but also their partners. Anne Speckhard and Vincent Rue observed that "Men who have been involved in an abortion often struggle with their internal self-concept of masculinity, feeling that they have failed to protect

---

492 Major, B. et al., op. cit., p. 780.
493 Hanna Söderberg, Lars Janzon and Nils-Otto Sjöberg, "Emotional distress following induced abortion. A study of its incidence and determinants among abortees in Malmö, Sweden", *European Journal of Obstetrics & Gynecology and Reproductive Biology*, 1998, 79, pp. 173-178.
494 Mary P. Conklin and Brian P. O'Connor, "Beliefs about the fetus as a moderator of post-abortion psychological well-being", *Journal of social and clinical psychology*, 1995, 14, 1, pp. 76-95.
495 Cf. part 4.1.
496 Hess, R.F., op. cit., p. 197.

and nurture. These feelings of failure and guilt are often generalized into many areas of the marital and familial relationships."[497]

However, studies pertaining to men's experience with a partner's abortion are limited in number.[498] One example is a prospective cohort study among Canadian men and women before and after abortion, by Pierre Lauzon et al.[499] Before the abortion, 56.9% of woman and 39.6% of men were much more distressed than their respective controls. Three weeks after the abortion, 41.7% of women and 30.9% of men were still highly distressed. Predictors of distress for women were fear of negative effects on the relationship, unsatisfactory relationships, relationships of less than 1 year, ambivalence about the decision to abort, not having a previous child, and suicidal ideation. Predictors of distress for men were fear of negative effects on the relationship, relationships of less than 1 year, preoccupation with the abortion and anxiety about its accompanying pain, negative perceptions of their own health, suicidal gestures in the past and suicidal ideation in the past year. Lauzon et al. conclude that being involved in a first-trimester abortion can be highly distressing for both women and men. Nearly one third of the men would have liked counselling. The authors suggest that the issue of fear of negative effects on the relationship should be raised routinely and explicitly in pre-abortion interviews.

It is remarkable that both Pierre Lauzon and second author Diane Roger-Achim at the time of publication practised at an abortion clinic in Montreal, Quebec. They used a self-administered questionnaire. Psychological distress was measured with the Ilfeld Psychiatric Symptom Index. However, two relative weaknesses of their study are the small sample size (113 men and 197 women) and the pretty high attrition rates (loss of cases in the course of the investigation) of 39% of the participating men and 36% of the women. They also did not look at long term effects of the abortion, either on the mental health of both partners or on their relationship.

---

[497] Anne Speckhard and Vincent M. Rue, "Complicated Mourning: Dynamics of Impacted Post Abortion Grief", in: *Journal of Prenatal and Perinatal Psychological Health*, 1993, 8, 1, pp. 5-32.

[498] Catherine T. Coyle and Vincent M. Rue, "Men's Perceptions Concerning Disclosure of a Partner's Abortion: Implications for Counseling", *European Journal of Counselling Psychology*, 2015, 3 (2), pp. 159–173.

[499] Pierre Lauzon, Diane Roger-Achim, André Achim and Richard Boyer, "Emotional distress among couples involved in first-trimester induces abortions", *Canadian Family Physician*, 2000, 46, pp. 2033-2040.

Qualitative research can shed some light on the long-term psychological effects of abortion on men, where large, quantitative research is lacking. Peter Petersen and Carmen Blaschke interviewed seven men, whose girlfriend had had an abortion one to five years previously, in interviews lasting between one and two hours.[500] These men were partners of women who attended Petersen's psychiatric practice in the 1980s, either for conflict management regarding their pregnancy or for an expert judgment on a psychiatric indication, one of the grounds on which an abortion is permitted in Germany.[501] Petersen noticed among these men the presence of a thick veil covering manifold emotions, such as a complete denial of any involvement, like 'an armour of ice': "I've got nothing to do with this". In other cases men's deeper feelings showed a chaotic panic at the thought of what had happened or signs of a heavy depression and feelings of guilt.[502] According to Petersen these hidden emotions have to do with a lack of the men's involvement in the decision to abort and also in the lack of any physical experience of the abortion itself, which can make it harder to deal with the situation.[503]

3.1.6 Recommendations for future research

From this part it can be concluded that, in order to make future research on psychological risks and effects of procured abortion representative for all women, control groups should include women with both planned and unplanned pregnancies. It would also be enriching to make use of different, both qualitative and quantitative research strategies. No interdisciplinary study could have been found which looks at both the psychological consequences of abortion and at the ethical or moral considerations of the decision-making process.

Ideally, a future quantitative study design should be large enough to produce statistically significant results. A control for possible confounding variables should be included. Therefore it is important to use both retrospective and prospective data, as has been the case in the 2008 study

---

500 Petersen, P., 1986, op. cit., pp. 258-269.
501 Based on the German criminal Code: § 218 StGB.
502 Petersen, P., 1986, op. cit., p. 259.
503 Ibid., pp. 259-262.

by David Fergusson et al.

Qualitative research gives insight into the long term mental health problems, although most studies work with small samples. With Priscilla Coleman et al. it is concluded that regarding post-abortion psychological research, there is a need for diversified research strategies.[504]

Few methodologically sound studies are available on mental health effects of abortion on men and the effects on relationships. It is recommendable that such studies will be done, for the sake of the men and women affected by negative mental health effects and to improve the social work that is being done before irreversible decisions are made.

3.2 Physical risks and effects of induced abortion on women

In the international literature there is a great quantity of medical and epidemiological data showing physical and psychological complications arising from induced abortion, occasionally with contradictory results. Research outcomes are analysed which investigate the relation between abortion and subsequent preterm birth. (3.2.1) A résumé is given of the heated debate among epidemiologists in the U.K. and other countries regarding a possible link of breast cancer after induced abortion. (3.2.2) Other studies deal with a possible association between abortion and subsequent suicide. (3.2.3) Finally, several studies point out a risk of complications after induced abortion, in particular the risk on chlamydia infections. (3.2.4)

3.2.1 Abortion and subsequent preterm birth

Preterm birth is associated with major birth defects, in particular with defects of the central nervous system. Research by Margaret Honein et al. shows that major birth defects were more than twice as common among preterm births (24–36 weeks) compared with term births (37–41 weeks gestation).[505]

A recent cohort study has been conducted in Scotland, among respectively

---

504 Coleman, P.K., 2005, op. cit., pp. 249-251.
505 M.A. Honein, R.S. Kirby, R.E. Meyer, J. Xing, N.I. Skerrette, N. Yuskiv, L. Marengo, J.R. Petrini, M.J. Davidoff, C.T. Mai, Ch. M. Druschel, S. Viner-Brown and L.E. Sever, "The Association Between Major Birth Defects and Preterm Birth", in: *Maternal and Child Health Journal*, 2009, 13, pp. 164-175.

120,033 women with a documented second pregnancy following an induced abortion; 457,477 women with a second pregnancy following live birth and 47,355 women with a second pregnancy after a miscarriage.[506] This study by Siladitya Bhattacharya et al. pointed out that induced abortion in a first pregnancy increased the risk of spontaneous preterm birth compared with that in primigravidae (women who are pregnant for the first time). They measured an adjusted Relative Risk (RR) of 1.37 (95% Confidence Interval (CI) 1.32 to 1.42) for women who have had an induced abortion. Compared to women with an initial live birth, the RR after induced abortion is 1.66 (95% CI 1.58 to 1.74). In comparison with women with a previous miscarriage, there is no evidence for a higher risk after induced abortion (adjusted RR 0.85, 95% CI 0.79 to 0.91).

A strength of this study is the large sample size. However, as the authors admit themselves, their study has some methodological limitations because of the unrecorded and missing data in relation to certain potential confounding factors, such as smoking data (only available for 50% of women) and marital status.[507] Therefore, the outcomes need to be compared with other research results.

In 2012, Reija Klemetti et al. presented their results of a nationwide study on birth outcomes after induced abortion in Finland.[508] Their study also has a very large sample size of more than 300,000 Finnish first-time mothers during 1996 and 2008. 31,083 women in this group have had one induced abortion, 4,417 women have had two induced abortions and 942 women have had three or more abortions. The other women have had no abortions and served as a reference group. The sample size made it possible to control the results for possible confounding factors, such as maternal age, marital status, socioeconomic position, urbanity, smoking during pregnancy, previous ectopic pregnancies and miscarriages. Their results showed that

---

506 Siladytia Bhattacharya, Alison Lowit, Sohinee Bhattacharya, Edwin A. Raja, Amanda J. Lee, Tahir Mahmood and Allan Templeton, "Reproductive outcomes following induced abortion: a national registerbased cohort study in Scotland", *British Medical Journal Open*, 2012, 2, 4, pp. 1-12.
507 Ibid., p. 6.
508 R. Klemetti, M. Gissler, M. Niinimäki and E. Hemminki, "Birth outcomes after induced abortion: a nationwide register-based study of first births in Finland", *Human Reproduction*, 2012, Nov., 27 (11), pp. 3315-3320.

after adjustment for these confounders, perinatal deaths and very preterm birth (< 28 gestational weeks) suggested worse outcomes after induced abortion, as can be seen in figure 8:

Birth outcome	Adjusted OR and 95% CI					
	0 versus 1 induced abortion		0 versus 2 induced abortions		0 versus 3 or more induced abortions	
	OR	CI	OR	CI	OR	CI
Very preterm <28 gestational week	1.19	0.98-1.44	1.69	1.14-2.51	2.78	1.48-5.24
Perinatal death	1.19	1.02-1.39	1.16	0.79-1.70	1.70	0.87-3.29

Figure 8: Adjusted Odds Ratios (OR) and 95% Confidence Intervals (CI) for birth outcomes of Finnish first-time mothers during 1996-2008, comparing those having had one or more previous induced abortion with those with a history of no induced abortion, by the number of abortions

Source: Klemetti, R. et al., 2012, op. cit., p. 3319.

The increasing odds ratios for both very preterm birth and perinatal death after one or more induced abortions exhibit a dose-response relationship: the more induced abortions a woman has undergone, the greater the risk of subsequent very preterm birth or perinatal death. Klemetti et al. caution that their study, because of its observational character, does not prove causality. However, in an earlier study, Pierre-Yves Ancel et al. have suggested that infectious diseases following abortion may account for the relationship with subsequent preterm delivery. By damaging the endometrium (the inner membrane of the uterus), surgical procedures applied at induced abortion could also lead to very preterm births in subsequent pregnancies, after placenta praevia and other types of maternal haemorrhage.[509] Klemetti et al. recommend that "health education should contain information of

---

[509] Pierre-Yves Ancel, Nathalie Lelong, Emiel Papiernik, Marie-Josèphe Saurel-Cubizolles and Monique Kaminski, "History of induced abortion as a risk factor for preterm birth in European countries: results of the EUROPOP survey", *Human Reproduction*, 2004, 19, 3, pp. 734-740, here pp. 738 and 739.

the potential health hazards of repeat induced abortions and that health care professionals should be informed about the potential risks of repeat induced abortions on infant outcomes in subsequent pregnancy".[510]

The outcomes presented by Bhattacharya et al. and Klemetti et al. are in line with earlier studies, as has been shown by Thorp et al. and in other research.[511] Their review shows that out of 24 studies that explored associations between abortion and subsequent preterm birth, 12 studies found an association with increased risk ratios which were consistently between 1.3 and 2.0. Moreover, 7 of the 12 studies identified a 'dose-response effect' with risk estimates rising as a woman had more induced abortions.

Induced abortion has not only been associated with subsequent preterm birth, but also with intrapartum infection and with subsequent placenta praevia. Kathrin Mühlemann et al. found that both women with a spontaneous or an induced abortion as their only previous pregnancy have a fourfold increased risk of intrapartum fever as compared to women with one prior live birth (odds ratio 4.3 (95% CI, 3.5-5.4)).[512] Intrapartum infection is associated with increased neonatal morbidity and death. Three studies reviewed by Thorp et al. found an association between induced abortion and subsequent placenta praevia, when the placenta positions itself in the lower part of the uterus and covers part or all of the cervix. If this

---

510 Klemetti, R. et al., op. cit., p. 3315.
511 Thorp, J.M. et al., op. cit., pp. 67-79. Thorp et al. looked at articles published in English between 1966 and 2002, using the MEDLINE database. Since then, these results have been confirmed by Ancel, P.-Y. et al., op. cit., pp. 734-740 and by P.S. Shah and J. Zao on behalf of Knowledge Synthesis Group of Determinants of preterm/LBW births, "Induced termination of pregnancy and low birthweight and preterm birth: a systematic review and meta-analyses", *British Journal of Obstetrics and Gynaecology*, 2009, 116, pp. 1425-1442; see also Laurence Henriet and Monique Kaminski, "Impact of induced abortions on subsequent pregnancy outcome: the 1995 French national perinatal survey", *British Journal of Obstetrics and Gynaecology*, 2001, 108, pp. 1036-1042 and Caroline Moreau, Monique Kaminski, Pierre-Yves Ancel, Jean Bouyer, Benoit Escande and Gérard Thiriez, Pierre Boulot, Jeanne Fresson, Catherine Arnaud, Damien Subtil, Loic Marpeau, Jean-Christophe Rozé, Françoise Maillard and Béatrice Larroque, "Previous induced abortions and the risk of very preterm delivery: results of the EPIPAGE study", *British Journal of Obstetrics and Gynaecology*, 2005, 112, pp. 430-437.
512 K. Mühlemann, M. Germain and M. Krohn, "Does an Abortion Increase the Risk of Intrapartum Infection in the Following Pregnancy?", *Epidemiology*, 1996, 7, 2, pp. 194-198.

situation remains so during pregnancy, birth will have to be by caesarean section. In some cases placenta praevia causes severe bleeding in the second half of pregnancy. Careful monitoring is necessary, because of the risk of neonatal death, especially at 37 or more weeks of gestation.[513]

Finally, Thorp et al. noticed that:

- epidemiological studies regarding an independent link between abortion and breast cancer show conflicting evidence and

- several studies pointed to an association between induced abortion and suicide or attempted suicide.[514]

These last two points need further consideration.

3.2.2 The association between abortion and breast cancer

The possible existence of a link between abortion and breast cancer has been the subject of a heated debate in recent decades, especially in the field of epidemiology. One major difficulty in determining a link between abortion and breast cancer is the long time span between most abortions and the possible development of breast cancer. For instance, in the UK between 2009 and 2011, an average of 80% of breast cancer cases were diagnosed in the over 50s, while most abortions and live births occur at ages under 30. Age-specific breast cancer incidence rates rise steeply from around age 30-34.[515]

According to Joel Brind, Angela Lanfranchi and others, induced abortion can be a risk factor for the development of breast cancer, because of the interruption of the hormonal growth process of mammalian breast cells. After an abortion more incompletely developed breast cells, which are vulnerable to the effects of carcinogens, remain in the woman's breasts.[516]

---

513 Cande V. Ananth, John C. Smulian and Anthony M. Vintzileos, "The effect of placenta previa on neonatal mortality: A population-based study in the United States, 1989 through 1997", *American Journal of Obstetrics and Gynecology*, 2003, 188, 5, 1299-1304.

514 Thorp, J.M. et al., op. cit., p. 73.

515 Cf. Cancer Research UK, "Breast Cancer (C50): 2010-2012 Average Number of New Cases Per Year and Age-Specific Incidence Rates per 100,000 Population, Females, UK".

516 Joel Brind, "The abortion – breast cancer connection", *National Catholic Bioethics Quarterly*, 2005 (c), pp. 303-329, esp. pp. 307-308; Angela Lanfranchi, "Normal Breast Physiology: the Reasons Hormonal Contraceptives and Induced Abortion Increase Breast-Cancer Risk", *Issues in Law & Medicine*, 2014, 29, 1, pp. 135-146.

The risk of developing breast cancer does not increase after a first trimester spontaneous abortion, because in those situations the produced levels of pregnancy hormones do not suffice for stimulating breast development.[517]

The problem in proving a causal, independent link between abortion and breast cancer is that many other risk factors and preventative factors are of influence, too. Known risk factors are: age;[518] reproductive history; family history of breast cancer; early age at menarche; age at menopause; use of oral contraceptives; Hormone Replacement Therapy (HRT); breast density; previous breast disease; bodyweight; fat intake; alcohol consumption; night shift work; etc.[519]

Research on preventative factors has found out that:

- Having given birth (parity) protects women against the development of hormonally responsive breast cancer, and the earlier the first full-term birth occurs, the greater the protection.[520]
- Breastfeeding gives additional protection.[521]
- Physical activity reduces the breast cancer risk, especially for post-

---

517 Lanfranchi, A., op. cit., p. 138.
518 For instance, Janet Daling et al. found that "among women who had been pregnant at least once, the risk of breast cancer in those who had experienced an induced abortion was 50% higher than among other women (95% CI 1.2-1.9)... Highest risks were observed when the abortion was done at ages younger than 18 years - particularly if it took place after 8 weeks' gestation - or at 30 years of age or older." Cf. Janet R. Daling, Kathleen E. Malone, Lynda F. Voigt, Emily White and Noel S. Weiss, "Risk of Breast Cancer Among Young Women: Relationship to Induced Abortion", *Journal of the National Cancer Institute*, 1994, 86, pp. 1584-1592, here p. 1584.
519 Cf. Cancer Research UK, "Breast cancer risk factors", on their website, accessed 14 December 2015. On contraceptives and HRT: World Health Organization International Agency for Research on Cancer, Press Release No. 167, 2005; Carlijn van Hoften, Huibert Burger, Petra H.M. Peeters, Diederik E. Grobbee, Paul A.H. van Noord and Hubert G.M. Leufkens, "Long-term oral contraceptive use increases breast cancer risk in women over 55 years of age: the DOM cohort", *International Journal of Cancer*, 2000, 87, pp. 591-594.
520 Kara Britt, Alan Ashworth and Matthew Smalley, "Pregnancy and the risk of breast cancer", *Endocrine-Related Cancer*, 2007, 14, pp. 907-933, here p. 923.
521 See also: Collaborative Group on Hormonal Factors in Breast Cancer, "Breast Cancer and breastfeeding: collaborative reanalysis of individual data from 47 epidemiological studies in 30 countries, including 50,302 women with breast cancer and 96,973 women without the disease", *The Lancet*, 2002, 360, pp. 187-195.

menopausal women.[522]

In 1996 the first meta-analysis of all 28 published reports which include specific data on induced abortion and breast cancer incidence was presented by Joel Brind et al.[523] The overall odds ratio (for any induced abortion exposure; n = 21 studies) was 1.3 (95% Confidence Interval (CI) of 1.2-1.4). This means that women who have had an induced abortion have a 1.3 times higher chance of getting breast cancer, compared to women in a control group who, at the time of the study had never been pregnant. No comparison has been made with women who had chosen to give birth, in order to calculate an independent risk of induced abortion. Brind's meta-analysis did not impose quality criteria on individual studies.

In the years after publication, his research has been criticised because of the possibility of reporting bias, in the sense that women with breast cancer who have had an induced abortion would be more likely to disclose the abortion in a retrospective interview than women in a healthy control group. In reaction to these critics, Brind has argued that despite its common use, there is no evidence for reporting bias.[524] A study by Holly Howe et al. which was based on foetal death records— and therefore did not make use of retrospective interviews—reported a 90 percent increase in breast cancer risk among women who had had an induced abortion (relative risk = 1.9).[525] Above that, the possibility of reporting bias has been investigated by Mei-Zu Tang et al., who conclude that women in a control group are not more reluctant to report a history of induced abortion than are women with breast cancer.[526]

---

[522] Cf. Cancer Research UK, "Breast cancer risk factors", on their website, accessed 14 December 2015.

[523] Joel Brind, Vernon M. Chinchilli, Walter B. Severs and Joan Summu-Long, "Induced abortion as an independent risk factor for breast cancer: a comprehensive review and meta-analysis", *Journal of Epidemiology and Community Health*, 1996, 50, 481-496.

[524] Joel Brind, "Induced Abortion as an Independent Risk Factor for Breast Cancer: A Critical Review of Recent Studies Based on Prospective Data", *Journal of American Physicians and Surgeons*, 2005 (a), 10, 4, pp. 105-110, esp. p. 105.

[525] Holly L. Howe, Ruby T. Senie, Helen Bzduch and Peter Herzfeld, "Early Abortion and Breast Cancer Risk Among Women Under Age 40", in: *International Journal of Epidemiology*, 1989, 18, pp. 300-304.

[526] Mei-Zu C. Tang, Noel S. Weiss, Janet R. Daling and Kathleen E. Malone, "Case-Control Differences in the Reliability of Reporting a History of Induced Abortion", *American Journal of Epidemiology* 151.12 (June 15, 2000): pp. 1139–1143.

Several studies conducted in the U.K. which denied a link between induced abortion and breast cancer have been criticised for underreporting.[527] For example, the study by Ben Goldacre among more than 350,000 women in the U.K. of whom 28,000 had developed breast cancer, relied entirely on medical records of abortion, from the National Health Service hospital records.[528] But in this case, "a simple perusal of statistics on induced abortion in the U.K. reveals that at least 15 percent of those women were abortion-positive, yet the records upon which the Goldacre study relied indicated that only just over 1 percent of the cancer patients—300 of them, to be exact—had an induced abortion on record."[529] Other prospective studies between 2001 and 2004 showed similar deficiencies.

In Scotland, David Brewster et al. performed a case-control study among 2,833 women with breast cancer who had had an induced abortion and 9,888 matched controls.[530] They found an odds ratio of 0.80 (95% CI 0.72-0.89) in women with a previous abortion and therefore concluded that these data do not support the hypothesis that induced abortion represents a substantial risk factor for the future development of breast cancer. But, according to Brind: "the proof of the distortion resulting from this is easily demonstrated by comparing the characteristics of Brewster's study population with the known patterns of the prevalence of abortion in Scotland. In Scotland, abortion is used primarily as a means to delay childbearing, and 58% of abortions are performed on nulliparous women.[531] In extreme contrast, in the Brewster study only 155 women—5.6% of the

---

527 J. Brind, 2005 (c), pp. 316-317 and 326. These studies were also included in a 2004 meta-study by the Collaborative Group on Hormonal Factors in Breast Cancer (V. Beral, D. Bull, R. Doll, R. Peto and G. Reeves), "Breast cancer and abortion: collaborative reanalysis of data from 53 epidemiological studies, including 83,000 women with breast cancer from 16 countries", *The Lancet*, 2004, Mar. 27; 363, pp. 1007-1016.
528 M.J. Goldacre, L.M. Kurina, V. Seagroatt and D. Yeates, "Abortion and Breast Cancer: A Case-Control Record Linkage Study", *Journal of Epidemiology and Community Health* 55.5 (May 2001), pp. 336–337.
529 J. Brind, 2005 (c), pp. 319-320.
530 David H. Brewster, Diane L. Stockton, Richard Dobbie, Diane Bull and Valerie Beral, "Risk of breast cancer after miscarriage or induced abortion: a Scottish record linkage case-control study", *Journal of Epidemiology and Community Health*, 2005, 59, pp. 283-287.
531 Nulliparous: a woman who has never given birth to a viable or live infant. S.K. Henshaw, "Induced abortion: A world review", 1990. In: *Family Planning Perspectives*, 1990, 22, pp. 76-89.

study population—had an abortion while nulliparous. Hence it is clear that the Brewster study's included population is wholly unrepresentative of the Scottish female population..."[532] It has been shown above that having children is a protective factor against breast cancer and therefore nulliparous women are more at risk.

Another big European study by Gillian Reeves et al. among 267,361 women, mostly aged between 35 and 65 and recruited between 1992 and 2000, did not show an independent link between induced abortion and breast cancer.[533] However, a serious difficulty with this study is the lack of any data shown regarding the age distribution of the participating women.[534]

In 2007, Karin Michels et al. found that among a predominantly premenopausal group of more than 100,000 American nurses between 29 and 46 years of age, neither induced nor spontaneous abortion was associated with the incidence of breast cancer.[535] And in 2008, Katherine DeLellis Henderson et al. concluded that among more than 109,000 American women from the California Teachers Study cohort, no statistically significant association between any measure of incomplete pregnancy and breast cancer risk could be found.[536]

However, the results of these latter studies also need to be questioned. Patrick Carroll points out three methodological problems regarding this

---

[532] Joel Brind, "Methodological concerns re: abortion and breast cancer in Scotland", *Journal of Epidemiology, Community and Health*, electronic letter published on 13 June 2005 (b).

[533] G.K. Reeves et al., "Breast cancer risk in relation to abortion: Results from the EPIC-study", *International Journal of Cancer*, 2006, 119, pp. 1741-1745.

[534] Joel Brind, "Breast cancer in relation to abortion: results from the EPIC-study. Letter to the editor.", *International Journal of Cancer*, 2008, 122, pp. 960-961. In her reply to Brind's letter, Gillian Reeves does not address this part of his criticism. Cf. Gillian Reeves, "Reply to: Breast cancer in relation to abortion: Results from the EPIC-study", *International Journal of Cancer*, 2008, 122, p. 962.

[535] Karin B. Michels, Fei Xue, Graham A. Colditz and Walter C. Willet, "Induced and Spontaneous Abortion and Incidence of Breast Cancer among Young Women. A Prospective Cohort Study", *Arch Intern Med*, 2007, 167, pp. 814-820.

[536] Katherine DeLellis Henderson, Jane Sullivan-Halley, Peggy Reynolds, Pamela L. Horn-Ross, Christina A. Clarke, Ellen T. Chang, Susan Neuhausen, Giske Ursin and Leslie Bernstein et al., "Incomplete pregnancy is not associated with breast cancer risk: the California Teacher Study", *Contraception*, 2008, 77, 6, pp. 391-396.

type of epidemiological research.⁵³⁷ Abortion did not become legal in most Western countries until the 1970s, and earlier abortions among older women are not recorded. Consequently, the older women, whose breast cancer incidence is known, have abortions not detectable by a longitudinal study, while the younger women, whose abortion history is known, tend to be too young to have experienced most of the modern increase in breast cancer. For example, the median age for breast cancer diagnosis in the United States is 61. Therefore, as is noted by Patrick Schneider et al. a cohort study needs to include four to five decades of data.⁵³⁸

A second problem is that epidemiological research is often biased because of underreporting by women who have had an induced abortion. Henderson et al. admit that underreporting of some 20% may have taken place in their cohort.⁵³⁹ Thirdly, Carroll remarks that epidemiological research such as the study by Henderson et al. follows from an "inappropriate comparison between women whose first pregnancy ended in abortion and those who were never pregnant, rather than to those who gave birth".⁵⁴⁰

It is a well-known fact that the incidence of breast cancer is higher in developed countries than in developing countries. In 2010, the cumulative probability of breast cancer incidence was 8.6 (95% CI 7.3-9.4) for developed countries and 3.8 (95% CI 3.4-4.1) for developing countries.⁵⁴¹ Still, also in the developing countries the incidence of breast cancer is rising. In recent years, a number of studies from countries like Bangladesh, China, India and Iran have reported a relative risk for women with a history of

---

537 Patrick Carroll, "The Breast Cancer Epidemic: Modeling and Forecasts based on Abortion and Other Risk Factors", Journal of American Physicians and Surgeons, 2007, 12, 3, pp. 72-78.
538 A.P. Schneider, Chr. M. Zainer, Chr. K. Kubat, N.K. Mullen and A.K. Windisch, "The breast cancer epidemic: 10 facts" in: *The Linacre Quarterly* 2014, 81 (3), pp. 244–277, here p. 263
539 Henderson, K.D.L. et al., op. cit., p. 395.
540 Patrick Carroll, "Legally Induced Abortion: The Demographic Profile and Hazards to the Health of Women", *Studies on Ethno-Medicin*, 2011, 5 (1), pp. 1-10.
541 Mohammad H. Forouzanfar, Kyle J. Foreman, Allyne M. Delossantos, Rafael Lozano, Alan D. Lopez, Christopher J.L. Murray and Mohsen Naghavi, "Breast and cervical cancer in 187 countries between 1980 and 2010: a systematic analysis", *The Lancet*, 2011, 378, pp. 1461–84.

induced abortion to develop breast cancer.[542] In particular, in Bangladesh the odds ratio found is very high: 20.62 for women with a history of induced abortion.[543] As explanation for the difference between these results and the above mentioned Western studies, Patrick Schneider notes that the more recent studies from developing countries have in their study design a sufficient time span between the history of abortion and a possible incidence of breast cancer. In the meantime, many of the Asian women participating in these studies have adopted "a Western life style in sexual and reproductive behavior".[544] What is meant here are the prevalence of delayed childbearing, nulliparity and the use of oral contraceptives, which, as has been shown above, are risk factors for the development of breast cancer. It is likely that in developing countries an association between abortion and breast cancer is more easy to detect, since there are less strong confounding factors than in Western countries.

The 2011 Guideline for counselling women considering termination of pregnancy of the Dutch Association of Abortion Specialists (NGvA) is silent on the issue of informing women of a possible association between induced abortion and breast cancer. In the 2011 RCOG guideline regarding the care of women requesting an induced abortion, a recommendation has been made that women should be informed that induced abortion is

---

542 Suraiya Jabeen, Musarrat Haque, Johirul Islam, Mohammad Z. Hossain, Atiya Begum and Abul Kashem, "Breast Cancer and Some Epidemiological Factors: a Hospital Based Study", *Journal of Dhaka Medical College*, 2013, 22 (1), pp. 61-66; Yubei Huang et al. found an odds ratio (OR) of 1.44 (95 % CI 1.29–1.59) for women who had at least one induced abortion (IA), a risk of 1.76 (95 % CI 1.39–2.22) and of 1.89 (95 % CI 1.40–2.55) for women who had at least two IAs and at least three IAs, respectively. Cf. Yubei Huang, Xiaoling Zhang, Weiqin Li, Fengju Song, Hongji Dai, Jing Wang, Ying Gao, Xueou Liu, Chuan Chen, Ye Yan, Yaogang Wang and Kexin Chen, "A meta-analysis of the association between induced abortion and breast cancer risk among Chinese females", in: *Cancer Causes Control*, 2014, 25, pp. 227–236; Ajeet Bhadoria et al. report an OR of 6.26 (95 % CI 4.16-9.41) for women with a history of abortions. Cf. A.S. Bhadoria, U. Kapil, N. Sareen and P. Singh, "Reproductive factors and breast cancer: A case-control study in tertiary care hospital of North India", *Indian Journal of Cancer*, 2013, 50, (4), pp. 316-321; Hajian-Tilaki and Kaveh-Ahangar showed that abortion is associated with an increased breast cancer risk (adjusted OR = 2.93 (95% CI 1.64–5.24). Cf. K.O. Hajian-Tilaki and T. Kaveh-Ahangar, "Reproductive factors associated with breast cancer risk in northern Iran", *Medical Oncology*, June 2011, 28 (2), pp. 441-446.
543 Jabeen, S. et al., op. cit., p. 63.
544 Schneider, A.P. et al., op. cit., p. 263.

not associated with an increase in breast cancer risk.[545] However, given the methodological problems with a lot of epidemiological studies and the recent results of studies in developing countries, this recommendation is likely to be premature.

3.2.3 The association between abortion and subsequent maternal mortality

In the first decade of the new millennium, the maternal mortality rate in England and Wales has been around 6/100,000 women. In comparison, in the Republic of Ireland, where induced abortion has long been illegal, the maternal mortality rate has been 3/100,000.[546] There is evidence that induced abortion is associated with a higher mortality rate in the year following the abortion. In their publication of 2004, Mika Gissler et al. found that the mortality rate for Finnish women within one year after having given birth was remarkably lower (28.2/100,000) than after a spontaneous abortion or ectopic pregnancy (51.9/100,000) or an induced abortion (83.1/100,000). After having differentiated between natural causes and violent causes for pregnancy-associated mortality, they showed that violent death causes (accidents, suicides or homicides) scored much higher after induced abortion (60/100,000) than after pregnancy or birth (9.6/100,000).[547] These results are important for counselling practices after an unintended pregnancy, since women are at a higher risk of being exposed to violence or other possible death causes within one year following termination of their pregnancy.

In a comment on the first results of this study, Gissler et al. admit that higher suicide rates after abortion could have been caused by other factors, such as the higher prevalence of depression among women who chose to terminate their pregnancy.[548] Other possible confounding factors are a

---

545 Royal College of Obstetricians and Gynaecologists, op. cit., p. 42.
546 Byron C. Calhoun, John M. Thorp and Patrick S. Carroll, "Maternal and Neonatal Health and Abortion: 40-Year Trends in Great Britain and Ireland", *Journal of American Physicians and Surgeons*, 2013, 18, (2), pp. 42-46.
547 Mika Gissler, Cynthia Berg, Marie-Hélène Bouvier-Colle and Pierre Buekens, "Pregnancy-associated mortality after birth, spontaneous abortion, or induced abortion in Finland, 1987-2000", *American Journal of Obstetrics and Gynecology*, 2004, 190, pp. 422-427.
548 Mika Gissler, Elina Hemminki and Jouko Lonnqvist, "Suicides after pregnancy in Finland, 1987-94: Register linkage study", *British Medical Journal*, 1996, 313, pp. 1431-1434.

lower social class, less social support or previous life events, such as prior reproductive history or exposure to violence.[549]

In order to control the conclusions of the Finnish research for duration, for socioeconomic circumstances and for the prevalence of a psychiatric history, David Reardon et al. undertook a similar retrospective study among 173,279 low income women who had received funding for either abortion or delivery in 1989 in the California Department of Health Services.[550] They controlled their sample for psychiatric claims women had made up to 1 year before the target pregnancy event. With this adjustment for psychiatric history, women who aborted had a significantly higher risk of death from suicide (relative risk of 3.12 (95% CI 1.25 – 7.78)) as well as for various diseases, such as cerebrovascular disease, mental disease and AIDS, compared to women who delivered and had no abortions. These elevated death rates were observed throughout the 8 years examined.[551]

In 1996, Helen Houston and Lionel Jacobson reported a significant association ($\chi^2 = 18.3$) between a history of taking a deliberate overdose requiring hospital treatment and procured abortion among 1,359 patients of a U.K. general practice.[552] More than two thirds of these overdoses occurred in women who were aged 19 years or less.

However, these studies have methodological shortcomings, such as the lack of basic demographic information known to be associated with mental health, including marital status and race; the lack of information about the motives for terminating the pregnancy and the lack of information about prior mental health history and exposure to violence.[553]

These findings point to the importance for controls of violence exposure in future research on pregnancy outcomes. As regards the counselling of

---

549 American Psychological Association, op. cit., p. 29.
550 David C. Reardon, Philip G. Ney, Fritz J. Scheuren, Jesse R. Cougle, Priscilla K. Coleman and Thomas W. Strahan, "Deaths Associated With Pregnancy Outcome: A Record Linkage Study of Low Income Women", *Southern Medical Journal*, 2002, 95, 8, pp. 834-841.
551 Relative risks for cerebrovascular disease 4.42 (1.06 – 18.48); for mental disease 3.21 (95% CI 1.11 – 9.27) and for AIDS 2.96 (95% CI 1.28 – 6.87). $P < .0001$ for all these outcomes. Reardon, D.C. et al., 2002, op. cit., p. 838.
552 Helen Houston and Lionel Jacobson, "Overdose and termination of pregnancy: an important association?", *British Journal of General Practice*, 1996, 46, pp. 737-738.
553 American Psychological Association, op. cit., pp. 22-29.

women who have an unplanned pregnancy, these results show the importance of bringing up and possibly dealing with relationship problems, because if these problems remain unnamed, the consequences might be severe.

3.2.4 Complications after induced abortion

The combination of chlamydia and induced abortion carries an additional risk of complications such as reduced fertility or infertility. Infection by *chlamydia trachomatis* is the most common bacterial sexually transmitted disease. In the Netherlands, the estimated prevalence of chlamydia has raised from 158/100,000 men and women in 2002 to 273/100,000 men and women in 2012.[554] In comparison, in 2009 the prevalence of chlamydia in the U.K. was 348.7/100,000 population, compared with 326.1 in 2008.[555]

Research shows that the risk of the infection spreading upwards along the reproductive tract is higher for women who have had an induced abortion.[556] Untreated chlamydia infections might lead to pelvic inflammatory disease (PID) which can then result in severe complications such as ectopic pregnancy, reduced fertility or infertility.[557]

3.3 Pregnancy or abortion? Psychological and relational factors

In order to contribute to the knowledge regarding the prevention of procured abortion, it is important to have an understanding of the reasons why women and their partners in some situations choose in favour of an abortion. In this part, the phenomenon of the increase of the number of abortions is seen in the light of the psychology of the agents, women and men who are confronted with an unintended pregnancy. The main reasons given by British and Dutch women (and sometimes by their partners) for deciding to abort, as well as the doubts they express, will be discussed. (3.3.1) In order to get more understanding of this process, some of the

---

554 F. van Aar, F.D.H. Koedijk, I.V.F. van den Broek, E.L.M. Op de Coul, L.C. Soetens, P.J. Woestenberg, J.C.M. Heijne, A.I. van Sighem, M.M.J. Nielen and B.H.B. van Benthem, *Sexually transmitted infections, including HIV, in the Netherlands in 2013*. National Institute for Public Health and the Environment, Bilthoven, 2014, p. 60.
555 Family Planning Association, "Factsheet Sexually Transmitted Infections", London, 2010, p. 1.
556 Makdoembaks, N., op. cit., p. 226.
557 Health Council of the Netherlands, *Screening for Chlamydia*. Publication no. 2004/07, The Hague, 2004, pp. 17 and 28-30.

results of the Dutch evaluation of the abortion legislation and praxis will be critically reviewed. After that, the focus will be on the relational factors influencing the decision making process among pregnant women and their partners (3.3.2).

In the literature, confirmation can be found for the fact that ambivalent thoughts and feelings are rather common for women and their partners when they are confronted with an unintended pregnancy. A distinction will be made between research on the development of the maternal-foetal attachment; research on the woman's memories of her own childhood, including possible experiences of sexual abuse and research on the woman's relationship with her husband or partner. Sometimes the ambivalence among pregnant women is the result of domestic violence. If the knowledge increases about why ambivalence exists among pregnant women and their partners, counsellors would be able to see more clearly how the prevention of abortion could be improved. In this regard, also the effects of abortion on the relationship will be investigated (3.3.3).

3.3.1 The reasons women give for requesting an abortion

When a woman is pregnant, all kinds of changes take place in her life. In their study of psychosocial adaptation to pregnancy, Regina Lederman and Karen Weis even speak of a paradigm shift, paradigm being understood here as a constellation of current self-image, beliefs, values, priorities, behaviour patterns, relationship with others, and set of problem-solving skills.[558] As a first step in the developmental process towards motherhood, they distinguish the acceptance of pregnancy. If this acceptance has taken place, the pregnant woman can gradually formulate a maternal role and develop a relationship with the coming child. Her relationship with her husband or partner has a strong impact on this process.

Especially when the pregnancy is not planned, all kinds of ambivalent thoughts and feelings might arise. A pregnant woman might initially feel that she and her partner are not able to raise a child together, while she would love to care for her child. Her partner might have doubts if he is ready to become a father, but he might also realise that the unborn child

---

558 Regina Lederman and Karen Weis, *Psychosocial Adaptation to Pregnancy. Seven Dimensions of Maternal Role Development*. Third edition, New York, 2009, pp. 2-29.

does not wait for him to be ready. Other pregnant women might expect difficulties because of their physical or mental condition. Again other couples might think that their family is already complete, or that they are not able to deal with a(nother) child financially. Expecting a child might drastically change study or career perspectives. In some cases the pregnancy could be the result of forced sexual intercourse. Or finally, the possibility exists that the future parents discover later during the pregnancy that there is a high chance that the child will be handicapped, which casts doubts on their ability or willingness to raise this child.

In all these situations, the woman might even consider an abortion. She might want to discuss this with her partner, and maybe with her own parents, a close friend, her G.P. or a counsellor. She then might decide to go to an abortion clinic or a hospital in order to have an abortion. She may be asked in retrospect what the reason or reasons were which led her to take this decision. Extensive research has been done in the Netherlands between 2003 and 2005 in the context of the evaluation of the abortion practice after the 1981 legalization.

3.3.1.1 The results of the evaluation of the Dutch abortion practice reviewed

The evaluation of the Dutch abortion practice has included research among women who have had an abortion, among their medical assistants, doctors and managers of abortion clinics, as well as representatives of professional associations and lobby organizations. Before the evaluation took place, the research program had been approved by the Minister of Health in 2003.[559]

An important aspect of the evaluation study by Mechteld Visser et al. is a diversified questionnaire, for women who considered an abortion in a clinic or hospital. Four clinics and five hospitals were selected, taking into account as far as possible representation across the regions. Women were asked at their first visit to the clinic or hospital to take home the questionnaire and to complete it within two weeks after their decision to abort or to bring their pregnancy to term. 317 women completed the form, which is a response of 52%. 255 women had their abortion in a clinic; 57 in a hospital. Only 1 woman who filled in the questionnaire decided not to have an abortion

---

559 Visser, M.R.M. et al., op. cit., p. 17.

after a consultation in a clinic; 3 of the participating women decided to bring their pregnancy to term after a consultation in a hospital.[560]

As regards the representation of the total population of women, three limitations need to be mentioned. Nearly two thirds (ca. 65%) of the participating women were of Dutch origin, which is a clear overrepresentation of the total population (with 42% of Dutch origin). Secondly, the socio-economic status of the participating women has not been taken into account. It could be the case for example that women within the same age group with a lower socio-economic status than the national average may answer the questionnaire differently. In this case, financial reasons could be mentioned more often, which would overemphasise the relevance of such reasons. For these women who came to the abortion clinic, financial problems could indeed be a reality, but maybe they had these problems already long before they visited the clinic. Mentioning it here could maybe hide other motives for the abortion. And thirdly, women with a clear psychopathology were not included in the research population. Visser et al. do not mention how many women were thus excluded from participation. But it is more than likely that by doing so, the average results are more positive than the real experiences of all women who visit an abortion clinic or hospital, including those with a psychopathology.

In the questionnaire the women were asked what their motives were for wanting an abortion. The women could give more than one reason, as many women did. The results are mentioned in figure 9:

---

560 Ibid., pp. 71-77 and 86-87.

Reasons	Clinic (%) Mentioned	Most important	Hospital (%) Mentioned	Most important
Financial reasons	46,7	11,6	50,0	12,5
No desire for children	31,8	7,1	23,2	12,5
No energy	26,7	10,1	23,2	7,5
House too small	26,3	1,0	35,7	5,0
Too young	25,1	7,6	32,1	7,5
Family complete	23,9	11,6	21,4	7,5
Education	23,1	5,6	26,8	5,0
Risk of health problem for the baby	16,5	5,6	16,1	< 5
Relationship too short	16,5	< 5	23,2	10,0
Broken relationship	16,1	5,1	16,1	< 5
Partner does not want pregnancy	15,3	< 5	23,2	5,0
Does not fit in with work	14,5	< 5	12,5	< 5
Not yet married	12,9	< 5	8,9	< 5
Own health at risk	11,4	< 5	10,7	7,5
No partner	10,6	< 5	10,7	< 5
Parents disagree	5,5	< 5	10,7	< 5
Relationship problems	9,8	< 5	14,3	7,5
Psychological problems	7,1	< 5	10,7	< 5
Pregnancy after unwanted sexual contact	2,4	5	< 5,4	< 5
Partner (probably) not the father	3,1	< 5	1,8	< 5
Refugee status	1,6	< 5	3,6	< 5
Family does not agree	2,7	< 5	1,8	< 5
Too old	9,0	< 5	3,6	< 5
Diverse	< 10	9,6	< 10	12,5

Clinics: N=255; n missing=0 (0%); Most important reason N=246.
Hospital: N=57; n missing=1 (2%); Most important reason hospital N=40.

Figure 9: Reasons Dutch women have for requesting an abortion

Source: M.R.M. Visser et al., 2005, op. cit., p. 83; percentages < 10 have been specified by Mechteld Visser after personal communication.

At first sight, a financial motive to have the abortion is the reason mentioned most often and is considered as the most important reason. Of course the costs of bringing up a child may weigh heavily on young couples. However, there are reasons to doubt this figure. At the time of their research, Visser et al. showed that in the majority of consultations in clinics and hospitals, other options than abortion were not even mentioned.[561] The possibility of carrying the pregnancy to term is discussed in 43% of consultations, adoption in 16% and professional support in only 10% of consultations. Visser et al. also found out that 80% of the participating women had not thought about support from professionals, family or friends when they decided to have the child aborted.[562] This percentage is at odds with the observation of Visser et al. that financial reasons were most important for the participating women. If this were indeed the case, one would expect that the percentage of women asking for professional support would be much higher.

If we look more closely to the different categories used by Visser et al. in figure 9, we see that relationship conflicts are split up into several subcategories: "Relationship too short", "Broken relationship", "Partner does not want pregnancy", "Not yet married", "No partner", "Relationship problems" and "Partner (probably) not the father". Together all these relationship conflicts and problems are mentioned more often than financial reasons. So, prudence is required, not to conclude too quickly that material reasons would be dominant for women when they decide for an abortion.

Often, more deeply lying reasons play a role, which come to the surface in personal interviews. In their research programme, Visser et al. made use of written questionnaires and did not include personal interviews. It is therefore worthwhile to compare the results of figure 9 with qualitative research, in particular by Ortrun Jürgensen, who took interviews in the neighbouring country of Germany among 49 women, six to twelve months after their abortion.[563] She found that, although doctors would often give a medical or social indication for an abortion, according to the interviewed women in almost two thirds of all cases the true reason for the abortion

---

561 Visser, M.R.M. et al., op. cit., p. 85; cf. part 1.5.2.
562 Ibid.
563 O. Jürgensen, in: Petersen, P., 1986, op. cit., p. 285.

was a relationship conflict. According to Jürgensen herself, the percentage of relationship conflicts was even higher, regarding 92% of all interviewed women, "most clearly expressed by the single and divorced women, deeply hidden by married women in 'frozen conjugal relationships'".[564]

A reason mentioned relatively often is the woman's lack of desire for children. The fact that many women mention this reason, is of course not surprising since they are visiting an abortion clinic or a hospital, in order to request an abortion. Other women consider themselves too young to become a mother or feel they have no energy to raise the child. Visser et al. did not further elaborate why the women mentioned these particular reasons. Other, comparable research on reasons women give for abortion has been reviewed by Maggie Kirkman et al.[565] They did not find a comparable British and only one Dutch study in the period between 1996 and 2007.[566] However, one similar study has been conducted in 2000 in Sweden, where 591 women were asked about their reasons to terminate their pregnancy.[567] According to Kirkman et al., reasons could be categorised into "Woman-Focused Reasons", "Other-Focused Reasons" and "Material Reasons".[568] These categories are not mutually exclusive and some categories can be classified into more than one subcategory. Among the reasons mentioned by the Swedish women, "Woman-Focused Reasons" and "Other-Focused

---

564 Ibid., pp. 285-286.
565 Maggie Kirkman, Heather Rowe, Annarella Hardiman, Shelley Mallet and Doreen Rosenthal, "Reasons women give for abortion: a review of the literature", *Archives of Women's Mental Health*, 2009, 12, pp. 365-378.
566 The Dutch study is by Marijke Korenromp et al. on the decision making process after a prenatal diagnosis of Down syndrome. Cf. part 5.3. Another review by Akinrinola Bankole et al. treated 32 studies conducted between 1967 and 1997 on reasons women give for abortion. But their review mainly focused on developing countries worldwide. Cf. Akinrinola Bankole, Susheela Singh and Taylor Haas, "Reasons why women have induced abortions: evidence from 27 countries", *International Family Planning Perspectives*, 1998, 24, pp. 117-127.
567 Margareta Larsson, Gunilla Aneblom, Viveka Odlind and Tanja Tydén, "Reasons for pregnancy termination, contraceptive habits and contraceptive failure among Swedish women requesting an early pregnancy termination", *Acta Obstetricia et Gynecologica Scandinavica*, 2002, 81, pp. 64-71.
568 Kirkman, M. et al., op. cit., p. 367.

Reasons" were mentioned much more often than "Material Reasons".[569] Similarly to the findings of Visser et al. and Petersen, these outcomes show that within the complexity of reasons women give for abortion, personal reasons and relationship problems are of more weight than material reasons.

3.3.1.2 Doubting the decision to abort

A significant percentage of Dutch women, varying from 24-37% has doubts before and during the consultation in an abortion clinic or hospital. 12-14% has severe doubts. However, a majority does not show these doubts to the physician or nurse.[570] The women who received the questionnaire at their first consultation in the clinic or hospital, were also asked to answer within two weeks after the abortion (or within two weeks after the decision not to abort), to what extent they could agree with the intervention. The degree of consent after the intervention shows a similarity with the doubts among women before and during the consultation. About three quarters of the women do not express doubts at any moment, while one quarter has doubts to some degree.[571] This figure indicates that the consultation itself neither changes the women's opinion significantly, nor takes away existing uncertainties about the desirability of the abortion. It has to be said that the degree of consent was only measured shortly after the intervention. Visser et al. do not give information on long term psychological effects of abortion.[572]

Results of comparable international research show higher percentages

---

569 In the category "Woman-focused reasons", most often mentioned reasons are: "Want to study first" (129 times), "Too young" (117 times) and "Want to work first" (100 times). "Women-focused reasons" are mentioned 649 times. Most often mentioned "Other-focused reasons" are: "Too early in the relationship" (107 times) and "Uncertain about relationship to partner" (99 times). "Other-focused reasons" are mentioned 528 times. Most often mentioned "Material reasons": "Poor economy" (166 times) and "Unsuitable housing" (51 times). "Material reasons" are only mentioned 217 times. I counted the reason "Family completed" (116 times) half of these in the category "Woman-focused reasons" and half in the category "Other-focused reasons"; the reason "Single" (69 times) I counted among "Woman-focused reasons." Cf. Larsson, M. et al., op. cit., p. 67.
570 Visser, M.R.M. et al., op. cit., pp. 84-85.
571 Ibid., p. 88.
572 The long term negative psychological effects have been discussed in part 3.1.3.

than those found in the Dutch evaluation. A Danish study by Charlotte Husfeldt et al. revealed that 44% of the women surveyed had doubts about their decision when the pregnancy was confirmed and 30% continued to express doubts when the abortion date arrived.[573] In qualitative studies, the results might even be more concerning. Anneli Kero, Ulf Högberg and Ann Lalos showed that of 221 interviewed Swedish women seeking an abortion, 46% said that their thoughts regarding termination evoked a conflict of conscience.[574]

Visser et al. found that the abortion itself slightly increases the degree of consent among women. But this phenomenon could also be caused by a reduction of cognitive dissonance, as has been described by Leon Festinger and others. According to this influential psychological theory, if a person holds two or more inconsistent cognitions, this arouses the state of cognitive dissonance, which is experienced as uncomfortable psychological tension. This will motivate the person to try to reduce the dissonance and achieve consonance.[575]

Applied to the issue of abortion, if a person believes that abortion is wrong in all or in certain cases, and then becomes directly involved in an abortion, as a mother or as a partner, this may cause cognitive dissonance. In order to strive towards consistency, a person may then start to rationalise the abortion for herself or himself, by thinking that: "the child did not have a good future anyway", "I was not ready to become a mother/father", "our relationship was heading towards an end anyway", etc.

When asked, many women will tell that undergoing an abortion is a drastic experience. But since the often complex decision making process has led to the result that they are no longer pregnant, often a form of relief will be the first, short term reaction. At the same time, earlier doubts are suppressed. In this way the cognitive dissonance has been reduced.

Complicating the appropriateness of the consultation is the fact that a majority of the women who had doubts about the abortion did not mention

---

573 Charlotte Husfeldt, Susanne Kierstein Hansen, Ann Lyngberg, Merete Nøddebo and Birgit Petersson, "Ambivalence among women applying for abortion", in: *Acta Obstetricia et Gynecologica Scandinavica*, 1995, Nov., 74, 10, pp. 813-817.
574 Kero, A., Högberg U. and Lalos, A., op. cit., p. 2567.
575 Leon Festinger, *A theory of cognitive dissonance*. Evanston, Il., 1957, pp. 2-3; Joel Cooper, *Cognitive Dissonance. Fifty Years of a Classic Theory*. London, 2007, pp. 6-7.

these doubts to the consultant. This is even more the case among women who do not have a Dutch origin.[576] It could mean that the real percentage of felt, unexpressed doubts is higher than Visser et al. suggest.

A very relevant question in this regard is why women who have doubts still choose an abortion. It is not unthinkable that social pressure from the woman's partner or family plays a role. Abortion after social pressure is illegal both in the U.K. and in the Netherlands. But if a woman remains silent about having been pressured, it can easily remain unnoticed during the intake consultation in the clinic. And tragically, when it remains unnoticed, no after care can be provided.

Still, according to Dutch managers of abortion clinics who have been interviewed for the evaluation, it is considered to be general policy that there is no intervention in the case of expressed doubts. When the counsellor observes uncertainty on the part of the woman, he or she will postpone the decision and possibly refer to a psychologist, a social worker or a doctor. Also in these cases alternatives are discussed. However, and this is typical for the decision-making process: in all abortion clinics it is stated that ultimately the woman decides if there is an emergency situation or not.[577]

3.3.2 Pregnancy or abortion: relational factors

In the previous part it has been shown that a quarter of the Dutch women who chose to have an abortion, have smaller or greater doubts with this decision. In the Netherlands alone this means 8.000 women on a yearly basis.[578] Now, the focus will be on relational factors which might play a role after a woman discovers she is pregnant, especially if this pregnancy is not planned.

3.3.2.1 Maternal-foetal attachment

It is common for women to experience some initial ambivalent thoughts and feelings when they discover that they are pregnant, even when their pregnancy is planned. Ambivalence is found to be expressed in two main

---

576 Visser, M.R.M. et al., op. cit., p. 84.
577 Ibid., p. 121.
578 If the same percentage could be applied to the U.K., this would mean that each year some 50.000 women doubt their decision to abort. However, scientific evidence is missing for this estimation.

areas: financial worries and anticipated changes in lifestyle, which includes possible motherhood-career conflicts. Concerns about an abnormal baby and physical discomfort are also mentioned, but less often, as reasons for an ambivalent attitude towards pregnancy.[579]

Empirical studies show that maternal attachment to the foetus usually increases during pregnancy, especially after ultrasound exposure and when the woman begins to experience foetal movement, which is usually after 16 weeks of pregnancy.[580] Psychologically this growing attachment during pregnancy can be based on an increasingly elaborate and personified internalised representation of the foetus. In a similar way, if abortion is considered, a positive resolution of the mechanism of cognitive dissonance could be reached by nourishing early maternal attachment.

Attachment is also manifested in behaviours that demonstrate care and commitment to the foetus. During the first and second trimester of the gestational period, these behaviours include nurturance (eating well, abstaining from cigarettes and alcohol), talking with the partner about the child and their future, reading about child development, naming the child, etc. On the other hand, negative cognitions and feelings regarding the foetus may be reflected in denial or suppression of its existence, for instance by paying no attention to antenatal health or preparation.[581]

3.3.2.2 Ambivalence because of memories of the woman's own childhood

There is support for the correlation between the woman's childhood memories of her own upbringing and the quality of maternal-foetal attachment. For instance, in a study of 171 Swedish women Anver Siddiqui et al. discovered that those women who recalled more emotional warmth from their mothers during childhood, demonstrated a higher maternal-

---

579 Lederman, R. and Weis, K., op. cit., pp. 50-54.
580 B. Sedgmen, C. McMahon, D. Cairns, R.J. Benzie and R.L. Woodfield, "The impact of two-dimensional versus three-dimensional ultrasound exposure on maternal–fetal attachment and maternal health behavior in pregnancy", *Ultrasound Obstetrics and Gynecology*, 2006, 27, pp. 245-251.
581 A.E. Reading, D.N. Cox, C.M. Sledmere and S. Campbell, "Psychological Changes Over the Course of Pregnancy: A Study of Attitudes Toward the Fetus/Neonate" *Health Psychology*, 1984, 3, p. 211; R. Hart, and C.A. McMahon, "Mood state and psychological adjustment to pregnancy", *Archives of Women's Mental Health*, 2006, 9, p. 330.

foetal attachment.[582] It has to be noted that this study focused on women in their third trimester of pregnancy. In this period, abortion is normally no longer a legal option. But it is no more than logical that these women must have had the same positive or negative memories of their own childhood during the first and second trimester.

If a pregnant woman has a history of being abused in her own childhood, this might affect the maternal-foetal attachment during her pregnancy. Ned Rodriguez et al. reviewed 33 empirical studies in order to investigate the relationship between childhood sexual abuse and PTSD.[583] They did not find studies which investigated the relationship between the more acute PTSD in sexually abused children and the chronic or delayed PTSD in adult survivors. However, in two studies among adolescents who were sexually abused in their childhood, a considerably higher PTSD prevalence or severe symptoms of PTSD have been reported, as well as attachment problems.[584]

It is further known that traumatic experiences can remain hidden for years in people's memory and then can come back when a traumatised person goes through a period of change.[585] If for instance a woman starts a new

---

[582] A. Siddiqui, B. Hägglöf and M. Eisemann, "Own memories of upbringing as a determinant of prenatal attachment in expectant women", *Journal of Reproductive and Infant Psychology*, 2000, 18, pp. 67-74.

[583] Ned Rodriguez, Hendrika van de Kemp and David W. Foy, "Posttraumatic Stress Disorder in Survivors of Childhood Sexual and Physical Abuse: A Critical Review of the Empirical Research", *Journal of Child Sexual Abuse*, 1998, 7, 2, pp. 17-45.

[584] In a sample of severely mentally ill youth, Jon McClellan et al. reported a 7% PTSD prevalence rate in the nonsexually abused group (n=226), 19% in the group with "isolated" incidents of child sexual abuse (CSA), 26% in the group with "intermittent" incidents of CSA (n=61) and 41% in the group with chronic CSA experiences (n=150). Cf. Jon McClellan, Julie Adams, Donna Douglas, Chris McCurry and Mick Storck, "Clinical characteristics related to severity of sexual abuse: A study of seriously mentally ill youth", *Child Abuse and Neglect*, 1995, 19, pp. 1245-1254.

Haviland et al. showed that among 37 physically and sexually abused adolescents in residential treatment, 22 (59.5%) had high scores for PTSD. These scores were positively correlated with object relations scores such as insecure attachment and egocentricity. Cf. M.G. Haviland, J.L. Sonne and L.R. Woods, "Beyond posttraumatic stress disorder: Object relations and reality testing disturbances in physically and sexually abused adolescents", *Journal of American Academy of Child and Adolescent Psychiatry*, 1995, 34, pp. 1054-1059.

[585] Cf. Mariéle Wulf, "Psychotrauma en het concept van het leven", *Minor geloof en cultuur, collegereeks 2011-2012, Christelijke ethiek in een postchristelijke cultuur*, 8, pp. 1-2. Unpublished manuscript.

relationship, she might feel secure enough to speak about her experiences of the past. As such, this is a positive development, although it can bring back pain from the past. If she is heard and supported, healing could take place. In some situations, it could be important that attention is given to these issues during a consultation with the G.P. or other professionals.

Other studies have shown a relationship between child sexual abuse and problems with psychosexual functioning during adulthood.[586] Women who are sexually abused during childhood, report higher levels of guilt feelings related to sexual experiences.[587] On the other hand, abused women reported more sexual behaviour which Robyn Walser and Jeffrey Kern have defined as "non-acceptable sexual behaviour" according to societal norms, using ratings for the average number of sexual partners per year, sexual intercourse experiences on first dates, the age of initial intercourse, etc.[588]

Guilt feelings after sexual abuse could arise when a woman begins to think that maybe she could have prevented the abuse. By blaming herself, the woman loses contact with her own reality of being a victim of abuse. In order to diminish her sense of guilt, she transforms herself psychologically from the victim into the perpetrator, so as to regain some sense of control. Similarly, traumatised persons often develop compulsive behavioural patterns.[589] Hypersexual behaviour, exposing or victimizing sexual behaviour are significantly associated with an onset of sexual abuse prior to seven years of age.[590]

Compulsive behavioural patterns such as sexual re-victimization or the transposition from victim to perpetrator can become critical when a woman becomes pregnant and has doubts about bringing her pregnancy to term.

---

[586] Scott D. Easton, Carol Coohey, Patrick O'leary, Ying Zhang and Lei Hua, "The Effect of Childhood Sexual Abuse on Psychosexual Functioning During Adulthood", *Journal of Family Violence*, 2011, 26, pp. 41-50.

[587] Robyn D. Walser and Jeffrey M. Kern, "Relationships Among Childhood Sexual Abuse, Sex Guilt, and Sexual Behavior in Adult Clinical Samples", *The Journal of Sex Research*, 1996, 33, 4, pp. 321-326.

[588] Ibid., pp. 323-324.

[589] Cf. Wulf, M., 2011, op. cit., p. 5. Unpublished manuscript.

[590] Jon McClellan, Chris McCurry, Marylin Ronnei, Julie Adams, Andrea Eisner and Mick Storck, "Age of Onset of Sexual Abuse: Relationship to Sexually Inappropriate Behaviors", *Journal of the American Academy of Child and Adolescent Psychiatry*, 1996, 34, 10, pp. 1375-1383.

An abortion could then seem to be a short term solution, but of course does not resolve the underlying psychological problems.

3.3.2.3 Ambivalence in the relationship with the partner

Mechteld Visser et al., in their evaluation of the Dutch abortion law, show that some 10% of the women who were interviewed did not tell anyone about their pregnancies.[591] Furthermore the investigators asked women who they considered the most important person with whom they should talk about the decision of whether or not to abort. In 70% of the women this was the partner, followed by a family member and/or a friend. Thus, it does sometimes happen that the partner is not involved at all in the decision to abort. It has to be noted that the husband or partner is not necessarily the begetter of the child.

Obviously these figures do not reveal the dilemmas and often real dramas that lie behind a decision to abort. In some cases, for instance, when the woman has had an affair, she might not want to speak about it, in order to save her relationship. It would be preferable that a woman avoids secrecy towards her husband about her pregnancy. Of course, speaking out makes her vulnerable, but it creates also the possibility for forgiveness and reconciliation. In some cases, the male begetter of the foetus might be involved in this process as well in taking some form of responsibility. But in other cases, this might not be humanly possible. Finally, there are also tragic cases in which adultery leads to alienation between the two partners or even separation. Even in such a tragic situation, it would be completely unjust to sacrifice the foetus.

The evaluation report hardly goes into this quite complicated matter. The authors do mention that in about half of the consultations in clinics or hospitals the opinion of people within the close circle is not discussed.[592] It is therefore unclear how there can be a decision-making process with all due care in these cases.

Among many couples, the news of a pregnancy will be greeted with joy and excitement. The new life that is on its way will bring along many questions about parenthood, the division of responsibilities, the organisation

---

591 Visser, M.R.M. et al., op. cit., p. 86.
592 Ibid., p. 86.

of the daily care, about expectancies with regard to the education the child will receive, etc. Unfortunately this sometimes creates tensions in the relationship between the father and mother with which they are unable to cope. In this study I have to pay attention mainly to the negative reactions which follow an unintended pregnancy, because these reactions could lead to the decision to abort.

Investigating possible negative reactions of men who hear that their partner is pregnant, several diverging reactions can become dominant. Peter Petersen distinguishes seven destructive forms of repression which he deduces from interviews with men who were facing an unintended pregnancy or who had already decided for an abortion.[593] In order to avoid repetition, his seven categories have been re-arranged them into five attitudes:[594]

1) Sometimes the message that his partner is pregnant, causes a man to panic. Suddenly his future plans seem to fall to pieces. The news might raise doubts about the strength of the relationship with his partner, or raise questions about his own identity in this relationship. He might want to walk away from the situation, leaving the mother to decide for herself. Other men immediately demand an abortion, either to save the relationship or in a deliberate attempt to break up. Psychosomatic complaints like headache, stomach pains or other stress symptoms might play a role in this attitude.

2) Other men might deny that the foetus is a human being, defining it as a lump of cells, as "something". With today's embryological knowledge, such a justification is not sustainable.[595] But if a man is not confronted with these findings, indifference might determine his attitude, leaving the decision and possible feelings of guilt to the mother.

3) Some men react by a mainly rational calculation of controllable factors such as time, money, energy, etc. and have difficulties in making an intuitive connection with the unborn human being which they have brought into existence.

4) Men can also display false modesty, by ignoring their responsibility:

---

593 Petersen, P., 1986, op. cit., pp. 274-275.
594 I have combined Petersen's categories of "narziβtische Panik" and "psychosomatische Beschwerden" into attitude 1 and the categories of "rationales Kalkül" and "definierter Termin" into attitude 3. Cf. ibid., pp. 274-275.
595 Cf. part 4.1.

"this is not my problem, she has to make a decision."

5) A fifth possible reaction is one of feelings of shame and/or guilt, which is reflected in the relationship with the partner, by quarrelling and making reproaches, without taking the interests of the unborn into account. This can then have a destructive outcome if an abortion is chosen.[596]

Of course these types of reactions might occur in combinations, attitudes may vary in the course of time, feelings may be left unsaid. Still, in each one of the negative reactions, an autonomous decision on the part of the woman becomes very hard or even an illusion. Each of the five attitudes also affects the partner. Because, if a man were to change his attitude, by no longer running away from his responsibility; by allowing himself to get attached to the unborn child instead of denying or ignoring its existence; by admitting and communicating his emotions and expectations; by expressing his opinion rather than evading from it; or by getting over shame and guilt, letting the unborn child in as part of the relationship; then all this would of course influence the attitude of the woman towards her child and her partner.

Usually, a woman will be very sensitive in seeing whether the man reacts with confidence and commitment when she tells him that she is pregnant. For her, there is the double weight of the physical changes that take place in her body and the questions that come up about raising the child and sharing responsibilities. In their study on partner support and pregnancy desirability, Charlan Kroelinger and Kathryn Oths show that a partner's reactions and feelings about a woman's pregnancy are reflected in women's experiences of wanting the pregnancy.[597] Women who lacked partner support were nearly twice as likely to express feelings of the pregnancy being unwanted than those who did experience their partner's social support. This social support has been expressed in terms of the woman's partner giving her comfort, love, status and/or help in case of emergency. Also a partner's financial support influences women's perception of the desirability of the pregnancy.[598] If a woman doesn't feel her partner's support during her early pregnancy, there is the risk that her considerations will incline towards an

---

596 Petersen, P., 1986, op. cit., pp. 274-275.
597 Charlan D. Kroelinger and Kathryn S. Oths, "Partner Support and Pregnancy Wantedness", *Birth*, 2000, 27, 2, pp. 112-119, esp. p. 115.
598 Ibid., 2000, p. 116.

abortion.

In order to show some examples of different attitudes of men who were involved in a decision to abort, some translated extracts of interviews which Basti Baroncini held with several Dutch men are given:

Willem, now 31 years of age, looks back on when he was 23, still studying and in a relationship with his girlfriend for half a year. "I was rather careless with contraception. I thought it was her responsibility and that I didn't need to worry about it. That was really a stupid mistake. But okay, one afternoon she called me to tell me that she was [...] pregnant. Straight away I thought: shit, this is inconvenient. I am completely unready for a child and I think as a couple we are not ready, either. Apart from that, the timing was very inconvenient. I had a busy study and did not want to be concerned with this in any way. In fact, I wanted to deny the problem."[599]

In this case, Willem's reaction shows an attitude of panic, followed by denial and leaving the final responsibility to his girlfriend, just as he had done earlier as regards contraception. Further on, Baroncini writes that their relationship breaks up, half a year after the abortion. Looking back, Willem tells that his ex-girlfriend had started to reproach him, because she had wanted to keep the baby, but she did not feel he had ever understood her situation. He disagreed, because he thought that they had taken the decision together. Above that, he thought that he had made clear to her that if she had decided to bring the pregnancy to term, he would have borne the consequences. A clear situation of painful miscommunication, followed by the sacrifice of a human life.

Of course, other and very different reactions are also possible. For instance, when the woman has already made up her mind and does not involve the man in her decision, he can experience a strong sense of powerlessness. This is the experience of Johan (33), whose girlfriend had an abortion:

"Glasses have been thrown through the room, yes. I was so angry with her because I felt I was not being heard or seen! Normally I do not react so physically: I would never do anything to her and I was myself most upset by these broken glasses, but it really was an expression of feelings of powerlessness. Besides the anger about the way the decision was taken, there was also anger about the

---

599 Basti Baroncini, *Man en abortus. Over de keuze, de ingreep en de verwerking*. Amsterdam, 2010, p. 46.

decision itself. I would have loved to see things differently. I was angry that I had lost a child. If the choice and the power had been mine, I would have acted very differently."[600]

Baroncini does not tell the other side of the story, so the exact reasons behind Johan's girlfriends choice to have an abortion remain unknown. Still, it seems that the sadness in this situation has two main causes: the decision making process, in which his opinion is ignored and the decision itself. Seven years after the abortion, they broke up. Looking back, Johan feels that the abortion has ever stood between them, although there also has been a certain resignation. "There was of course love between us and above that we found it a challenge to see if we could come out of this difficult situation together having learnt something from it."[601]

It is clear that in both cases the decision making process is crucial. In the first case it would have been reasonable to have encouraged Willem to take a more responsible attitude towards parenthood, rather than being in denial. In Johan's case, it is the other way round. His desire to become a father had been denied and there was no open communication or genuine search for alternatives.

If the ambivalence in one's attitude is recognised and discussed, conversion could take place, on the part of the woman, or the man, or both. Using Bernard Lonergan's expression, an intellectual conversion could have taken place when there is a changed insight into what the child, which is growing in the mother's womb, is really like.[602] This is an important matter to consider especially for the man, since he does not experience the living human being inside himself. On the other hand, in cases like that of Johan and his girlfriend, a growth in authenticity could have taken place when his feelings and judgement as the begetter of the child had been taken seriously.

---

600 Ibid., p. 41.
601 Ibid., p. 232.
602 Lonergan, B., op. cit., p. 238. Lonergan considers intellectual conversion as the elimination of the myth that knowing is like looking, that objectivity is seeing what is there to be seen. This myth does not take into account the actual meaning of what is seen.

3.3.2.4 Pregnancy and domestic violence

About one in four British women between 16 and 59 years of age has experienced domestic violence throughout their lifetime. In a national survey in 1996, young women aged 20 to 24 reported the highest levels of domestic violence: 28% said that they had been assaulted by a partner at some time, and 34% had been threatened or assaulted.[603] Later research among pregnant women in an inner-London hospital confirmed these figures. In this research, 3% of women had experienced domestic violence during the current pregnancy, a percentage which is also found in similar studies.[604]

There is a growing recognition of the importance of handling the problem of domestic violence. The British Government wants to increase the early identification of victims of domestic violence by making domestic violence part of routine inquiry and comprehensive assessment processes in a number of primary health and social care settings.[605] The Crime and Disorder Act (1998) provides a legal power to share information between health care workers and other professionals in the educational, criminal justice and social welfare fields, in order to protect domestic violence victims.[606]

In the Netherlands, the prevalence of domestic violence is measured differently, on the basis of yearly police figures. Here, the estimated number of victims was ca. 197,000 per year, in the period 2006-2007. This number includes threats, as well as physical, psychological, sexual and other kinds of violence. The category of persons between 18 and 30 years of age has the highest estimated number of victims. In more than 60% of all cases the partner or ex-partner are indicated as suspects.[607]

In figure 9, part 3.3.1.1, domestic violence is not mentioned as a possible

---

603 Catriona Mirrlees-Black, *Domestic violence: findings from a new British Crime Survey self-completion questionnaire*. Home Office Research Study 191. London: Home Office, 1999, pp. 18-20.
604 Loraine Bacchus, Gill Mezey and Susan Bewley, "Domestic violence: prevalence in pregnant women and associations with physical and psychological health", *European Journal of Obstetrics & Gynecology and Reproductive Biology*, 2004, 113, pp. 6-11.
605 Home Office, *Domestic Violence. A National Report*. London, 2005, p. 25.
606 Home Office, *Safety and justice: sharing personal information in the context of domestic violence – an overview*. London, 2004, p. 2.
607 H.C.J. van der Veen and S. Bogaerts, *Huiselijk geweld in Nederland. Overkoepelend syntheserapport van het vangst-hervangst-, slachtoffer- en daderonderzoek 2007-2010*, Meppel, 2010, pp. 67-69.

reason for women to choose to have an abortion. The questionnaire included categories as "relationship problems", "own health at risk" and "pregnancy after unwanted sexual contact". However, it is remarkable that domestic violence is not mentioned once in the evaluation report. It is important that G.P.'s or health care professionals during a first consultation in an abortion clinic are attentive to the possibility of domestic violence. In this regard, Canadian researchers Dominique Bourassa and Jocelyn Bérubé plead for routine assessment for intimate partner violence among women who consider an abortion and visit a family planning clinic.[608] If no attention is given to a situation of domestic violence, there is a great risk that in the decision making process abortion is chosen while the real difficulties the woman is faced with are not properly dealt with.

3.3.3 The quality of the relationship after abortion

If a procured abortion has a negative impact on a woman's or a man's mental health, then it can be expected that the quality of their relationship after abortion is also at risk. A prospective Swiss study by Francesco Bianchi-Demicheli et al. pointed out that 31% of women, interviewed six months after their abortion reported at least one sexual dysfunction, correlated with anxiety and symptoms of depression.[609]

Priscilla Coleman et al. investigated associations between abortions and relationship functioning among more than 1,500 American men and women.[610] After adjusting for covariates, they found out that women who had experienced an abortion with their current partner, compared with women without a history of abortion, were 116% more likely to argue about children, 75% more likely to argue about money, 80% more likely to argue about the partner's relatives and 99% more likely to argue about the respondent's relatives. These women and women who had experienced

---

608 Dominique Bourassa and Joselyn Bérubé, "The prevalence of intimate partner violence among women and teenagers seeking abortion compared with those continuing pregnancy", *Journal of Obstetrics and Gynaecology Canada*, 2007, 29, 5, pp. 415-423.
609 Francesco Bianchi-Demicheli, Eliane Perrin, Frank Lüdicke, Patrizia Bianchi, Dominique Chatton and Aldo Campana, "Termination of pregnancy and women's sexuality", *Gynecological and Obstetrical Investigation*, 2002, 53, pp. 48-53.
610 Priscilla K. Coleman, Vincent M. Rue and Catherine T. Coyle, "Induced Abortion and intimate relationship quality in the Chicago Health and Social Life Survey", *Public Health*, 2009, 123, pp. 331-338.

an abortion in a previous relationship also reported elevated sexual risks. Similarly, men whose partners had experienced an abortion in the current relationship were more likely to report arguing and conflicts than men with no partner history of abortion.[611] However, a weakness of this study is the inability to control for pre-abortion relationship problems, as the authors admit themselves.[612]

Reviewing earlier studies on the relation between induced abortion and psychosexuality, Bianchi-Demicheli et al. report of four studies between 1963 and 1999. Three of these four studies show severe methodological limitations, such as the lack of a control group, lack of retrospective data and small sample sizes.[613] Similarly, Zoë Bradshaw and Pauline Slade have looked at the post-1990 literature concerning psychological experiences and sexual relationships prior to and following procured abortion. Again, they make a mention of studies with methodological deficiencies: no control group, unstandardized measurement or an effect measurement of short duration.[614] The presence of a control group is needed in order to get insight into the quality of the women's relationship before the abortion took place, in comparison to a group of women who did not have an abortion. It has to be known if the women of the sample group would not already qualify their relationship as more troubled in comparison to a control group. If this would be the case, then a large decrease in satisfaction after the abortion would be more unlikely, since the relationship was already problematic.

The findings presented in part 3.3 indicate that in the consultations in Dutch abortion clinics and hospitals relationship problems are often underestimated. From literature research it is known that pregnancy often comes along with ambivalent feelings for both women and men. To take these feelings seriously and to consider both partner's views on parenthood is essential for an authentic decision making process, which often requires professional help.

---

611 Ibid., p. 334.
612 Ibid., p. 337.
613 Francesco Bianchi-Demicheli, Regina Kulier, Eliane Perrin and Aldo Campana, "Induced abortion and psychosexuality", *Journal of Psychosomatic Obstetrics and Gynecology*, 2000, 21, pp. 213-217.
614 Zoë Bradshaw and Pauline Slade, "The effects of induced abortion on emotional experiences and relationships: A critical review of the literature", *Clinical Psychology Review*, 2003, 23, pp. 929-958, especially pp. 941-943 and Appendix A.

For women who have strong doubts in bringing their pregnancy to term, the underestimation of relationship problems in counselling sessions could lay serious hindrances for their growth towards motherhood. For men who do not agree with an abortion, a decision making process in which they are ignored might turn out to be a very sorrowful episode in their lives, with long-lasting effects on their feelings of self-worth and sometimes with a definitive impact on their relationship. When there is no open atmosphere to discuss alternatives to abortion with experts in this field, ways to find support for preparing both partners for responsible parenthood, might be blocked.

In other situations, a history of child abuse, domestic violence or other traumatic experiences hinder a normal maternal attachment to her child. In those cases it would be preferable that during a first consultation these issues are properly addressed and therapeutic care is offered, rather than seeking an abortion which is only an escape-route from the problems which need to be faced.

3.4 The abortion legislation in the U.K. and the Netherlands does not guarantee women's autonomy

In the course of the 19th and 20th centuries, the legal discourse in both the U.K. and the Netherlands shows a clear shift in the focus of attention from the protection of the child to the autonomous decision of the woman, whereas the man has been absent in the legal framework ever since.

At the time when abortion became legal, politicians in the U.K. and in the Netherlands stated that their intention was to keep the abortion number low and that doctors had to guarantee that there was no other way to end the emergency situation than by terminating the woman's pregnancy. However, since then there has been little political will to promote alternatives for legal abortion.

A real problem of the Dutch abortion legislation is the intrinsic contradiction of the two principles of the protection of unborn human life and the woman's right to assistance in case of an unintended pregnancy. As soon as this woman's right is filled in with a 'right' to abortion, it becomes impossible to uphold both principles at the same time, because they exclude one another. In the Netherlands, abortions are described as inescapable emergency situations, without giving criteria to what this means and without discussing alternatives in a majority of consultations, despite a legal obligation to do so. The fact that abortions are offered free of charge, makes even more clear that there are no real stimuli to look for alternatives.

The British abortion praxis legitimises almost all situations in which abortion is chosen by referring to the risk of mental health problems for the women involved if they brought their pregnancy to term. In the U.K., a political discussion on ethical aspects of abortion has been explicitly ruled out. By doing so, questions regarding the moral status of the foetus have been ignored. Similarly, in the Netherlands the Government did neither formulate emergency criteria for abortion, or stimulated further research to the prevention of abortion.

Within feminist thought, several authors point at the limitations of the ideal of autonomy and at the desire for inclusiveness of men in making reproductive choices. An autonomy approach based on available opportunities could bring women in a disadvantageous negotiating position compared to men. Applied to the issue of abortion, Kantian philosophy could be helpful if the focus is on an increase of a woman's and a man's capabilities. On the other hand, if counsellors have insufficient attention for the possibilities a woman has to bring her pregnancy to term, her autonomy may also be impeded. The autonomy of the pregnant woman could be directly threatened when the male begetter reacts negatively or with indifference on her pregnancy. In these cases, the legal opportunity of autonomous choice could become a threefold emergency, in which a decision has to be made: at first, a women may feel forced to take a decision in favour of abortion; secondly, the autonomous decision could become a moral dilemma, especially if decisions are required, such as in the case of a prenatal diagnosis of a foetal anomaly; thirdly, a decision is required which, reasonably considered, cannot be demanded from no one because they go against a person's own autonomy and freedom and against the life and flourishing of another human being.[615]

For these reasons, women's autonomy cannot be guaranteed by the current abortion legislation in the U.K. and the Netherlands. Evidence has been presented that women are struggling with mental and physical

---

615 Cf. Wulf, C.M., 2013 (b), op. cit., pp. 334-335.

health problems after abortion, sometimes many years later. Fergusson et al. conclude that experiencing a procured abortion implies an increased risk of mental health problems for women of about 30%. Various international studies point at the risk of preterm births in pregnancies following an abortion. Other research points out an increased risk of complications after procured abortion in the case of an existing chlamydial infection. Finally, several studies conclude that there is a link between procured abortion and the risks of suicide, psychiatric admission or self-harm. The conclusion must be that because of these risks and effects on their mental and physical health, for many British and Dutch women human autonomy is not guaranteed by the current abortion legislation. In many cases, the opportunity of autonomous choice becomes a situation of real emergency and not of freedom. The legislator could increase human autonomy by introducing measures to stimulate preventive counselling and by offering alternatives for abortion for every woman who seeks help. In this way, attention is paid to the real and often hidden problems that women carry with them when they enter an abortion clinic or hospital. Further, strict emergency criteria need to be formulated and maintained. Often, abortion is performed as a kind of symptom management, which does not help women in the long run. Aftercare in which only a medical check takes place and in which information on contraception is provided, is often much too limited as regards the possible long term psychological and psychosocial problems.

In situations where insufficient attention is paid to underlying relationship conflicts, a decision in favour of abortion could not only have negative consequences for the woman and the child, but could also affect the man's self-esteem, in particular when he would have had a positive attitude towards the child. Often, the involvement of the male begetter in the decision making process is crucial. In other, often very tragic situations, more attention should be given to a history of domestic violence, before a decision is made.

Chapter 4

The human embryo, its rights and its dignity

In his essay on the foundation of morality, Paul Ricoeur remarks that the passage from the idea of the preferable to the idea of a norm starts when we begin to consider what is not preferable as something deviant. The essence of a norm, of a prohibition is "not to positively designate what is preferable, but to negatively designate what is deviant as what is not to be done".[616]

In chapter 3, it has been shown that the value of physical and mental health of women could be at risk after an induced abortion. Sometimes, men suffer as well from negative mental health effects after an abortion and also the quality of their relationship could be under threat. So far, not much has been said of the object of every abortion: the human embryo. Within the scientific discourse, one usually speaks of an embryo, after ten weeks gestation the term foetus is also used. This distinction between an embryo and a foetus does not have any legal significance. However, in 1990 another legal distinction was introduced with the enactment of the British Human Fertilisation and Embryology Act. This Act allows the experimentation with embryos up to fourteen days after conception. The Dutch legislation regarding the use of gametes and embryos was enforced in 2002 and has

---

616 Ricoeur, P., 1978, op. cit., p. 184.

a similar approach and constraints.[617] Although a detailed discussion of the implementation of both acts is beyond the scope of this study, this introduction of a threshold of fourteen days has had consequences for the philosophical and theological thinking on the status of the human embryo and the morality of abortion.

In *Oneself as another*, Ricoeur takes up the question of abortion, as part of his study on the self and practical wisdom.[618] He admits that on the basis of biological criteria, the embryo is a biological individual from the moment of conception. But he wonders "whether practical wisdom, without entirely losing this biological criterion from sight, must not take into account the phenomena of thresholds and stages that put into question the simple alternative between person and thing".[619] In other words, his goal is to show both the credibility of the demand for universalization and the contextual character of the application of moral rules. In fact, in this dialectical approach, Ricoeur does not take a definitive position in the debate, leaving room for a "critical solicitude", where moral judgments are the result of the

---

617 It will be shown that both the British and the Dutch legislator has chosen to maintain a gradualist approach, which allows the use of human embryos under certain constraints, such as the permission of a local authoritative body and a time limit of fourteen days after fertilisation. Cf. Wet van 20 juni 2002, houdende regels inzake handelingen met geslachtscellen en embryo's (Embryowet), in: *Staatsblad van het Koninkrijk der Nederlanden*, Den Haag, 2002, nr. 338, art. 2 and art. 24, lid e. Other countries, like Australia, Belgium, India, Japan and Singapore have a similar time limitation as the U.K. and the Netherlands. Cf. House of Commons Science and Technology Committee, *Human Reproductive Technologies and the Law. Fifth Report of Session 2004-2005, Volume I*, London, 2005, p. 22; Ibid., *Volume II, Oral and written evidence*, p. 345.
618 Ricoeur, P., 1992, op. cit., pp. 240-296.
619 Ibid., p. 271. In order to dissociate the biological criterion from what he calls an underlying "substantialist ontology", Ricoeur refers to the pragmatic or gradualist viewpoint, which has been dominant in the British abortion debate. (cf. part 4.3) According to a pragmatic viewpoint the question of knowing how the embryo is to be treated is itself to be free of any ontological criteria. However, an objection must be made against the position that the biologic criterion is necessarily connected with a so-called "substantialist ontology". Already Thomas Aquinas argued that the human soul, the first principle of life, is not a body, but an act of a body. (cf. Th. Aquinas, *Summa Theologica (S.T.)*, I, q. 75, a. 1. It is very well possible to think of the biological nature of human beings without falling into a reductionist viewpoint which a substantialist ontology would imply. After Aquinas, in 1312 the Council of Vienna declared that the human soul is not a separate nature, but forms a unity with the living body. (cf. part 6.2.1.3)

good counsel of wise and competent men and women.[620] His suggestion to take into account the phenomena of thresholds and stages comes close to a gradualist position. Within the juridical interpretation of the gradualist approach, a right of the human embryo to live is not acknowledged from the moment of conception, but only after a certain period of gestation.[621]

In many Western countries the discussion on the status of the human embryo has not led to a full protection of rights for early human embryos. Some bioethicists, such as Julian Savulescu or Baruch Brody, even hold that an embryo cannot be a human being if it does not have a functioning brain, which starts at around six weeks after conception.[622] It seems that their conclusion is based on the empiricist assumption that knowing is like looking.[623] The question "Who can be considered a human being?" cannot be answered only by looking at a developing embryo, but it is also an ontological question, to which a valid answer can only be given based on the experiences, understanding, judgements and beliefs of a certain community. Or, in Bernard Lonergan's words: "The reality known is not just looked at; it is given in experience, organized and extrapolated by understanding, posited by judgment and belief."[624]

First, a brief sketch is given of normal embryonic and foetal development. (4.1) After having seen the normal embryonic development and having contemplated its meaning, the question comes up whether the value of the unborn human life needs to be protected by a certain norm. As Paul Ricoeur has remarked, the introduction of a norm within the ethical debate could cause a scission, "as soon as the preferable is opposed to the desirable, what is worthwhile to what I desire".[625] Applied to the abortion dilemma: it can be argued that giving birth to a child is something worthwhile, but a

---

620 Ricoeur, P., 1992, op. cit., p. 273; cf. Charles E. Reagan, *Paul Ricoeur. His Life and His Work*. Chicago, 1996, p. 94.
621 Cf. part 4.3.1.
622 Julian Savulescu states that "we only begin to exist when our brains start to function", in: Julian Savulescu, "Abortion, embryo destruction and the future of value argument", in: *Journal of Medical Ethics*, 2002, 28, 3, pp. 133-136. Similarly Baruch Brody remarks that: "What is essential for being human is the possession of the potential for human activities that comes with having the structure required for a functioning brain." Cf. Baruch Brody, *Abortion and the Sanctity of Human Life: A Philosophical View*. Cambridge, Ma., 1975, pp. 113-114.
623 Cf. part 2.2.6.
624 Lonergan, B., op. cit., p. 238.
625 Ricoeur, P., 1978, op. cit., p. 184.

pregnant woman may not experience it this way.

This is why national and international legal systems have tried to find a balance between on the one hand the protection of unborn human life and on the other hand the desires of the individual. The analysis of some of the main international documents on the rights of the unborn child and of the relevant European jurisprudence shows that there is indeed no consensus within the juridical and political discourse on the rights of the unborn child. (4.2) Therefore, a reflection is required on the use of the term 'dignity' in relation to the unborn child. The introduction of the term 'dignity' prepares the ground for an extended discussion on the ontological status of the human embryo. (4.3)

4.1 Embryonic and foetal development

During the past decades, the knowledge of embryonic and foetal development has increased enormously. Already in 1978, Franz Böckle stated that there is consensus among ethicists about the fact that from conception onwards we are dealing with life that is unchangeably specifically human.[626] This consensus has undoubtedly contributed to a more nuanced view of the nature of an abortion. The growing insight in embryonic and foetal development, however, has not resulted in a change of policy with regard to legal abortion. As a criterion for the legality of abortion both the British and Dutch lawmakers have chosen for a limit of 24 weeks. After this time of gestation, the human embryo is normally capable of viability outside the womb. By using viability as a criterion for illegal abortions, a legal distinction has been introduced between unborn human beings on the one hand and viable persons with a right to life on the other hand.

In this regard, Christopher Kaczor notes that in fact physiological dependency, such as the unborn child's dependency of the mother, has no relationship to personhood.[627] A pregnant women with a habit of smoking or alcohol consumption might severely harm the unborn child's interests. In the Dutch legal practice it has happened that an unborn child has been placed under supervision of a regional youth care agency because

---

626 Franz Böckle, in: Anselm Hertz et al., *Handbuch der Christlichen Ethik, Band 2*, Freiburg, 1978, p. 36.
627 Kaczor, C., op. cit., p. 69.

the mother's lifestyle could be a threat for him.[628] In particular, the first trimester of pregnancy is critical because several foetal abnormalities might develop during that developmental stage. So, it is clear that the interests of the human embryo with regard to its survival and its health begin to manifest themselves long time before foetal viability. The fact that these interests are not consciously experienced by the unborn child itself, is of no relevance when his or her life or health are directly under threat.

In general, it needs to be remarked that human existence is per definition a limited existence. With all other organisms we share that our existence is always on its way to development. Being human means being limited and dependant in his relations with other persons and with regard to material things. These existential human conditions do not determine the value of individual human beings. Every human being carries with him a certain potentiality, which either will be or will not be realised.[629]

In his study on the human person, Günter Rager presumes the following hypothesis: if we as adults were to identify ourselves with the person we were at our early childhood, and if we could accept the idea of continuity in our identity from the very beginning, then it seems obvious that we could also identify with our beginnings as a zygote.[630] But then, if we have value as adults, we would also have value from our earliest beginnings.

The conclusion must be that it is inconsistent to say that adult life has value and embryonic life does not have value, since both are different stages of human life. In the case of a developing embryo, one can understand that an embryo has the potential to grow into an adult person. Seen from a theological point of view, this potentiality must be there already from conception onwards, although it is not yet fully unfolded.[631] As regards the right to life of human embryos, this thought has ethical relevance: if the essence of this organism is being considered by ways of its potential

---

628 Court of Utrecht, 3 June 2004, in: *Tijdschrift voor Familie- en Jeugdrecht*, 2005, n. 89. The Court based her verdict on Art. 2, BW (Civil Law), which says "the child of which a woman is pregnant is considered as being born, as often as his interest requires so." It is important to notice that the mother agreed with the supervision.
629 Wulf, C.M., 2011, op. cit., pp. 414-419.
630 Günther Rager, *Die Person. Wege zu ihrem Verständnis*. Fribourg, 2006, p. 188.
631 Cf. Wulf, C.M., 2010, op. cit., p. 13.

development, then the embryo's right to life cannot be denied.[632] Yet, in current philosophical discussions, such a metaphysical understanding of personality is criticised.[633]

The main criterion for legal abortion, viability, can be defined as the ability of the human embryo to survive after a premature birth in an extra uterine environment. Philosophers like Christopher Kaczor, Julian Savulescu and Peter Singer have argued that viability is an inappropriate legal and ethical criterion for personhood.[634] Savulescu notes that viability is dependent on the state of technology.[635] Over the last 30 years, it has dropped from 28 weeks to 24 weeks, or sometimes even less. But, as Kaczor concludes, "it is nonsensical to believe that technology determines who is or is not a person, since technology bears no necessary relationship to personhood".[636]

Before the moment of viability, there has already been a constant and remarkable development of the embryo, right from the very beginning. Some of the main biological characteristics of this development will therefore be summarised first.

A human zygote or embryo is formed in a process that lasts 20 to 22 hours after penetration of the egg by a sperm.[637] When the fertilisation process is complete, 46 chromosomes provide the blueprint for the embryo's physical development. Because the zygote, the newly formed cell, consists of 23 chromosomes from each parent, its genome is distinct from that of the mother and the father. Except for the possibility of monozygotic twins, of which I will speak later, the zygote is genetically unique, with a DNA pattern which no one else has. The sex of the embryo is determined by whether the sperm contributes an X or a Y chromosome to the zygote.[638]

From the time of fertilisation onwards, embryonic development is

---

632 Rager, G., op. cit., pp. 185-188; cf. Wulf, C.M., 2011, op. cit., p. 416.
633 Cf. part 4.3.2.1.
634 Kaczor, C., op. cit., pp. 68-71; Julian Savulescu, "Is current practice around late termination of pregnancy eugenic and discriminatory? Maternal interests and abortion", in: *Journal of Medical Ethics*, 2001, 27, 1, pp. 165-171; Peter Singer, *Rethinking Life & Death: The Collapse of Our Traditional Ethics*. New York, 1994, p. 102.
635 Savulescu, J., 2001, op. cit., p. 168.
636 Kaczor, C., op. cit., p. 70.
637 Norman Ford S.D.B., *The Prenatal Person. Ethics from Conception to Birth*. Malden, MA., 2002, p. 55.
638 Moore, K.L. and Persaud, T.V.N., op. cit., pp. 33-35.

characterised by an intrinsic finality, very different from that of gametes (male sperm or female egg-cells). Gametes, with 23 chromosomes each, are clearly oriented towards combining with each other, and if they fail in that, they die. The intrinsic finality of a human embryo after fertilisation has been described by Patrick Lee as follows:

> [T]he direction of this organism's growth and the orientation of its homeostatic operations - for example, the maintenance of a constant temperature, pressure, salt and potassium levels - is towards its own survival and flourishing, a distinct end from the survival and flourishing of the mother, in whose body this distinct organism resides. ... The human embryo possesses the internal resources and the active disposition needed to develop himself or herself into full maturity. And unless deprived of a suitable environment, or prevented by accident or disease, the embryo *will* actively develop itself in its own distinct direction, toward its own survival and maturity. The direction of its growth is not extrinsically determined, but is in accord with the genetic and epigenetic within it. The human embryo is, then, a whole (though immature) and distinct human organism.[639]

About 30 hours after fertilisation, the division of the zygote into blastomeres begins. When there are 12 to 32 blastomeres, the developing human is called a morula. While further cleavage takes place, a fluid-filled space appears inside the morula. Then the blastomeres are split into a thin, outer cell layer, the trophoblast, which will further develop into the embryonic part of the placenta, and a group of centrally located blastomeres, which gives rise to the embryo. Some six days after fertilisation, the blastocyst, as it is called by then, searches for a spot to implant in the uterus.

During the second week, a rapid proliferation and differentiation of the trophoblast takes place. As of the fourteenth or fifteenth day, early formation of the central nervous system, backbone, and spinal column begins, with the appearance of the so-called primitive streak. During week 3, the gastrointestinal system has also begun to develop with the kidneys, liver, and intestines forming. The heart has begun to form. The embryo's tiny heart begins to beat by day twenty-one. During week 5 the brain has developed into five areas and some cranial nerves are visible. Arm and leg

---

639 Lee, P., op. cit., pp. 73-74.

buds are visible and the formation of the eyes, lips, and nose has begun. In week 7 the embryo has developed its own blood type, distinct from the mother's. The eyes have a retina and lens. The major muscle system is developed and the embryo is able to move.

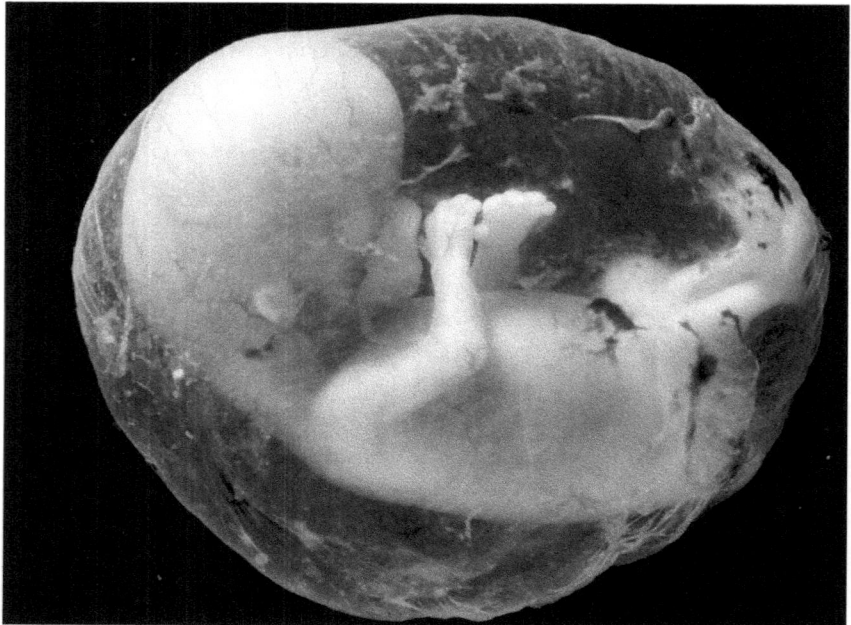

Figure 10: Eight weeks-old human embryo in uterus (56 post-ovular days)
Photo: Steve Allen/Getty Images.

The embryo is reactive to its environment inside the amniotic sac in which it moves. Hands and feet can be seen.

From week 9 the embryonic period is over and the foetal stage begins. At the end of the first trimester (12 weeks) most major organs and tissues have developed and red blood cells are now produced in the liver. The face is well formed and the eyes are almost fully developed. Arms, hands, fingers, legs, feet, and toes are fully formed. Testosterone is produced by the testes in the male foetus.

Between week 13 and 16 muscle tissue is lengthening and bones are hardening. The liver and other organs produce appropriate fluids. Eyebrows and eyelashes appear and the foetus makes active movements including kicks and even somersaults. Sex organs are visible on ultrasound scans as of 14-16 weeks. Around week 20 the foetus begins to hear.

In the British and Dutch abortion legislation, viability is an important criterion for the legal protection of foetuses.[640] Although there is no sharp limit of development, age, or weight at which a foetus becomes viable, experience has shown that from an age of 22 weeks, viability increases, as long as the foetus has enough birth weight (more than 500 gram).[641] Viability further depends on the presence of intensive care units for premature babies. During the last few decades, the available technology has lowered viability limit considerably and further developments in this area are promising.[642]

From an ethical point of view it has been argued that neither viability nor sentience are tenable criteria for ascribing the status of personhood to human embryos. The sentience argument has been used in the political discussion in order to defend the current abortion legislation. In 2007, the British House of Commons Science and Technology Committee concluded that "while the evidence suggests that foetuses have physiological reactions to noxious stimuli, it does not indicate that pain is consciously felt, especially not below the current upper gestational limit of abortion".[643] The RCOG states that the lack of cortical connections before 24 weeks implies that foetal pain is not possible until after 24 weeks.[644]

As regards foetuses' physiological reactions, Neena Modi and Vivette Glover mention evidence that the human foetus is able to mount various stress responses from early in gestation.[645] Xenophon Giannakoulopoulos

---

[640] Cf. parts 1.1 and 1.2.
[641] Moore, K.L. and Persaud, T.V.N., op. cit., p. 103.
[642] Kaczor, C., op. cit., pp. 70 and 215-230, in which he speaks of the possibility, the advantages and objections of artificial wombs.
[643] House of Commons Science and Technology Committee, *Scientific Developments Relating to the Abortion Act 1967. Twelfth Report of Session 2006/2007, Volume I*, London, 2007, p. 25.
[644] Cf. Royal College of Obstetricians and Gynaecologists, *Fetal Awareness. Review of Research and Recommendations for Practice. Report of a working party.* London, 2010, p. 24.
[645] N. Modi and V. Glover, "Fetal pain and stress", in: K.J.S. Anand, B.J. Stevens and P.J. McGrath, *Pain in Neonates, 2nd Revised and Enlarged Edition*. Pain Research and Clinical Management, Vol. 10, Amsterdam, 2000, pp. 217-227.

et al. showed a more rapid increase in noradrenaline with procedures that involve piercing the foetal abdomen with a needle, from as early as 18 weeks gestation.[646] Their results indicate that the foetus is capable of mounting an independent noradrenaline stress response from 18 weeks gestation.

The thalamus, located in the centre of the brain, is playing a central role in pain processing. During foetal development, neural connections to the thalamus are present by 20 weeks gestation; connections to subplate neurons are present by 17 weeks with intensive differentiation by 25 weeks; a functional spinal reflex is present by 19 weeks. Therefore, although the foetus may not be able to perceive pain from a cortical level before 24 weeks, he or she may be able to perceive noxious stimuli causing stress responses.[647]

It has been argued by Sumner that as soon as a foetus develops the capacity to feel pleasure or suffer pain, he or she would begin to have interests and therefore also rights.[648] However, an important philosophical objection against the use of sentience as a criterion for personhood has been put forward by Kaczor. He points out the fact that human persons have very different capacities for pain or pleasure:

> [D]ifferences in human sentience are not confined to the time of gestation. The kung fu master can put his arms around a burning cauldron, endure the searing of flesh, and carry the weighty object. The proverbial princess cannot stand the pea under her multiple matrasses. Many men cannot bear the least discomfort, and many women endure childbirth without anesthetic. Certain injuries and diseases greatly hinder the human capacity for pain, as do drugs of various kinds, as do differences in degrees of concentration and experience. Since adult human beings differ rather radically in their capacity for pain or pleasure, this should lead to the conclusion that they differ rather radically in terms of personhood. If degrees of sentience gives rise to degrees of rights, then not only are all human beings not equal, not all human persons are equal.[649]

---

646 Xenophon Giannakoulopoulos, Jerónima Teixeira, Nicholas Fisk and Vivette Glover, "Human fetal and maternal noradrenaline responses to invasive procedures", *Pediatric Research*, 1999, 45, pp. 494-499.
647 Lowery, C.L. et al., op. cit., pp. 275 and 280.
648 L.W. Sumner, *Abortion and Moral Theory*. Princeton, 2014; cf. Kaczor, C., op. cit., p. 74.
649 Kaczor, C., op. cit., p. 76.

The conclusion that not all human persons would be equal is at odds with the Universal Declaration on Human Rights, which states that "dignity is inherent ... to all members of the human family" and that all human beings are "free and equal in dignity and rights".[650]

Further, if the experience of pleasure and pain would be a criterion for the wrongness of killing a human being, then persons who are in surgery under anaesthesia or in a temporary coma would also be excluded from their right to life.[651] Finally, the scientific literature has reported cases of congenital insensitivity to pain, a (very rare) condition caused by a genetic mutation, which renders human beings totally insensitive to pain.[652] It is clear that people suffering from this disease must be considered persons in a juridical sense. Given the above mentioned arguments, the conclusion must be that sentience is not an apt criterion for personhood.

Summarizing it can be said that the development of an embryo is autonomous, continuous, coordinated and gradual. The chromosomal structure of the embryo is specifically human according to number, form, and functioning. The embryonic development is characterised by an intrinsic finality, guided by the DNA in the cell core, which is present and active in its specific combination from the moment of conception.[653]

4.2 The right to life and the dignity of the unborn child in international documents and in European jurisprudence

International declarations and conventions on human rights are binding for Nations states who have signed them. A treatment of the relevant United Nations and European documents is therefore necessary to get a clear sight of the international juridical framework, which sets boundaries for the national abortion legislations. Above that, European jurisprudence, in particular from the European Court for Human Rights, has relevance for the national regulations of procured abortion in the U.K. and in the Netherlands. For this reason, some verdicts of this European Court will be

---

650 General Assembly of the United Nations, *Universal Declaration of Human Rights*, 1948, Preamble and Article 1. Cf. part 4.2.
651 Cf. Kaczor, C., op. cit., p. 75.
652 Cf. Kaczor, C., op. cit., p. 77.
653 W.J. Eijk, "The status of the human embryo", in: Eijk, W.J. et al., (eds.), op. cit., pp. 136-162, here p. 158; cf. F. Böckle, *Handbuch der Christlichen Ethik, band 2*, 1978, p. 36.

discussed, too.

Pieter Willem Smits has analysed the genesis of four documents of the General Assembly of the United Nations which are relevant for the right to life of the unborn child.[654] These documents are: the Universal Declaration of Human Rights (1948), the International Covenant on Civil and Political Rights, the Declaration of the Rights of the Child and the Convention on the Rights of the Child. To this list the Universal Declaration on Bioethics and Human Rights, which appeared in 2005, certainly needs to be added.[655]

From the genesis of the first four documents mentioned above, it is clear that immediately there were different opinions among the delegates about the question when human life and therefore the right to life begins. Some countries, like Lebanon and Chile, argued that this right begins at conception, but the delegates of the U.S., the U.S.S.R. and the U.K. declared themselves against such a definition. Proposals to introduce the phrase that the right to life begins at conception in both Art. 3 of the Universal Declaration which states that: "Everyone has the right to life…" and in Art. 6 of the International Covenant, saying: "Every human being has the inherent right to life…" could not rely on a majority of votes.[656]

The General Assembly of the United Nations opens the Universal Declaration on Human Rights, stating that "dignity is inherent … to all members of the human family" and that all human beings are "free and equal in dignity and rights".[657] Commenting on this preamble, Roberto Andorno states that the term "inherent" means "involved in the constitution or essential character of something" or "intrinsic". Thus, dignity is inseparable from the human condition. It is an unconditional worth that everyone has simply by virtue of being human. "The same idea can be expressed by saying that all human beings are 'persons'. Indeed, the term 'person' is not merely descriptive or generic (like for instance 'mammal'), but prescriptive,

---

[654] Pieter W. Smits, *The right to life of the unborn child in international documents, decisions and opinions*, dissertation Faculty of Law, University of Leiden, the Netherlands, 1992, here pp. 5-74.
[655] United Nations Educational, Social and Cultural Organization, *Declaration on Bioethics and Human Rights*. Paris, 2006.
[656] Smits, P.W., op. cit., pp. 10-12 and 17-22.
[657] General Assembly of the United Nations, *Universal Declaration of Human Rights*, 1948, Preamble and Article 1; cf. part 4.1.

a *nomen dignitatis.*"⁶⁵⁸ However, the term 'dignity' has not been defined in the Universal Declaration of Human Rights, nor in later United Nations declarations, nor in international law.

The same differences of opinion played a role in the debates on the Declaration and the Convention of the Rights of the Child. Although the preamble of the Declaration states that the child "…needs special safeguards and care, including appropriate legal protection, before as well as after birth" and Principle 4 states that the child has the right to "…prenatal and postnatal care", an attempt by the Italian delegate to introduce the formula "from the moment of conception", failed.⁶⁵⁹

In 2005, the United Nations Educational, Social and Cultural Organization (UNESCO) adopted by acclamation in its General Conference the Declaration on Bioethics and Human Rights. The declaration aims at promoting respect for human dignity and the protection of human rights, consistent with international human rights law. However, as has been the case with earlier declarations and also in international law, a definition of what is meant by human dignity, is lacking.⁶⁶⁰

Given the fact that in many countries, including the United Kingdom and the Netherlands, viability of the foetus outside the womb has been chosen as a decisive criterion for legal protection, the Declaration of Bioethics and Human Rights does not mention the unborn child. However, tension remains between the determination of rights of new-born infants and the respect for human autonomy. In this regard the Declaration states that "For persons who are not capable of exercising autonomy, special measures are to be taken to protect their rights and interests."⁶⁶¹

4.2.1 The European Convention of Human Rights

Within the European context there is the European Convention of Human Rights formulated in 1950, which states in Article 2, part 1, that:

---

658 Roberto Andorno, "Human Dignity and Human Rights as a Common Ground for a Global Bioethics", *Journal of Medicine and Philosophy*, 2009, 34, pp. 223-240, here p. 209. Cf. Robert Spaemann, *Persons*. Translated from the German by Oliver O'Donovan, Oxford, 2006, pp. 16-17.

659 Smits, P.W., op. cit., pp. 33-37.

660 Andorno, R., op. cit., p. 229.

661 United Nations Educational, Social and Cultural Organization, *Declaration on Bioethics and Human Rights*. Paris, 2006, Art. 5.

"Everyone's right to life shall be protected by law."[662] However, the genesis of this statement does not reveal if this is also true for the unborn child. In this regard, Smits remarks that: "Having studied the geneses described before, it is striking that the question of when the right to life arises has been discussed repeatedly; however, the issue when life begins has been largely neglected."[663]

Given the fact that the international legislature had not answered the question when the right to life begins, this question was left to the national Constitutional courts. Smits treats these decisions of national Constitutional courts in Europe in chronological order and successively examines cases in Austria, France, Italy, Germany and Spain.[664] In the case of Paton versus United Kingdom, as will be shown later on, the European Commission of Human Rights specifically refers to the decision of the Austrian Court. Therefore, we have to deal with this decision first.

In 1974, The Austrian Constitutional Court decided against an application of the European Convention by the Government of the *Land* of Salzburg. The Salzburg Government objected to § 97 (1) of the Austrian Penal Code, which stated that abortion is not punishable when the termination of pregnancy is carried out by a physician after preceding medical consultation and within the first three months from the beginning of the pregnancy. Such is the practice which is nowadays legalised in many European countries. According to the Salzburg Government, the time limitation of three months could not be reconciled with Article 2 of the European Convention, which in Austria has the force of a constitution. Further, the Government argued that the term 'life' in Article 2 had to be interpreted as biological-physical existence, adding that it related to a purely natural concept, which simply signified 'having life', in contrast to 'not yet alive' or 'dead'. Referring to the literature concerning, on the one hand, Article 2 of the Convention and, on the other hand, Article 2(2) of the West German Constitution, which had the same historical background, the Salzburg Government pointed out that most of the authors took the view that Article 2 of the Convention and Article 2(2) of the German Constitution were to be construed as also

---

662 Council of Europe, "The European Convention on Human Rights", art. 2.
663 Smits, P.W., op. cit., p. 74.
664 Smits, P.W., op. cit., pp. 88-133.

applying to the unborn. They also made reference to Article 4 par. 1 of the American Convention, stressing that as stated therein the right of life has to be protected by law and, in general, from the moment of conception. It noted that the limitation laid down in the phrase "in general" clearly shows the possibility of indications but that in principle the duty of protection is applicable.[665]

Smits then gives the line of argumentation of the Austrian Government in reaction to the Salzburg plea. In summary, they point out that "the relation between the pregnant woman and her foetus is unique and that the foetus which develops from the fertilized ovum is a part of the woman's body and only becomes viable long after the period of 12 weeks. In view of the valuation of the life of the foetus in criminal law in general and of the harm caused by a pregnancy to the woman, it seems admissible to decide on a conflict between the interests of the foetus and those of the woman in averting the injuries of an unwanted pregnancy in favour of the pregnant woman."[666]

However, biologically speaking it is just not correct to presuppose the foetus a part of the woman's body.[667] Or, as Smits comments: "[The Austrian Court] did not pay attention to the argument of the Salzburg Government that the term 'life' in Article 2 of the Convention had to be construed as the biological-physical existence and to its statement about the way in which the human being comes into being at the moment of fusion of the sperm and the ovum and the process of development started then, a process without any caesura in organic respect in which birth is of no importance for identity."[668]

Further, the Austrian Government argues that at the time the European Convention was drawn up, an abortion act had been in force in Denmark since 1937, in pursuance of which the pregnant woman was not punishable when her pregnancy was terminated by a doctor, even if the woman knew that there were no legal grounds for abortion. After the Convention was

---

665 Decision of 11 October 1974, cf. Smits, P.W., op. cit., pp. 88-97. The complete text of the Salzburg plea can be found in Wolfgang Waldstein, *Das Menschenrecht zum Leben. Beiträge zu Fragen des Schutzes menschlichen Lebens.* Berlin, 1982, Appendix A, pp. 131-149.
666 Smits, P.W., op. cit., pp. 90-91.
667 Cf. part 4.1.
668 Smits, P.W., op. cit., p. 96.

ratified, liberalised abortion regulations had been prepared and made in different Member States.[669]

The Austrian Court concludes that Article 2 of the Convention "does not contain a definition of life as protected by this provision, adding that it has not been established at what time life begins. However, a consideration of the text of Article 2 as a whole in its context does not support the view that the provision also includes germinal (unborn) life."[670]

This decision sets the tone for further European jurisprudence. In 1980, the case of Paton versus The United Kingdom is brought before the European Commission of Human Rights.[671] William Paton, a citizen of the U.K., complained that the Abortion Act of 1967 violates Articles 2 and/or 5, 6, 8 and 9 of the European Convention of Human Rights. Paton had previously tried to prevent the termination of his wife's pregnancy, but the U.K. High Court of Justice had refused his application. In her considerations, the Commission is referring to the view of the Austrian Constitutional Court that Article 2 does not cover unborn life. In order to formulate her own view, the Commission then examines if Article 2, in the absence of any explicit reference to unborn life, is to be interpreted:

1) as not covering the foetus at all;

2) as recognizing a 'right to life' of the foetus with certain implied limitations; or

3) as recognizing an absolute 'right to life' of the foetus.[672]

First, the Commission excludes the third interpretation, starting with the following presupposition: "The 'life' of the foetus is intimately connected with, and cannot be regarded in isolation of the life of the pregnant woman."[673]

Again, this presupposition is just not true in a biological sense. Although the lives of the foetus and the woman are indeed intimately connected, biologically speaking it makes no sense to say that the life of the foetus could

---

669 Ibid., pp. 93-94.
670 Ibid., pp. 94-95. The original text of the Austrian Court can be found in Waldstein, W., op. cit., Appendix B, pp. 150-163.
671 Decision of the Commission as to the admissibility of Application No. 8416/78, 13 May 1980, in: European Commission of Human Rights, *Decisions and Reports*, 1980, 19, p. 244. Cf. Smits, P.W., op. cit., pp. 145-157.
672 Ibid., consideration n. 17.
673 Ibid., consideration n. 19.

not be regarded apart from of the life of the pregnant woman. A whole scientific discipline, embryology, has been devoted to the life of the foetus, whose development is unique, gradual, continuous and coordinated.

In this regard, Smits remarks that the Commission leaves open the question of whether Art. 2 of the Convention also covers prenatal life.[674] Indeed, there is no definitive affirmation of this kind in the Commission's considerations. The Commission argues that if Art. 2 of the Convention has to be seen as absolute, then this would mean that the life of the foetus would be regarded as being of a higher value than the life of the pregnant woman. However, this interpretation does not necessarily follow. One only has to look at the text of the Convention itself to see that certain limitations are already set to the right of life of every human being. Art. 2, part 2 says that "deprivation of life shall not be regarded as inflicted in contravention of this article when it results from the use of force which is no more than absolutely necessary: (a) in defence of any person from unlawful violence; (b) in order to effect a lawful arrest or to prevent escape of a person lawfully detained, or (c) in action lawfully taken for the purpose of quelling a riot or insurrection."[675]

Now for a foetus it would be quite impossible to enforce any unlawful violence towards the mother, or to escape, or to quell a riot or insurrection. Art. 2, part 2 is therefore irrelevant to unborn life. But a different, possible interpretation of Art. 2, part 1 would be that both the life of the mother and the life of the foetus are to be equally protected. This conclusion had been drawn by the German Federal Constitutional Court in 1975, stating that: "no distinction can be made between the various stages of developing life before birth or between born and unborn children. 'Everyone' in the meaning of Art. 2(2) of the Constitution is 'every living human being', in other words: every human individual possessing life; 'everyone' therefore includes unborn human beings."[676]

If we then go back to the decision of the European Commission in the case of Paton versus the U.K., the Commission, having excluded an absolute right to life of the foetus, finds that authorization by the U.K.

---

674 Smits, P.W., op. cit., p. 156.
675 Council of Europe, "The European Convention on Human Rights", art. 2.
676 Decision of the German Federal Constitutional Court of 25 February 1975, in: Smits, P.W., op. cit., pp. 109-122.

authorities of the abortion is compatible with the first sentence of Art. 2(1) because, if one assumes that this provision applies at the initial stage of the pregnancy, the abortion is covered "by an implied limitation of the right to life of the foetus, protecting the life and health of the woman at that stage".[677]

Suddenly, in its considerations the Commission speaks of the "protection of the life of the woman". Before that, it was not clear at all that the life of Paton's wife was at stake. In the vast majority of cases the life of the woman is not at stake in a decision in favour of an abortion. On the other hand, the 'right to life' of the foetus is indeed limited by the abortion, even in an absolute way. Therefore, assuming that the abortion in the case of Paton's wife did not take place in a life threatening situation, the decision of the European Commission expresses that the protection of the woman's quality of life is considered as of more value than the life of the foetus.

In other words, the implicit presumption of the British Abortion Act means that a legal inequality exists between the right to life or health of the woman and the right to life of the foetus. The same legal inequality can be found in the various laws on abortion in the Netherlands and other European nations. This inequality, by which the 'right to life' of the foetus is limited by the mother's rights and interests, is confirmed by the controversial case *Vo versus France*, brought before the European Court of Human Rights in 2004.[678]

4.2.2 The right to life in the case of Vo versus France

The tragic case of *Vo versus France* involved an involuntary termination of pregnancy caused by negligence of the acting doctor G., who was working at the Lyons General Hospital. He had confused the six months pregnant Mrs. Thi-Nho Vo, who came to the hospital for a medical examination, with another Vietnamese woman, also with the name Vo, who visited the hospital to have a contraceptive coil removed. Before the doctor realised he had the wrong patient in front of him, he had pierced the amniotic sac in Mrs. Thi-Nho Vo's womb. One week later, her pregnancy was terminated

---

677 Decision of the Commission as to the admissibility of Application No. 8416/78, 13 May 1980, consideration n. 23. Cf. Smits, P.W., op. cit., p. 155.
678 European Court of Human Rights, *Case of Vo versus France*. Application No. 53924/00, 8 July 2004. In: Idem, *Report of Judgments and Decisions*, no. VIII, 2004.

on health grounds. Mrs. and Mr. Vo lodged a criminal complaint, alleging unintentional injury to Mrs. Vo entailing total unfitness for work for a period not exceeding three months and unintentional homicide of her child. After an initial acquittal of Dr. G., the Lyons Court of Appeal found him guilty of both offences. The Court of Appeal motivated its verdict by referring to the French Civil Code, Article 16 and the Voluntary Termination of Pregnancy Act, section 1, which both state that the law should guarantee respect of every human being from the beginning of life, adding that "these statutory provisions cannot be regarded as mere statements of intent, devoid of any legal effect".[679]

However, the Court of Cassation, on an appeal on points of law by Dr. G., reversed the judgment of the Lyons Court of Appeal, concluding that Dr. G. could only be held liable for unintentional injury to Mrs. Vo. He could not be held liable for unintentional homicide of her child, since, according to the French Criminal Code, the embryo could not be considered a person.

After the final verdict by the Court of Cassation, Mrs. Vo decided to bring a complaint to the European Court of Human Rights. In the starting point for its verdict, the Court concludes that in the various European laws on abortion "the unborn child is not regarded as a 'person' directly protected by Article 2 of the Convention and that if the unborn does have a 'right' to 'life', it is implicitly limited by the mother's rights and interests."[680]

As regards the French current legal situation, the Court remarked that "[i]t is clear... that in France the nature and legal status of the embryo and/or foetus are currently not defined and that the manner in which it is to be protected will be determined by very varied forces within French society."[681] The Court also observed that at European level there is also no consensus on the nature and status of the embryo and/or foetus and that "[a]t best, it may be regarded as common ground between States that the embryo/foetus belongs to the human race. The potentiality of that being and its capacity to become a person – enjoying protection under the civil law, moreover, in many States, such as France, in the context of inheritance and gifts, and

---

679 Ibid., p. 7.
680 European Court of Human Rights, *Case of Vo versus France*, 2004, n. 80.
681 Ibid., n. 83.

also in the United Kingdom [a reference is made to *Paton versus the U.K.*, W.B.] – require protection in the name of human dignity, without making it a 'person' with the 'right to life' for the purposes of Article 2".[682]

Commenting on these verdicts, Britta van Beers states that the logic of the subsequent Court of Cassation's jurisprudence in various earlier judgments is not very clear, because of a poor motivation.[683] In different verdicts, concerning cases of an involuntary termination of pregnancy, after a medical mistake or after a car accident, the Court decided that the health care practitioner or the driver involved had not committed involuntary homicide.[684] However, in the case of an eight month old foetus, who died as the result of a car accident, one hour after his birth, the verdict of involuntary homicide was acknowledged by the same Court.[685]

This juridical distinction between on the one hand an unborn child and on the other hand a child after a premature birth has raised a lot of criticism, which resulted in an attempt by the French MP Jean-Paul Garraud to amend the Civil Code in such a way that *involuntary* termination of pregnancy would become a criminal offence. However, the amendment was withdrawn after the first reading, out of fear that legal possibilities for *voluntary* termination of pregnancy would also be limited.[686] If in the case of Mrs. Vo's unborn child the right to life had been acknowledged by the European Court of Human Rights, then such a verdict could have had implications for abortion legislations in European Nation states.

Analysing the *Vo versus France* case, it is clear that the European Court of Human Rights is confronted by its boundaries as regards the question whether or not the human embryo needs to be considered as a person. In its concluding paragraphs, the Court states that "there is no European consensus on the scientific and legal definition of the beginning of life"

---

682 Ibid., n. 84.
683 Britta C. van Beers, *Persoon en lichaam in het recht. Menselijke waardigheid en zelfbeschikking in het tijdperk van medische biotechnologie.* Dissertation Law Faculty of the Free University of Amsterdam (VU), 2009, here p. 252.
684 Ibid.; cf. Jean Pradel, "La seconde mort de l'enfant conçu (à propos de l'arrêt d'Assemblée plénière du 29 juin 2001)", *Recueil Dalloz*, 2001, 36, pp. 2907-2913.
685 Cf. Cour de cassation, (Chambre criminelle) de la France (French Court of Cassation) 2 December 2003, in: *La Semaine Juridique*, 2004, 15, p. 682.
686 Beers, B.C. van, op. cit., p. 253; Florence Bellivier and Pierre Egea, "Les chemins de la liberté (petite leçon de biopolitique)", *Recueil Dalloz*, 2004, 10, pp. 647-652.

and that therefore the legal definition of the human person has been left to the discretion of States.[687]

The Court acknowledges that defining the human being has "legal, medical, philosophical, ethical or religious dimensions".[688] Given these various dimensions, it does not come as a surprise that the judges of the Court were divided on the matter. German judge Georg Ress of the Court submitted a dissenting opinion, in which he explained his interpretation of Art. 2 of the European Convention of Human Rights, stating that: "Historically, lawyers have understood the notion of 'everyone' ('*toute personne*') as including the human being before birth and, above all, the notion of 'life' as covering all human life commencing with conception, that is to say from the moment an *independent existence* develops until it ends with death, birth being but a stage in that development."[689]

Given the context of international Human Rights documents, in which the term 'dignity' has not been defined and given the fact that the European Court of Human Rights did not define the juridical meaning of the notion of 'everyone' in Article 2 of the Convention, the legal recognition of the dignity of the human embryo is most insecure.

4.2.3 The legal recognition of the dignity of the human embryo within the European context

The various decisions of the national Constitutional Courts in Europe regarding the legal protection of the embryo give reason for some reflections on the use of the term dignity within the European juridical context.

The decision of the German Federal Constitutional Court of 25 February 1975, which has been pointed out above, serves as an early example of the way in which the term dignity has been used in European legislation. The Court proposed that Article 2 (2) of the German Constitution also protects the developing life in the mother's womb as an independent legal

---

[687] European Court of Human Rights, *Case of Vo versus France*. 8 July 2004, n. 82. Literally, the Court states here that "It follows that the issue of when the right to life begins comes within the margin of appreciation which the Court generally considers that States should enjoy in this sphere, notwithstanding an evolutive interpretation of the Convention."

[688] Ibid.

[689] Dissenting opinion of Judge G. Ress, in: European Court of Human Rights, *Case of Vo versus France*. 8 July 2004, p. 51.

interest. In its considerations, the German Court referred to Article 1 (1) of the German Constitution, which states that the dignity of man shall be inviolable.[690] This statement on human dignity is different from the Dutch Constitutions, in which the term 'dignity' is not mentioned. In the U.K., judges have started developing a concept of dignity by drawing on the common law and by interpreting the Human Rights Act 1998, which does not enshrine human dignity.[691]

Historically, within the European context the dignity protection duty seems to have been a creation of German constitutional law.[692] The German Court added to its decision that where human life exists, it is entitled to human dignity and that it is not decisive whether the person entitled to this dignity is conscious or himself capable of preserving it. According to the Court, human life constitutes the vital basis of human dignity and is to be considered as a precondition for all other fundamental rights. The State has the obligation to protect the developing life in principle even against the mother. However, further in its considerations the Court argues that there could be circumstances in which the law cannot prescribe that the pregnant woman should give priority to the rights of the unborn child.[693]

So, in its decision, the German Court considers human dignity as a precondition for all other fundamental rights, but then leaves room for circumstances in which the penalization of abortion is cancelled.

In the context of international conventions and declarations, respect for human dignity is a requirement which has been increasingly voiced in

---

690 Basic Law for the Federal Republic of Germany (Promulgated by the Parliamentary Council on 23 May 1949; cf. Smits, P.W., op. cit., p. 109.
691 Catherine Dupré, "Dignity, Democracy, Civilisation", *Liverpool Law Review*, 2012, 33, pp. 263-280, here p. 268. Both the British Human Fertilization and Embryology Act 1990 and the Dutch Embryo Act 2002 do not mention human dignity. The preamble of the Dutch Embryo Act speaks of "respect for human life".
692 Catherine Dupré, "Human Dignity in Europe: A Foundational Constitutional Principle", *European Public Law*, 2013, 19, 2, pp. 319-340, here p. 336.
693 Smits, P.W., op. cit., pp. 113-114. The Court mentions four indications: the risk of the woman's life or the risk of serious injury to her health; a eugenic indication, an ethical (criminological) indication and the social or hardship ground. These indications have been integrated into the German Criminal Code. Cf. Ibid., pp. 116-117. I will not further deal with these indications, since I have limited this research to the case studies of the U.K. and the Netherlands.

recent years.[694] The Charter of Fundamental Rights of the European Union (signed and proclaimed in the year 2000 by the European Parliament, the Council of the European Union and the European Commission) mentions human dignity in the first article: "Human dignity is inviolable. It must be respected and protected."[695] With the coming into force of the Treaty of Lisbon in 2009, the Charter has become directly enforceable by the E.U. and national courts.

The Lisbon Treaty introduces the possibility of a European Citizens' Initiative, a petition by at least one million E.U. citizens to change E.U. legislation. In 2014, a public hearing took place in the European Parliament of the European Citizens' Initiative 'One of us', after a petition had been signed by 1.7 million European citizens. The petition proposed a ban on E.U. funding for "activities which presuppose the destruction of human embryos, in particular in the areas of research, development aid and public health".[696] The 'One of Us' proposal explicitly excluded abortion as an objective for legislative change, since abortion legislation is not an E.U. competence, but a competence of Member States. In her reply, the European Commission stated that E.U. primary legislation "explicitly enshrines human dignity, the right to life, and the right to the integrity of the person". For this reason, the Commission did not see a need to propose changes to the E.U. Financial Regulation.[697]

4.3 The status of the human embryo

An essential question in the political and societal debate on abortion is from what moment in the embryonic development it is reasonable to speak of the beginning of personhood. Since, if it were to be recognised that an embryo has the status of a person at some stage in his or her development, then it would follow that the embryo also has rights and in particular the right to live. A closely related metaphysical question concerns whether the

---

694 Deryck Beyleveld and Roger Brownsword, *Human Dignity in Bioethics and Biolaw*. Oxford, 2001, p. 1.
695 Charter of Fundamental Rights of the European Union, in: *Official Journal of the European Communities*, 18 December 2000, p. 9.
696 European Parliament, Press release *European Parliament hearing on 'One of Us' European Citizens' Initiative*, 9 April 2014.
697 European Commission, *Communication on the European Citizens' Initiative 'One of us'*. Brussels, 28 May 2014.

embryo can be considered a human being endowed with a soul from the moment of fertilisation. (4.3.1) In this part, the phenomena of monozygotic twins and spontaneous abortions will be addressed since these phenomena are used as arguments to deny 'ensoulment' at fertilisation.

It is clear from the beginning that the question of ensoulment is indeed a metaphysical question, and therefore every attempt to falsify the possibility of the existence of a human soul in the unborn or the new-born, will fail. On the other hand, it is also impossible to demonstrate ensoulment of a human embryo in an experimental, empirical setting.[698]

With regard to the personhood of the embryo, arguments are given by contemporary philosophers such as Ronald Dworkin, Jeff McMahan and Hugo Tristram Engelhardt.[699] (4.3.2) These authors deny the personhood of (early) embryos. Others, on the contrary, have pointed at the active, specifiable potentiality of the human embryo. (4.3.2.1) Finally, it is argued by Robert Spaemann and others that personhood starts at conception.[700] (4.3.2.2)

4.3.1 The status of the early human embryo

In 1990 the British Parliament enacted the Human Fertilisation and Embryology Act, according to which it is allowed to experiment with embryos up to fourteen days after conception. The Act further established the Human Fertilisation and Embryology Authority, which may grant licences for infertility treatment services, for the storage of gametes and embryos and for research projects in the area of embryology.[701]

The report of the Warnock Committee was the basis for this Act.[702] This Committee, presided by philosopher Mary Warnock, had the task of advising the British Government on legislation regarding the various treatments for infertility and research on embryos. It had "to consider

---

698 R.J. White, "Cold War against the Vatican?", *Nature*, 1995, 374, p. 589.
699 Cf. Ronald Dworkin, *Life's dominion. An Argument about Abortion and Euthanasia.* London, 1993; Jeff McMahan, "Cloning, killing, and identity", *Journal of Medical Ethics*, 1999, 25, pp. 77-86; H. Tristram Engelhardt jr., *Manuale di bioetica,* Milano, 1999.
700 Spaemann, R., op. cit.; Grisez, G., 1970, op. cit., pp. 306-346.
701 Human Fertilisation and Embryology Act 1990, in: *United Kingdom Public General Acts,* 1990, chapter 37, art. 3 and 11.
702 Mary Warnock (ed.), *A Question of Life. The Warnock report on Human Fertilisation and Embryology.* Oxford, 1985.

recent and potential developments in medicine and science related to human fertilisation and embryology; to consider what policies and safeguards should be applied, including consideration of the social, ethical and legal implications of these developments; and to make recommendations."[703] A long list of scientific, religious and non-governmental organisations and individuals who submitted written or oral evidence to the Committee is included in the report.

The Warnock Committee did not pay attention to alternatives which would help couples with their desire to have children while at the same time fully respecting the status of the human embryo, such as Fertility Care, foster care or adoption.[704] Fertility Care is an example of a method which seeks to improve a diminished fertility and to normalise disorders in the functioning of the reproductive organs. The method includes both guidance which serve to make optimal use of the natural means to determine the moment of ovulation, as well as specific medicines and surgical interventions to restore fertility where it is lacking.[705]

The Warnock Committee did not deal with the issue of abortion, although they admitted that this issue is "in some sense related".[706] The Committee's agenda was fully determined by the recent scientific and medical developments, whereas the question as to how society wants to protect human embryos already in a state of development from being aborted, was ignored.

As regards the status of the embryo, the Warnock Committee took a gradualist position. This position accepts that the human embryo is morally significant, but its rights increase gradually during its formation. In the biological development of the human individual, the Committee took as reference point the formation of the primitive streak, which is the first identifiable sign of the formation of the central nervous system, backbone, and spinal column), at about fifteen days after fertilisation. According to the Committee, "this marks the beginning of individual development of

---

703 Ibid., p. 4.
704 The issues of foster care and adoption will be treated in part 7.1.3.
705 L.J.M. Hendriks, "Medical Responsibility for the Transmission of Human Life", in: Eijk, W.J. et al., (eds.), op. cit., pp. 205-238, here p. 232.
706 Warnock, M., op. cit., p. 5.

the embryo."[707] While acknowledging that "the embryo of the human species should be afforded some protection in the law"[708], the Committee recommended that "no live human embryo derived from *in vitro* fertilisation, whether frozen or unfrozen, may be kept alive, if not transferred to a woman, beyond fourteen days after fertilisation, nor may it be used as a research subject beyond fourteen days after fertilisation. This fourteen day period does not include any time during which the embryo may have been frozen."[709] Further, the Committee stated that as long as the embryo had the capacity to split into two genetically identical embryos, it could not be regarded as an individual and therefore neither as a human individual. The embryo could only be considered an individual after the formation of the primitive streak, because then the embryo would lose its capacity to split.[710]

The report of the Warnock Committee has had a long lasting influence on the regulation of infertility treatments and embryo research in the U.K and other countries like the Netherlands, where the limit of fourteen days serves as a time limit for the experimentation with embryos. In 2004 the British Government announced that the 1990 Human Fertilisation and Embryology Act would be revised. Following a year of inquiry and collecting evidence, the Government stated that "the gradualist approach to the status of the human embryo as originally proposed by the Warnock Committee…continues to be appropriate."[711] Still, as came out in 2006, in a House of Commons debate on the preparation of the new act, Mary Warnock herself admitted that the fourteen days limit is "arbitrary"[712]. Despite this objection, the 2008 Human Fertilisation and Embryology Act remained unchanged as regards the fourteen days limitation.[713]

The assumption of the Warnock Committee that the formation of the primitive streak marks the beginning of the development of an individual,

---

707 Ibid., p. 66.
708 Ibid., p. 63.
709 Ibid., p. 66.
710 Ibid., pp. 59 and 66.
711 Secretary of State for Health, *Government Response to the Report from the House of Commons Science and Technology Committee: Human Reproductive Technologies and the Law*, London, 2005.
712 B. Iddon, MP, in: House of Commons debates, Hansard, session 2005-2006, vol. 448, column 544.
713 Human Fertilisation and Embryology Act 2008, in: *United Kingdom Public General Acts*, London, 2008, chapter 22.

seems to be at odds with the conclusion of part 4.1. There it has been shown that the embryonic development is characterised by an intrinsic finality, guided by the DNA in the cell core, which is present and active in its specific combination from the moment of conception. It is therefore necessary to look at the arguments which have been brought in to support the gradualist position as taken by the Warnock Committee and others. The first argument concerns the possibility of monozygotic twins up to fourteen or fifteen days. It will be shown how monozygotic twinning can also be explained if one supports the immediate ensoulment thesis.

A second argument brought in by defenders of the gradualist position, is the reality of spontaneous abortions. It will be argued later that this reality does not have relevance for the *moral* valuation of procured abortion.[714]

4.3.1.1 Monozygotic twinning

According to the Warnock Committee, an embryo could not be regarded as a human individual, as long as it has the capacity to split into two genetically identical embryos. However, an objection against the Warnock position is the fact that so far it has never been observed that a genetically identical twin originates by splitting of the embryonic shield.[715] In fact, much is still unknown as to how monozygotic twinning exactly takes place. Basically, there are two possibilities: the zygote's potentiality to twin is either passive, which means that it could be activated by forces outside the embryo, or active, because of its inclusion in the embryo's genetic structure.[716]

Among animals, a form of passive twinning can for example be found among earthworms, which have the capacity to continue living as two individuals when they are split in two. Theoretically, it is possible that a similar form of asexual reproduction exists among human embryos in the early phase of embryonic development, before the formation of the primitive streak, although so far no proof of such a possibility exists.[717]

The phenomenon of splitting of living organisms, in particular plants and animals such as earthworms, was already observed by Aristotle. He asks

---

714 In part 4.3.1.3.
715 W.J. Eijk, in: Eijk, W.J. et al., (eds.), op. cit., p. 147.
716 Kaczor, C., op. cit., p. 127; for the distinction between active and passive potentiality, which goes back to Aristotle, see part 4.3.2.1.
717 W.J. Eijk, in: Eijk, W.J. et al. (eds.), op. cit., p. 148.

himself what this splitting means in relation to the soul of these organisms. In *De anima* he has described the soul as the source of such phenomena as the "capacity for nutrition, sensation, thought and motion". He then continues to say that in the case of the nutritive and sensitive powers "the soul of each individual ... though actually one, is potentially several souls."[718] The word 'soul' here needs to be interpreted as 'principle of life' and not as 'individual'. Kevin Flannery makes this passage more clear. "There are present in the parts, such as the parts of earthworms, sources of movement that can survive a division. While still within the body of the original earthworm, they are in potency; after a division, the ancillary sources of movement become central sources and we have new substances."[719]

Nowadays, it is known to biologists that the majority of monozygotic human twins develop by division of the embryoblast, which already takes place at the end of the first week after fertilisation. Other monozygotic twins develop even earlier by separation of embryonic blastomeres. Recent evidence shows that cells in the mouse embryo can differ in their individual developmental properties as early as the four-cell stage. Other research shows that already in the two-cell stage, blastomeres in mice have different developmental characteristics.[720] But it is clear that one needs to be careful with interpretations of scientific research on animals regarding their significance for our understanding of early human development. Likewise, it is imprudent to draw conclusions with political consequences and repercussions for the required respect for human embryos, when this

---

718 Aristotle, *De anima*. Translated into English by R.D. Hicks, Amsterdam, 1965, Book II, 2, (413b18-19), p. 55. This passage is analysed by Kevin L. Flannery S.J., "Applying Aristotle in contemporary embryology", in *The Thomist*, 2003, 67, pp. 249-278.
719 Flannery S.J., K.L., op. cit., p. 274.
720 Marie-Elena Torres-Padilla, David-Emlyn Parfitt, Tony Kouzarides and Magdalena Zernicka-Goetz, "Histone arginine methylation regulates pluripotency in the early mouse embryo", *Nature*, 445 (2007), pp. 214-218. Karolina Piotrowska-Nitsche, Aitana Perea-Gomez, Seiki Haraguchi and Magdalena Zernicka-Goetz, "Four-cell stage mouse blastomeres have different developmental properties", *Development*, 132, 3 (2004), pp. 479-490. Berenika Plusa, Anna-Katerina Hadjantonakis, Dionne Gray, Karolina Piotrowska-Nitsche, Agnieszka Jedrusik, Virginia Papaioannu, David M. Glover and Magdalena Zernicka-Goetz, "The first cleavage of the mouse zygote predicts the blastocyst axis", *Nature*, 434 (2005), pp. 391-395. More general information on the developing embryo can be found in: Moore, K.L. and Persaud, T.V.N., op. cit., p. 147.

decision is taken without the necessary scientific evidence.[721]

4.3.1.2 Ensoulment: delayed or immediately at fertilisation?

The example of the splitting of earthworms illustrates that, possibly, the twinning of animal or even human embryos could be caused by an external force and that individuality of two (or more) embryo's already existed before the actual splitting of the original embryo. But this possibility does not provide certainty when answering the question as to whether the beginning of a human individual starts immediately at fertilisation or at a later stage of embryonic development. Empirically, it is impossible to prove and therefore also to falsify any ensoulment thesis. However, in the course of the centuries, philosophers and theologians sought to integrate empirical data with their belief in the existence of a unique and immortal human soul, the principle of life and the precondition for all rational, sensitive and vegetative activities.[722] The question regarding the ensoulment of the human embryo is very relevant for the abortion dilemma, because it determines the question of the personhood of the embryo and therefore also about their worthiness of protection. In the course of history, both theories of immediate and of delayed ensoulment have been defended.

One early theory of delayed ensoulment has been developed by Aristotle. He thought that the ensoulment of a human embryo took place in an indirect way. Based on observations without any modern equipment, he wrongly presupposed that the embryo sprung from the menstrual blood, which would remain in the uterus during pregnancy. With the semen, the menstrual blood would receive three kinds of soul in potential: a vegetative soul, a sensitive soul, and a rational soul. The semen and the embryo were assumed to have the vegetative soul potentially, but not actually, until the embryo absorbs nourishment. Likewise, the sensitive soul and the rational soul, which comes from outside the body and which has a divine origin,

---

721 Cf. W.J. Eijk, in: Eijk, W.J. et al. (eds.), op. cit., p. 147.
722 The next chapter deals with the writings of Augustin (6.1.1.1) and Thomas Aquinas (6.1.1.2) on the human soul. The Catechism of the Catholic Church (CCC) states that "in Sacred Scripture the term 'soul' often refers to human life or the entire human person. But 'soul' also refers to the innermost aspect of man, that which is of greatest value in him, that by which he is most especially in God's image: 'soul' signifies the spiritual principle in man." Cf. CCC, 1997, n. 363.

must be possessed potentially before they are possessed in actuality.[723]

According to Aristotle, the soul could be considered the form of a natural body which has in it the capacity of life.[724] After analysing aborted embryos, he stated that a male embryo is ensouled by a rational soul on the fortieth day and a female embryo on the eightieth day. These kind of philosophical constructions have had a large following for many centuries.[725]

For instance, in the Jewish tradition, the philosopher Philo (25 B.C. – c. 41 A.D.) could argue that, as long as the child was still in the mother's body and connected to her womb, it had to be considered "a part of the mother, according to natural scientists who have dedicated their lives to pure science, and the most eminent doctors..."[726]

When in 1827 Karl Ernst von Baer discovered the egg-cell (or ovum) in humans and animals and also the mechanism of fertilisation, there was evidence that the human body did not begin as a clot of blood, but as a living, fertilised egg-cell. For many natural scientists and theologians, this discovery was a reason to accept the hypothesis of an immediate ensoulment

---

[723] Aristotle, *De Generatione Animalium*. Translated into English by Jonathan Barnes (ed.), The Complete Works of Aristotle, Vol. I, Princeton, 1985, *Generation of animals*, I, 19-20, (727a-729a), pp. 1128-1132; II, 4, (738b), p. 1146; II, 3, (736b), p. 1143; cf. W.J. Eijk, in: Eijk, W.J. et al. (eds.), op. cit., p. 150.

[724] Aristotle, *De Anima*, Book II, I, (412a), p. 49.

[725] According to Aristotle, the limbs and also the penis of aborted male embryos are already differentiated at forty days gestation, whereas aborted female embryos only show differentiation after the first three months of gestation. He also states that the first movement of male embryos occurs about the fortieth day, of female embryos about the ninetieth day. Cf. *Historia Animalium*, VII, c. 3. (583 b 2-5). Translated into English by J.A. Smith and W.D. Ross, (eds.), The Works of Aristotle, Vol. IV, Oxford, 1956. Among Aristotle's followers on this point are St. Albert the Great and St. Thomas Aquinas, cf. part 6.1.1.3.

More recent research shows that when gender comparisons are made, most studies report no differences for growth or movement patterns between male and female foetuses regardless of gestational age. One exception is the study of Robert Almli et al. Using ultrasonography from 30 weeks gestation onwards, they found that male subjects displayed greater numbers of leg movements per minute than female subjects during both antenatal and postnatal development. Cf. C. Robert Almli, Robert H. Ball and Mark E. Wheeler, "Human Fetal and Neonatal Movement Patterns: Gender Differences and Fetal-to-Neonatal Continuity", *Developmental Psychobiology*, 2001, 38, pp. 252-273, here pp. 253 and 261. Of course, these results do not prove anything as regards ensoulment.

[726] Philo of Alexandria, *De specialibus legibus*, Book III, 20, 117. German translation by: L. Cohn, I. Heinemann, M. Adler and W. Theiler, *Über die Einzelgesetze*, III. Buch, 20, 117, Berlin, 1962, p. 219.

at the moment of conception. The distinction made by Aristotle between male and female ensoulment could no longer be sustained.[727]

In recent years, scientists who accepted the immediate ensoulment thesis, have tried to give an answer to the question of the possibility of monozygotic twinning during the first two weeks after fertilisation. A first possible solution is provided by Benedict Ashley and Albert Moraczewski, who state that only if an early embryonic cell is removed from the original embryo, then a new soul is infused. With this theory, the means by which the egg is fertilised, spontaneously or artificially by In Vitro Fertilisation (IVF) or similar techniques, are irrelevant to the creation of an ensouled human being. The argument they offer is that monozygotic twinning is not normal, but exceptional behaviour for an early embryo. It might be so that an early human embryo consists of pluripotent or even totipotent cells; but each of them only develops into a mature human being once they are separated from the others.[728]

Rose Koch-Hershenov gives a second possible solution to the question of monozygotic twinning. In her view, "when two genetically identical embryos develop from what appears to be a single fertilized egg, this is not a case of a single human being dividing into two, but of two human beings separating. These two human beings are each composites of a soul and body (matter) and each came into existence at fertilisation when two souls were infused into the unicellular body. Upon infusion, the souls of each of these human beings are collocated, sharing the same matter."[729]

One strength of this latter solution is that it can accommodate the

---

[727] Cf. W.J. Eijk, in: Eijk, W.J. et al. (eds.), op. cit., p. 151.

[728] Benedict Ashley and Albert S. Moraczewski, "Is the Biological Subject of Human Rights Present from Conception?", in: Peter J. Cataldo and Albert S. Moraczewski, *The Fetal Tissue Issue: Medical and Ethical Aspects*, Braintree, MA, 1994, p. 49. The term 'totipotency' of an early embryonic cell is used in the scientific literature to refer to the capacity a cell has, if separated from the embryo, to become a complete separate embryo. Koch-Hershenov argues that this terminology should not be confused with the capacity of early embryonic cells to replace any other embryonic cell, with regard to function. These undifferentiated stem cells could better be called 'pluripotent', since there is no scientific evidence that they are really 'totipotent' in the sense that every stem cell possesses the intrinsic capacity to become a new embryo. Cf. Rose Koch-Hershenov, "Totipotency, Twinning, and Ensoulment at Fertilization", *Journal of Medicine and Philosophy*, 31, 2006, pp. 139-164.

[729] Koch-Hershenov, R., op. cit., p. 158.

anomalous cases of monozygotic twinning in which the twins fail to separate and so are 'conjoined twins'. Even though they share body parts to some extent, in most cases, each conjoined twin is an individual organism. An extreme example of this is the case of the dicephalus, a conjoined twin which shares all the organs beneath the cerebrum (the upper brain). The two cerebrums make possible two distinct streams of consciousness. This example makes it more plausible to believe that two human beings (or two persons) can share the material dimensions of the same early embryo, or even the unicellular zygote which is, by any biologist's definition, an organism. This renders plausible the thesis that two twin human beings, and thus two souls, are present from fertilisation in the same cell(s) prior to the fission which takes place with monozygotic twinning.[730]

Another argument for this so-called hylomorphic metaphysics, the basis of which was already laid by Thomas Aquinas, is that the configuring activity of the soul can provide metaphysical explanation for the regular growth and development of the embryo from the moment of conception.[731] An account of this regular growth and development is lacking in theories as stated by Barry Smith and Berit Brogaard and others, who deny that the pre-15 or pre-16 day embryo is a human being.[732]

Given the results of recent research on monozygotic twinning, it can be tentatively concluded that at least the vast majority of human beings begin to exist at conception.[733] According to Ashley and Moraczewski, the life of *nearly all* human beings starts at conception. Koch-Hershenov's theory leaves open the possibility that *all* human life starts at conception. The possibility of monozygotic twinning is in itself no sustainable argument against the immediate ensoulment thesis.

Finally, a phenomenological argument could be brought in against the

---

730 Ibid., pp. 159-160.
731 Ibid., p. 152. According to Aquinas, the soul is created in the body, and souls are produced simultaneously with human bodies, at the culmination of human generation. Cf. Eleonore Stump, *Aquinas*. London, 2003, p. 207. She refers to Aquinas' *Summa Theologica*, Ia, 118, 2-3. His vision on the human soul will be briefly explained in part 6.1.1.3.
732 Barry Smith and Berit Brogaard, "Sixteen Days", *Journal of Medicine and Philosophy*, 2003, 28, 1, pp. 45-78, especially p. 69. Also in the Warnock report, no account is given for the normal, regular growth and development before and after fourteen days.
733 Cf. Kaczor, C., op. cit., pp. 103-104.

thesis that an embryo could not be regarded as a human individual, as long as it has the capacity to split into two genetically identical embryos. The argument which is often heard is that genetic uniqueness is an accidental feature, not an essential feature of a person. Even if all parameters which characterise a person (all spiritual, emotional and physical characteristics) were known and if all external factors which determine a person were calculable, then still would a person's behaviour be incalculable beforehand. The totality of a person's qualities, or in one word someone's individuality, must be considered as an essential feature of the human person and therefore a precondition for freedom.[734]

4.3.1.3 Spontaneous abortions

Still, another argument has been brought into the discussion against the immediate ensoulment thesis and also in relation to the morality of abortion: the phenomenon of spontaneous abortions. Spontaneous abortions might happen because of chromosomal abnormalities in the foetus' tissue, because of a disease of the mother, such as collagen vascular disease, insufficiently controlled diabetes, hormonal factors, maternal infections or tumours, or because of stress.[735] About 15% to 20% of known pregnancies terminate in spontaneous abortions. Threatened abortion, defined as vaginal bleeding before 20 weeks gestation, occurs in about 30% to 40% of all pregnancies. It is often not possible to differentiate clinically between threatened abortion, completed abortion and ectopic pregnancy in an unruptured tube.[736]

The fact that there are spontaneous abortions does not deny the fact that generally speaking, embryos have the capacity to develop into a full-grown human being, but it only illustrates that, because of certain internal, genetic causes or external circumstances, not every embryo will develop

---

[734] Cf. Wulf, C.M., 2011, op. cit., pp. 260-261. On the other hand, freedom - and love - are also preconditions for the self-realization of every individual. Cf. ibid., pp. 264-266.

[735] For an overview of studies on the association between stress and reproductive failure, see: Katrina Nakamura, Sam Sheps and Petra Clara Arck, "Stress and reproductive failure: past notions, present insights and future directions", *Journal of assisted reproduction and genetics*, 2008, 25, pp. 47-62. They state that "the overall weight of evidence supports the plausibility of a stress trigger to human reproductive failure." Ibid., p. 57.

[736] T.G. Stovall, "Early Pregnancy Loss and Ectopic Pregnancy", in: J.S. Berek, E.Y. Adashi and P.A. Hillard, (eds.), *Novak's Gynecology*, Thirteenth edition. Philadelphia (etc.), 2002, pp. 507-542, here p. 507.

into a foetus or an infant.

Further, the fact that there are many spontaneous abortions is not relevant for the moral question of how to treat the unborn. Spontaneous abortions do not legitimise the deliberate killing of a foetus. This can be illustrated by the fact that in normal circumstances, in case of a wanted pregnancy, social conventions dictate that the embryo receives from the mother and from all other caregivers the protection that is needed to grow into a foetus and an infant.

4.3.2 The personhood of the embryo

The key argument for many scientists who favour legal abortion is that an embryo might be a developing human being, but could not be considered a person in an anthropological or juridical sense, since being a person would imply a developed capacity for reasoning, willing, desiring and relating to others. Ronald Dworkin states that "it is not in any way presumed that the foetus is a person with rights or interests of its own."[737] Hugo Tristram Engelhardt argues that a human being becomes a person only after circa one year, when the brain has become so full-grown as to support the above mentioned functions.[738] According to Jeff McMahan, the human person begins to exist when the brain in his or her body first acquires the capacity to support consciousness, which is normally approximately 28 to 30 weeks after fertilisation.[739] Finally Bonny Steinbock adheres to a theory of psychological continuity.[740] According to this view, a first-trimester foetus does not have a personal identity, because there is no continuity of experiences, which are related by memories, desires, feelings, intentions and the like. She concludes that "unless there is conscious awareness of some

---

[737] Dworkin, R., op. cit., p. 48. Dworkin seems to overlook the importance of the genetic argument, that after its formation the zygote already contains all the genetic material that is decisive for the development of its later personality.

[738] Engelhardt, H.T., op. cit., p. 160. It needs to be said, that Engelhardt later declared that the Manual does not represent his own opinion and that in fact he holds a Christian position. More on Engelhardt can be found for example in Cataldo Zuccaro, *Bioetica e valori nel postmoderno. In dialogo con la cultura liberale*, Brescia, 2003, pp. 48 and further.

[739] McMahan, J., 1999, op. cit., 25, pp. 77-86.

[740] Bonny Steinbock, "Why Most Abortions Are Not Wrong", in: R.B. Edwards and E. Bittar, (eds.), *Advances in Bioethics. Bioethics for medical education*. Volume 5, 1999, pp. 245-267.

kind, a being does not have a life to lose".[741]

It has to be noticed that among the followers of the idea of belated personhood, the valuation of human life differs. Some, like Dworkin, try to find a way of "how best to respect a conviction that almost everyone shares, whether for philosophical or religious reasons: the life of any human creature, in any form, has intrinsic or sacred value."[742] Others argue that human dignity has to meet certain qualitative demands of physical, mental and social well-being, and that life as such has no intrinsic value.[743]

There is a biological and a philosophical argument against all these different notions of personhood. Considering the biological development of the early embryo, it is well known that there is no specific moment of a substantial change in the nervous system's development, which would mark the beginning of personhood or the delayed infusion of a rational soul. Rather, the development of a human embryo is unique, gradual, continuous and coordinated from the moment of conception.[744] This pleads against the indication of the beginning of personhood at some later stage during pregnancy.

From a philosophical point of view, Don Marquis has shown that Steinbock's theory of psychological continuity leads to the very implausible conclusion that "the first-trimester foetus that was my precursor was a different individual from me", since it existed weeks before I did.[745] This earlier precursor either ceased to exist when sentience began, or it continues to exist as a biological organism. But this latter solution implies that we as persons are not the same individual as our biological organism, which is again very implausible.

If personality is thus reduced to certain specific brain functions or related to unproven philosophical constructions, a dualism is introduced between on the one hand human beings with a human body and on the other hand human persons, defined as human beings with a human consciousness. This

---

[741] Ibid., p. 249.
[742] Dworkin, R., op. cit., p. 12.
[743] For instance H. van den Enden, *Abortus: pro/contra. Een critische analyse*. Baarn, 1971. Cf. Bruijn, J. de, op. cit., p. 186.
[744] Cf. part 4.1.
[745] Don Marquis, "Why Most Abortions are Immoral", in: R.B. Edwards and E. Bittar (eds.), *Advances in Bioethics. Bioethics for medical education*. Volume 5, 1999, pp. 215-244.

dualist thinking has far reaching ethical consequences: embryos, foetuses and new-borns are no longer considered as human persons with a right to life and a physical integrity which needs to be fully respected.[746] In this kind of dualist thinking the argument of the active potentiality of a human embryo is missing.

4.3.2.1 The active, specifiable potentiality of the human embryo

In the last decades, the dualism in the writings of Engelhardt and others has been criticised by Francis Wade and later by Massimo Reichlin, by ways of a reappraisal of Aristotelian metaphysics.[747] Engelhardt states that two distinct stages could be distinguished in the development of man: the first stage, that of 'human being', is the achieving of biological qualities; the second stage, that of personal being, is the actuality of one who can participate in social roles. He contends that "it is easier to construe the situation as a development from biological properties to personal properties with a consequent *essential* and *substantial* change in the significance of the bearer of the properties."[748]

Reichlin and Wade reject this dualism by making use of Aristotle's understanding of active potentiality. For a proper understanding of the term potentiality in the Aristotelian sense, it has to be distinguished it from possibility and probability. According to writers as Mary Warnock, potentiality stands for the possibility of future change. "If x is potentially y, this means that x may be y in certain circumstances."[749] Indeed, possibility corresponds to a general sense of potentiality as understood by Aristotle, but he distinguished active potentiality – which means a being's inherent capacity to autonomously develop itself – and passive potentiality – which only implies the capacity to undergo modifications from external agents.[750]

---

746 For a more extended discussion of the 'identity theory of mind', on which this idea of personhood is based, see W.J. Eijk, in: Eijk, W.J. et al. (eds.), op. cit., pp. 64-67.
747 Francis Wade S.J., "Potentiality in the abortion discussion", *Review of Metaphysics*, 1975, 29, pp. 239-255. Massimo Reichlin, "The argument from potential: a reappraisal", *Bioethics*, 1997, 11, 1, pp. 1-23.
748 H. Tristram Engelhardt, "The Ontology of Abortion", *Ethics*, 1974, 84, pp. 217-234, here p. 225. (italics mine).
749 Mary Warnock, "Do Human Cells Have Rights?", *Bioethics*, 1987, 1, 1, pp. 1-14, here p. 12.
750 Aristotle, *Metaphysics*. Edited and translated into English by J. Warrington, London, 1956, p. 235 (Book Θ, Ch. 7, 1049). Cf. Reichlin, M., op. cit., p. 4 and pp. 13-17.

More recently, the same distinction as has been made by Warnock returns in Guido de Wert's reflection on the abortion debate.[751] Speaking of an embryo as a "potential person", he considers the following argument: "…[I]f Y is a potential X, then it follows that Y is not X and that therefore there is no reason to treat Y as X." Mariéle Wulf criticises this argument as follows:

> Here, Y and X are seen as two different objects. However, because we are speaking of a human being, one should not speak of Y and X, but instead of X_1 and X_2 on two different moments in time. The difference between X_1 and X_2 regards time and possible development, because development is an essential characteristic of a living being.[752]

In order to make this distinction clear in the context of human biology: a human gamete only has a remote sort of passive potentiality, because gametes do not have an individual capacity to undergo modifications, but rather the possibility that two entities unite in order to form a new individual which is distinct from the two originals. On the other hand, the embryo has in itself the potential for full personhood and does not receive it from outside. This is an example of an active potentiality towards which the embryo has a natural tendency.[753]

A second distinction which needs to be made is between an active specifiable potentiality, for example the potential of a child to become a musician and an active natural potentiality, for example the potential of an embryo to have an intellectual life. This latter potential means that an embryo has a natural tendency to develop the biological structures enabling him or her to have an intellectual life, when conditions permit, whereas the question of whether a child will become a musician mostly depends on personal preferences, inclinations and choices and again on certain favourable conditions.[754]

Further, potentiality should not be confused with probability. The

---

751 Guido de Wert, "Abortus", in: Marcel Becker, Bas van Stokkom, Paul van Tongeren and Jean-Pierre Wils (eds.), *Lexicon van de ethiek*, Assen, 2007, pp. 1-3.
752 Wulf, C.M., 2013 (a), op. cit., p. 68.
753 Reichlin, M., op. cit., pp. 4-14.
754 Francis Wade follows Max Scheler in this distinction, cf. Max Scheler, *The Human Place in the Cosmos*. Translated from the German by Manfred S. Frings, Illinois, 2009, in particular pp. 21-25. Cf. Wade S.J., F.C., op. cit., p. 243 and Reichlin, M., op. cit., pp. 14-15.

latter term indicates a certain chance, for instance the probability that a pregnancy ends in a spontaneous abortion. But, as Reichlin notes: "speaking of potentiality of a being implies affirming something about the nature of that being, something about the kind of being it actually is: the biological facts about it cannot be but *a posteriori* confirmations and empirical expressions of an underlying ontological structure."[755] Therefore, a proper understanding of the concept of potentiality "does not refer to the mere possibility of acquiring new capacities by means of an external agent, nor to the probability rate of the realization of such empirical mutations; rather, it refers to an inherent dynamic principle which rules the process of development of that being towards the progressive and never ending actualization of its already present nature".[756]

The argument of active potentiality has been overlooked by Jeff McMahan, who claims that the early foetus "cannot have an interest in becoming a person".[757] According to him, we are 'embodied minds', but the early foetus does not fall under this definition. McMahan admits that his theory of 'embodied minds' does not answer the question of how mind and brain are related.[758] Therefore, this theory could not provide an explanation of the unity of mind and body.

These types of thinking do not give a satisfying answer to the observations that the earliest development of a human embryo shows an intrinsic finality to grow into a human being with a future of value. This intrinsic finality has been determined under the influence of the chromosomal structure which is complete after fertilisation. Therefore, it is necessary to look further in order to come to a more complete description of personhood, in which these modern biological insights are integrated. In order to do so, the question needs to be asked what arguments could be given to ascribe the qualification of personhood to human embryos.

---

755 Reichlin, M., op. cit., p. 11.
756 Ibid., p. 22.
757 Jeff McMahan, *The Ethics of Killing. Problems at the Margins of Life*. Oxford, 2002, p. 305.
758 Ibid., p. 88.

4.3.2.2 The difference between 'something' and 'someone'

At first there is a preliminary remark to make on personhood. The argumentation that personhood starts at conception, has a *biological* and a *philosophical* component. Earlier it has been indicated by a number of biological facts that generally speaking, human life begins at conception.[759] The exception of monozygotic twinning has also been considered, about which two different metaphysical theories exist, the one of Ashley and Moraczewski saying that ensoulment takes place on two different moments, first at conception and then at the moment of twinning, and the other of Koch-Hershenov, stating that before twinning, two souls share the same cellular body.[760]

Still, the conclusion that the life of all human beings starts at conception (as Koch-Hershenov maintains) or that the life of nearly all human beings starts at conception (as Ashley and Moraczewski maintain), is not the same as saying that the embryo is a person from the very beginning. This depends on the philosophical interpretation of personhood.

Robert Spaemann offers a clear and extended philosophical analysis on personhood and the difference between 'something' and 'someone'.[761] He rejects the opinion, as stated by some in the abortion debate, that embryos (like little children) are persons only *in potential*. This, so he argues, is impossible. Personhood is not the result of a developmental process, but always the characteristic structure of this development. Our biological functioning, for instance, the acts of eating and drinking, are personal. Otherwise there would not exist preferences, aversions, etc. Also our family relationships are highly personal. We know from experience that the relationship of parents towards their child is characterised from the beginning onwards by treating the child as a person, not as a 'something'. This should be essential for a psychologically healthy upbringing.

Treating a child as a person with dignity and treating oneself as a person with dignity requires the abilities to deal in a reasonable, sensitive way with the surrounding world. As persons we have essential relations with matter,

---

759 In part 4.1.
760 In part 4.3.1.1.
761 Spaemann, R., op. cit., pp. 238-248.

space and time. These relations have ethical relevance.[762] Even from the very beginning of the human existence, in the mother's womb, the choices made by parents as regard their lifestyle, could have ethical implications for their child.

Spaemann concludes that there can be only one criterion for personality: the biological belonging to the human species. Therefore the beginning and the end of human life cannot be separated from the beginning and the end of personhood. His conclusion is shared by Norman Ford, who notices that "human nature usually enables foetuses to develop to the stage where, without ceasing to be the same living human individuals, they can exercise intellectually self-conscious, free and moral acts. They are persons with potential, not potential persons."[763]

---

[762] Wulf, C.M., 2013 (a), op. cit., p. 41.
[763] Norman Ford, "The Moral Significance of the Human Foetus", in: Richard E. Ashcroft et al., 2007, 387-392. It must be said that in an earlier work, Norman Ford speaks of a zygote as a potential person, because of the possibility of monozygotic twinning up to the formation of the primitive streak. From an ethical point of view, he adds that "The argument for respecting human zygotes as potential persons based on their natural actual and proximate potency to become human individuals in the Creator's plan, in my view, suffices to justify a duty of absolute respect for embryos and their formative process from the beginning of the zygote." Cf. Ford S.D.B., N.M., 2002, op. cit. p. 68.

Chapter 5

Towards an authentic and responsible reproductive decision making process

In the previous chapter, it has been argued that foetuses need to be considered as persons with a potential to grow out into individuals able to exercise intellectually self-conscious, free and moral acts. Inevitably, the question comes up how to make responsible reproductive choices, especially when circumstances for pregnant women and their partners are difficult.

The main focus in this chapter is on several philosophical currents which can be influential with regard to reproductive decision-making processes. (5.1) Paul Ricoeur's phenomenological approach offers various insights in the relation between self-esteem and the other, which becomes acute with regard to the question of responsibility towards the unborn child. (5.1.1) However, within other philosophical currents, it is presupposed that as regards reproductive choices, decisions are being made based on rational choice. Therefore, part 5.1.2 deals with the rational choice theory on fertility. The rational choice theory presumes that the consequences of a reproductive choice can be overseen. In part 5.1.3, it will be shown that this type of consequentialist reasoning is problematic in relation to abortion. In particular, both the rational choice theory and a consequentialist decision-making model do not take into account the future of value argument, which has been put forward by Don Marquis. (5.1.4) In these models an integral view on human dignity is also lacking. (5.1.5)

Other philosophical views have strongly influenced the abortion debate. As a representative of contemporary liberal philosophy, John Rawls' view on abortion will be considered. (5.1.6) Finally, the principles of respect for every basic value in every act and the principle of acts with double effect, as have been described by Germain Grisez and John Finnis, will be discussed. (5.1.7 and 5.1.8)

In parts 5.2 and 5.3, the focus is on the consequences of the developments in prenatal diagnosis for reproductive decision-making process. Especially when a foetal anomaly has been detected, parents can be faced with very complicated situations.

In the final part of this chapter, an ethical conclusion will be formulated with regard to procured abortion. (5.4)

5.1 Various philosophical views on reproductive decision making

The search in this chapter is for an authentic and responsible reproductive decision making process. Authenticity can be described as a characteristic of a person, who lives from out of his most inner depth. He knows what is meaningful and what is not; he knows his worth and his dignity and is therefore able to esteem the worth and dignity of every other human being.[764] Charles Taylor has shown that in modern times, the term 'authenticity' has become ambivalent.[765] In adopting the ideal of authenticity, people often give support to a certain kind of liberalism, more specifically the liberalism of neutrality. It holds that "a liberal society must be neutral on questions on what constitutes a good life. The good life is what each individual seeks, in his or her own way, and government would be lacking in impartiality, and thus in equal respect for all citizens, if it took sides on this question".[766] As regards procured abortion, this type of reasoning could either lead to a subjectivist stance, which many today accept and would say, for instance: "Abortion is right for those who think it is right, and wrong for those who think it is wrong", or to a relativist stance, which would imply that the morality of abortion is relative to the particular culture in which one lives.[767] These types of thinking leave aside the dignity of the foetus and in particular its future value, as will be argued shortly afterwards.

For Ricoeur, the notion of an authentic self always goes together with a responsible self. As Ann Marie Mealey puts it: "For Ricoeur, the fostering of self-development is as important as the fostering of the development

---

[764] Cf. Wulf, C.M., 2011, op. cit., p. 280.
[765] Cf. Charles Taylor, *The Ethics of Authenticity*. Cambridge, Ma. and London, 1992, pp. 17-21.
[766] Ibid., pp. 17-18. As representatives of this current, Taylor mentions John Rawls, Ronald Dworkin and Will Kymlicka.
[767] Grisez, G., 1970, op. cit., pp. 270-273.

of the other."⁷⁶⁸ Although he starts his search for the ethical aim with the notion of freedom, there can be no true freedom without responsibility. Or, in other words, in Ricoeur's view there is no such thing as freedom for oneself without the obligation of providing freedom for another.⁷⁶⁹

In the next part, Ricoeur's phenomenological approach will be further elaborated, because it has a lot to offer to the understanding of ourselves in relation to others, which could be helpful with regard to the abortion dilemma.

5.1.1 The ethical intention in relation to others: Paul Ricoeur

In his study on the self and the ethical aim, Ricoeur defines an 'ethical intention' as "aiming at the 'good life' with and for others, in just institutions".⁷⁷⁰ In his analysis on the self and the ethical aim, he describes how the second component of the ethical aim, which he calls solicitude with and for Others, links up with the first one, that of self-esteem, aiming at a good life.⁷⁷¹ Following Emmanuel Levinas, Ricoeur uses the word 'Other' (with a capital 'O') as a metacategory, which transcends the first-order discourse to which belongs the categories or existentials such as persons and things.⁷⁷² The phenomenological hermeneutic of the self, as has been elaborated by Levinas and by Ricoeur, is closely connected with various modalities of passivity of the self. This phenomenology produces a new dialectic of the Same and the Other, "which in many ways, attests that the Other is not only the counterpart of the Same but belongs to the intimate constitution of its sense."⁷⁷³ For instance, in the field of linguistics, the speaker's self-designation appears to be intertwined with the speech situation, in the sense that every participant is affected by the speech addressed to him or to her. In the situation of an unintended pregnancy, a woman's self-designation will be affected by her partner's attitude towards her and towards the foetus. If a man accepts the givenness of the unborn

---

768 Ann Marie Mealey, *The Identity of Christian Morality*. Farnham, 2009, p. 69.
769 Ibid.
770 Ricoeur, P., 1992, op. cit., p. 172.
771 Ibid., pp. 180-194.
772 Ibid., p. 298.
773 Ibid., p. 329; cf. Emmanuel Levinas, *Totality and Infinity. An essay on exteriority*. Translated into English by Alphonso Lingis. The Hague, 1979, pp. 33-108.

child, this could positively influence the woman's self-designation and it could deepen their relationship. Likewise, a man's self-designation will be affected by his partner's attitude towards him and towards the foetus. If a man starts to value the woman's love or affection for their unborn child, this will also undoubtedly have an effect on his own self-designation. This might then have an effect on the way she looks at him as the begetter of the child.

In a similar way, a woman's self-designation might also be affected by her parents' reactions or by other person's reactions if she tells them she is pregnant. This goes for a man's self-designation too if he tells his parents or other persons what has happened. Now, when it comes to the concrete realization of the ethical aim, a paradoxical situation could arise when there is a tension between the aim of self-esteem and the aim of solicitude with and for others. If the ethical aim of self-esteem becomes enclosed in itself, then the reflection on openness towards the other could be in great danger. For instance, if a man remains fixed on his own career perspectives and tries to derive his self-esteem from this perspective only, without showing the courage to take a leap into the deep end, or the willingness to take upon himself the responsibility of fatherhood, the result could be that he will not only loose the foetus, but also that the relationship with his partner could be under severe threat. This is obvious in the situation that she wants to keep her child. However, also if the woman decides to have an abortion because of his attitude towards her and towards the foetus, this could work out very negatively for their relationship.[774]

In *Oneself as Another*, Ricoeur elaborates on a possible solution to the paradox between solicitude and self-esteem, by starting with the thesis that solicitude is not something added on to self-esteem from outside but on the contrary, solicitude unfolds the dialogic dimension of self-esteem.[775] He does so by referring once more to Aristotle, who sees friendship as a phenomenon which makes a transition possible between the aim of the 'good life' and the virtue of justice.[776] Friendship itself is a virtue, an excellence in Aristotelian terms, at work in deliberate choices, while at the

---

774 Cf. part 3.3.2.3.
775 Ricoeur, P., 1992, op. cit., p. 180.
776 Aristotle, *Nichomachean Ethics*, VIII, 9, pp. 218-219.

same time it could be seen as a condition for happiness.[777]

Friendship is thus described as a need of a man in search for happiness. Friendship works toward establishing the conditions for the realization of life, considered in its intrinsic goodness and its basic pleasure.[778]

An intriguing question which arises from this phenomenological description of friendship, is whether it is possible to establish a friendship with an unborn child. As every pregnancy is unique, an answer to this question would be completely personal for every expectant mother or father. It is just remarkable how Ricoeur's analysis of Aristotle's treatise on friendship could be applicable in the situation of an expectant parent. Aristotle considers a friend to be "another self".[779] The greatest good a friend desires for his friend is to stay just as he is.[780]

It must be said that Aristotle emphasises the mutuality of friendship. According to the idea of mutuality, each loves the other just as he is.[781] The unborn child, of course, does not have the full capacity to love its mother or father in the sense of 'love' as a conscious emotion or as a virtue. The parents however do have a capacity to love their child in this sense. Aristotle describes the idea of mutuality in friendship as a form of reciprocity, which is not based on utility, where one loves the other for the sake of some expected advantage, or for pleasure, but which is based on the idea that the other could remain who he or she is.

With this description of friendship, Ricoeur then returns to the features which can be attributed to solicitude.[782] As a first feature, he mentions the initiative of the other in the intersubjective relation, referring to the phenomenology of Levinas.[783] In Levinas's analysis on exteriority and the face, the face of the Other "appears" as an epiphany which opens humanity. He commands as a master, he commands justice and he forbids murder.[784]

Ricoeur, however, goes further in order to give solicitude a more

---

777 Ibid., IX, 9, pp. 236-238.
778 Ricoeur, P., 1992, op. cit., p. 186.
779 Aristotle, *Nicomachean Ethics*, IX, 4, op. cit., p. 230.
780 Ricoeur, P., 1992, op. cit., p. 184; cf. Aristotle, *Nicomachean Ethics*, VIII, 7.1159a11-12.
781 Aristotle, *Nicomachean Ethics*, VIII, 3, p. 211.
782 Ricoeur, P., 1992, op. cit., pp. 188-194.
783 Ibid., p. 188.
784 Ibid., p. 189; cf. Levinas, E., 1979, op. cit., pp. 199 and 213.

fundamental status than obedience to duty.[785] In doing so, he describes the status of solicitude as "that of *benevolent spontaneity*, intimately related to self-esteem within the framework of the aim of the 'good' life."[786] The inverse situation from that of instruction by the other is the suffering of the other.

Here, it is necessary to pause for a moment in order to illustrate the analysis of solicitude with the act of procured abortion. Apart from the motives someone may have in favour of abortion, it is clear that with the act of abortion every benevolent spontaneity in the reciprocal relationship of the mother and the foetus comes to an abrupt end. In the discussion between defenders and adversaries of legal abortion, it has often been argued that the foetus does not suffer because of the inability to experience pain.[787] In this regard, Ricoeur's description of suffering is very relevant, because suffering is not defined solely by physical pain, nor even by mental pain, but by the reduction, even the destruction of the capacity for acting, of being-able-to-act, experienced as a violation of self-integrity.[788] In reaction, one could argue that a foetus is unable to experience its own suffering as a violation of self-integrity because it does not possess the full capacity of self-consciousness.[789] This might indeed be true, but on the other hand, after procured abortion *any* development of a present or future capacity of the foetus has become impossible, including the capacity of self-consciousness. This is why Ricoeur's definition of suffering is so meaningful in relation to procured abortion, because the very nature of this act means the destruction of *every* present or future capacity of the foetus. It is a reductionist view of the reality of a developing foetus if one only considers the capacity to consciously experience pain.

Paul Ricoeur has yet a third dimension in his definition of an ethical intention, besides the aim of the 'good life' and the realization of this aim with and for others. This third dimension has to do with the addition 'in just

---

785 Ricoeur, P., op. cit., 1992, p. 190.
786 Ibid.
787 The question whether pain perception - or sentience - is an apt criterion for personhood, has been discussed in part 4.1.
788 Ricoeur, P., 1992, op. cit., p. 190.
789 As for instance the Royal College of Obstetricians and Gynaecologists has stated, cf. part 4.1.

institutions'.⁷⁹⁰ He assumes that living well is not limited to interpersonal relations but extends to the life of institutions. By the term 'institutions' is meant the structure of living together as this belongs to a historical community – people, nation, region and so forth. Secondly, Ricoeur asserts that justice "presents ethical features that are not contained in solicitude, essentially a requirement of equality".⁷⁹¹

The first question he brings up in this regard is how authorities could be rescued from the ephemeral: from the temporal condition which institutions have. Often in modern political structures we can see the ephemeral at work, when short term achievements prevail over long term interests. Authors like Hannah Arendt, to whom Ricoeur refers, have challenged modern politics by pointing out the right of every individual to have rights. She argues that the right of every individual to belong to humanity, should be guaranteed by humanity itself.⁷⁹²

Reflecting on the horrendous experiences of the Jewish ghettos and concentration camps, Arendt concludes that the right to have rights is even more fundamental than the right of justice or of freedom. The right to have rights means to live in a framework where one is judged by one's actions and opinions, as well as the right to belong to some kind of organised community.⁷⁹³

For Arendt, the event of natality, of birth, could be seen as an ontological foundation for human rights.⁷⁹⁴ In the experience of birth, Arendt sees the human capacity to relate to one's own potentiality for beginning, an event of novelty and unprecedented potentiality for the new.⁷⁹⁵

Peg Birmingham comments that Arendt is indebted to Augustine's insight *"Initium ergo ut esset, creatus est homo, ante quem nullus fuit"*. ("That there might be a beginning, man was created before whom nobody was.")⁷⁹⁶ By means

---

790 Ricoeur, P., 1992, op. cit., pp. 194-202.
791 Ibid., p. 194.
792 Hannah Arendt, *The Origins of Totalitarianism*. New York, 1966, p. 298.
793 Ibid., pp. 296-297.
794 Peg Birmingham, *Hannah Arendt & Human Rights. The Predicament of Common Responsibility*. Bloomington, In., 2006, p. 12.
795 Patricia Bowen-Moore, *Hannah Arendt's Philosophy of Natality*. New York, 1989, p. 2.
796 Hannah Arendt quotes Augustine's *Civitas Dei*, Book XII, ch. 20, in her essay 'Understanding and Politics', in: Hannah Arendt, *Essays in Understanding 1930-1954*. Edited by Jerome Kohn. New York, 1994, p. 321.

of this principle of beginning, Arendt pleads for a radical reformulation of the modern framework of human rights, in a way that the rights of freedom and agency are rooted in the more fundamental right of action and speech.[797]

According to Hannah Arendt, human power corresponds to the human ability not just to act, but to act in concert. Our life-story proceeds as a compromise from the encounter between the events initiated by man as the agent of action *and* the interplay of circumstances induced by the web of human relationships.[798] Along with Arendt, Ricoeur notices the difficulty that often human power becomes invisible because it is so extensively covered over by relations of domination.[799] In relation to the abortion dilemma, human power could for instance be overshadowed by the domination of economic or financial requirements, which might become a blockade for solicitude. In the lives of young people who are facing parenthood, a positive attitude of their employer, educational institute or health insurance company could be very important. It could be lifesaving, if they show a willingness to contribute to a constructive planning of future arrangements. Still, research shows that the most important factors in determining whether a pregnancy would end in abortion are marital status, being single and socio-economic status.[800] On the other hand, a negative domination of family or professional relations could threaten the autonomous choice to bring a pregnancy to term.

The second question raised by Ricoeur with regard to just institutions has to do with equality, which can be defined as the ethical core common to distributive and reparative justice.[801] At first sight, it seems difficult to apply this definition in the case of procured abortion, since after an abortion it is

---

797 Birmingham, P., op. cit., p. 36.
798 Paul Ricoeur, "Action, story and history: on re reading *The Human Condition*", in: Garrath Williams (ed.), *Hannah Arendt. Critical Assessments of Leading Political Philosophers. Vol. III. The Human Condition.* Abingdon, 2006, p.49.
799 Ricoeur, P., 1992, op. cit., pp. 196-197.
800 Philippe Combes, Marie-Cécile Gaillard, Jacques Pellet and Jacques Demongeot, "A score for measurement of the role of social vulnerability in decisions on abortion", *European Journal of Obstetrics & Gynecology and Reproductive Biology*, 2004, 117, pp. 93-101, here p. 100; part 3.3.1 deals in an extensive way with the reasons women have for an abortion.
801 Ricoeur, P., 1992, op. cit., p. 201.

no longer possible to bring about distributive or reparative justice towards the foetus. Still, the issue of equality has been put forward by several authors with regard to selective abortion after prenatal diagnosis. For instance, Erik Parens and Adrienne Asch argue that selective abortion expresses negative or discriminatory attitudes not merely about a disabling trait, but about those who carry it.[802] They point to the risk that with prenatal diagnosis, one single trait stands for the whole human being. Similarly, people with disabilities could encounter a discriminatory attitude, when they have the experience of being overlooked because of some single trait they bear. Prenatal testing could repeat and reinforce that same tendency toward letting the part stand for the whole.

Parens and Asch conclude that discrimination against people with disabilities often involves a tendency to allow the part to stand for the whole.[803] This kind of discrimination leads to profound misconceptions, which are widespread in society. Assessing the well-being of a disabled child, people tend to focus on the child's disability rather than on the child's personality. Or, assessing the well-being of parents with a disabled child, people tend to see the hindrances parents are confronted with, rather than their adaptational strategies. Evidence in this regard shows surprising results. For instance, a review by Philip Ferguson, Alan Gartner and Dorothy Lipsky concludes that "aggregate patterns of over-all adjustment and well-being to be similar across groups of families with or without children with disabilities".[804] These authors do not deny that families are often distressed upon first learning that their child has a disability. And they acknowledge that families with children who evince significantly challenging behaviour, experience more disruption than do other families. On average, however, families that include disabled children fare no better or worse than other families. Another study by Jo Ann Blier Blaymore et al. showed that pediatricians tended to overestimate the negative effects of a certain

---

802 Erik Parens and Adrienne Asch, "The Disability Rights Critique of Prenatal Genetic Testing. Reflections and Recommendations", *The Hastings Center Report*, 1999, 29, 5, pp. S1-S22.
803 Ibid., p. S15.
804 Philip M. Ferguson, Alan Gartner and Dorothy K. Lipsky, "The Experience of Disability in Families: A Synthesis of Research and Parent Narratives", in: Erik Parens and Adrienne Asch, *Prenatal Genetic Testing*, Garrison, New York, 2000, e-book, location 1177.

disability on a child in comparison to the child's parents. They also tended to underestimate the positive effects of the disability on the family.[805]

It is therefore fundamental to recognise that questions of identity and of personal well-being do not depend on just one part of the whole person, but indeed on the person as a whole. Otherwise, injustice towards persons with disabilities will continue to lurk. Respect for the equality of persons is arguably one of the most substantive values available to us. As Ricoeur concludes: "Equality provides to the self another who is an *each*...The sense of justice presupposes solicitude, to the extent that it holds persons to be irreplaceable. Justice in turn adds to solicitude, to the extent that the field of application of equality is all of humanity."[806]

5.1.2 Rational choice theory on fertility

In our postmodern era, Ricoeur's phenomenology is just one, albeit widely respected philosophical current among other. Similarly, in the human sciences there are several different approaches to reproductive decision-making processes. According to the Dutch sociologist Mark Levels, the dominant theory among sociologists and demographers to describe and explain differences in reproductive decisions among women is the rational choice theory on fertility.[807] This theory presupposes that reproductive decision-making involves rational deliberations about costs and benefits. Defenders of the theory assume that people aim to maximise their welfare as they conceive it by comparing costs and benefits. Further, adherents of this theory recognise the importance of altruism within families. They presuppose that "many parents are altruistic toward children in the sense that the utility of parents depends positively on the utility of their children".[808]

Some adherents of the rational choice theory try to explain differences in reproductive decisions of various groups of women (for example women of different educational levels or religious and non-religious women) by

---

805 J.A. Blier Blaymore, J. Liebling, Y. Morales and M. Carlucci, "Parents' and Pediatricians' Views of Individuals with Meningomyelocile", *Clinical Pediatrics*, 1996, 35, 3, pp. 113-117.
806 Ricoeur, P., 1992, op. cit., p. 202.
807 This originally economic theory has been developed by H. Leibenstein in 1957 and advanced by G.S. Becker and others. Cf. Levels, M., op. cit., pp. 91-92.
808 G.S. Becker and R.J. Barro, "A Reformulation of the Economic Theory of Fertility", *The Quarterly Journal of Economics*, 1988, 103, 1, pp. 1-25, here p. 3.

comparing economic costs, opportunity (or career) costs, moral and social costs.[809] But these costs are incomparable. We cannot oversee the social costs of abortion because of the unknown qualities of the child and the unknown benefits for the people who would have received the child into their families, into their circle of friends, into the society as a whole, if the child had been born. Likewise, it is impossible to express the moral costs of abortion in a similar unit as economic costs or opportunity costs.

Choosing abortion based on a weighing of costs and benefits has been regarded by Germain Grisez as a form of utilitarianism.[810] According to utilitarianism the moral good or evil of human acts is determined by the results of the acts. For the utilitarian the good includes every sort of enjoyment, desirable experience and implies a minimum of pain, anguish or boredom. With this definition, it is easy to see that abortion would be justified in a number of cases, since not always the greatest utility is reached with the birth of a baby.

Grisez calls utilitarianism a secular ethic in the sense that it has developed as a "new morality" in a conscious reaction to traditional religious ethics. But to consider utilitarianism as the dominant secular ethic in Western society, in particular as regards reproductive decisions, would be too simple. This would for instance imply that modern women and men choosing an abortion only look at whatever will give the greatest profit for themselves and maybe for their family. Maybe some people do choose in this way, if the choice for an abortion is an escape from facing the real problems in their lifestyle or in their relationship and if possible solutions related to the upbringing of their child are not seriously looked at. In these cases, the decision to abort is not in accordance with the law, because the legislation both in the U.K. and the Netherlands requires a situation of urgency. But in many situations the idea of an 'easy way-out' does not do justice to the real convictions of those who are faced with an unintended pregnancy. In reality many women who consider abortion, often together with their partner, do seriously weigh all the relevant factors in their lives, before taking a decision.

---

809 For example Mark Levels states that "religious women face more moral and social costs for not having children, for practicing contraception and, most importantly, for having an abortion than non-religious women". In: Levels, M., op. cit., p. 105.
810 Grisez, G., 1970, op. cit., pp. 287-307 and G. Grisez, *The Way of the Lord Jesus, Vol. II, Living a Christian Life*, Quincy, Ill., 1993, p. 490.

5.1.3 Consequentialism and abortion

The main problem with this form of so-called rational decision-making is that it must be considered as a form of consequentialism.[811] The essential problem of consequentialist reasoning is the impossibility of invoking consequences in the evaluation of the act. In the case of procured abortion, one never knows what the life of the child would be like if it were to be born. One can only say with certainty that by being aborted, the embryo will be deprived of his or her earthly life.

Before one chooses to eliminate the human life, one has only a remote experience of its value, its uniqueness. Maybe the parents have seen the child moving on the ultrasound images, or maybe the mother has felt the child in her womb. But the child's personality will never be known. Therefore, it is impossible to make a proper judgement, as if the advantages of the choice to abort were in proportion to the disadvantages, since the seeming advantages of abortion are in reality largely unknown. And even if the abortion would bring a certain 'good' to the life of the woman and her partner, this good would be incommensurable to the good that giving birth would bring, simply because the different forms of goods, or of the 'lesser evil', are objectively incommensurable. Above that, the number of possible alternative choices which one could make, are in fact unlimited, which is another reason for the impossibility of calculating consequences. Because of the universal scope of this principle of practical reasonableness, John Finnis has integrated the problem of consequentialism in his natural law theory.[812]

5.1.4 The future of value argument

For Don Marquis, the certainty that with the act of abortion a foetus is deprived of his or her further life as a human being has been the starting point for an account of the immorality of the act.[813] His argument, which is also called the 'future of value account', is that abortion deprives the foetus of a future like ours, which is potentially valuable. He builds up this argument by showing why killing an adult human being is *prima facie*

---

811 Cf. Finnis, J., op. cit., pp. 115, 117 and 124-125.
812 Ibid.
813 Don Marquis, "Why abortion is immoral", *Journal of Philosophy*, 1989, 86, 4, pp. 183-202.

seriously wrong:

> What primarily makes killing wrong is ... its effect on the victim. . . The loss of one's life deprives one of all the experiences, activities, projects, and enjoyments that would otherwise have constituted one's future. Therefore, killing someone is wrong, primarily because the killing inflicts (one of) the greatest possible losses on the victim.[814]

Marquis subsequently argues that killing a foetus is in this sense identical to killing an adult:

> The future of a standard foetus includes a set of experiences, projects, activities, and such which are identical with the futures of adult human beings and are identical with the future of young children. Since the reason that is sufficient to explain why it is wrong to kill human beings after the time of birth is a reason that also applies to foetuses, it follows that abortion is prima facie seriously morally wrong.[815]

Various authors have made objections against the future of value account. David Boonin states that the fact that a preconscious foetus has the *capacity* to desire a future like ours does not suffice to defend an account of the moral wrongness of killing the foetus.[816] However, he overlooks the fact that Marquis is not only speaking of a capacity to desire a future like ours, but of *having* a future like ours in the first place. This is illustrated by Pedro Galvão, who shows that Boonin in his attempt to reject the future of value account has misrepresented Marquis' view.[817] In a way similar to Boonin, Galvão points out two versions of the future of value account, principle A (Marquis' own view) and principle B (Boonin's interpretation of Marquis' view):

A) If an individual P has a future like ours, then P has a right to life

and

B) If an individual P has a future like ours (F) and if either P now desires that F be preserved, or P will later desire to continue having the experiences contained in F (if P is not killed), then P has a right to life.

---

814 Ibid., p. 189.
815 Ibid, p. 192.
816 David Boonin, *A Defense of Abortion*. Cambridge, 2003, p. 83.
817 Pedro Galvão, "Boonin on the future-like-ours argument against abortion", *Bioethics*, 2007, 21 (6), pp. 324-328.

Galvão then argues that by the standards of parsimony principle A is superior to principle B. However, Boonin completely focuses on the second part of principle B, by treating the foetal capacity to desire a future like ours and by concluding that having this capacity is insufficient for an account of the wrongness of killing. He omits the fact that, generally speaking, a foetus not only has this capacity, but already *possesses a future like ours*, if it is not killed. Therefore, his argument falls short.

In another attempt to reject Marquis' account, Carson Strong states that "the foetus is not deprived of *everything* that the adult is deprived of in being killed. Specifically, a foetus is not deprived of the continuation of its plans and projects. There is no interruption of ongoing plans when a foetus is killed."[818] Underlying Strong's point of view is the idea that the criterion for personhood is the possession of self-consciousness. Similarly, other authors have argued that the wrongness of killing is based on respect for the autonomous and authoritative determination of the person's will not to be killed.[819]

A major problem with this type of thinking is that it does not offer an explanation for the wrongness of killing infants and young children, because they too are not deprived of the continuation of plans and projects when they are killed. Since we believe that the killing of infants and young children is seriously wrong, the 'personhood objection' as brought forward by Strong and others, is a highly insufficient argument against the 'future of value account'.[820] The 'future of value account' does explain the wrongness of killing infants and young children, just as it seeks to explain in a secular way the wrongness of the deliberate killing of human embryos.[821]

---

[818] Carson Strong, "A critique of 'the best secular argument against abortion'", *Journal of Medical Ethics*, 2008, 34, pp. 727-731, here p. 730.

[819] Cf. McMahan, J., 2002, op. cit., p. 257, where he quotes Warren Quinn, "Abortion: Identity and Loss", *Philosophy and Public Affairs*, 1984, 13, pp. 24-54, here p. 49.

[820] Cf. Marquis, D., 1989, op. cit., p. 192.

[821] Marquis has nuanced his 1989 essay, explicating that a 'future-like-ours' entails a typical human's future and therefore does not entail a future of human-like animals, although he admits that animals do have futures of value. In: Don Marquis, "Strong's objections to the future of value account", *Journal of Medical Ethics*, 2011, 37, pp. 384-388.

5.1.5 A bioethical view on human dignity

Closely related to the future of value argument is the plea for recognition of human dignity. In the public discussion about questions of modern medicine and biology, the dignity of human beings plays an important, perhaps even central role.[822] The constitutions of many Western countries have adopted the concept of human dignity and not infrequently give it the status of being the highest principle of law. In many influential documents on the level of international and supranational relations, human dignity occupies a core position.[823]

Still, the concept of 'human dignity' is controversial, as bioethicist Markus Rothhaar clearly indicates: "This overwhelming presence of human dignity in public space stands in marked contrast to the reserve, even the scepticism of experts in matters of applied ethics, including medical ethics."[824]

This scepticism has to do with the problem of defining what the concept of human dignity entails. While acknowledging this definition problem, John Finnis remarks that the notion of human dignity has to do with the recognition of the literally immeasurable value of human personality in each of its basic aspects.[825] Still, the concept of human dignity has an important place in Finnis' natural law theory. Within natural law theory, casuistry comes about in terms of 'direct' choices or intentions, as against 'indirect' effects, as will be shown further on in this chapter, by the application of the principle of double effect with regard to procured abortion.[826] Such judgments are arrived at by a steady determination to respect human good in one's own existence, rather than by trading off that good against some vision of future 'net best consequences'.[827]

The immeasurability of human personality does not imply that the concept of human dignity cannot be described at all. In order to provide greater clarity regarding the significance of the concept of human dignity within the field of bioethics, Daniel Sulmasy distinguishes three different

---

822 Markus Rothhaar, "Human dignity and human rights in bioethics: the Kantian approach", *Medical Health Care and Philosophy*, 2010, 13, pp. 251-257.
823 Cf. part 4.2.
824 Rothhaar, M., op. cit., p. 251.
825 Finnis, J., op. cit., p. 225.
826 Cf. part 5.1.8.
827 Cf. part 5.1.3; Finnis, J., op. cit., p. 226.

aspects of human dignity:

1) attributed dignity: the worth or value that human beings confer upon others by acts of attribution. It is even possible to attribute worth or value upon oneself using the word dignity.

2) intrinsic dignity: the value that human beings have simply by virtue of the fact that they are human beings. This sense of dignity is therefore prior to human attribution.

3) inflorescent dignity: the value of a process that is conducive to human excellence or the value of a state of affairs by which an individual expresses human excellence.[828]

This third sense of dignity is used to refer to a state of virtue—a state of affairs in which a human being habitually acts in ways that expresses the intrinsic value of the human being.[829]

Sulmasy then argues that intrinsic dignity is foundational from a moral point of view.[830] In doing so, he uses an axiological argument, based on classical theories of value, which hold that whatever is intrinsically good is worthy of being valued in itself.[831] He concludes that "'Intrinsic dignity' is just the name we give to the special type of intrinsic value that belongs to members of natural kinds that have kind-specific *capacities* for language, rationality, love, free will, moral agency, creativity, aesthetic sensibility, and an ability to grasp the finite and the infinite."[832]

From this notion of intrinsic dignity, various moral norms can be

---

[828] Daniel P. Sulmasy O.F.M., "Dignity and Bioethics: History, Theory and Selected Applications", in: President's Council on Bioethics, *Human Dignity and Bioethics. Essays Commissioned by the President's Council on Bioethics*. Washington D.C., 2008, pp. 469-501.

[829] Ibid., p. 473. Carlo Leget comments on this third meaning of dignity that it can be considered as a further refinement of the intrinsic version of dignity and that it cannot stand on its own. He offers as third version of dignity "something that people experience of themselves". However, I think that Leget's third version of dignity is better to be considered as attributed dignity, in the sense of the value people attribute to their own quality of life. Cf. Carlo Leget, "Analyzing dignity: a perspective from the ethics of care", *Medical Health Care and Philosophy*, published online 12 July 2012.

[830] Sulmasy O.F.M., D.P., op. cit., pp. 474-478.

[831] Sulmasy's theory of intrinsic value follows Holmes Rolston III's *Environmental Ethics* (Philadelphia: Temple University Press, 1988), who aligns with the views of Kant, Brentano, Broad, Ross, and others, that whatever is intrinsically good is worthy of being valued in itself. Cf. Sulmasy O.F.M., D.P., op. cit., p. 500.

[832] Ibid., p. 475, italics are mine.

derived, also with regard to the status of the embryo. The key-word here is capacity. The intrinsic value of human kind is, according to Sulmasy, not based on the active expression by an individual of any one (or even several) of the particular characteristics that confer intrinsic dignity on human kind as a whole.[833] Infants, severely mentally ill persons or comatose persons lack one or more of the above mentioned capacities, but obviously they share in human dignity.

Similarly, embryos, being a member of the human natural kind, will normally develop into human beings with the capacities for language, rationality, love, etc., even though these capacities are not yet actively expressed. Sulmasy therefore concludes that, "if a human embryo is a member of the human natural kind, then it has all the intrinsic dignity of the human natural kind".[834] Of course, this conclusion has far reaching implications for the moral dilemma of abortion.

5.1.6 Contemporary liberal philosophy and abortion: John Rawls

Within postmodern society, Sulmasy's conclusion has not reached a consensus. On the contrary, individual freedom of choice is often valued more than communal solutions for individual problems. Among contemporary philosophers the view can be found that the problem of abortion has to do with a weighing of different values, according to one's personal convictions. One of the representatives of liberal philosophy, John Rawls, has put forward his vision of political liberalism, with implications for the abortion debate.

John Rawls has developed the idea of a well-ordered society, in which citizens are able to live as free and equal persons and which is effectively regulated by a public political conception of justice.[835] He calls his idea of justice as fairness a "highly idealized concept" which is "limited to the domain of the political and its values", because he presumes the postmodern society as essentially pluralistic, with no reasonable religious,

---

833 Ibid., p. 490.
834 Ibid., p. 491.
835 John Rawls, *Political Liberalism*. New York, 1993, here p. 35.

philosophical or moral doctrine affirmed by all citizens.[836] This limitation influences his ethical point of view regarding abortion. Rawls' political conception of justice has as subject the main political, social and economic institutions. These form the basic structure of society. Essential for the subject of abortion is Rawls' assumption that the members of society "enter it only by birth and leave it only by death".[837] His political conception of justice follows from this assumption about personhood. According to Rawls, "each person has an equal claim to a fully adequate scheme of equal basic rights and liberties". Further, he holds as a principle of justice that "social and economic inequalities are to be to the greatest benefit of the least advantaged members of society".[838]

In theory, these two principles of justice could be applied to human embryos. It could be argued in particular that human embryos of parents who decide to have an abortion are among the least advantaged members of society. But with his conception of a person, Rawls has excluded the application of these two principles of justice to unborn human life.

When Rawls discusses the issue of abortion, he presumes a reasonable balance between the three following political values: the due respect for human life, the ordered reproduction of political society over time, including the family in some form, and finally the equality of women as equal citizens.[839] He then states, without discussing the question in general, that during the first trimester of pregnancy, the political value of equality of women overrides the other two values. Beyond this term, he presumes that a reasonable balance may allow her such a right in certain circumstances.

In fact, Rawls argues that he deliberately avoids using a metaphysical concept of the person because he assumes that there is no accepted understanding of what a metaphysical doctrine is.[840] For the sake of his political conception of justice, he puts people's comprehensive doctrines

---

[836] Ibid., pp. 35-38. Rawls admits that among other matters, the justice of and in the family is omitted in his conception of justice as fairness. Still, he believes, without treating this aspect of justice, that "the alleged difficulties in discussing problems of gender and the family can be overcome". Ibid, p. XXIX of the Introduction.
[837] Ibid., pp. 11-12.
[838] Ibid., pp. 5-6.
[839] Ibid., p. 243fn.
[840] Ibid., p. 29fn.

behind a "veil of ignorance", thus stressing their political autonomy.[841] Here, we have to question his argumentation. He presumes that in his presentation of justice as fairness and in the underlying ideas and conceptions, no particular metaphysical doctrine about the nature of persons, distinctive and opposed to other metaphysical doctrines, appears among its premises, or seems required by its argument.[842] But, as has been pointed out above, by presuming that human personhood starts at birth, Rawls is implicitly making use of a metaphysical concept of the human person which denies the continuity of human existence and development before and after birth. Therefore, these metaphysical presuppositions and the concept of the human person have to be accounted for in the abortion debate, because decisions are at stake about life or death of human beings.[843]

More in general, John Finnis states that for the sake of a 'democratic' impartiality, Rawls does not attribute intrinsic value to basic forms of good as truth, play, art of friendship, without giving a satisfactory reason for such a radical emaciation of the human good.[844]

Rawls further states that "if metaphysical presuppositions are involved, perhaps they are so general that they would not distinguish between the metaphysical views – Cartesian, Leibnizian or Kantian; realist, idealist or materialist – with which philosophy has traditionally been concerned. In this case they would not appear to be relevant for the structure and content of a political conception of justice one way or the other."[845]

Against this view it needs to be brought in that several philosophers of the previous century have pointed out the shortcomings of the metaphysical presuppositions of the Enlightenment thinkers. Emmanuel Levinas for instance has criticised the idealistic conception of the subject for stressing too much the rational 'I' and by doing so neglecting 'You', both as alterity

---

841 Ibid., pp. 24-25.
842 Ibid., p. 29fn.
843 Cf. Wulf, C.M., 2013 (b), op. cit., pp. 241-242.
844 Finnis, J., op. cit., p. 106.
845 Ibid.

(the other) and as transcendence (the Other).[846] The monadic assumption (the pure I) of the idealist thinking is at the origin of a philosophy in which the I is in danger of break off communication, wanting to claim the other for oneself.[847]

Charles Taylor, in his analysis of the ethics of authenticity, argues that the more self-centred and 'narcissistic' modes of contemporary culture are inadequate. To put it more concretely, modes that opt for self-fulfilment without regard to the demands of our ties with others, destroy the conditions for realizing authenticity itself.[848] Among the arguments he mentions, there is one of particular interest for the abortion debate. This has to do with the question of identity. Our identities are formed in dialogue with others. This dialogue takes place continuously in a partly overt and partly internalised way. So, identity is not something which is fixed at a certain point in time. Rather, men and women form identities as persons in relationships which are more than just instrumental.[849] Therefore, the quality of this dialogue with others will determine our present and future identity. For instance, men might show panic, anger or other forms of impulsive or even irresponsible behaviour after the discovery of an unintended pregnancy.[850] These reactions can, if they are not properly addressed, make a woman decide for an abortion which she might not have chosen if her partner had reacted differently. Or, on the contrary, a woman might already have made up her mind in favour of an abortion, without having consulted her partner. In other cases, both man and woman might initially agree about having an abortion. The point is here that both their future identities depend heavily on the outcome of their dialogue, on their listening to the opinions of significant others, as well as on the values they have internalised as their own. It may require a conversion of heart to open oneself to see the value of the new life which has just begun.

---

846 "A turning on the basis of the face of the other, in which, at the very heart of the phenomenon, in its very light, a surplus of significance is signified that could be designated as glory." In: Emmanuel Levinas, *Alterity & transcendence*. Translated into English by Michael B. Smith, New York, 1999, pp. 26-27; See also Wulf, C.M., 2010, op. cit., pp. 51-53.
847 Cf. Wulf, C.M., 2010, op. cit., p. 52.
848 Taylor, Ch., 1992, op. cit., p. 35.
849 Ibid., pp. 52-53.
850 Cf. part 3.3.2.3.

The renewed attention given to the other/Other in contemporary philosophy has ethical consequences which are not taken into consideration by Rawls, especially with regard to a revaluation of parenthood. Birth can be understood in terms of a gift which is given by the Other and through which an other is given in responsibility, promise and forgiveness.[851] In this sense, Lisa Guenther has applied Lévinas's thought by interpreting birth as "an ethical gift", a gift that "already implicates me in a radical responsibility for Others".[852] This interpretation not only has implications for women, but also for men, because birth is not only a moment in time, but it implies a continuous (re)creation of the conditions that allow a child to live and flourish.[853]

It has been pointed out that Rawls deliberately avoids using a metaphysical concept of the human person. Finnis, Lévinas, Guenther and Taylor have shown that metaphysical views on the human person, which according to Rawls are irrelevant for a political conception of justice, also have implications for the ethical view on unborn human life.

5.1.7 The principle of respect for every basic value in every act

Robert Spaemann states that personhood does not begin at some point during foetal development, but already at the completion of fertilisation. With this conclusion it becomes clearer to see the intrinsic moral problem of procured abortion. The intrinsic dignity of the foetus, both in the here and now and in the future has already been considered with the help of the potentiality argument and the future of value argument.[854] Other moral philosophers, such as Germain Grisez and John Finnis have followed a

---

851 Cf. Lisa Guenther, *The Gift of the Other: Lévinas and the Politics of Reproduction*. New York, 2006, pp. 46-41.
852 Ibid. p. 4.
853 I leave aside here the political implications of a politics of maternity, which Silvia Benso mentions, commenting on Guenther's book. While Guenther stresses the right to reproductive choices, Benso pleads for stimulating parental rights in order to establish equality between the sexes, such as the right to paid maternity leave, parental leave to care for either young or sick children, the right to flexible work schedule, the right to affordable, quality child care, etc. Cf. Silvia Benso, "The Gift of the Other: Levinas and the Politics of Reproduction. Book review", *Dialogue*, 2007, 46, 2, pp. 409-411, here 411.
854 Cf. parts 4.3.2.1 and 5.1.4.

different line of thinking, but arrive at the same conclusion.[855]

In order to come to a revaluation of abortion, Grisez presents a list of basic human goods, among which life itself is the first, including health and safety.[856] He distinguishes between four reflective or existential goods and three non-reflective or substantive goods. As existential goods he mentions self-integration; practical reasonableness or authenticity; justice and friendship; religion or holiness. Substantive goods are: life and health; knowledge of truth; activities of skilful work and of play.[857]

Finnis, while admitting that his account of basic forms of human good is substantially similar to Grisez's list, stresses that there is no objective hierarchy amongst each of the basic goods.[858] As a principle of practical reasonableness, he states that "one should not choose to do any act which of itself does nothing but damage or impede a realization or participation of any one or more of the basic forms of good".[859] In a positive way, this principle implies respect for every basic value or good in every act. According to Finnis, this principle of practical reasonableness must be considered a principle of natural law.[860]

5.1.8 The principle of acts with double effect in relation to abortion

In the abortion debate, the argument is often been raised that life would only be worth living when certain quality standards are met. This presumption needs further consideration as regards the often painful dilemmas future parents are facing after the diagnosis of a handicapped child.[861]

Grisez concludes that there are only a few exceptions in which the principle of proportionality could be applied in decisions favouring abortion. These are situations in which the principle of acts with double

---

855 Grisez, G., 1970, op. cit., pp. 307-321; Finnis, J., op. cit., pp. 81-99 and pp. 118-124.
856 Grisez, G., 1970, op. cit., pp. 312-313.
857 Grisez, G., 1983, op. cit., pp. 121-125
858 Finnis, J., op. cit., pp. 92-95 and p. 98.
859 Ibid., p. 118.
860 Ibid., pp. 118-125; cf. part 5.1.3. Finnis' natural law theory has been described as "remarkably and distinctively modern, post-Kantian in its individualistic stress on obligation as selfundertaken commitment." In: Haakonssen, K., op. cit., p. 1210.
861 Cf. parts 4.5 and 4.6.

effect is applied.⁸⁶² In some cases the foetus' death may be accepted in order to save the mother. The four conditions of the principle of double effect are fulfilled simultaneously when: 1) some pathology threatens the lives of both a pregnant woman and her child; 2) it is not safe to wait or waiting surely will result in the death of both; 3) there is no way to save the child and 4) an operation that can save the mother's life will result in the child's death. These types of cases, to be diagnosed by the medical profession, are for example involving ectopic pregnancy (implantation of the embryo outside the uterus)⁸⁶³ or the removal of a cancerous gravid uterus. In these exceptions the killing is indirect in order to combat the pathology and therefore unintentional. These abortions "have both the good effect of protecting human life and the bad effect of destroying it."⁸⁶⁴

When life itself is a basic form of human good, the ethical conclusion which follows and which I share, is that in all other cases, apart from the above mentioned exceptions, ways must be sought to avoid an abortion. It's important to stress here that every time one speaks of a decision in favour of procured abortion, it has to be taken into account that such a decision is not only the woman's responsibility, but it always involves other persons taking part in the decision, the male begetter of the child in the first place, their families, close friends and especially the doctor who is executing the abortion and his staff members who are involved in the decision making process. And finally, society in general is also directly involved, in particular those members of society who carry political responsibility, because attractive alternatives to abortion should be offered.

5.2 The medicalization of pregnancy: prenatal diagnosis, foetal treatment and perinatal palliative care

The legal and political discourse on abortion is characterised by a process of medicalization.⁸⁶⁵ Not only the problem of abortion has been medicalised, but pregnancy as such. This latter development could be seen

---

862 Cf. part 1.1.2.
863 It is estimated that in the U.K. around 1 in 90 pregnancies develops into an ectopic pregnancy. This is around 11,000 pregnancies a year, cf. NHS, "Ectopic pregnancy", on their website, accessed 10 December 2015.
864 Grisez, G. 1993, op. cit., p. 502.
865 Cf. part 1.6.

for instance in the growing influence of prenatal diagnosis, especially when the difficult moral question is at stake what to do when a hereditary disease or a chromosome deviation of the embryo has been detected. In this part, the quickly developing areas of prenatal diagnosis, foetal treatment and perinatal palliative care will be sketched. The aim of this part is not to be complete, but to give an impression of the dilemmas parents can be faced with after a diagnosis of a serious disease or impairment has been detected.

Prenatal diagnosis has been developed since the seventies of the past century.[866] Since then the available techniques have been improved considerably. The possibilities to detect genetic deviations of the embryo in the early phases of pregnancy have increased. At the same time, smaller, not life threatening deviations can be discovered. The application of these techniques has become safer, although there is still a chance to disturb the pregnancy itself. For instance, if an increased risk on Down's syndrome or an inherited disease is detected, a woman can decide to undergo further testing at a centre for prenatal research in order to get more certainty. This follow-up testing can consist of a chorionic villus sampling or amniocentesis. Both tests involve a small risk of miscarriage. This occurs in three to five of every thousand women to receive testing.[867] For other anomalies, follow-up tests consist of an extensive ultrasound scan or an amniocentesis.[868] Despite the medical progress, there are still many hereditary illnesses that cannot be detected before birth.

During the 1990s, prenatal screening for Down's syndrome has become widespread in the U.K. The proportion of Health Authorities or Boards offering multiple marker serum screening for Down's syndrome to all

---

[866] Cf. V.G.H.J. Kirkels et al., *Annalen van het Thijmgenootschap*, 1991, 79, 2.
[867] Rijksinstituut voor Volksgezondheid en Milieu (RIVM, the Dutch National Institute for Public Health and the Environment), *Informatie over de screening op Downsyndroom*, brochure, Bilthoven, 2011, p. 15. Earlier research in the U.K. pointed at a risk of 0.9% for both amniocentesis and chorionic villus sampling. Cf. R.E. Gilbert, C. Augood, R. Gupta, A.E. Ades, S. Logan, M. Sculpher and J.H.P. van der Meulen, "Screening for Down's syndrome: effects, safety, and cost effectiveness of first and second trimester strategies", *BMJ*, 2001, 323, pp. 1-6.
[868] Mohangoo, A.D. and Buitendijk, S.E., op. cit.

pregnant women increased from 56% in 1994 to 69% in 1998.[869] After the introduction of multiple marker serum screening, the percentage of women receiving prenatal diagnosis of Down's syndrome in England and Wales remained relatively constant at approximately 70% in older women, but increased in younger women.[870]

Before 2007, in the Netherlands there were some commonly accepted indications to apply prenatal diagnosis. These indications were:

- a high-risk of a chromosome deviation, when the mother is older than 36 years, when there was an earlier birth of a child with a non-hereditary chromosome deviation, or when one of the parents carries a hereditary chromosome deviation.

- a high-risk of other hereditary diseases or a deformation of one or more parts of the body, found after biochemical research of the amniotic fluid or an echogram.

In 2007, the Dutch Government introduced the 20 weeks ultrasound scan (in Dutch: Structureel Echoscopisch Onderzoek, SEO), which is offered to all pregnant women and reimbursed by all health insurance companies. Before this introduction, ca. 90% of the pregnant women already received such an ultrasound scan, with or without medical indication.[871] The SEO has as objective to assess the foetus for physical defects. Examples of anomalies which can be detected with the SEO are Down's syndrome, spina bifida (Latin for: split spine) and anencephaly[872]. The SEO consists of two parts: a first trimester screening on Down's syndrome and a 20 week ultrasound scan.

A few years before the introduction of SEO, Matthijs van den Berg et al. did research among 962 Dutch women on informed decision making in the

---

[869] N.J. Wald, W.J. Huttly and C.F. Hennessy, "Down's syndrome screening in the UK in 1998", in: *The Lancet*, 1999, 354, p. 1264.

[870] E. de Souza, E. Alberman and J.K. Morris, "Down's syndrome: screening and antenatal diagnosis regionally in England and Wales 1989-2008", *Journal of Medical Screening*, 2010, 17, 4, pp. 170-175.

[871] D. Oepkes and J. Wieringa, "Recht op prenatale kennis", *Medisch contact*, 2008, 63, 31-32, pp. 1296-1298.

[872] Anencephaly is a serious birth defect in which a baby is born without parts of the brain and skull.

context of prenatal screening.[873] They state that informed decision making in this context needs to meet the following three criteria: 1) the choice of accepting prenatal screening versus declining it must be based on knowledge about characteristics of the tested disorder(s), the screening test itself and the meaning of the possible test results. 2) an informed decision implies an evaluation of the alternatives, thinking about the consequences, weighing up the pros and cons. 3) The informed decision needs to be consistent with the decision maker's values.[874]

The results of their inquiry shows that 49% of the women could be classified as not having made an informed decision: 16% due to insufficient knowledge, 21% due to lack of deliberation and 12% due to value-inconsistency.[875] These findings are in accordance with many other international studies.[876]

Josephine Green et al. show that in relation to informed decision making about prenatal screening, not only the knowledge of the woman, but also of her partner is often insufficient.[877] For example, as regards carrier screening for the chronic lung disease cystic fibrosis, unsatisfactory levels of understanding were revealed. They found out that many of the men were reliant on their partners for information. Since the women themselves were often poorly informed, low levels of understanding in men were – with hindsight – only to be expected.

What has not been said so far, is that because of the increased usage of prenatal diagnosis, parents are confronted with new and extremely difficult questions about the continuation or termination of the pregnancy, especially when a serious impairment has been detected: questions regarding the expected quality of life of their child, regarding the possibilities to raise the

---

873 Matthijs van den Berg, Daniëlle R.M. Timmermans, Leo P. ten Kate, John M.G. Vugt and Gerrit van der Wal, "Informed decision making in the context of prenatal screening", *Patient Education and Counseling*, 2006, 63, pp. 110-117.
874 Ibid., pp. 112-113.
875 Ibid., p. 113.
876 Cf. J.M. Green, J. Hewison, H.L. Bekker, L.D. Bryant and H.S. Cuckle, "Psycho-social aspects of genetic screening of pregnant women and newborns: a systematic review", *Health Technology Assessment*, 2004, 8, pp. 1-124.
877 Ibid., p. 77.

child themselves or to make use of the available professional help.[873]

It has been shown that the percentages of British and Dutch parents who decide for an abortion after the detection of the Down's syndrome, are between 80 and 95%.[879] There is no cure for Down's syndrome, but there are a number of treatments such as physiotherapy, speech therapy or occupational therapy, that can help someone with the condition to lead a healthy, active and more independent life.[880]

As regards abortion after the diagnosis of spina bifida, the figures are similar to those for Down's syndrome, circa 80% in the Netherlands.[881] At the same time, the possibilities of prenatal and neonatal treatment of this and certain other anomalies have quickly expanded, especially since the 1990s and are even more promising for the future.[882] For instance, Alex Eggink reports that for a selected number of patients with spina bifida, prenatal closure of the defect resulted in a better neurological outcome than postnatal surgical repair. Foetal treatment of spina bifida takes place around the 26th week of pregnancy. However, prenatal surgery of spina bifida is associated with an increased risk of preterm birth and obstetric complications.[883]

So far, most treatments of spina bifida take place after birth. The consequences of spina bifida are diverse, such as mobility problems in various degrees, incontinence and a bigger chance of a mental retardation. On the other hand, many children with spina bifida have normal intellectual

---

878 In parts 7.3 and 7.4 the possibilities of counselling and pastoral care in general and after prenatal diagnosis will be dealt with.
879 Cf. parts 1.4.1.4 and 1.4.2.
880 Cf. NHS, "Living with Down Syndrome" on their website, accessed 20 October 2015.
881 Klazien Bron and Eelco Kruidenier, *20-weken echo en spina bifida*. Utrecht, 2011, p. 70.
882 On foetal and neonatal treatment, see for instance: D.J. Sahn and G. Mack, "Fetal cardiology/past and future", in: Linsey Allan, Lisa Hornberger and Gurleen Sharland, *Textbook of Fetal Cardiology*, London, 2000, pp. 1-15; Ivan Rebeyka, "Fetal cardiac surgery", in: Ibid., pp. 525-533. Alan Flake gives examples of disorders such as anaemia, pulmonary immaturity, biochemical defects, cardiac arrhythmias and endocrine deficiencies which are amenable to prenatal therapy. Cf. Alan W. Flake, "Fetal Therapy. Medical and Surgical Approaches", in: Robert K. Creasy, Robert Resnik and Jay Iams (eds.), *Maternal-fetal Medicine. Principles and Practice*. Fifth Edition, Philadelphia, Pennsylvania 2004, pp. 483-494, here p. 484.
883 Alex J. Eggink, "Foetale therapie voor spina bifida", *Nederlands Tijdschrift voor Geneeskunde*, 2012, 156: A4924. Eggink points at the possibility for a referral to the Gasthuisberg Hospital in Leuven (Belgium), specialised in foetal therapy.

capabilities and manage to follow regular education.[884]

Sometimes, after the diagnosis of a lethal foetal abnormality, perinatal palliative care could be offered as an alternative to termination of pregnancy. After 22 weeks, termination of pregnancy usually includes feticide. Research to the alternative of perinatal palliative care for foetuses with a lethal anomaly is scarce, but promising.[885] For instance, Andrew Breeze et al. have investigated 20 diagnoses of lethal foetal abnormalities after 18 weeks gestation in Addenbrooke's Hospital in Cambridge, U.K.[886] The abnormalities included 12 renal tract abnormalities, 3 skeletal dysplasias and 5 trisomy's. 40% of parents chose to continue the pregnancy and pursue perinatal palliative care, including postnatal counselling. This and other research shows that most babies with lethal abnormality were born alive when the parents continued the pregnancy.[887] Perinatal palliative care avoids the psychological effect of abortion on parents and clinicians.[888] Byron Calhoun et al. notice that parental response to the perinatal hospice in which palliative care had been offered, was "overwhelmingly positive".[889]

From this part, it is concluded that often by ways of prenatal diagnosis, also a prenatal selection takes place, in the sense that parents give their approval or disapproval of the physical condition of the foetus. This development has been be associated with eugenics.[890] Among others, Jürgen Habermas uses the term liberal eugenics, by which he means a practice that entrusts decisions about any interventions into the genome of a foetus

---

[884] Bron, K. and Kruidenier, E., op cit., p. 74.
[885] Charlotte Wool, "Systematic Review of the Literature. Parental Outcomes After Diagnosis of Fetal Anomaly", *Advances in Neonatal Care*, 2011, 11, 3, pp. 182-192.
[886] A.C.G. Breeze, C.C. Lees, A. Kumar, H.H. Missfelder-Lobos and E.M. Murdoch, "Palliative care for prenatally diagnosed lethal fetal abnormality", *Archives of Disease in Childhood. Fetal and Neonatal edition*, 2007, 92, pp. F56-F58.
[887] Ibid., p. F58; cf. Byron C. Calhoun, Peter Napolitano, Melissa Terry, Carie Bussey and Nathan J. Hoeldtke, "Perinatal hospice. Comprehensive Care for the Family of the Fetus with a Lethal Condition", *Journal of Reproductive Medicine*, May 2003, pp. 343-348; Michelle D'Almeida, Roderick F. Hume, Anthony Lathrop, Adaku Njoku and Byron C. Calhoun, "Perinatal Hospice: Family-Centered Care of the Fetus with a Lethal Condition", *Journal of American Physicians and Surgeons*, 2006, 11, 2, pp. 52-55.
[888] Breeze, A.C.G. et al., op cit., p. F56.
[889] Calhoun, B.C. et al., op. cit., pp. 343-348, cf. Wool, Ch., op. cit, p. 189.
[890] Beers, B.C. van, op cit., pp. 350-351.

to the discretion of the parents.⁸⁹¹ Reflecting on the juridical and ethical consequences of the progress in biology and biotechnology, Habermas warns for a decay of the distinction between persons and matters, in the case of the birth of a handicapped child, which is then considered as a matter of damage.⁸⁹² Habermas notices that for instance, granting 'wrongful birth' claims to parents after an incorrect or incomplete prenatal diagnosis, could imply a denial of the child's inherent human dignity, by reducing the person and the life of the child to a product, or to a matter with a certain price.⁸⁹³

5.3 Parental dilemmas after a diagnosis of a serious impairment of the foetus

Earlier, Don Marquis' future of value argument for the immorality of procured abortion was dealt with.⁸⁹⁴ Against this argument, Carson Strong states that the future of value account could not be applied in the case of terminally ill patients or in the case of severely cognitively impaired patients, because they too would not have a "future like ours".⁸⁹⁵ As regards terminally ill patients, Marquis argues that if their lives contain some pleasures, they have futures of value, even though their prospective futures are much shorter than ours.⁸⁹⁶ More fundamentally, Ezio di Nucci supports Marquis' argument because, stating that terminally ill patients or severely cognitively impaired patients do not have a valuable future violates the principle of equality.⁸⁹⁷ It would mean that we would have to evaluate and rank experiences, activities, projects and enjoyments and from there make a judgment on the wrongness of killing certain patients.

Equality is about values and about rights. When it comes to the

---

891 Jürgen Habermas, *The Future of Human Nature*, translated from German by Hella Beister and William Rehg, Cambridge, U.K., 2003, p. 78; or in the original edition, Jürgen Habermas, *Die Zukunft der menschlichen Natur. Auf dem Weg zu einer liberalen Eugenik?* Frankfurt, 2005, p. 86.
892 Habermas, J., 2005, op. cit., pp. 29-30; quoted in: Beers, B.C. van, op. cit., p. 299.
893 Beers, B.C. van, op cit., p. 300.
894 Cf. part 5.1.4.
895 Strong, C., op. cit., p. 729.
896 Marquis, D., 2011, op. cit., p. 385.
897 Ezio Di Nucci, "On how to interpret the role of the future within the abortion debate", *Journal of Medical Ethics*, 2009, 35, pp. 651-652. The equality argument has also been mentioned by Paul Ricoeur, cf. part 5.1.1.

rights of foetuses, there is ambivalence in the current system of national and international rights. Within international law, there is no explicit acknowledgement of foetuses as persons. Foetuses have a right to a certain degree of legal protection (in particular after 24 weeks gestation), but as a consequence of legalizing abortion, in many cases their rights are not acknowledged. In those cases, the woman's right to an autonomous choice prevails. The question which can be raised during every decision making process after the discovery of an unintended pregnancy is: what does this autonomous choice tell us about the value of the life of *this* foetus? And what can be said in general of the value of every foetal life?

These questions become even more probing when it comes to the rights of foetuses with a serious impairment.[898] The difficulties of informed decision making of pregnant women and their partners with regard to prenatal testing have been shown in the previous part. Once the diagnosis of a serious impairment has been made, parents give both child related motivations, as well as motives of self-interest. On the one hand, they may feel committed to their unborn child, while on the other hand, they may feel shocked and bewildered at the reception of the diagnostic results and at the perspective of a decision making process which they have to go through.[899]

Marijke Korenromp analysed the decision making process of 71 Dutch women who had their pregnancy terminated after the diagnosis of Down syndrome.[900] She reports that the main child related motivations for these women to choose an abortion were: the prognosis that the child would never be able to function independently; the anomaly was considered too severe; the burden for the child was considered too heavy; worries about the care of the child after the death of the parent(s) and uncertainty about the consequences of the anomaly. The main motives of self-interest women gave were: the burden was considered too heavy for my other child(ren),

---

[898] I will not deal here with the disability critique and disability rights theory in general, since this is beyond the scope of this research. For an extensive treatment of the main issues in this area, I refer to Parens, E. and Asch, A. (Eds.), 2000, op cit.

[899] Hilmar H. Bijma, Agnes van der Heide and Hajo I.J. Wildschut, "Decision-Making after Ultrasound Diagnosis of Fetal Abnormality", *Reproductive Health Matters*, 2008, 16 (31 Supplement), pp. 82-89; Wool, Ch., op. cit., p. 183.

[900] Korenromp, M.J., op. cit., pp. 119-130.

for myself or for my relationship; I did not want a handicapped child and I thought I would be unhappy if I had this child. 21% of women reported considerable doubt.[901] Motives of self-interest may lead to feelings of guilt after the decision to abort has been made.[902]

Since the introduction of ultrasound technology some forty years ago, many more couples are faced with real dilemmas, which have become manifest in very different ways and circumstances. Some of them have witnessed how an initially wanted pregnancy turned out into a tragic and painful period of 'inescapable' questions and decisions.[903]

As regards the search for an authentic reproductive decision making process, the principal problem of consequentialist reasoning has been shown.[904] The same principle objection can be made in relation to decisions in favour of an abortion of an unborn child for whom a certain or probable handicap has been discovered during prenatal diagnosis. With all the available prenatal tests, the medical staff and parents might be inclined to focus on the child's limited physical or mental capacities, if it were to be born. But the child's character, its ability to cope with his or her physical or mental limitations, the possible moments of the child's happiness and the possible richness the child might bring to the family, are all still hidden and can only be revealed gradually. This is why consequentialist reasoning falls short after the diagnosis of a probable serious impairment of the foetus.

Still, the reality is that in many cases couples decide to have an abortion after the prenatal diagnosis of an expected serious impairment of the foetus. The large majority of couples who are faced with a diagnosis of a serious foetal impairment will very carefully gather all relevant information about the disease or handicap, the future perspectives, the possibilities of treatment and support by the social service sector, associations and the possible help of family members and peers. More than likely, they will also investigate the possibilities of raising a child with such an impairment and reflect on their own attitude towards the expected capacities and limitations

---

901 Ibid., p. 123.
902 Ibid., p. 127; cf. part 3.1.3.
903 For a personal description of the variety of dilemmas Dutch parents have been facing after prenatal diagnosis, I refer to Maarten Slagboom's *Echo. Prenataal onderzoek en keuzevrijheid*. Amsterdam, 2011.
904 In part 5.1.3.

of their future child.

When it comes to raising children with or without impairments, various ethicists have argued that initial parental commitment has to be unconditional. Children need security and recognition in order to test out what can be relied upon in their experience and what cannot. Security and recognition can be provided by parents or by other educators. But, as Alasdair MacIntyre points out, an important difference is that in the case of parents, providing security and recognition requires that they "make the object of their continuing care and their commitment *this* child, just because it is their child for whom and to whom they are uniquely responsible".[905] This commitment holds for parents of normally developing, healthy children just as much as for parents of children who suffer disfigurement or brain damage.[906] Of course parental duties can be transferred to some extent by adoption in a case of need, but there should be a serious concern to safeguard the interests of the child.

If a child of certain parents became disabled during his or her childhood years, the parents would still love the child and respect and promote his or her interests.[907] Generally, if parents are asked why they love their child, they would not say that they love him or her because of the child's particular array of traits, but rather because it is their child they love. This is why Hugh LaFollette speaks of a rigid, rather than a historical relationship between parents and their (very young) children.[908] He also mentions as another characteristic that the relationships between parents and their (very young) children are non-reciprocal. The very young child is not yet able to reciprocate the parents' care.

The same characteristics could be applied to the relationship of a man and a woman with their expected child, once they have accepted their responsibility as future parents. The unborn child is yet unable to give any affection in return for all the efforts the future parents are making during the woman's pregnancy. Therefore, the future parents' love for the unborn

---

905 Alasdair MacIntyre, *Dependent Rational Animals. Why Human Beings Need the Virtues.* London, 1999, p. 90.
906 Ibid., p. 91.
907 Cf. Helen Watt, "Preimplantation Genetic Diagnosis: Choosing the 'Good Enough' Child", *Health Care Analysis*, 2004, 12, 1, pp. 51-60, here p. 53.
908 Cf. Hugh LaFollette, *Personal Relationships: Love, Identity, and Morality.* Oxford, 1996, p. 11.

could be considered as one of the highest forms of solicitude and love, just as in the case of parental love for a very young child. Both forms of love are unreciprocated and also rigid, in the sense that the future parents love the unborn as parents love the new-born, come what may.

5.4 An ethical conclusion on procured abortion

So far, in national and international law, there is no explicit recognition of the foetus as a person. It needs to be said that this situation is unlike the foetal homicide legislation in many states in the U.S. In 2015, 38 states have foetal homicide laws, meant to prevent violent acts against pregnant women. Of these 38 states, 23 states have foetal homicide laws that apply to the earliest stages of pregnancy, although they make an exception for abortion.[909] It is remarkable that, for the purpose of criminal homicide or assaults, 6 states define foetuses as persons and 17 states use the term "unborn child".[910] However, as a consequence of legalizing abortion, foetal rights are often not acknowledged.

In part 4.1 it has been pointed out that foetal interests begin to manifest themselves long time before foetal viability. The use of sentience as a criterion for the beginning of personhood leads to situations of inequality. Therefore, I have argued that neither viability nor sentience are appropriate criteria for the recognition of personhood. Instead, the principle of double effect could serve as a valid legal tool in order to distinguish between medically necessary and other abortions.

The comparative analysis of European international law has shown that despite some recognition of the need to protect the dignity of the human embryo, this has not resulted in a recognition of the right to life in the sense of Article 2 of the European Convention of Human Rights. From a bioethical point of view, however, the inherent dignity of the human embryo should be distinguished from attributed dignity and recognised as such.

---

909 National Conference of State Legislatures, "Fetal homicide laws", on their website, accessed 23 December 2015.
910 For instance, the state of Kentucky defines an unborn child as "a member of the species *Homo sapiens* in utero from conception onward". Cf. Kentucky Revised Statutes, chapter 507A.010. The states of Alabama, Kansas, Louisiana, Ohio, South Dakota and Tennessee explicitly use the term 'person' for a human embryo or foetus at any stage of gestation in utero.

In chapter 4 it has been shown that embryonic development is unique, gradual, continuous and coordinated. No moment of substantial change could be indicated in the development of the embryo or neonate, to mark the beginning of personhood. Therefore it has been concluded that theories of belated personhood show a dualism between human beings on the one hand and human persons on the other, with far reaching ethical consequences. This dualism could be avoided when the human embryo is considered a person from the moment of conception. The biological argument which has been given for this ethical stance is that the zygote forms the beginning of a human being. A philosophical argument has been provided by Robert Spaemann, who concludes that it is impossible to be a person only in potential. The beginning and the end of human life cannot be separated from the beginning and the end of personhood.

As regards the decision of procured abortion, it has been argued that decisions which go against life itself, cannot be reasonably demanded from no one.[911] According to Mariéle Wulf, in these decision making processes, the two following guiding principle are applicable:

1) a free decision should not destroy freedom itself, because this goes against human dignity; 2) every free decision should take into account the greater possibility of life itself.[912]

One could argue that the first guiding principle has received a place in the British and Dutch abortion legislation, since it considers a forced abortion as illegal. But, as we have seen, in many other situations women may feel forced to undergo an abortion, because of a lack of cooperation of their partner or because of a lack of support from significant others. In those situations, the essential freedom of the unborn child should prevail over the accidental freedom of the mother, which consists in the realization of her immediate future plans. To the mother, support should be given, so that she does not need to give up on herself.[913]

In these and other situations, also the second guiding principle should be followed. Life could only be weighed up against life.[914] Only if the life of the mother is at direct threat and if the foetus has no chance of survival,

---

911 Cf. part 3.4
912 Wulf, C.M., 2013 (2), op. cit., p. 335; cf. part 6.1.3.2.
913 Wulf, C.M., 2013 (2), op. cit., p. 335.
914 Ibid.

such as in case of ectopic pregnancy, procured abortion could, morally speaking, be performed in order to save the mother's life. In other cases alternatives for procured abortion should be sought, because every human life is worthy of protection.

The fundamental problem in the current British and Dutch legislation is that the unborn child has not been recognised as another person with a right to life. If one does not recognise the other as a person, then the other human being runs the risk of being treated as an object, of which one can get rid of in case one expects psychological, social or economic difficulties. According to Ricoeur, self-respect reaches its full meaning when respect for the norm will have blossomed into respect for others and for "oneself as another".[915] One passes from the aim of the good life to the sense of justice by way of solicitude for the other. This solicitude can become real when individual solicitude for the other is stimulated and also when collective solicitude is realised in just institutions. Or, in other words, if a pregnant woman is convinced according to her conscience that she cannot take care of the child herself, then alternatives need to be offered to her, so that the life of the unborn child can be saved. In chapter 7 it will be made clear how this solicitude for the other can be realised with regard to alternatives for abortion.

So far, it must be concluded that in the current abortion legislation in the U.K. and the Netherlands, the dignity of the unborn child is not sufficiently recognised and respected. For many British and Dutch women, human autonomy cannot be guaranteed either by the current abortion legislation, because in many cases the opportunity of an autonomous choice becomes an emergency situation. So, both principles of human autonomy and of the dignity of the unborn child cannot be guaranteed in the current legislation. Therefore the third principle mentioned in the introduction, the criterion of universality, cannot be applied either to the current abortion legislation in both countries.

For this reason, it is needed to look further and to consider how the current abortion legislation and praxis could possibly be corrected, in order to do justice to both principles of human autonomy and the dignity of the unborn child. Such a correction requires a considerable effort from

---

915 Ricoeur, P., 1992, op. cit., p. 203.

various scientific disciplines, as well as political and public support. Before making recommendations for the future care of pregnant women, their partners and their offspring in the U.K. and the Netherlands, it will first be investigated how in the course of history within the area of moral theology a search has taken place for the universalisation of the ethics of abortion.

Chapter 6

A historical search for a universalization of the ethics of abortion

According to Paul Ricoeur, the idea of law should add to our notions of value, norm and imperative a requirement for universality, a potential universalization.[916] As regards the protection of the value of women's health and also as regards the legal norm of autonomy, it has been shown that this requirement is lacking in the current abortion legislation in the U.K. and the Netherlands. Scientific evidence indicates that about 20% of all women have negative psychological effects after induced abortion.[917] Qualitative research confirms that women, when they are asked in more depth and after a longer period of time, are likely to indicate a relationship conflict as the true reason for their abortion.[918]

This scientific evidence indicates that both the value of women's health, the principle of women's autonomy in relation to significant others and the future value of the life of the foetus cannot be sufficiently protected with the current British and Dutch abortion legislation. The essential problem with the current abortion legislation is that it seeks to protect a relative value at the cost of a basic form of human good, which is the life of the foetus.[919] Freedom is not a value in itself, it is only a relative value because it has another objective, another value as its aim.[920] Freedom could be abused if it is only aimed at one's personal interests.

In her book on the history and methods of moral theology, Mariéle

---
916 Ricoeur, P., 1978, op. cit., p. 187.
917 Cf. part 3.1.3.
918 Cf. part 3.3.1.1.
919 Finnis, J., op. cit., pp. 86-87; Grisez, G., 1970, op. cit., pp. 312-313.
920 Wulf, C.M., 2013 (2), op. cit., p. 336.

Wulf mentions four basic values which in modern and postmodern times often have been threatened by the abuse of freedom: autonomy, creativity, friendship and love and finally discovering and living the truth.[921] Autonomy is a basic value, which could be threatened if it is undermined by any form of addiction. In relation to the decision-making process after the discovery of an unintended pregnancy, human autonomy could be overshadowed by the fear of binding oneself in a loving relationship or by an inclination to focus solely on one's own career perspectives.

The second basic value concerns the creativity to develop or to found something new. The process of creating something new is one of the most important human inclinations. However, in our world the process of creativity is often threatened by violence and destruction. Even a new, human life could be threatened in this way.

As a third basic value, friendship and love are mentioned. It is in friendship and love that the human person could develop himself in relation to others and by doing so, discover one's self-esteem. It is obvious, however, that love could be perverted to no more than sexuality, friendship to mutual self-interest. Thus, in another way freedom could be abused.

The fourth basic value regards discovering and living the truth, which runs the risk of being substituted by lies or ideologies, or of being overruled by all sorts of different opinions. So it could happen that a young pregnant woman is heavily influenced in her decision by her partner's attitude, by her parents, by her employer or by other persons in her peer group to choose for an abortion against her tacit desire to become a mother.

People could live their lives to the full if these four basic values are being safeguarded in a positive way, if one's autonomy is supported, if one's creativity is stimulated, if one's yearning for genuine love is answered and if one has found satisfaction in one's search for the truth.[922] If these conditions are fulfilled, people could use their freedom in a positive way, related to some other aim, the ethical aim of the 'good life'. For this reason Ricoeur states that the problem of the recognition of the freedom of the other is the central phenomenon of ethics.[923]

---

921 Wulf, C.M., 2013 (2), op. cit., p. 337.
922 Ibid, pp. 337 and 341.
923 Ricoeur, P., 1978, op. cit., p. 178.

He notes that during the first stage of moral reflection, a certain inclination could be set aside by reason of its purely epistemic inadequacy with respect to the criterion of universality.[924] It has already been pointed out that Ricoeur proposes two questions as a criterion of universality: "Would I want everyone else to do the same?" and "Could my desire serve as a universal law?"[925] For the reasons which have just been mentioned, the threat of the four basic values and the violation of the dignity of the unborn child, the two questions which Ricoeur proposes have to be answered in the negative as regards the option of procured abortion and its current legalisation in the U.K. and the Netherlands, except for the cases which have been discussed earlier, cases in which the life of the mother is directly at stake.[926]

In his study on the self and the moral norm, Ricoeur introduces the idea of respect as a motive which has an element of passivity at the heart of the principle of autonomy: "Respect is self-esteem that has passed through the sieve of the universal and constraining norm."[927] The norm of respect owed to persons is connected to the dialogic structure of the ethical aim, that is, to solicitude. It is in the Golden Rule that Ricoeur sees an appropriate transitional formula between solicitude and the second Kantian imperative, which is the notion of the person as an end in himself or herself.[928] The Golden Rule in its positive formulation: "Treat others as you would like them to treat you" is mentioned twice in the Gospels. (Lk. 6, 31 and Mat. 7, 12) In its negative formulation: "Do not do unto your neighbour what you would hate him to do to you", it can be found in Hillel, in the Babylonian Talmud.[929] All these statements enunciate a norm of reciprocity.[930]

In the Introduction to this research, it has been pointed out that as a final step in his attempt to offer a foundation for morality, Ricoeur inserts the evangelical perspective in the ethical order.[931] By doing so, his search

---

924 Idem, 1992, p. 207.
925 In the Introduction to this research.
926 Cf. part 5.1.8.
927 Ricoeur, P., 1992, op. cit., p. 215.
928 Ibid., p. 219; cf. part 2.2.2.
929 "Shabbath Hillel", in: Isidore Epstein (ed.), *Hebrew-English edition of the Babylonian Talmud*, translated into English by H. Freedman, London etc., 1972, p. 31a.
930 Ibid.
931 Ricoeur, P., 1978, op. cit., pp. 189-191.

for a foundation of moral philosophy comes to an end.⁹³² However, for a moral theologian, it is where the search for universalization actually begins. Especially during the last decades, this search has taken new directions. After the call of the Second Vatican Council for an openness to the world and for a service to be offered to humanity, the focus of attention within theological research has been on human experience and practice.⁹³³ The opening up of the object of 'practice' initially led to a move within theological research to the social and human sciences, as has been the case in the earlier chapters of this study on the abortion practice.

Now, a historical analysis will be made of the moral theological views regarding abortion within the Catholic Church throughout the centuries. (6.1) This limitation has been made out of the presupposition that the Church doctrine has some valuable insights to offer to society, insights which have been developed out of a Judeo-Christian tradition of more than two millennia. In particular, the historical development of the Church doctrine on abortion will be evaluated for its consistency. It will be shown that the doctrinal development has been influenced by scientific discoveries within the field of embryology. The chapter closes with a treatise on the Christian interpretation of human conscience, because of the importance of the role of conscience with regard to (reproductive) decision making. (6.2)

6.1 Abortion in the teaching of the Catholic Church

In this part, the historical developments in teaching of the Catholic Church about procured abortion will be reviewed. Research in this area has already been done in the seventies of the previous century, in particular and in great detail by John Connery and also by Germain Grisez and John

---

932 At the end of *Oneself as another*, in the study 'What ontology in view?', he remarks: "Perhaps the philosopher as philosopher has to admit that one does not know and cannot say whether this Other, the source of the injunction, is another person whom I can look in the face or who can stare at me, or my ancestors for whom there is no representation, to so great an extent does my debt to them constitute my very self, or God - living God, absent God - or an empty place. With this aporia of the Other, philosophical discourse comes to an end." Cf. Ricoeur, P., 1992, op. cit., p. 355.
933 Second Vatican Council, *Gaudium et Spes*, n. 2-3; cf. Fortin-Melkevik, A., op. cit., pp. 101-111.

Noonan.[934] I will therefore focus on the main arguments in the Church's teaching throughout the centuries against procured abortion in general and then on the arguments which are brought to the fore in some exceptional cases in which procured abortion could be allowed, according to this teaching.

From the Jewish religion and culture, the radical rejection of procured abortion was quickly introduced in the first Christian writings after the Gospels and the New Testament letters. Throughout the centuries, many important authors in the history of the Church, such as Augustine and Thomas Aquinas and have considered the issue of abortion. The Old and New Testament writings were interpreted by various authors of the early Church and the Middle Ages (6.1.1). The Church teaching with regard to abortion was refined during the Renaissance and the Enlightenment. (6.1.2) The Church's teaching and practice developed further in the twentieth century, especially after the instruction on procured abortion of 1974 and in the writings of Pope John Paul II. (6.1.3) The Magisterial point of view on abortion will be dealt with in relation to prenatal diagnosis and the expectance of a handicapped child. (6.1.4) The Magisterial view on abortion does not stand on itself, but has a strong relation with the teaching of family values and virtues. (6.1.5) Finally in relation to the Church' point of view regarding abortion, the relevant articles in canon law will be considered. (6.1.6)

6.1.1 Sacred Scripture, early Christianity and the Middle Ages

A first reference to abortion can be found in what is probably the oldest book in Sacred Scripture, the book of Exodus.

6.1.1.1 The Old Testament

In the Old Testament there is one text that explicitly deals with abortion, namely in Exodus 21, 22-25. In fact, the passage is on involuntary abortion. The text reads as follows: "When people who are fighting injure a pregnant woman so that there is a miscarriage, and yet no further harm follows, the one responsible shall be fined what the woman's husband demands, paying

---

934 Grisez, G., 1970, op. cit.; John T. Noonan, Jr., *The morality of abortion. Legal and historical perspectives.* Harvard U.P., 1970; John Connery S.J., *Abortion: The development of the Roman Catholic Perspectives.* Loyola University Press, 1977.

as much as the judges determine. If any harm follows, then you shall give life for life, eye for eye, tooth for tooth, hand for hand, foot for foot, burn for burn, wound for wound, stripe for stripe."[935]

This fragment from the book of the Covenant protects the rights of a husband regarding the unborn life in his pregnant wife. The unborn human life is considered as precious. Among the people of ancient Israel, a childless couple was seen as a misfortune, whereas a marriage with many children was seen as a blessing. Especially if the wife were to die in a conflict or if she were to be made infertile this was considered to be a crime where a death sentence might be the consequence. Although this punishment may sound extremely severe to our ears, it had in fact been introduced in order to limit possible acts of revenge.[936]

The husband's commitment towards the child is also made clear: he is the one who can ask for a penalty in the situation where the child did not survive the fight but his wife was not otherwise wounded. The height of the penalty is then determined by independent judges, whose judgement is on God's behalf (cf. Deuteronomy 1, 17).

Important for the development of the Christian tradition is the Greek translation of the original Hebrew version of the book of the Covenant. This translation, which is known as the Septuagint, was produced in Alexandria during the third and second centuries B.C.. The English translation of the same passage from Exodus in the Septuagint is as follows: "If two men strive and smite a woman, and her child is imperfectly formed, he shall be forced to pay a penalty; as the woman's husband shall lay upon him, he shall pay with a valuation. But if he be perfectly formed, he shall give life for life, eye for eye, tooth for tooth, hand for hand, foot for foot, burning for

---

[935] The Bible translation used is the New Revised Standard Version, Catholic Edition, Oxford/New York, 1999. The text is commented on by Connery S.J., J., op. cit., p. 8.
[936] According to modern commentators this sentence is one of the rare cases in which the so-called retaliation law (*ius talionis*) is applicable. Later Semitic jurisprudence would further limit the retaliation law by other forms of compensation. Frank C. Fensham, *Exodus*. Nijkerk, 1970, pp. 155-156. Cf. J.F. Craghan, "Exodus", in: Erik Eynikel, Ed Noort, Tjitze Baarda and Adelbert Denaux (eds.), *Internationaal Commentaar op de Bijbel*, Kampen, 2001, Vol. 1, p. 497.

burning, wound for wound, stripe for stripe."[937]

So, in the Hebrew text, a line is drawn between the death of the foetus because of a miscarriage and the death or injury of the mother. In the Greek text however, the distinction is between the perfectly formed and the imperfectly formed foetus. The abortion of the formed foetus is considered homicide, whereas the abortion of the imperfectly formed foetus is penalised as something less than homicide.

On this difference between the Hebrew and the Greek version of this passage of Exodus, Connery comments that it is difficult to explain the difference as a mistaken translation. Rather, the emphasis on formation of the foetus coincides with Greek and particular Aristotelian thought on the status of the foetus. Aristotle held that life was present in the embryo from conception, but only at a vegetative level. The rational soul was infused only when the foetus was formed. As we have seen, this theory was based on a wrong presupposition that an embryo is formed out of sperm and menstrual blood.[938]

In a detailed comparison of the Masoretic (the Hebrew text of the Jewish Bible) and the Greek translation, Nina Collins shows that the latter has been the outcome of extended oral debate on the basic meaning and practical implications of the Hebrew law, which took place among the Jews some time before the translation of the Pentateuch into Greek.[939] According to rabbinic commentary on Exodus 21, 22 it is argued that the value of the foetus may be related to the length of time the child had spent in the womb. If the foetus is formed as a man, someone who killed the child, should be charged with a death penalty, because the foetus is made in the image of God (cf. Genesis 9, 6). When this comment is followed, then the harm mentioned in verse 21, 23 can imply harm to the formed foetus alone (as in the Septuagint) *or* to both the foetus and the mother (as in the Masoretic text). This latter option corresponds with another philosophical school in the Greek world, Stoicism, which was also very influential during

---

[937] *The Septuagint Version of the Old Testament and Apocrypha. With an English translation and with various readings and critical notes.* Translated by L.C.L. Brenton, Grand Rapids, Mich., 1971.
[938] In part 4.3.1.2; Cf. Connery S.J., J., op. cit., pp. 17-23 and 57.
[939] N.L. Collins, "Notes on the text of Exodus XXI 22", in: *Vetus Testamentum* XLIII, 3, 1993, pp. 289-301; Connery S.J., J., op. cit., pp. 23 and 57.

the period of the Roman republic. According to the Stoics, a foetus had to be considered part of the mother until birth, when it received an *anima* by breathing.

Interpreting the passage of Exodus 21, 22-25, Noonan makes the point that these verses are referring to a conflict which leads to a miscarriage and do not explicitly speak of a *procured* abortion.[940] But in contrast with Noonan, Connery argues that the Septuagint text does have implications for the moral vision on procured abortion, which was considered wrong, at least for the formed foetus. "In imposing the penalty for homicide on the abortion of the formed foetus, even if it was caused by a third party, the law makes the life of the foetus the real issue, rather than any possible violation of the rights of the parents... Abortion was allowed only when necessary to save the life of the mother. There is no evidence for any other exception."[941]

Connery's argument is supported by several authors in the Jewish tradition, such as philosopher Philo of Alexandria (25 B.C. – 41 A.D.) and historian Flavius Josephus (37 – 100 A.D). Philo takes over from the Septuagint the distinction between the formed and the unformed foetus, but he does not mention the husband as the one who can desire a penalty. Rather, he states that any man who beats a pregnant woman, so that she suffers a miscarriage, has to pay a penalty as long as the foetus is unformed and deserves a death sentence, when the foetus is formed. The husband himself is not exempted.[942]

Philo compares this crime with another form of injustice, which is the act of abandoning a child. According to Philo, abandoning children was rather common among the surrounding peoples in his days. For him it is clear that both causing a miscarriage and abandoning a child are crimes which the lawmaker has forbidden. Both acts are to be considered as crimes against the human species.[943]

---

940 Noonan also mentions the letter of St. Paul to the Galatians (Gal. 5, 20) as a possible reference to abortion, more specifically by the term *pharmakeia*, or sorcery. Noonan, Jr., J.T., 1970, op. cit., pp. 9-11. But according to Connery it is unlikely that St. Paul used this term to indicate abortion. Connery S.J., J., op. cit., pp. 34-35.
941 Connery S.J., J., op. cit., pp. 18 and 21.
942 Philo of Alexandria, *De specialibus legibus*, book III, 19, 108-109. In German translation, Band 2, Berlin, 1962, pp. 216-217.
943 Ibid., book III, 20, 117-118, pp. 219-220.

Unlike Philo, Flavius Josephus departs from the Hebrew original. But he adds as a reason for fining the man who caused a miscarriage: "... since he has diminished the population, through the destruction of what was in the belly."[944] It must have been clear to him that the miscarriage meant the loss of a human being, not only for the parents, but for the society as a whole. In *Contra Apionem,* Josephus makes a comparison between contraception, abortion and infanticide, stating that "the law prohibited women from causing the seed to miscarry and from destroying it. But if it were to become evident, she would be an infanticide, obliterating a soul and diminishing the human race."[945] According to John Barclay, who mentions various other commentators, the phrase "But if it were to become evident..." refers to cases in which it is clear that the woman caused an abortion, thus indicating that in other cases, such as spontaneous or accidental abortions, the woman could not be held responsible.[946]

So, both Philo of Alexandria and Flavius Josephus conclude from the phrase of Exodus that procured abortion is wrong. Of course, this passage has to be seen in the context of the whole book of Exodus. The fifth commandment of the Decalogue, "you shall not murder" (Exodus 20, 13; Deuteronomy 5, 17) and its further specification in Exodus 23, 7, "do not kill the innocent or those in the right", are clear in their condemnation of the destruction of an innocent human being's life.[947] According to modern exegetic commentaries, the book of Exodus and the other four books of the Pentateuch (Genesis, Leviticus, Numbers and Deuteronomy) form a compound document written by various authors from the tenth to the sixth century B.C.[948] Both the Decalogue and the book of the Covenant (Exodus 20, 22 – 23, 19) are associated with the tradition of the Elohist, an author of the ninth or eighth century B.C.[949] The exodus of the people of

---

944 Flavius Josephus, *Antiquitates,* book IV, 278. English translation and commentary by Louis H. Feldman, *Judean Antiquities, 1-4,* in: Steve Mason (ed.), *Flavius Josephus. Translation and Commentary.* Vol. 3, Leiden, 2000, pp. 448-449.
945 Flavius Josephus, *Contra Apionem,* book II, 202. English translation and commentary by John M.G. Barclay, *Against Apion,* in: Steve Mason (ed.), *Flavius Josephus. Translation and Commentary.* Vol. 10, Leiden, 2007, p. 285.
946 Ibid., p. 285.
947 Cf. Catechism of the Catholic Church, 1997, n. 2258 and 2261.
948 J.F. Craghan, in: Eynikel, E. et. al. (eds.), op. cit., p. 469.
949 Ibid.

Israel out of Egypt, led by Moses, has been placed by many experts in the middle of the thirteenth century B.C.[950] The Elohist has probably inserted the Decalogue and the book of the Covenant as originally independent traditions within the description of the theophany at mount Sinai, during which the will of JHWH was revealed to Moses.[951]

In the words of Matthew the Evangelist, Jesus reminds his disciples of the commandments of the Decalogue, with the intention to bring the fulfilment of the ancient writings in the Law and the Prophets (cf. Matthew 5, 17-20). To the fifth commandment, Jesus adds that not only those who murder are liable to judgment, but all who are angry at their brother or sister (Matthew 5, 21-22). Leske comments that according to Jesus' words, a violation of the fifth commandment does not occur only in the specific action of murder, but also in words and thoughts. Every time when one deliberately uses violence against another, whether it be in a physical, mental or spiritual way, the commandment is violated.[952]

6.1.1.2 Early Christianity

The texts quoted above from Sacred Scripture have had a great influence on the Christian tradition. As regards the passage on abortion from the book of Exodus (21, 22-25), the Septuagint version was even more influential than the original Hebrew text. The early Christians "inherited from the Jews their general respect for human life at all stages, an attitude which put them in conflict, as were the Jews themselves, with the surrounding Roman world, where both abortion and infanticide were widely accepted."[953] Similarly, Noonan states that the Christian teaching on abortion has to be seen in the context of the commands of the Old Testament to love God with all your heart (Deuteronomy 6, 5) and to love your neighbour as yourself (Leviticus 19, 18). The foetus as human is a neighbour; his life has parity with one's own.[954]

A first clear condemnation of abortion and infanticide in Christian teaching is found in the *Didachê*: "You shall not kill the foetus by abortion,

---

950 Ibid., p. 460.
951 Ibid., pp. 494-495.
952 A. Leske, in ibid., p. 1480.
953 Connery S.J., J., op. cit., pp. 18-32, here p. 21.
954 Cf. Noonan, Jr., J.T., 1970, op. cit., p. 58.

or destroy the infant already born."⁹⁵⁵ Similar condemnations are found in other early Christian writings, such as the letter of Barnabas, the Apocalypse of Peter and in the *Embassy for the Christians*, written by the second century philosopher Athenagoras.⁹⁵⁶

These writers argue against procured abortion and infanticide by focusing on the immorality of destroying a foetus or new-born. Another second century Christian author, Clement of Alexandria, points out the dehumanizing effect of procured abortion for the women themselves: "Our whole life would go by in a natural way, if we control our desires from the beginning and do not kill the new human life which comes into being by God's providence; but because such women use fully destructive means to abort, in order to hide their fornication and by doing so, destroy not only the foetus, but also their humanity." Clement goes on with a plea to exercise marital chastity and natural fertility planning, because "nature does not ever give the opportunity for conjugal union."⁹⁵⁷

In *Apologeticum*, Tertullian (ca. 155 – 240 A.D.) holds that we are not allowed to kill the fruit in the womb. "It does not make a difference, if someone steals life after birth or destroys life, which is still developing. What is to become a man, is already a man."⁹⁵⁸

This teaching by Tertullian meant a break with the existing Roman law of the time, which did not condemn the destruction of the unborn human life as homicide. In fact, Tertullian laid the foundation for a Christian penal

---

955 Didachê, or the teaching of the twelve apostles, 2,2, transl. by James A. Kleist S.J., Westminster, Mar. 1948. The time of composition of the Didachê must be at least as early as the first half of the second century.

956 Epistle of Barnabas, the, 19, 5; 20, 2, translated by James A. Kleist S.J., Westminster, Mar. 1948. Apocalypse of Peter, the Akhmim fragment, 26, in: Montague R. James, *The Apocryphal New Testament*, London, 1975, p. 509. Athanagoras, *Embassy for the Christians*, 35. Transl. and annotated by J.H. Crehan, S.J., Westminster, Mar., 1956. Commentaries on these works can be found in Connery S.J., J., op. cit., pp. 33-45 and Noonan, Jr., J.T., 1970, op. cit., pp. 9-11.

957 Clement of Alexandria, *Der Erzieher*, Buch II, 10, 96, 1. Transl. into German by O. Stählin, München, 1934, p. 103.

958 Tertullian, *Apologeticum*, 9, 8. Transl. into Dutch and commented by Chr. Mohrmann, Utrecht, 1951, p. 32. This argument of active potentiality has already been elaborated in part 4.3.2.1.

law in this matter.[959]

Despite the influence of the Septuagint in the early Church, the Hebrew original formed the basis for a translation in Latin by Jerome (ca. 347 – 419/420 A.D.), which later became known as the Vulgata. In the Vulgata, the distinction between the formed and the unformed foetus, as had been introduced in the Septuagint version of Exodus 21, 22-23, was no longer made. Just as in the Hebrew Bible, the extent of the punishment after an abortion caused by a fight between men varied according to the damage that had been done to the foetus and to the mother.[960]

Augustin (354 – 430 A.D.) speaks of abortion in relation to Christian marriage. He argues that when a married couple use drugs to cause sterility, or destroy the foetus already conceived, in fact "they are not husband and wife, and if they were such from the beginning, they did not come together in marriage, but rather in debauchery. But if both of them are not such people, I venture to say: either she is in some sense the prostitute of her

---

959 Cf. Chr. Mohrmann, in: Tertullianus, *Apologeticum,*, Utrecht, 1951, footnote on p. 32. In Roman law the foetus was never considered a human person with rights accordingly. For instance, in his *Digest*, Roman emperor Justinian writes: *Partus enim antequam edatur mulieris portio est vel viscerum.* ("[T]he child is part of the woman or her insides before it is born.") Cf. Theodor Mommsen, Paul Krueger and Alan Watson (eds.), *The Digest of Justinian.* Philadelphia, Pennsylvania, 1985, Vol. II, 25, 4, 1, 1.
The first piece of Church legislation dates from the year 305, when at Elvira in today's Spain it was determined in canon 63 that if a woman who was baptised committed adultery in the absence of her husband and then destroyed the child, she was not to be restored to communion with the faithful even at the end of her life. Canon 68 states that if a catechumen did the same thing, she may be baptised at the end of her life. *Concilium Eliberitanum*, c. 63, in: Sacrorum conciliorum nova et amplissima collectio, Mansi, J.D., Vol II, ab anno CCCV ad annum CCCXLVI, orig. ed. Florence, 1759, reprod. Paris, 1901, p. 16. Canon 63 was mitigated a few years later at the Council of Ancyra in 314 A.D., by making a gradual reconciliation with the church community possible. Cf. *Concilium Ancyranum*, c. 21, in: Mansi, J.D., Vol II, 1901, p. 514. This possibility was then reinforced at the first great ecumenical Council of Nicaea in 325 A.D. in canon 13, stating "in the case of anyone whatsoever who is dying and seeks to share in the Eucharist, the bishop upon examining the matter shall give him a share in the offering." Cf. Heinrich Denzinger, *Enchiridion symbolorum definitionum et declarationum de rebus fidei et morum. / Kompendium der Glaubensbekenntnisse und kirchlichen Lehrentscheidungen.* Freiburg, 2005, pp. 65-66.
960 Cf. *Biblia Sacra iuxta Latinam vulgatam versionem.* Ad codicum fidem iussu Pii PP. XI, Vol. II, Exodi et Levitici, Rome, 1929.

husband, or he is an adulterer toward his wife."⁹⁶¹

Crucial for the issue of abortion is the question of the beginning of human life. As we have seen, it was only in the nineteenth century that the human egg-cell was discovered.⁹⁶² Neither Jerome or Augustine had knowledge of the complete formation of genetic material at conception. This might have lead Jerome to the conclusion that an abortion is not considered as homicide "until the fused elements in the womb have taken up the form of members."⁹⁶³ Augustine asks himself if it is possible for living foetuses to share in the resurrection of the body. He admits that he is not sure of the answer, but he does not see "how they fail to share in the resurrection of the dead unless they are not counted in the number of the dead."⁹⁶⁴ Indeed, "no Christian ought to doubt: that the bodies of all men who have been born and are to be born, and have died and are to die, will rise again." But regarding the underlying question: *When* a human being starts to live in the womb, Augustine admits that he does not know whether man can answer it.⁹⁶⁵ In another work, when he speaks of the passage of Exodus 21, 22-25, he leaves open the possibility that the unformed foetus might be animated. But again he shows his caution: "This is a large question and not one to be decided precipitously."⁹⁶⁶

Others, like Tertullian held that the seed of the soul was implanted at the same time as the seed of the body. But he assumed that the soul was a corporal substance, which originated in the seed.⁹⁶⁷ Two centuries later, this

---

961 Augustine, *De nuptiis et concupiscentiis*, I, 17. Transl. and commented by R.J. Teske, S.J., *Answer to the Pelagians, II: Marriage and Desire*, in: J.E. Rotelle, O.S.A., The works of Saint Augustine. A Translation for the 21ˢᵗ Century, Part I, Vol. 24, New York, 1998, pp. 39-40.

962 In part 4.3.1.2.

963 Jerome, *Letter 121 Ad Algasiam*, 4, "Sicuti enim semina paulatim formantur in uteris: et tam diu non reputatur homicidium, donec elementa confusa suas imagines membraque suscipiant…" Cf. Saint Jérôme, *Correspondance*, Vol. VII, Transl. in French by J. Labourt, Paris, 2003, p. 22.

964 Augustine, *Civitate Dei*, Book XXII, 13, transl. by W.M. Green, *City of God*, Vol. VII in: J. Henderson, (ed.), The Loeb Classical Library no. 417, Cambridge/London, 1972, p. 273.

965 Augustine, *Enchiridion de fide, spe et caritate*, 86, transl. by B.M. Peebles, *Faith, hope and charity*, in: R.J. Deferrari, (ed.), The Fathers of the Church, Vol. 2, New York, 1947, p. 442

966 Augustine, *Quaestionum in heptateuchum, libri VII*, in: Corpus Scriptorum Ecclesiasticorum Latinorum, vol. 28, 80, New York, 1895, pp. 146-148; cf. Connery S.J., J., op. cit., 1977, p. 57.

967 Tertullian, *Über die Seele (De Anima)*, 37, 5. Transl. into German and commented by J.H. Waszink, Zürich, 1980.

assumption is extensively contradicted by Augustine, in his commentary on the book of Genesis, on which he had worked for some fifteen years.[968] In it, he argues that the soul of each man is created by God in his image. After its creation out of nothing, the soul is not of a bodily, but of a spiritual material.[969] Augustine further explains his motivation for needing to go on at length with regard to this matter: "to refute those who believe that a person's soul, like flesh from flesh, is made by the parents..."[970] On the contrary, if the human soul was corporal, then it would also be passible, which could not possibly be reconciled with the verse of Genesis 1,27 that man is created in God's image. The first part of this verse: "God created man in his own image", had to refer to the soul, because the soul, like God, is immortal, whereas the second part of the same verse: "male and female he created them", referred to the body.[971]

In Augustine's *Answer to Julian*, an anti-Pelagian work which he wrote in reaction to Julian's *To Turbantius*, he denies that the foetus belongs to the woman's body, but the child must have its own condition, since, sometimes the child will be baptised shortly after birth, while the mother is not leading a Christian life, whereas in other cases the child dies before it is baptised, while the mother is a Christian. According to Augustine, the body of a baptised woman could be considered a temple of God, in which the Holy Spirit dwells.[972] But the child is not a temple of God, unless it is reborn through the sacrament of baptism. When a child dies before it is baptised, Augustine even writes that "it justly fall[s] under the heavy yoke of the children of Adam...".[973] Although he admits that he is not sure of the answer himself, he asks the rhetorical question: "Who has ever doubted that unbaptized little ones who have only original sin and are not burdened by

---

968 Augustine, *De Genesi ad litteram*, transl. and annotated by E. Hill O.P., *On Genesis: The Literal Meaning of Genesis*, in: J.E. Rotelle, O.S.A. (ed.), The works of Saint Augustine. A Translation for the 21st Century. Part I, Vol. 13, New York, 2002.
969 Ibid., Book VII, 7 (5) – 43 (28).
970 Ibid., Book X, 1 (1).
971 Ibid., Book III, 34 (22); Book VI, 31 (20) and Book VII, especially the conclusive part 43 (28).
972 Cf. Rom, 5,5.
973 Augustine, *Contra Iulianum*, Book VI, 14, 43. Transl. and commented by R.J. Teske, S.J., *Answer to the Pelagians, II: Answer to Julian*, in: J.E. Rotelle, O.S.A., The works of Saint Augustine. A Translation for the 21st Century, Part I, Vol. 24, New York, 1998, pp. 503-504; Cf. John, 3, 3-22.

any personal sins will suffer the lightest punishment of all?"[974]

Here, it must be added that the traditional teaching of the theory of *limbo*, elaborated by theologians in the centuries after Augustine, which entails that the souls of infants who die subject to original sin and without baptism, neither merit the beatific vision, nor yet are subjected to any punishment, because they are not guilty of any personal sin, has never entered into the dogmatic definitions of the Magisterium, and is not mentioned in the Catechism of the Catholic Church.[975] In 2007, a document published by the International Theological Commission and approved by Pope Benedict XVI, concluded that "there are theological and liturgical reasons to hope that infants who die without baptism may be saved and brought into eternal happiness, even if there is not an explicit teaching on this question found in Revelation."[976]

In the Eastern Church there is an important contribution to the discussion of abortion by Basil the Great (330 – 379). In a letter to Amphilochius, bishop of Iconium, in which he is describing the discipline of the Church, he states that anyone who purposely destroys a foetus, will pay the penalty of homicide.[977] Basil adds that "we do not further investigate the subtlety of a formed or an unformed foetus".[978] To him this is not relevant, because the penalty will not only vindicate the death of the foetus, but also of the mother, who often suffered death after the attempt to abort her foetus. In these cases there were two victims. However, the penalty for the abortionist who provided the lethal drugs, and for the woman should not extend for more than ten years of excommunication, after which a gradual reconciliation with the church community could be possible. Curing, so he said, did not depend on the length of time, but on the way the penitence was done.[979]

---

974 Augustine, *Contra Iulianum*, Book V, 11, 44, in: J.E. Rotelle, O.S.A., 1998, p. 461.
975 The Catechism teaches that infants who die without baptism are entrusted by the Church to the mercy of God, as is shown in the specific funeral rite for such children. Cf. Catechism of the Catholic Church, 1997, nr. 1261.
976 International Theological Commission, *The hope of salvation for infants who die without being baptised*, Vatican, 2007, foreword.
977 Basil the Great, *Epistle nr. 188*, c. II, in: J.P. Migne, *Patrologia Graeca*, Vol. 32, Turnhout, 1961, p. 671; J. Connery, S.J., 1977, pp. 49-50.
978 '*De formato autem aut informi subtilius non inquirimus.*' In: J.P. Migne, 1961, Vol. 32, p. 671.
979 Idem. Indicating this ten years penalty, Basil followed the Council of Ancyra of 314. See footnote 959; cf. Connery S.J., J., op. cit., pp. 47-48.

6.1.1.3 The Middle Ages

In the year 692, the ecumenical Council of Trulla of the Greek Church, held in Constantinople, imposed the penance for homicide both on those who give abortifacients and on women who take them. Several decades later, in 868, the Council of Worms prescribed that a voluntarily aborted foetus before term by a woman was to be considered a homicide. More and more, both in the Eastern and in the Western Church, the canon on abortion of the Council of Ancyra of the year 314 became general church discipline. Like the Council of Ancyra, the Councils of Trulla and Worms did not make a distinction between the animated and unanimated foetus in considering procured abortion as homicide.[980]

Another development during the Middle Ages was the individual use of penitential books. Penances usually entailed fasting, for instance one, three or seven years on bread and water. The woman's poverty could mitigate the penance. If it was clear that the abortion followed fornication, the penance could be augmented. Some of the Medieval penitential books made a

---

[980] Council of Ancyra, see footnote 959. *Concilium Trullanum (Quinisextum)*, c. 91. In: J.D. Mansi, Vol. XI, 1901, p. 982; *Concilium Wormatiense*, c. 35. In: J.D. Mansi, Vol. XV, 1960, p. 876. It has to be said, that in the centuries to come, the distinction between the animated and the unanimated foetus would reappear in several ecclesiastical writings on abortion, also at the highest level of authority. In 1214, Pope Innocent III answered in a letter to a Carthusian prior that one of his monks who had made a woman pregnant, could continue his ministry "if the conceptus was not yet living" *(vivificatus)*. Twenty years later, this letter is included in a collection called the *Decretales* published by Raymond of Pennaforte and authorised by Pope Gregory IX. Cf. Innocentius III, "Letter to a Carthusian prior as of Oct. 4, 1211", in: A. Potthast, (ed.) *Regesta Pontificum Romanorum*, Berlin, 1874, p. 372, nr. 4312; cf. Gregory IX, "Decretales", Lib. V, Tit. XII, c. 20, in: E.A. Friedberg and A.L. Richter, (eds.), *Corpus Iuris Canonici. Editio Lipsiensis Secunda*, Leipzig 1879. But in the same book of the *Decretales*, in c. 5, Raymond of Pennafort has included a passage which he ascribes to the Council of Worms and which says that all efforts to prevent conception or offspring are classified as homicide. So there is a discrepancy between the two passages, which lead to a controversy up to the end of the thirteenth century. Connery and Jones are among the authors who have analyzed this controversy. Both conclude that the confusion was dispelled by the general acceptance of the distinction between intentional homicide and real or actual homicide. It was only to the latter that the Church attached an irregularity. It has to be borne in mind that in the centuries before the discovery of the egg-cell, the seed was seen as the source of life and therefore also sterilisation was considered as homicide. But for abortion of the unanimated foetus, as well as for sterilisation, a lesser sacramental penance was imposed. Cf. Connery S.J., J., op. cit., p. 103; David A. Jones, *The Soul of the Embryo*, London, 2004, pp. 69-71.

distinction between penances depending on the age of the foetus.⁹⁸¹ When the penance was fulfilled, the penitent could be reconciled with the Church community.⁹⁸²

Important for the future discussion of abortion is Thomas Aquinas' commentary on the *Sentences*, where he takes up the question of the time of ensoulment of the embryo. Unaware of the mechanism of fertilisation, he adopts from Aristotle the distinction regarding the time of male (40 days) and female ensoulment (90 days).⁹⁸³ Aquinas states that the soul is the first principle by which the body lives. Now the intellect, which is the form of the human body, is multiplied according to the number of bodies. As a new body is generated, God gives a new soul to the body, and body and soul become a human being.⁹⁸⁴

Some decades after Aquinas' death, the Catholic doctrine on the unity of the human body and soul was confirmed, which states that one has to consider the soul as the 'form' of the body. The Council of Vienna in 1312 stated that the body made of matter becomes a living, human body, because of its spiritual soul.⁹⁸⁵ Therefore, according to this doctrine, a living, human body cannot exist without a soul. In the sixteenth century the fifth Council of Lateran confirms the belief in the immortality of the soul as a dogma of Catholic faith.⁹⁸⁶

Aquinas' view on the (belated) ensoulment of the embryo does not mean that he thought that abortion was permissible. In his *Summa Theologica* he states that one who strikes a pregnant woman (and causes an abortion)

---

981 Jones mentions the Irish canons (late seventh century), the Bigotian Penitential (early eighth century), the Old Irish Penitential (early ninth century) as well as Anglo-Saxon penitentials. In: Jones, D.A., op. cit., pp. 67-68. See also the commentary at the previous footnote.
982 Connery S.J., J., op. cit., pp. 65-87.
983 Thomas Aquinas, *Scriptum super Sententiis Petri Lombardi*, 3, d.3, q.5, a.2 ad responsio. Edited by M.F. Moos, O.P., Paris, 1956, pp. 145-146. Cf. Reichlin, M., op. cit., p. 16. On the distinction between male and female embryos, see footnote 725.
984 Thomas Aquinas, *Summa Theologica (S.T.)* I, q.76 a. 1-2. and *S.T.* I, q. 90 a. 2-3. Edition in Latin, Ottawa, 1953, Vol I, pp. 447-453 and pp. 559-561; see also in Holy Scripture, Gen. 1,27 and Gen. 2,7. According to St. Thomas, the human soul is both incorporeal, subsistent and incorruptible. (*S.T.* I, q. 75 a. 2 and 6). in ibid., p. 440.
985 Catechism of the Catholic Church, 1997, n. 365; cf. Council of Vienna in 1312, in: Denzinger, H., op. cit., nr. 902, p. 391.
986 The 5ᵗʰ Council of Lateran, 1513, in: Denzinger, H., op. cit., nr. 1440, pp. 482-483.

is charged with homicide, even though the agent may not have intended to cause an abortion.[987] Above that, in the same question he answers that it is in no way lawful to slay the innocent.[988]

6.1.2 The Renaissance and the Enlightenment

Although the opinions on animation of the embryo differed, it has to be noted that the Catholic tradition has always taught against abortion in general.[989] Towards the end of the Middle Ages for instance, Antoninus writes a widely reproduced *Confessionale*, in which he repeats the traditional condemnation of abortion. Everyone who cooperates in an abortion is guilty of the sin, which is classified under homicide. Further he writes that the sin is committed whether or not the procedure is effective and whether or not the foetus is animated.[990]

Towards the end of the 16th century two papal constitutions appeared regarding abortion. In the first one, *Effrenatam* of 1588, Sixtus V fully reconfirms the early Christian teaching on abortion and formalizes the penalty of excommunication for mothers who undergo abortion and for those who advise or execute abortion.[991] Absolution of the excommunication he reserves for the Holy See. But a few years later, experience showed that this severe sanction did not work effectively and could even lead to serious spiritual harm. Sixtus' successor Pope Gregory XIV argued that "the eternal Pastor had come to save and not to perish human souls..." Therefore, in 1591, he removed the reservation of absolution to the Holy See, in order that people could go to confession. The local bishop could grant certain delegated priests the faculty to absolve in these matters.[992]

In the century which followed the appearance of the two papal decrees, the

---

987 Th. Aquinas, *S.T.*, II-II, q. 64, a.8; cf. Connery S.J., J., op. cit., pp. 111.
988 Th. Aquinas, *S.T.*, II-II, q. 64, a.6.
989 Grisez, G., 1970, op. cit., pp. 165-177 and Connery S.J., J., op. cit., p. 105.
990 Antoninus of Florence, *Confessionale Anthonini*. Parijs, 1517, p. 51 (*De homicidio*), cf. Grisez, G., 1970, op. cit., p. 166. St. Antoninus (1389-1459) was a Dominican moralist and Archbishop of Florence.
991 Sixtus V, Effrenatam. In: F.L. Ferraris, *Bibliotheca canonica iuridica moralis theologica*, 1885, pp. 36-38.
992 Gregory XIV, "Sedes apostolica pia mater", in: Ibid. pp. 38-39. In particular par. 2: "... aeternumque Pastorem ..., qui venit animas hominum salvare, non perdere..." Cf. Grisez, G., 1970, op. cit., p. 168.

moral theological debate centred on the question of whether exceptions on the abortion prohibition could be allowed in certain cases or circumstances. In neither of the two decrees is any exception mentioned. Tomas Sanchez considers the case of an indirect abortion of a "not yet animated foetus", executed in order to save the life of the mother. He accepts this particular case, by quoting several other authors as precedents.[993] Some decades later Joannis de Lugo further specifies three conditions under which an indirect abortion could be chosen: when the life of the mother is in serious danger; when the object of the treatment itself is not the killing of the child, but this effect is truly incidental; and when no delay is possible, in order to let the child be born and baptised. One can recognise in these conditions mentioned by De Lugo the principle of double effect.[994]

In the beginning of the 17th century, the first influences of the scientific revolution appear to be clear. In 1620, Thomas Fienus publishes a biomedical treatise on the formation of the foetus.[995] In it he argues that the soul must be infused around the third day after conception, which of course means a breaking with the Aristotelian and the early Christian teaching on animation. His main argument is that the soul must organise the body; nothing else can do so. Soul is what distinguishes the living and developing from what is not alive. Fienus states that the soul has a rational character from the outset.

When in 1869 canon law was reorganised, Pope Pius IX included among those who incur automatic excommunication "those procuring abortion, if successful", without distinguishing whether the foetus was animated or not. According to Grisez, "this act endorsed the growing awareness that the old distinction between animated and non-animated foetuses was grounded neither in experimental evidence nor necessary reasons."[996] Some years later, in 1879, a scientific plea for the immediate animation theory appears,

---

[993] T. Sanchez S.J. *De sancto matrimonii sacramento disputationum*, Antwerp, 1614. I consulted the edition of Viterbo, 1754, vol. III, book IX, question 20, no. 7-9. Cf. Grisez, G., 1970, op. cit., p. 168.
[994] Cf. part 5.1.8; Joannis de Lugo S.J., *Disputationes scholasticae et morales*, vol. VI, *De Iustitia et Iure*, Paris, 1869, disp. 10, sect. 5, q. 132-133 (p. 80). Cf. Connery S.J., J., op. cit., pp. 175-180.
[995] Thomas Fienus, *De formatrice fetus liber*. Antwerp, 1620, pp. 161, 184 and 199. Thomas Fienus was a professor of medicine at Louvain, Belgium. Cf. Grisez, G., 1970, op. cit., p. 170
[996] Ibid., p. 177.

by the hand of an anonymous writer in *Nouvelle Revue Théologique*.[997] In the first part the writer shows that the arguments for delayed animation derived from Scripture and the tradition of the Church are inconclusive.[998] Following Fienus and other scientists, the author then develops the line of reasoning that if the principle of formative development is immanent, then animation must be immediate.[999] Finally, the author shows that also the arguments of modern biology weigh heavily in favour of the immediate animation theory. By this time the human ovum had been discovered and it was known that the embryonic development started at fertilisation. Quoting a Parisian physician, the author states that "since the foetus receives the principle of life from the moment of conception, there is no further reason to distinguish between a foetus from nine months and the fertilized egg, some hours after conception."[1000] He concludes that "the Church can no longer sustain on reasonable grounds that a foetus could be given life without a rational soul."[1001]

Since then, ecclesiastical authorities have assumed that animation with a human soul must occur at once. So, it has been pointed out that throughout the ages the Catholic Church has been consistent in her condemnation of procured abortion as homicide. In the nineteenth century the early Christian writings which did not make a distinction between the formed and the unformed foetus, were confirmed by medical discoveries. The idea that the Catholic Church would have changed her position on abortion after 1870, cannot be sustained.[1002]

---

997 Anonymus, "De animatione foetus", *Nouvelle revue théologique*, 1879, 11, pp. 163-186.
998 Cf. part 6.1.1; Grisez, G., 1970, op. cit., p. 178.
999 Cf. John Haldane and Patrick Lee, "Aquinas on Human Ensoulment, Abortion and the Value of Life", *Philosophy*, 2003, 78, pp. 255-278.
1000 Anonymus, 1879, p. 185. The quoted physician is Dr. Cazeaux and his article has been published in the *Gazette médicale*, 10 February 1852.
1001 Ibid., p. 186.
1002 It would be wrong to conclude that the Catholic Church has ever be permissive towards abortion before the presupposed ensoulment of the foetus. In 2001, this point of view has again been raised in a debate in the House of Lords by the Anglican Bishop of Oxford, Richard Harries, who suggested that it was only in the 19th century that the position of the Catholic Church became firmed up and that "earlier Christian thought on this subject indicates an awareness of a developing reality, with developing rights [of the human embryo] as we would put it." House of Lords, January 21st 2001, cf. *Hansard*, 621, 16, cols. 35-37. David Albert Jones contradicts this line of thought, which also has been brought forward by the Anglican theologian G.R. Dunstan and others, in his extended historical analysis on the status of the human embryo in the Christian tradition in: Jones, D.A., op. cit., esp. pp. 57-74.

6.1.3 The twentieth and twenty-first century

In 1930 in his encyclical *Casti connubii* Pius XI stated that the lives of both mother and child "are equally sacred and no one, not even public authority, can ever have the right to destroy them."[1003] Therefore it is the task of state authorities to protect the unborn. His successors Pius XII and John XXIII repeat the same Church doctrine on the illicitness of abortion.[1004] However, new accents are also made, due to the rapidly changing post-war context and the ever advancing medical technology. In 1951, so three years after the appearance of the United Nations Declaration on Human Rights, Pope Pius XII states that the inviolability of human life is "a fundamental right of the human person".[1005] The Pope makes this statement a few years after the failure of several countries to include in the Human Rights Declaration the phrase that human life should be protected from the moment of conception.[1006]

In the same discourse, Pius XII makes clear what, according to the teaching of the Church, are the boundaries of direct and indirect abortion. "We have on purpose always used the expression '*direct* attack on the life of the innocent', '*direct* killing'. For if, for instance, the safety of the life of the mother-to-be, independently of her pregnant condition, should urgently require a surgical operation or other therapeutic treatment, which would have as a side effect, in no way willed or intended yet inevitable, the death of the foetus, then such an act could no longer be called a *direct* attack on innocent life. With these conditions, the operation, like other similar medical interventions, can be allowable, always assuming that a good of great worth, such as life, is at stake, and that it is not possible to delay until after the baby is born or to make use of some other effective remedy."[1007] The Popes' view on what could be defined as an indirect abortion is similar

---

1003 Pius XI, *Casti Connubii*, n. 64., Vatican, 1930.
1004 Pius XII, *Discorsi e Radiomessagi di Sua Santità Pio XII*, 1944, 6, 183ff.; John XXIII, encyclical *Mater et magistra*, AAS 53 (1961), p. 447, cf. *De abortu procurato*, n. 7.
1005 Pius XII, "Discorso di Sua Santità Pio PP. XII ai partecipanti al convegno del 'Fronte della famiglia' e della federazione delle associazioni delle famiglie", in: Pius XII, *Discorsi e Radiomessaggi di Sua Santità Pio XII*, 1951, 13, pp. 413 – 418.
1006 Lebanon and Chile suggested to introduce a text in the Universal Declaration to acknowledge a right to life to the unborn; cf. part 4.2.
1007 Pius XII, op. cit., pp. 413-418, cf. Grisez, G., 1970, op. cit., pp. 182-183.

to the application of the principle of acts with double effect.[1008]

6.1.3.1 The rise and decline of youth care, the care for unmarried mothers and their children in Catholic institutions in the twentieth century

From the second half of the 19th century and up to the 1970s, caring for unmarried mothers and their children was task taken on by many congregations of religious sisters, catholic lay-organizations and organizations of other Christian denominations in the Netherlands and the U.K.[1009] These institutions provided alternatives for women with unintended pregnancies who did not consider abortion. For example, in 1948, *'Moederheil'* (Salvation for mothers), run by the Little Sisters of Saint Joseph, was the largest of transitional houses for unmarried mothers in the Netherlands. From 1924 to 1948, the sisters accommodated more than 2,000 women, while more than 10,000 women visited their clinic for child-bearing.[1010] Many of the children who were placed in these religious institutions came from families or mothers with all kinds of problems. Children with mental, physical or social retardations received care and education while living in religious boarding schools. In 1967 in the Netherlands there were still 95 of these schools for special lower education.[1011]

Recently, the care provided by Dutch institutions belonging to the Catholic Church, as well as other Dutch institutions for youth care has been

---

1008 Cf. part 5.1.8; cf. Biemans, W.J.A., "Procured Abortion", in: Eijk, W.J. et al. (eds.), op. cit., p. 172.

1009 The history of these congregations is well documented, for example in: Annelies van Heijst, Marjet Derks and Marit Monteiro, *Ex Caritate. Kloosterleven, apostolaat en nieuwe spirit van actieve vrouwelijke religieuzen in Nederland in de 19ᵉ en 20ᵉ eeuw*. Hilversum, 2010, pp. 380-397. José Eijt, *We waren er altijd. Zusters in zorg en verpleging. Franciscanessen van de H. Elisabeth 1880-2009*. Rotterdam, 2009, pp. 335-360; José Eijt and Suzanne Hautvast, *Een missie in de marge. Dochters van Onze Lieve Vrouw van het Heilig Hart in Nederland en Indonesië 1911-2000*. Hilversum, 2002, pp. 162-169. A description of the situation of religion and society in England in the 19th and 20th centuries can be found in: Hugh McLeod, *Religion and Society in England 1850-1914*. Basingstoke, 1996; Callum G. Brown, *Religion and Society in Twentieth-Century Britain*. Harlow, 2006 and Hugh McLeod, *The Religious Crisis of the 1960s*. Oxford, 2007.

1010 Heijst, A. van et al., op. cit., p. 389.

1011 Marieke Hilhorst, *Instellingen voor onderwijs en opvoeding aan meisjes van zustercongregaties. Historische achtergronden en ontwikkelingen tot 1970*. In: Wim Deetman et al., 2013, pp. 283-304, here p. 288.

subjected to historical investigations.[1012] Jeroen Dekker et al. notice that in the period before the Second World War, the work in the religious institutions for child protection had not been professionalised very much.[1013] Only in the 1960s, new pedagogical and developmental psychological insights became integrated in their youth care. According to Marieke Hilhorst, until then in many boarding schools for girls there had been a pedagogical climate characterised by fear, punishment and repression.[1014] Already in the 1940s and 1950s, this had led to criticism, not only from societal groups but also from within the Church.[1015] The growing influence of the Charismatic Movement in the 1960s in the U.K. and elsewhere, needs to be added to these developments.[1016]

In 2011 the Commission of Inquiry into the sexual abuse of minors in the Roman Catholic Church, chaired by Wim Deetman, stated as interim conclusion that "inadequate supervision appears to have been a specific problem in Catholic boarding schools and boarding institutions, children's homes, seminaries and orphanages."[1017]

Annelies van Heijst describes how in the 1960s and 1970s both the societal significance and the esteem within the Church of active female religious congregations diminished.[1018] The ideals of equal rights for everyone and social support for vulnerable groups replaced their works of charity. Against the background of a general criticism towards institutions which were considered as authoritarian, the sister congregations had to legitimise

---

1012 Wim Deetman, Nel Draijer, Pieter Kalbfleisch, Harald Merckelbach, Marit Monteiro and Gerard de Vries, *Seksueel misbruik van minderjarigen in de Rooms-katholieke Kerk*. Amsterdam, 2011; W.J. Deetman et al., *Seksueel misbruik van en geweld tegen meisjes in de Rooms-katholieke Kerk. Een vervolgonderzoek*. Amsterdam, 2013 and Jeroen Dekker et al., *Jeugdzorg in Nederland, 1945-2010. Resultaten van deelonderzoek 1 van de commissie-Samson: Historische schets van de institutionele ontwikkeling van de jeugdsector vanuit het perspectief van het kind en de aan hem/haar verleende zorg*. Groningen, 2012.
1013 J.J.H. Dekker et al., op. cit., p. 33; Cf. Deetman, W.J. et al., 2013, op. cit., p. 39.
1014 Hilhorst, M., op. cit., p. 294.
1015 Ibid., p. 298.
1016 McLeod, H., 2007, op. cit., pp. 138-139.
1017 Deetman, W.J. et al., 2011, op. cit., p. 72. At the same time, it is noticed that as regards the risk of being sexually abused, there is no significant difference between Catholic and other institutions. Cf. ibid., p. 266.
1018 Annelies van Heijst, *Liefdewerk. Een herwaardering van de caritas bij de Arme Zusters van het Goddelijk Kind, sinds 1852*. Hilversum, 2002, pp. 267-282;

themselves. They tried to do so by calling their charity works 'social', in order to show that these works were significant not only for the Church, but for society as a whole. According to Van Heijst this interpretation only partly sufficed, because it left out the religious dimension of the charity works.[1019]

During the 1960s and 1970s, charity works organised by active religious sister congregations for unmarried women and their children rapidly diminished. This development took place as part of major changes within the Church and Western European society: the cultural revolution, the process of secularization and the diminishing number of men and women entering religious life.[1020] In society as a whole, religion was more and more considered as a private matter.[1021] As a result of the increasing prosperity and the emancipation of women, the need for institutional care for newborns diminished. At the same time when the religious institutions for unmarried mothers and their children gradually disappeared, a tendency developed to put up new-borns for adoption or to place them in foster care families.[1022] But even more influential in this regard were the decreasing birth rate, the increasing use of contraceptives and the increasing number of abortions.[1023] On these and other developments, the Church reacted in the 1960s, in particular at the Second Vatican Council.

6.1.3.2 The Second Vatican Council and beyond

The Second Vatican Council refers to abortion twice in its pastoral constitution on the Church in the modern world, *Gaudium et Spes*. This document is among the most important messages of the Council, in which is set forth how the Church conceives its relation to the modern world. *Gaudium et Spes* stresses the social nature of man, the growing human interdependence and the respect for the human person. Further, it expresses how the Church wants to put itself at the service of humanity.[1024]

1019 Ibid., p. 273.
1020 Dekker J.J.H. et al., op. cit., p. 37; Hugh McLeod, "The Sixties: Writing the Religious History of a Crucial Decade", *Kirchliche Zeitgeschichte*, 2001, 14, pp. 36-48.
1021 Van Heijst, A., op. cit., p. 273.
1022 Cf. Eijt, J., op. cit., p. 358 and Deetman, W.J., 2013, op. cit., pp. 94-96.
1023 Cf. parts 1.4.1, 1.4.2 and 1.4.3.1.
1024 Second Vatican Council, *Gaudium et Spes*, 1965, n. 3.

The first reference to abortion in *Gaudium et Spes* is in a list of acts opposed to human life, such as murder, genocide, abortion, euthanasia, and wilful self-destruction; acts which violate the integrity of the human person, such as torture, or which insult human dignity, such as slavery, prostitution and the selling of women and children.[1025] The Council lists these acts in a chapter called "The community of mankind", indicating that acts like abortion are not only an individual decision, but always take place in a societal context which facilitates such a decision. Here, *Gaudium et Spes* opposes an individualistic morality and wants to encourage citizens to participate in common endeavours which promote the dignity of man.[1026]

In a second reference to abortion, *Gaudium et Spes* mentions that from the moment of conception life must be guarded with the greatest care.[1027] In the same part the Council makes a mention of circumstances that can play a role for married couples who do not want, at least temporarily, to increase their families.[1028]

In the summer of 1968, a few years after the Second Vatican Council, Pope Paul VI promulgates the encyclical letter *Humanae Vitae*, in which he repeats the traditional rejection of abortion.[1029] However, abortion is not central in this document. In *Humanae Vitae*, the Church's doctrine on conjugal love and its unifying and procreative meaning is set out. Referring to natural law, *Humanae Vitae* condemns methods of artificial birth control, unless they have a therapeutic goal, whereas recourse to the to the non-fertile days of the woman's cycle ('natural family planning') is considered licit for married couples, because it makes use of a natural disposition.[1030]

This teaching has caused so many diametrically opposed reactions that

---

[1025] Ibid., n. 27.
[1026] Ibid., n. 30-31. The opposition to an individualistic morality does not mean that *Gaudium et Spes* rejects human autonomy per se. It states in n. 36 that "If by autonomy of earthly affairs we mean that created things and societies themselves enjoy their own laws and values which must be gradually deciphered, put to use, and regulated by men, then it is entirely right to demand that autonomy." At the same time, it "warns against a false concept of the autonomy of earthly realities, one which would maintain that 'created things are not dependent on God and that man can use them without reference to their Creator'." Cf. Ibid., n. 36.
[1027] Ibid., n. 51.
[1028] Ibid.
[1029] Paul VI, Encyclical *Humanae Vitae*, Vatican, 1968, n. 14.
[1030] Ibid., n. 14-16.

the essential message of the encyclical has been lost many times in the many discussions to which it gave rise. In order to understand the Church's teaching on the regulation of birth better, it is necessary to look at the assumptions, which are clearly explained in *Humanae Vitae*. In fact, the teaching on regulation of birth is based on the Church's view on love, marriage and natural law.

Firstly, when the Church speaks of love, it is referring to the Biblical meaning of love which is, according to the first letter of St. John, that "God is love".[1031] Following *Gaudium et Spes*, Paul VI's encyclical expresses as a first doctrinal principle that this love gets its full expression in marriage. In Scripture and in the Magisterial teaching, marriage is described as "the wise and provident institution of God the Creator, whose purpose was to effect in man His loving design."[1032]

Humanae Vitae describes five essential characteristics of the Biblical concept of married love: a love which is fully human, total, faithful, exclusive and fecund.[1033] Thus, the encyclical provides a very positive vision on married love, in which the gift of oneself is central, out of love for the partner's sake. Children are considered as the supreme gift of marriage, which contribute in the highest degree to their parents' welfare.

From these principles and characteristics, it follows that the teaching on abortion and contraceptive behaviour is related to the teaching on conjugal love and sexuality. In this regard, the magisterial declaration *De abortu procurato* of 1974 enters into the discussion on what is supposed to be meant by

---

1031 1 John, 4:8.
1032 Paul VI, op. cit., n. 8, see also *Gaudium et Spes*, 49, which adds the following Scriptural references: Genesis 2:22-24; Proverbs 5:15-20 and 31:10-31; Tobit 8:4-8; Song of Solomon 1:2-3; 1:16; 4:16; 5:1; 7:8-14; 1 Corinthians 7:3-6; Ephesians 5:25-33. *Gaudium et Spes*, n. 50 treats the fruitfulness of marriage.
1033 Paul VI, op. cit., n. 9. This teaching on conjugal love had already been the subject of reflection of several earlier Conciliar documents, papal instructions and encyclicals. Cf. *Catechismus Romanus Concilii Tridentini*, part. II, Ch. VIII; Pius XI, Encyclical *Casti Connubii*, in AAS XXII (1930), pp. 559-561; Pius XII, AAS XLIII (1951), p. 843; AAS L. (1958), pp. 734-735; John XXIII, encyc. *Mater et Magistra*, in AAS LIII (1961), p. 447; *Gaudium et Spes*, n. 51.

sexual freedom.[1034] What is at stake here are the values of love and freedom, in connection with sexuality and fertility. It is argued that sexuality as an act of authentic love has an intrinsic orientation towards the possibility of new life. Suppressing this possibility by ways of contraception bears the risk of self-centeredness, and may even lead to a hostile attitude towards new life. From there it is only a small step towards abortion, if contraception should fail.[1035] It is for this reason that the Church sees abortion and contraception as being in line, although both acts differ in their consequences.

Humanae Vitae points out the possible consequences for society of methods of artificial birth control.[1036] It could open the way for marital infidelity and a general lowering of moral standards, that will in particular affect the young. Secondly, a man who grows accustomed to the use of contraceptive methods may forget the reverence due to a woman. By disregarding her physical and emotional equilibrium, or worse, by reducing her to being a mere instrument for the satisfaction of his own desires, he might no longer consider her as his partner whom he should surround with care and affection.

Thirdly, *Humanae Vitae*, not only being written for a Catholic audience but for all men of good will, points out the risk of governments favouring or even imposing contraceptive methods or abortion. For instance, the recent history in the Far East shows that sex-selective abortion can become

---

1034 "The same must be said of the claim to sexual freedom. If by this expression one is to understand the mastery progressively acquired by reason and by authentic love over instinctive impulse, without diminishing pleasure but keeping it in its proper place - and in this sphere this is the only authentic freedom - then there is nothing to object to. But this kind of freedom will always be careful not to violate justice. If, on the contrary, one is to understand that men and women are 'free' to seek sexual pleasure to the point of satiety, without taking into account any law or the essential orientation of sexual life to its fruits of fertility, then this idea has nothing Christian in it. It is even unworthy of man. In any case it does not confer any right to dispose of human life - even if embryonic- or to suppress it on the pretext that it is burdensome." (Congregation for the Doctrine of the Faith, 1974, n. 16.).

1035 This view has been elaborated in the writings of Pope John Paul II, in particular in the encyclicals *Veritatis Splendor*, 1993, n. 80 and *Evangelium Vitae*, 1995, n. 13, as will be shown.

1036 Paul VI, 1968, n. 17.

a frightening reality.[1037] Even within Europe, sex-selective abortion occurs despite legal restrictions.[1038]

However, both from within the Catholic Church as from outside, *Humanae Vitae* is particularly criticised regarding the issue of contraception, as Joseph Komonchak illustrates: "Almost since the day it was issued, *Humanae Vitae* has been the *signum cui contradicetur* [a sign of contradiction[1039]] which Pope Paul VI anticipated it might become. The encyclical met with an opposition and dissent stronger and more public than any papal statement within memory, and the controversy that ensued quickly excited profound and even violent emotions and reactions. If emotions are somewhat calmer today and a certain peace, or at least truce, now rules over the Church's pastoral practice, opinions have not ceased to be divided on the subject and authority of the encyclical."[1040]

In the modern world, a growing plea for autonomy in relation to birth control characterised the years immediately following *Humanae Vitae*. At the same time in various parts in the world legislation was developed in order to legalise abortion.

During these years, the Episcopal conferences of England and Wales and the Netherlands protested against (possible) legalization of procured abortion.[1041] For instance, in 1974 the Dutch bishops argued that an essential aspect of the decision to abort, the killing of a human being in development, is often obscured in the public discussion on procured abortion. As regards the prevention of abortion, they state that "all available individual and social

---

1037 Amartya Sen provides the following statistical data: as compared to the biologically common ratio being 95 girls born to 100 boys, the Indian ratio is 92,7 girls for 100 boys, the South-Korean ratio is 88/100 and the Chinese ratio is 86/100. In: Michelle Webber and Kate Bezanson (eds.), *Rethinking Society in the 21ˢᵗ Century: Critical Readings in Sociology*. Toronto, 2008, p. 206.

1038 Cf. part 1.5.1 and 1.5.2.

1039 Paul VI, 1968, n. 18.

1040 Komonchak, Joseph A. "*Humanae Vitae* and Its Reception: Ecclesiological Reflections", in: *Theological Studies*, 39, 1978, pp. 221-257. See also Janet E. Smith, *Humanae Vitae a generation later*. Washington D.C., 1991. Of her book, chapter 6 in particular gives an overview of both positive and negative reactions from theologians and lay people on *Humanae Vitae*.

1041 Bishops' Conference of England and Wales, *Statement concerning moral questions*. London, 1970, pp. 15-16; Bisschoppen van Nederland, *Bisschoppelijke verklaring over abortus arte provocatus*. Utrecht, 1974.

help needs to be promised and guaranteed, for the woman who considers abortion and if necessary for the child itself. We do not say this only to the professional caregiver, but to all who are involved in the situation and of whom help might be expected, especially the woman's husband, friend or partner, her parents and her family."[1042]

In the same year, the Congregation for the Doctrine of the Faith published the declaration *De abortu procurato*.[1043] In the instruction the traditional doctrine of the Church on direct abortion is once more affirmed. Pope Paul VI, "speaking of this subject on many occasions, has not hesitated to declare that this teaching of the Church 'has not changed and is unchangeable'."[1044]

The declaration *De abortu procurato* does not teach in a definitive way on the moment of ensoulment:

> This declaration expressly leaves aside the question of the moment when the spiritual soul is infused. There is not a unanimous tradition on this point and authors are as yet in disagreement. For some it dates from the first instant; for others it could not at least precede nidation. It is not within the competence of science to decide between these views, because the existence of an immortal soul is not a question in its field. It is a philosophical problem from which our moral affirmation remains independent for two reasons: (1) supposing a belated animation, there is still nothing less than a human life, preparing for and calling for a soul in which the nature received from parents is completed, (2) on the other hand, it suffices that this presence of the soul be probable (and one can never prove the contrary) in order that the taking of life involves accepting the risk of killing a man, not only waiting for, but already in possession of his soul.[1045]

Since the question of the moment of the infusion of the spiritual soul cannot be decided in a scientific manner and because of that, always an

---

[1042] Bisschoppen van Nederland, 1974, 1-5. Three years earlier, on 24th February 1971, the Dutch Episcopate had already published a letter in which abortion on request was rejected. However, in this letter they acknowledged that in some cases a choice between one life and another was inevitable, cases in which one's conscience had to decide. Archief van de Kerken XXVI (1971), p. 235. Cf. Bruijn, J. de, op. cit., p. 204.
[1043] Congregation for the Doctrine of the Faith, Declaration *De abortu procurato*, 1974.
[1044] Ibid., n. 7.
[1045] Ibid., footnote n. 19.

uncertainty remains if people have to make a decision regarding the life or death of a foetus, decisions like these could cause a moral dilemma. Such a dilemma could for instance be experienced by parents who are expecting a child with a probable handicap and who often feel that they have to decide about the life of their child. In this regard, it is stated by Mariéle Wulf that a free, moral decision should take into account the greater possibility, the greater life. A decision which is contrary to life, should not be taken.[1046] As a theological reason for this rule, she mentions that "every decision against life and against the flourishing of life is a decision against the Holy Spirit".[1047]

The instruction on respect for human life in its origin and on the dignity of procreation, known as *Donum Vitae* of 1987, states that: "from the moment of conception, the life of every human being is to be respected in an absolute way because man is the only creature on earth that God has wished for himself and the spiritual soul of each man is immediately created by God; his whole being bears the image of the Creator."[1048] In their document of 2005, "Cherishing Life", the Catholic Bishops' Conference of England and Wales also state that "[t]he dignity of each human being is founded on his or her creation in the image and likeness of God (Genesis 1:26-27)."[1049]

In 2008, the Congregation for the Doctrine of the Faith confirmed both the principles and moral evaluations of *Donum Vitae*, in their instruction *Dignitas Personae*: "If *Donum Vitae*, in order to avoid a statement of an explicitly philosophical nature, did not define the embryo as a person, it nonetheless did indicate that there is an intrinsic connection between the ontological dimension and the specific value of every human life. Although the presence of the spiritual soul cannot be observed experimentally, the conclusions of science regarding the human embryo give 'a valuable

---

[1046] Wulf, C.M., 2013 (b), op. cit., pp. 334-335.
[1047] Ibid., p. 335. According to St. John, Jesus tells his disciples: "It is the spirit that gives life." (John, 6, 63) According to Teresa Okuze, this passage in John's Gospel is about the faith in God's and Jesus' power to give life with the means that they choose. Cf. T. Okuze, "Johannes", in: Eynikel, E. et al. (eds.), op. cit., Vol. 2, p. 1704. In the Nicene Creed, the Holy Spirit is entitled as "the Lord and Giver of life".
[1048] Congregation for the Doctrine of the Faith, Instruction *Donum Vitae*, 1987, Introduction, n. 5, cf. Pius XII, *Humani Generis*, n. 36, Vatican, 1950.
[1049] Catholic Bishops' Conference of England and Wales, *Cherishing Life*, London, 2004, n. 39.

indication for discerning by the use of reason a personal presence at the moment of the first appearance of a human life: how could a human individual not be a human person?"[1050] Indeed, the reality of the human being for the entire span of life, both before and after birth, does not allow us to posit either a change in nature or a gradation in moral value, since it possesses *full anthropological and ethical status*. The human embryo has, therefore, from the very beginning, the dignity proper to a person."[1051] One of the characteristics of a human life in the embryonic stage and beyond is that it "exists within a network of relationships: as the offspring of a mother and a father and as the gift of God the creator."[1052]

During the pontificate of John Paul II, the Magisterium reiterated that direct abortion must be seen as an 'intrinsically evil act'.[1053] Intrinsically evil acts are acts which *per se* and in themselves, regardless of circumstances, are always seriously wrong by reason of their object. The Second Vatican Council itself, in discussing the respect due to the human person, gives a number of examples of such acts, among which homicide, genocide, abortion, euthanasia and torture are mentioned.[1054] In 1993 Pope John Paul II rejects the application of consequentialist theories in cases that are to be judged as "intrinsically evil".[1055] It has to be noted that this typology does not categorise the person, but only the act itself.[1056]

The encyclical *Evangelium Vitae* by John Paul II does not bring a new position of the Catholic Church on abortion, but brings certain nuances and interconnections, such as the relation between Church and State. What is at stake here is the complex relation and the tensions which can exist between universal moral norms and democratically chosen legislation.

John Paul II reflects on the purpose and competence of civil law, which

---

1050 Congregation for the Doctrine of the Faith, Instruction *Dignitas Personae*, Vatican, 2008, n. 5; cf. Idem, *Donum Vitae*, 1987, I, 1.
1051 Congregation for the Doctrine of the Faith, 2008, op. cit., n. 5; cf. Catechism of the Catholic Church, Vatican, 1997, n. 2274.
1052 Catholic Bishops' Conference of England and Wales, 2004, n. 55.
1053 John Paul II, 1993, op. cit., n. 80.
1054 Ibid.; cf. John Paul II, Postsynodal Apostolic Exhortation *Reconciliatio et Paenitentia*, Vatican, 1983, n. 17; cf. Second Vatican Council, *Gaudium et Spes*, n. 27.
1055 John Paul II, 1993, op. cit., n. 75 and 79.
1056 For the application of this distinction between intrinsically evil acts and mortal sins, see part 7.8.

is that of "ensuring the common good of people through the recognition and defence of their fundamental rights, the promotion of peace and of public morality... Civil law must ensure that all members of society enjoy respect for certain fundamental rights which innately belong to the person, rights which every positive law must recognize and guarantee. First and fundamental among these is the inviolable right to life of every innocent human being."[1057]

He then addresses politicians who are faced with legislative proposals for a more restrictive abortion law, when it is not possible to completely abrogate the existing legislation by a majority of votes. In such a case, an elected official could justifiably support proposals aimed at limiting the harm done by such a law and at lessening its negative consequences at the level of general opinion and public morality.[1058]

While distinguishing clearly between abortion and contraception, the encyclical further warns against a certain "contraceptive mentality" that is present in modern society.[1059] This tendency is reinforced by the introduction of chemical products that act as contraceptives or abortifacients, such as the morning-after pill, or as abortifacients only, such as the abortion pill RU486. In this regard, the English and Welsh bishops call upon pharmaceutical companies that they are honest and explicit in saying how their drugs achieve their effects so that the public can make properly informed decisions.[1060]

John Paul II sees the danger of a cultural climate with reductionist and materialistic tendencies, according to which sexuality is depersonalised and exploited, whereas procreation is seen as an enemy which is to be avoided in sexual activity.[1061] On the other hand he recalls the fundamental goodness that human life characterizes, since man "is a manifestation of God in the world, a sign of his presence, a trace of his glory".[1062] The Pope is referring to the first chapter of the book of Genesis, which says that "God created humankind in his image".[1063] Perhaps the main intention of *Evangelium*

[1057] John Paul II, 1993, op. cit., n. 71, which refers to the Second Vatican Council document *Dignitatis Humanae*, n. 7.
[1058] John Paul II, 1993, op. cit., n. 73.
[1059] Ibid., n. 13.
[1060] Catholic Bishops' Conference of England and Wales, 2004, n. 176.
[1061] Ibid., n. 23.
[1062] Ibid., n. 34.
[1063] Cf. Gen., 1, 26-27.

Vitae is to direct attention to the loving care of God for every creature, including the unborn. One of the many Biblical quotations is from Jeremiah: "Before I formed you in the womb I knew you, and before you were born I consecrated you" (Jer. 1,5).

John Paul II does not explicitly mention the word 'person' in his definition of abortion. But he affirms that the human being is to be respected and treated *as a person* from the moment of conception.[1064] His way of thinking has similarities with Robert Spaemann's point of view. He stated that the only criterion for personality is the biological belonging to the human species.[1065]

Pope John Paul II shows that he is well aware of the painfulness that often accompanies the woman's decision to carry out an abortion, "out of a desire to protect certain important values such as her own health or a decent standard of living for the other members of the family." He continues: "Sometimes it is feared that the child to be born would live in such conditions that it would be better if the birth did not take place. Nevertheless, these reasons and others like them, however serious and tragic, can never justify the deliberate killing of an innocent human being."[1066] A crucial difference between this argument and some defenders of abortion, for instance Judith Jarvis Thomson or Daniel Callahan, is that they argue that the right to life of the unborn is subject to discussion in certain circumstances, whereas John Paul II states that under no circumstances whatsoever there is a right to directly kill the unborn.[1067]

According to Pope Francis, the defence of unborn life is closely linked to the defence of each and every other human right. He states that it "involves

---

[1064] John Paul II, 1995, op. cit., n. 60.
[1065] Cf. part 4.3.2.2. In 1983 Pope John Paul II made a similar statement in his speech to the World Medical Association: "La nature biologique de chaque home est intangible en ce sens qu'elle est constitutive de l'identité personelle de l'individu dans tout le cours de son histoire. Chaque personne humaine, dans sa singularité absolument unique, n'est pas seulement constituée par son esprit, mais par son corps. Ainsi, dans le corps et par le corps, on touche la personne elle-même dans sa réalité concrète. Respecter la dignité de l'homme revient par conséquent à sauvegarder cette identité de l'homme *corpore et anima unus*, comme dit le Concile Vatican II." In: *Acta Apostolicae Sedis*, 1984, 76, p. 393; cf. Demmer, K., 1985, op. cit., pp. 136-137.
[1066] John Paul II, 1995, op. cit., n. 58, cf. Congregation for the Doctrine of the Faith, 1974, n. 14.
[1067] The arguments of Thompson, Callahan and others have been discussed in part 2.2.7.

the conviction that a human being is always sacred and inviolable, in any situation and at every stage of development. Human beings are ends in themselves and never a means of resolving other problems."[1068] On the other hand, he is aware that "we have done little to adequately accompany women in very difficult situations, where abortion appears as a quick solution to their profound anguish, especially when the life developing within them is the result of rape or a situation of extreme poverty."[1069]

As regards situations of rape, it needs to be mentioned that a difference has been made in the writings of the Church Magisterium between abortion and emergency contraception after rape. The Catholic Archbishops of Great Britain clearly state that a woman is entitled to defend herself against the continuing effects of rape by seeking immediate medical assistance with a view to preventing conception. Once conception has occurred, the newly-conceived child needs to be protected.[1070] This view is in line with the argument that an embryo, contrary to a gamete, has a future of value.[1071]

Finally, Pope Francis' encyclical *Laudato Si'* points at the incompatibility of the justification of abortion with a concern for the protection of nature. This encyclical, named after the famous canticle of praise by Francis of Assisi, is at the same time an appeal to take the care of the earth, our common home, more seriously and also an expression of admiration of the beauty of creation. Pope Francis underlines the importance of the concern for other vulnerable beings and this includes human embryos, even if their presence may be uncomfortable and creates difficulties.[1072]

6.1.4 The Magisterium's reaction to prenatal diagnosis

In reaction to the technological progress in prenatal diagnosis and all the questions that this raises, the Magisterium has not remained silent. Three documents are of particular interest here, the Instruction *Donum*

1068 Francis, apostolic exhortation *Evangelii Gaudium*, Vatican, 2013, n. 213.
1069 Ibid., n. 214.
1070 Catholic Archbishops of Great Britain, *Abortion and the right to live*. London, 1980, n. 21. The ethical directives of U.S. Roman Catholic bishops for Catholic health-care facilities have a similar line of reasoning. Cf. United States Conference of Catholic Bishops. *Ethical and religious directives for Catholic Health Care Services*. Washington DC, 2009, n. 36.
1071 Cf. part 5.1.4.
1072 Francis, Encyclical letter *Laudato Si'*, on care for our common home. Vatican, 2015 (a), n. 120.

Vitae of the Congregation for the Doctrine of the Faith (CDF) of 1987, a document of the British Episcopate on prenatal diagnosis and the more recent Instruction *Dignitas Personae*, also of the CDF, of 2008.[1073]

Already in the introduction of *Donum Vitae* ('The Gift of Life') it is stated that the scope of this instruction is not "to intervene on the basis of a particular competence in the area of the experimental sciences; but having taken account of the data of research and technology, it intends to put forward, by virtue of its evangelical mission and apostolic duty, the moral teaching corresponding to the dignity of the person and to his or her integral vocation." The instruction then formulates moral criteria as regards the applications of scientific research and technology, especially in relation to human life and its beginnings. These criteria are "the respect, defence and promotion of man, his primary and fundamental right to life, his dignity as a person who is endowed with a spiritual soul and with moral responsibility and who is called to beatific communion with God."

Both documents acknowledge that in some cases the application of prenatal diagnosis is meant to promote the health of the embryo and the mother. Obviously, in those cases this application is judged as morally justifiable and yet it remains important to take into consideration the risks of prenatal tests.[1074] Further, *Donum Vitae* points out that parents, relatives or anyone else would act contrary to the moral law if they would have the deliberate intention of having or advising an abortion should the results of prenatal tests confirm the existence of a malformation or abnormality. In particular, the instruction speaks of illicit cooperation if the specialist is deliberately contributing to establish or favour a link between prenatal diagnosis and abortion.[1075]

The instruction *Dignitas personae* ('The dignity of the person') confirms completely the principles and moral evaluations of *Donum Vitae*.[1076] The document does not enter into forms of prenatal diagnosis, other than pre-implantation diagnosis, which it rejects because it "is directed toward

---

1073 Catholic Bishops of Great Britain, Joint Committee on Bioethical Issues, "Antenatal Tests: What You Should Know. Answers to questions which face every pregnant mother", in *Briefing*, 19:3 (3 Feb. 1989) 50-56; cf. *Medicina e Morale*, 40:1 (1990), 149-158.
1074 Cf. part 5.2.
1075 *Donum Vitae*, part 1, question 2.
1076 Congregation for the Doctrine of the Faith, *Dignitas Personae*, Vatican, 2008, n. 1.

the qualitative selection and consequent destruction of embryos, which constitutes an act of abortion."[1077]

6.1.5 Abortion in relation to the Magisterial teaching of family values and virtues

The Magisterial stance on the protection of unborn life is closely connected with the teaching on other values, in particular those concerned with marriage and family life. In 1981, John Paul II pointed at the positive and negative aspects in the situation of families in today's global society.[1078] On the one hand, he welcomes the "more lively awareness of personal freedom and greater attention to the quality of interpersonal relationships in marriage, to promoting the dignity of women, to responsible procreation, to the education of children." On the other hand, he remarks that "signs are not lacking of a disturbing degradation of some fundamental values: a mistaken theoretical and practical concept of the independence of the spouses in relation to each other; serious misconceptions regarding the relationship of authority between parents and children; the concrete difficulties that the family itself experiences in the transmission of values; the growing number of divorces; the scourge of abortion; the ever more frequent recourse to sterilization; the appearance of a truly contraceptive mentality."[1079]

Thirty years have passed since John Paul II wrote down these words and since then, divorce rates in the Western world have increased further, whereas the number of marriages has decreased.[1080] It is remarkable

---

[1077] Ibid., n. 22.
[1078] John Paul II, Apostolic exhortation *Familiaris Consortio, on the role of the Christian family in the modern world.* Vatican, 1981.
[1079] Ibid., n. 6.
[1080] Francis Fukuyama describes how in virtually all modernizing societies, the role of the family has diminished in importance. For instance, from 1972 to 1994, the divorce rates in the U.K. and the Netherlands have climbed from respectively 1,3 and 0,9 per 1,000 inhabitants to 3,1 and 2,3 per 1,000. Cf. Fukuyama, F., op. cit., pp. 36-47 and 292. Between 1982 and 2009, the percentage of married men in the U.K. has dropped from 50 to 40%; in the Netherlands these percentages were respectively 48% and 42%. Cf. UN Demographic Statistics, "Population by marital status, age, sex and urban/rural residence", UNdata, accessed 15 December 2015. In parts 1.4.1.4 and 1.4.2 it has been shown that abortion rates in the U.K. and the Netherlands are much lower among married women.

that John Paul II often refers to the *totality* of conjugal love, just as his predecessor Paul VI did in *Humanae Vitae*.[1081] But John Paul II in his writings gives more attention to the spiritual and physical dimensions of this totality, especially in what has become known as the theology of the body.[1082] A central element in this theology is the sacramentality of the human body, a sacrament being a "visible sign of the hidden reality of salvation."[1083] John Paul II calls the body the "primordial sacrament", instituted by God at the dawn of creation.[1084] The essence of what it is that, according to John Paul II, human male bodies and human female bodies make visible about God, is thus summarised by Paula Jean Miller:

> When we act in a truly human way (and we can act only in and through our bodies), we are images of how God acts. The human person, embodied as male and female, makes visible a God who both gives and receives in selfless and unconditional love. We know this by revelation in Scripture, as well as through reason in our own human experience. When a man and a woman love each other absolutely and fully, their love is often blessed with the gift of a child, a third person who embodies their love and makes it incarnate for the world. The way a man and a woman love each other in marriage is to make visible to the world this God who is two Persons, who love each other so fully and absolutely that their love is a third Person, the Holy Spirit of love. God is a communion of three Persons in love; the human family is its created image.[1085]

Pope John Paul II published his theology of the body in a series of audiences, held between 1979 and 1984. In one of these audiences, he gave pastoral and moral directions on the principle of responsible parenthood.[1086]

1081 Cf. part 6.1.3.2.
1082 For a brief introduction of the theology of the body, see for instance: Paula Jean Miller F.S.E., "The Theology of the Body. A New Look at *Humanae Vitae*.", *Theology Today*, 57, 2001, 4, pp. 501-508.
1083 Catechism of the Catholic Church, 1997, n. 774.
1084 John Paul II, *General Audience, 20 February 1980, Man Enters the World As a Subject of Truth and Love*. Vatican, 1980.
1085 Miller F.S.E., P.J., op. cit., p. 504.
1086 John Paul II, General Audience of Wednesday 1 August 1984 on Responsible Parenthood, in: *L'Osservatore Romano, Weekly Edition in English*, 6 August 1984, p. 1.

This principle is directly related to the problem of abortion and to means of contraception, since when man and woman have a commitment to responsible parenthood, this means that they cannot act arbitrarily as regards their procreation. Already in the encyclical *Humanae Vitae*, Paul VI indicates that the human mind discerns biological laws that apply to the human person, in relation to the procreative faculty of men.[1087] As regards the diversity of these laws, Paul VI refers to the teaching of Thomas Aquinas, who discerns in the human person several natural inclinations to what is good, such as an inclination towards the preservation of his own being, which he shares with all substances; an inclination to sexual intercourse and the education of offspring, which man shares with all animals; and finally a natural inclination to reason, which is specific to man.[1088] Exercising responsible parenthood, man will make use of his reason and his will, so as to control his innate drives and emotions. Likewise, couples practicing responsible parenthood, will discern if they wish to have more children, or "for serious reasons and with due respect to moral precepts, decide not to have additional children for either a certain or an indefinite period of time".[1089] John Paul II states, just as his predecessors did, that only natural ways of regulating fertility are morally acceptable, since they make use of the method of self-mastery, which corresponds to the fundamental constitution of the person.[1090] According to the criterion of truth, the conjugal act signifies not only love, but also potential fecundity.[1091]

It has been argued by Charles Curran that the papal talks of John Paul II on the theology of the body lack a recognition of historical development regarding the Church's teachings on marriage and sexuality.[1092] At the same time, Curran acknowledges that, while John Paul's anthropology and

---

[1087] Paul VI, 1968, n. 10.
[1088] Th. Aquinas, *S. T.,* II, I, q. 94, a. 2.
[1089] Paul VI, 1968, n. 10.
[1090] John Paul II, general audience of Wednesday, 22 August 1984 on the Church's Position on Transmission of Life, in: *L'Osservatore Romano, Weekly Edition in English*, 27 August 1984, p. 7.
[1091] Ibid., cf. Paul VI, 1968, n. 12.
[1092] Charles E. Curran, *The Moral Theology of Pope John Paul II*, Washington D.C., 2005, pp. 179-184. He mainly refers to the writings of John Noonan on contraception and the indissolubility of marriage, cf. John T. Noonan, Jr., *Contraception. A History of Its Treatment by the Catholic Theologians and Canonists*. Enlarged Edition, Cambridge (Ma.) and London, 1986.

metaphysics insist on a natural law approach, he also developed personalist arguments in order to defend the existing papal teaching on marriage and sexuality.[1093]

John Noonan concludes his historical analysis of the Church's teaching on contraception with the observation that at the core of this teaching five propositions can be found, which represent underlying values. These propositions are that procreation is intrinsically good; procreation of offspring reaches its completion only in their education; innocent life is sacred; the personal dignity of a spouse is to be respected and marital love is holy.[1094] Despite these constant, underlying values, the Church's doctrine on marriage and sexuality shows an historical development, influenced by changes in theological thinking, scientific discoveries and cultural shifts in society.[1095]

One example of how scientific discoveries have influenced the Church' teaching on family values and virtues, can make this more clear: in recent decades, there is a growing attention for natural ways of fertility regulation, both within and outside the Church. The Catholic Church has indeed supported and encouraged the promotion of natural fertility planning, such as the Billings' method. However, as Thérèse Jacob-Hargot has remarked, this method is primarily 'natural'. It is not only called 'natural' since it makes use of physiological signs of fertility, without any negative health or environmental effects, but also because it makes use of specifically human capacities: reason, will, intelligence and imagination.[1096]

6.1.6 Abortion and canon law

The Church legislation, stated in canon law is clear in regard to abortion, though some nuances are also made. While applying canon law, it must always be kept in mind that penances are meant to reconcile the believer with the merciful God.

1093 Curran, Ch. E., op. cit., pp. 116-117.
1094 Noonan, Jr., J.T., 1986, op. cit., p. 533.
1095 For a further treatment of this historical development of the Church' teaching on contraception, which is beyond the scope of this study, I refer to the earlier quoted work by John Noonan.
1096 Thérèse Jacob-Hargot, *Pour une libération sexuelle véritable*. Langres – Saint Geosmes, 2010, pp. 121 and 124.

The canonical penance against those who committed 'a crime against life', which is automatic excommunication, includes those who actively cooperated to procure a completed abortion.[1097] The Pontifical Commission for the Authentic Interpretation of the Code of Canon Law declares that the canonical concept of abortion is "the killing of the foetus in whatever way or at whatever time from the moment of conception".[1098] However, in assessing a canonical penalty, the penal authority must consider various factors affecting imputability, e.g., age, ignorance or fear.[1099] In practice, a confessor might remit a penalty, since this excommunication would rarely be formally declared. While counselling the penitent about the moral evil of abortion, the confessor should also consider possible mitigating circumstances which preclude the incurring of the penalty.[1100] Usually the penalty in the case of a procured abortion can only be remitted by the bishop or by a priest with a special faculty. For the occasion of the extraordinary Jubilee of Mercy, which started 8 December 2015, Pope Francis has conceded to all priests "the discretion to absolve of the sin of abortion those who have procured it and who, with contrite heart, seek forgiveness for it".[1101]

A politician or legislator is not to be considered a necessary accomplice, which would lead to automatic excommunication. However, an individual bishop might take a decision to impose a canonical penalty on a politician or legislator in order to correct error and repair scandal. This must be done according to the Church penal and procedural law.[1102]

1097 *Codex Iuris Canonici*, Vatican, 1983, n. 1398 and 1329, § 2 on complicity in a delict, when their assistance is indispensable for the abortion. The complicity might include parents of the aborted foetus, their families, doctor, nurses, etc. The canon does not apply to administrators of clinics and hospitals or to political officials facilitating abortions by advocating abortion rights and voting to fund abortions, however morally questionable their behaviour. Cf. John P. Beal, James A. Coriden and Thomas J. Green (eds.), *The New Commentary on the Code of Canon Law* /Commissioned by the Canon Law Society of America, Mahwah, N.J., 2000, p. 1603.
1098 Cf. Congregation for the Doctrine of the Faith, 2008, note 46.
1099 *Codex Iuris Canonici*, 1983, n. 1323-1327, cf. Beal, J.P. et al. (eds.), op. cit., p. 1603.
1100 Cf. *Codex Iuris Canonici*, 1983, n. 1357 and 1323-1324 and ibid., p. 1603.
1101 Francis, "Letter of his Holiness Pope Francis according to which an indulgence is granted to the faithful on the occasion of the extraordinary Jubilee of Mercy", Vatican, 2015 (b).
1102 R.O. Morrissey, *The Canonical Effects of Abortion in the 1983 Code of Canon Law. Dissertatio ad lauream in Facultate Iuris Canonici apud Pontificiam Universitatem S. Thomae in Urbe*. Rome, 1995, p. 71.

Further, it needs to be noted that members of religious institutes, secular institutes or societies of apostolic life must be dismissed for committing such an offense, unless in exceptional cases.[1103] Anyone who has procured a completed abortion or positively cooperated cannot be ordained.[1104] Those who are ordained and are in similar circumstances, are considered irregular in regard to exercising orders already received.[1105] In the last two cases a dispensation reserved to the Apostolic See can be granted.[1106]

It can be concluded that with regard to abortion, canon law is applicable in cases when someone has deliberately chosen to abort or when someone has actively cooperated to procure a completed abortion.

Canon law provides two articles on the possibility of baptizing aborted foetuses and new-borns in danger of death. Can. 871 states that if possible, aborted foetuses are to be baptised when they are alive. Since it is highly unlikely that an ordained person, a catechist or another person designated to baptise will be present for the baptism of a foetus, the Catholic baptismal ritual reminds pastors of their obligation to instruct lay people, especially "midwives, family or social workers or nurses of the sick, as well as physicians and surgeons" on how to baptise.[1107]

Can. 867, part 2 states that an infant in danger of death needs to be baptised without any postponement. Besides administering the sacrament, it is clear that an important aspect of the work of clergy and hospital chaplains regards the communication with family members, which can be particularly relevant in their coping process with illness and death and sometimes in making difficult treatment decisions.[1108]

1103 *Codex Iuris Canonici*, 1983, n. 695, 729, 746 and Beal, J.P. et al. (eds.), op. cit. p. 1603.
1104 *Codex Iuris Canonici*, 1983, n. 1041, 4° and ibid., p. 1603.
1105 *Codex Iuris Canonici*, 1983, n. 1044, § 1, 3° and ibid., p. 1603.
1106 *Codex Iuris Canonici*, 1983, n. 1047, § 3, cf. ibid., pp. 1603 and 1226.
1107 Beal, J.P. et al. (eds.), op. cit., p. 1060; the quotation is from the General introduction on Christian initiation, Roman Ritual for the baptism of children. Cf. Nationale Raad voor Liturgie, *Liturgie van de sacramenten en andere kerkelijke vieringen. Het doopsel van kinderen*, Zeist, 1993, n. 17. When there is no priest or deacon available and when there is a life threatening situations, baptism is administered validly by any believer, even by anyone with a good intention, if water is poured on the child (on the head, if possible), while saying the words: "I baptise you in the name of the Father and the Son and the Holy Spirit." Cf. ibid., n. 16 and 23.
1108 On the role of the clergy and the hospital chaplain (ordained or not ordained) in relation to pain and pain management, see David F. Kelly, *Contemporary Catholic Health Care Ethics*. Washington D.C., 2004, pp. 226-228.

6.2 The Christian interpretation of human conscience throughout the centuries

The Church acknowledges the binding character of a person's conscience.[1109] At the same time the Church' teaching confirms that the dignity of human conscience is derived from the universal and objective norms of morality, or, in other words, from the truth about moral good and evil.[1110]

In the course of the centuries, Doctors of the Church and many theologians have interpreted the Biblical meaning of human conscience. As regards the Christian interpretation of formation of conscience, on the level of ethical foundations, man finds himself in front of an horizon of divine obligation.[1111] The formation of conscience takes shape in dialogue, in relation between God and man.

Within Sacred Scripture, a certain obligation always originates in the word of God.[1112] The Old Testament writings do not explicitly use the word 'conscience', because this word does not exist in Biblical Hebrew. Instead, both in the Old and the New Testament one can find the term 'heart', referring to the interior centre of man, the origin of personhood and of ethical decisions. (Proverbs 12, 20; Sirach 13, 25; Psalm 17, 3; Psalm 51, 10; Matthew 6, 21) The heart forms the place of faith (John 14, 1), of doubt (Mark 11, 23), it could be pure (Matthew 5, 8), hardened (Mark 3, 5) or far removed from God (Matthew 15, 8). Evil intentions could arise from the heart (Matthew 15, 19) On the other hand, according to Matthew, Jesus insists on the greatest and first commandment from the law of Moses: "You shall love the Lord your God with all your heart, and with all your soul, and with all your mind." (Matthew 22, 37) The heart forms the place for the relationship with God. Therefore, Christian ethics always has a relation to the Creator and to creation.[1113]

In Sacred Scripture the term 'conscience' (in Greek: *syneidesis*) can mainly be found in the Pauline corpus. In his letters, St. Paul mentions the human conscience in relation to the moral value of one's own or others'

[1109] Cf. part 2.3.1.
[1110] John Paul II, 1993, n. 60.
[1111] Wulf, C.M., 2013 (b), op. cit., p. 328.
[1112] Wulf, C.M., 2013 (a), op. cit., p. 55.
[1113] Wulf, C.M., 2013 (a), op. cit., pp. 55-56.

behaviour. Still, already in the Pauline corpus several different meanings of the term 'conscience' can be traced, which have been further developed in later centuries in the tradition of the Church and in the various scientific traditions. Salvatore Privitera and Livio Melina et al. distinguish four different meanings of 'conscience' which can be found in Holy Scripture:[1114] firstly a parenetic (exhortative) meaning, which describes the submission to authorities, "not only because of wrath, but also because of conscience" (Romans 13,5); secondly, an intellectual meaning, according to which conscience is described as a cognitive faculty, able to discern between good and evil (examples of this kind of discernment can be found in Romans 2, 18 and Philippians 1, 9); thirdly, a psychological meaning, like in Romans 2, 15. Here, conscience is considered as an interior witness of the godly law, which is written in the hearts of heathens as well as Jews.[1115] Finally, the term conscience is used as in the Old Testament meaning of 'heart', out of which both good and bad actions can arise. (Hebrews 9, 14) This is also called the dimension of the will, in which conscience represents the active centre of decision.

In these different ways conscience enables one to assume responsibility for the acts performed.[1116] In order to act responsibly, the Church Magisterium points out the necessity of the formation of conscience, so that it is informed and the person is able to formulate moral judgments based on reason and enlightened by faith.[1117]

In the Middle Ages, the theological question comes up of the possibility of an erroneous conscience.[1118] It is Thomas Aquinas who offers the key to the answer, proposing the distinction between two levels of human

---

1114 Melina, L., et al., op. cit., pp. 599-600; see also Salvatore Privitera, "Coscienza", part IV, Integrazione, in: Francesco Compagnoni, Giannino Piara and Salvatore Privitera, *Nuovo dizionario della teologia morale*, Cinisello Balsamo (Milano), 1990, pp. 200-202.
1115 Cf. Rudolf Bultmann, *Theology of the New Testament*. Translated in English by K. Grobel, Waco, Texas, 2007, pp. 217-218 and A.F.N. Lekkerkerker, *De brief van Paulus aan de Romeinen*, vol. I, Nijkerk, 1971, p. 100.
1116 Catechism of the Catholic Church, 1997, n. 1781.
1117 Ibid., n. 1783-1785.
1118 Cf. part 2.3.1.

conscience: the *synderesis* and the true and proper conscience.[1119] As a sign of the image of God in us, the *synderesis* is indelible and infallible. In this way, every decision of human conscience stands before the call of truth.[1120] For every human person, conscience forms the place where he could encounter the sacred.[1121]

However, error could enter human thought and behaviour in the moment of application of human conscience, which is the work of practical reason. In this sense, the formation of conscience is essential in order to adequately fulfil its task.[1122]

At the Second Vatican Council, the way in which human conscience functions, is described as follows:

In the depths of his conscience, man detects a law which he does not impose upon himself, but which holds him to obedience. Always summoning him to love good and avoid evil, the voice of conscience when necessary speaks to his heart: do this, shun that. For man has in his heart a law written by God; to obey it is the very dignity of man; according to it he will be judged. Conscience is the most secret core and sanctuary of a man. There he is alone with God, Whose voice echoes in his depths.[1123]

Although this text confirms the traditional doctrine, it is noted that

---

[1119] Thomas Aquinas, *Questiones disputatae De veritate*, 16 and 17, translated in German by Edith Stein, *Übersetzung Des Hl. Thomas von Aquino Untersuchungen über die Wahrheit, I, Eingeführt und bearbeitet von Andreas Speer und Francesco Valerio Tommasi*. Edith Stein Gesamtausgabe, 23, Freiburg 2008, pp. 450-475. Cf. Melina, L. et al., op. cit., p. 601; cf. part 2.3. Likewise, St. Alphonsus Liguori speaks of the relation between Godly law and human conscience, in describing a true conscience as the obligation to inquire the truth in moral matters, so that our judgments are conform the Godly law. The Godly law is the remote or material law of our actions; the proximate and formal law is our conscience. Since the goodness or evil of actions is apparent to us insofar as conscience graps them, conscience is defined by De Liguori as the dictate of reason by which we judge what is to be done, or avoided, in the here and now. Alphonsus de Liguori, *Theologia Moralis, Lib. I, Tract. III, Cap. II, Art. 1*. Edited by J. Aertnys, C.SS.R., and C.A. Damen, C.SS.R., Torino, 1947, p. 71; Ibid., *Lib. I, Tract. III, Cap. I*, p. 69; cf. Frederick M. Jones C.SS.R., *Alphonsus de Liguori. Selected writings*. New York, 1999, p. 323.

[1120] Cf. Eberhard Schockenhoff, *Wie gewiss ist das Gewissen? Eine ethische Orientierung*. Freiburg, 2003, pp. 166-169. He refers for instance to the Pastoral Constitution *Gaudium et Spes*, n. 50, speaking of conjugal love, which is revealed, protected and impelled by the divine law to its true fulfillment.

[1121] Wulf, C.M., 2013 (a), op. cit., p. 57.

[1122] Cf. Catechism of the Catholic Church, 1997, n. 1783.

[1123] *Gaudium et Spes*, n. 16.

an amplified hermeneutic horizon is introduced. Beyond the scholastic distinctions, in this description the profound ontological dimension of human conscience is valued in its religious and responsible nature, with Augustinian resonances.[1124]

It needs to be said that a Christian is free in his conscience. No one has the right to force someone to act in a manner contrary to his conscience. Nor, on the other hand is he or she to be restrained from acting in accordance with his conscience.[1125] The role of the Church is to put herself "always and only at the service of conscience".[1126]

1124 Cf. Melina, L. et al., op. cit., p. 604.
1125 Second Vatican Council, *Declaration on Religious Freedom Dignitatis Humanae*, Vatican, 1965, n. 3; Catechism of the Catholic Church, 1997, n. 1782; Wulf, C.M., 2013 (a), op. cit., p. 57.
1126 John Paul II, 1993, n. 64.

Chapter 7

Abortion prevention, sex education, counselling and pastoral care

In the previous chapters it has been pointed out that the value of women's health, the principle of women's autonomy in relation to significant others and the future value of the foetus cannot be sufficiently protected with the current British and Dutch abortion legislation. Therefore, it is necessary to look for ways to stimulate the prevention of procured abortion and to sustain responsible parenthood. These aims will be the focus of this chapter and the next.

With regard to abortion prevention it is important to increase the knowledge about the ways in which professionals, volunteers and families in British and Dutch societies could contribute to providing alternatives to abortion. (7.1) In this chapter, possible alternatives to abortion will be investigated, including their main goals and their organisational structure in the U.K. and the Netherlands. (7.1.1) The state of affairs regarding Sex and Relationships Education (SRE) in primary and secondary schools in the U.K. and the Netherlands will be summarised and discussed. (7.1.2)

It has been shown that in the Netherlands, about a quarter of all women revealed doubts before and after the intervention, some of them very serious.[1127] These findings are a strong indication for psychological complications in the years after the abortion, especially since a majority does not show these doubts to the consultant. Therefore, high quality standards for counselling pregnant women and their partners are required.

Counselling and pastoral care could be helpful during the decision-making process after the discovery of an unintended pregnancy (7.3) or after prenatal diagnosis (7.4) and in the education of virtues (7.5). The role

---

1127 Cf. part 3.3.1.2.

men could play in these decision-making processes and the way in which they could more actively share in the responsibilities of parenthood will also be investigated. If necessary, legal measures can be taken in order to prove fatherhood (7.6). Even when an abortion has already taken place, pastoral care can be helpful in the process of reconciliation. (7.7)

The restriction of abortion laws can only be executed in a just way if at the same time there are sufficient means for couples in difficulty to receive assistance in fulfilling their parental responsibilities. This is required because it belongs to the undisputed rights of children.

7.1 Alternatives to abortion in the U.K. and the Netherlands

The following alternatives to abortion can be distinguished: the support of parenthood, coming from professional agencies, from volunteers (including family and peers) and/or from the Government. In this part, the organisational structure of these alternatives in the U.K. and the Netherlands will be evaluated. After that, the alternatives of adoption and foster care are considered.

7.1.1 Personal assistance and financial support after an unintended pregnancy in the U.K.

In the U.K. several private organisations take care of women who are in need of help because they are facing an unintended pregnancy that, after due consideration, they still want to bring to term. For example, LIFE offers free confidential counselling, also after abortion and pregnancy loss, and gives practical help on an on-going basis. Their services are available to men and women, teenagers, single people and couples. LIFE is an organisational member of the British Association of Counsellors and Psychotherapists (BACP) and adheres to its Code of Ethics. In 2008 LIFE Housing had 32 houses nationwide, each suitable for 4-7 service users and is locally funded by 23 Supporting People Administering Authorities since 2000. Between 2007 and 2010, they provided accommodation for nearly 400 women per year. LIFE offers a skills programme for their service users, focusing on for example kitchen skills, health and safety issues and budgeting. Support, which is based on an individual support plan, can be continued for two years, depending on the mother's needs. The reported tenant satisfaction rate was 93% in 2010/11, whereas the void rate in their houses was 8%. LIFE has also established community support services in places like Belfast and Hampshire.[1128] Despite these positive results, LIFE faces serious financial problems, which in 2010 were resolved by expanding fundraising and by a severe pruning of staff salaries and other expenditures.[1129] In 2013, LIFE still has 23 houses and five community services across the U.K.

Comment on Reproductive Ethics (Corethics) was founded in 1994 by Josephine Quintavalle and Margaret Nolan. As a public interest group its focus is on ethical dilemmas surrounding human reproduction, particularly the new technologies of assisted conception. Corethics holds the absolute respect for the human embryo as a principal tenet.[1130]

Since 1966, the Society for the Protection of the Unborn Child (SPUC) has operated as a pressure group, not as a registered charity. SPUC was founded to uphold the principle of respect for human life, in particular the life of the unborn child. The society's constitution is non-religious, endorsing the recognition by the world community in the 1959 United Nations Declaration of the Rights of the Child that the child "needs special safeguards and care, including appropriate legal protection, before as well as after birth."[1131] The SPUC's lobbying work concentrates on the U.K. Parliaments and Assemblies, as well as the European Parliament. SPUC also focuses on press and media releases and on educational activities.[1132]

Abortion Recovery Care & Helpline (ARCH) is an organization which offers help for women, men and families to restore their lives and relationships after an abortion experience. ARCH offers free, confidential one-to-one counselling, telephone counselling and group counselling. ARCH provides speakers for schools, colleges and other groups as well as contributions to the media.[1133]

SPUC and ARCH support the Silence No More Awareness campaign. This international campaign started in 2002 and seeks to expose and heal

---

1128 Cf. Life, *Annual Review 2010/11*, Lemington Spa, 2012, p. 7.
1129 According to Prof. J. Scarisbrick, national chairman of LIFE, *Annual Review 2010/11*, p. 2.
1130 Cf. www.corethics.org, accessed 14 December 2015.
1131 United Nations Declaration of the Rights of the Child, 1959, preambula.
1132 Cf. www.spuc.org.uk, accessed 14 December 2015.
1133 Cf. www.archtrust.org.uk, accessed 14 December 2015.

the secrecy and silence surrounding the emotional and physical pain of abortion. As of February 2015, the Silent No More Awareness Campaign has held 1,436 gatherings in 17 countries including the U.K. and the Netherlands with a total of 5,934 women and men sharing their abortion testimonies.[1134]

The ProLife Alliance has been founded as a British political party, but nowadays aims at education and campaigning in the areas of abortion, euthanasia, human cloning and embryo abuse.[1135] In 2011, after a five year legal conflict, the Department of Health fulfilled a Freedom of Information Request from the ProLife Alliance, by publishing data on the number of abortions after the discovery of foetal anomalies, including cleft palates and Down's syndrome.[1136]

7.1.2 Personal assistance and financial support after an unintended pregnancy in the Netherlands

Already in the 1970s, before the time of legalization of abortion, in the Netherlands little political was shown to offer material support to women who wanted to bring an unplanned pregnancy to term, but did not have sufficient means to do so.[1137] In 2011, it is still the case that the infrastructure is largely lacking in the Netherlands to offer any substantial help to this category of women. Pro-life organizations and organizations involved in social work do not have the means to provide this kind of assistance on a national scale. For instance, Siriz (formerly called VBOK ['Vereniging ter Bescherming van het Ongeboren Kind'] is the largest Dutch pro-life organization, founded in 1971.[1138] After the legalization of abortion in 1981, VBOK changed its strategy from protesting against legalization to offering assistance to pregnant women and young mothers. In 2012, Siriz had one

---

1134 Cf. www.silentnomoreawareness.org/about-us/, accessed 14 December 2015.
1135 Cf. www.prolife.org.uk, accessed 31 December 2015.
1136 Cf. Claire Bates, "Revealed: The thousands of pregnancies aborted for 'abnormalities' including cleft palates and Down's syndrome", *Daily Mail*, 5 July 2011.
1137 In part 2.1.3.
1138 Driving forces behind the foundation and initial governance of the VBOK are Prof. Dr. W.P. Plate, obstetrician; Prof. Dr. G.A. Lindeboom, internist and writer in medical history; Prof. Dr. T.K.A.B. Eskes, gynaecologist; Dr. H. Rottinghuis, gynaecologist; baron C.J. Schimmelpenninck van der Oye; Mrs. C.A.H. Haitsma Mulier-van Beusekom, editor; P.M. Beijerbergen van Henegouwen S.J., priest and H.J. Ogilvie, G.P. Cf. VBOK, 1996, p. 30.

house in the city of Gouda where pregnant women could go, as well as thirteen care stations and eleven host families.[1139] By the end of 2008, for the first time in their history, Siriz/VBOK received financial support from the state.[1140] In 2013, the total amount of national and local governmental support has been € 703,180.--.[1141] In comparison, in 2012 Dutch abortion clinics received € 13,2 million as subsidies.[1142] As regards the requests made to Siriz for care facilities, there is still an increasing demand. In 2010, of the 49 applications, 33 women could not be placed.[1143] In 2012, there were 60 applications; 22 women have been placed and accompanied.[1144]

Organizations for social work such as FIOM, mainly offer consultation on a large number of issues and, if needed, refer to places offering accompaniment or day-care centres for children. Among the obstacles to offering assistance are the complexity of organizations and financial regulations, the limited availability of information in languages other than Dutch, the limited number and high costs of day care centres and the long waiting lists for housing.[1145] After a substantial reduction in subsidies in 2012, FIOM is reforming herself into a knowlegde-center, which provides training for care-givers in the area of decision-making after the discovery of an unintended pregnancy.[1146]

Stirezo Pro Life is a foundation that wants to encourage a development in society in which the right to life, freedom and the inviolability of personhood are guaranteed from the moment of conception until death.[1147] Stirezo tries to reach this goal by referring to other organisations and information, networking and providing assistance if desired.

1139 Siriz, *Jaarverslag 2012*, Amersfoort, 2013, pp. 8-9.
1140 VBOK, *Jaarverslag 2008*, Amersfoort, 2009, p. 44.
1141 Siriz, *Ontwikkeling en groei. Jaarverslag 2013*, Amersfoort, 2014, p. 53.
1142 Cf. part 1.2.1.
1143 Siriz, *Jaarverslag 2010*, p. 13.
1144 Siriz, 2013, p. 17.
1145 According to the FIOM-brochure "*Leuk om jong moeder te zijn?*" (Is it nice to be a young mother?), Den Bosch, 2005. FIOM (Federatie van Instellingen voor Ongehuwde Moeders) is founded in the 1930s and has had as one of its core messages the maintenance of the bond between the (unmarried) mother and child. Cf. Deetman, W.J., 2013, op. cit., p. 89.
1146 FIOM, Maaike Smulders and Monique van den Heuvel, (red.), *Choice. Jaarmagazine 2013*, Den Bosch, 2014, p. 4.
1147 Cf. www.stirezo.nl, accessed 31 December 2015.

Finally, Timon, a foundation that has a Christian basis and gives assistance and accompaniment to teenagers and young adults, has a capacity of some fifteen communes in the central region of the Netherlands, which are open for all, regardless of their religion or their philosophy of life.[1148]

In some other cases, when the mother is not able to raise the child herself, adoption preceded by temporary accommodation in a foster family could be an option.

7.1.3 Adoption and foster care

In 2011, 560 children were adopted in the Netherlands. Most of these children came from abroad. The number of children being adopted in the Netherlands is decreasing.[1149] On the other hand, the number of newly placed foster children has strongly increased, from almost 2,000 children in 1995 to almost 9,000 in 2009.[1150]

In 2007, 4,637 children were adopted in England and Wales. This number includes both children from within the U.K. and overseas adoptions.[1151] In 2015, this figure has risen to 5,715.[1152] In the same year, the number of foster children in the U.K. has grown to more than 64,000.[1153]

Among children who were born in the U.K., Barbara Maughan et al. found that adoptees performed more positively than children from similar birth circumstances who had not been adopted, on tests at school. This advantage was retained at school-leaving age and in later adult qualifications.[1154] This difference can be explained because of the higher average socioeconomic status and better material circumstances of families who adopt a child, as well as the more favourable educational environment of the adoptive

---

1148 Cf. www.timon.nl, accessed 14 December 2015.
1149 Cf. Centraal Bureau voor de Statistiek, "Aantal adopties sinds de jaren zestig niet meer zo laag", on their website, accessed 27 December 2015.
1150 Graaf, Arie de, "Gezinnen in beweging", in Bucx, F. (ed.), *Gezinsrapport*, Sociaal Cultureel Planbureau, Den Haag, 2011, p. 82-96, here p. 85.
1151 Office for National Statistics, *Marriage, Divorce and Adoption Statistics, Series FM2 2006*. Newport, 2009, p. 105.
1152 AdoptionUK, "Adoption facts and figures", on their website, accessed 27 December 2015.
1153 Fostering Network, "Statistics on children in care", on their website, accessed 27 December 2015.
1154 B. Maughan, S. Collishaw and A. Pickles, "School Achievement and Adult Qualifications among Adoptees: A Longitudinal Study", *Journal of Child Psychology and Psychiatry and Allied Disciplines*, 1998, 39, 5, pp. 669-685.

homes and of the parental interests in education.[1155]

When adoption is considered, it is important to notice the difference between the legal family ties and the so-called adoption triangle (the three parties involved in an adoption: the biological parents, the adoptive parents and the child).[1156] When an adoption takes place, the legal family ties between the biological parents and the child cease to exist. However, in some cases contact between the child and its biological parents remains possible. In those cases, the court may need to decide how the adoption triangle will function in practice.

Pien Bos et al. have found that among Dutch mothers who put up their child for adoption, often ambiguous feelings, conflicting loyalties and changeable opinions and circumstances play a role in their decision and their inner life.[1157] Some mothers expressed fear of damaging one's reputation, fear of violence (sometimes associated with crimes of honour) and shame during and after the decision making process regarding adoption. Others suffered from cumulative traumatizing experiences. Especially for some of the mothers who were still minors, the irreversibility of the decision to put up their child for adoption weighed heavily on them. In many cases, foster care is a more acceptable alternative for parents who are not able to raise their child themselves. Foster care takes place on a temporary basis and is closer to the natural situation, since foster parents are sought as close as possible to the child's home address, often among relatives or friends. On the other hand, a reason for concern is that foster children often fall behind their peers at school and are more likely not to be in education, employment or training at the end of their teenage years.[1158]

Social work organizations, like the British Association for Adoption and Fostering (BAAF) and the Fostering Network in the U.K. or FIOM in the

---

1155 Ibid., p. 683.
1156 The full procedure for adoption in the Netherlands is explained by the Stichting Adoptievoorzieningen on www.adoptie.nl. For adoption and fostering regulations in the U.K., see http://www.baaf.org.uk. Both sites accessed 14 December 2015.
1157 Pien Bos, Fenneke Reysoo and Astrid Werdmuller, *'In één klap moeder, en ook weer niet.'* Onderzoek naar demografische en sociaal-economische kenmerken en motieven van vrouwen die tussen 1998-2007 in Nederland hun kind ter adoptie hebben afgestaan. Den Bosch, 2011, pp. 158-161 and 165.
1158 Fostering Network, "Head, Heart, Hands. Introducing social pedagogy into foster care", London, 2013, p. 4.

Netherlands, or pro-life organizations like Life, Siriz or *Schreeuw om Leven Hulpverlening* accompany or advise young mothers on the emotional, social and legal dimensions of putting up a child for adoption or of placement in foster care. Despite the positively changing attitudes regarding adoption and foster care, it still is a delicate issue, often subject to prejudices. It needs to be treated with great care, because of the emotional dimension for both mother and child, but also because it could mean the salvation of a life that otherwise would be lost.

7.2 Sex and Relationships Education (SRE) in the U.K. and the Netherlands

It has been shown that the teenage pregnancy rate in the U.K. is much higher than in the Netherlands.[1159] In 2013, the British Office for Standards in Education, Children's Services and Skills (Ofsted) reported that the quality of sex and relationships education (SRE) in schools in England was "not yet good enough".[1160] Five years before, the SRE Review steering group had reached a consensus on three conclusions that are relevant in relation to abortion:

1) In SRE a stronger focus needs to be made on 'relationships' and the skills and values that young people need as they progress through childhood and adolescence, into adulthood.

2) The work of SRE should be within a clear and explicit framework of values including mutual respect, rights and responsibilities, gender equality and acceptance of diversity.

3) SRE should be inclusive and meet the needs of all young people, recognising that existing SRE provision does not always take sufficient account of issues such as sexuality, disability, ethnicity and faith.[1161]

Other conclusions of the steering group drew attention to the need for more information, advice and support for young people on sex and relationships and a better communication between schools, parents and professional advisers.

1159 In part 1.4.3.
1160 Office for Standards in Education, Children's Services and Skills, *Not yet good enough: personal, social, health and economic education in schools*. Manchester, 2013, p. 1.
1161 Department for Children, Schools and Families (DCSF), *Review of Sex and Relationships Education (SRE) in Schools. A report by the External Steering Group*, London, 2008.

The 2013 Ofsted report is critical on what has been achieved so far. Based on the Ofsted findings, the House of Commons Education Committee stresses the need for parental consultation and engagement in the provision of SRE. The Committee further states that the existing right of a parent to withdraw their child from elements of SRE must be retained.[1162]

If SRE is not delivered well, for instance with a one-sided focus on birth control, there is a risk of deterioration of the rates of STI's. David Paton has examined the impact of an increase in access to family planning on teenage pregnancy and STI-diagnosis rates in England.[1163] He has used data from the Department of Health on numbers of free family planning clinic sessions, held between 1998 and 2001 (including those in schools). His analysis shows that clinic sessions are significantly associated with more STI diagnoses among teenagers. It appears that this adverse relationship is driven by the promotion of abortifacient emergency birth control pills at family planning clinics.[1164]

As regards the Netherlands, Lotje Bagchus et al. state that an early start of SRE is important for the development of healthy and safe sexual behaviour and the prevention of risky sexual behaviour at a later age.[1165] They estimate that in 2010, some 20% of the primary schools in the Netherlands pay attention to SRE.[1166] Their research confirms that teachers and directors of primary schools, staff members of the Community Health Services (GGD) and parents see the importance of SRE. Parents indicate that they appreciate the attention for the psychosocial development of their children more than the education on sexuality, STI's, contraception and procreation. On the whole, the pupils themselves appreciate the SRE lessons.[1167]

Marianne Cense et al. have investigated determining factors for a successful implementation of a frequently used educational project on

---

1162 House of Commons Education Committee, *Life lessons: PSHE and SRE in schools. Fifth Report of Session 2014-2015*. London 2015, p. 4.
1163 Paton, D., 2007, op. cit., pp. 281-308.
1164 Ibid., p. 301.
1165 Lotje Bagchus, Marloes Martens and Maria van der Sluis, *Relationele en seksuele vorming in het basisonderwijs. Een effect- en procesevaluatie van de lespakketten 'Relaties en seksualiteit' en 'Lekker in je vel'*. Amsterdam, 2010, p. 2.
1166 Ibid., p. 3.
1167 Ibid., pp. 147-152.

relations and sexuality for primary schools.[1168] Their research group consists of 321 teachers and staff members of Dutch primary schools. The schools are divided into four groups with different signatures: public, Roman catholic, protestant or other. In general, the respondents do not see religious conviction or the pupil's background as a constraining factor for SRE. However, for many Christian schools it is important that Christian teachings are integrated within SRE. This is the reason that some schools have not made use of any of the existing methods.[1169]

Looking at the contents of SRE at Dutch secondary schools, it becomes clear that the knowledge and the values that are being transmitted, are strongly influenced by the possible risks of unsafe sexual behaviour. Ine Vanwesenbeeck et al. have investigated the effectivity of a renewed SRE program among 1,590 Dutch secondary school pupils between 1999 and 2002.[1170] They did not only find an increase in knowledge of sexual risks, but also a change of attitudes among the pupils who have worked with the program. They have more positive attitudes towards the use of contraceptives and they think in a more liberal way of gender roles in the area of sexuality. The appreciation of the relational and the physical aspects of sexuality, the awareness of the gravity of STI's and the risk perception towards STI's, AIDS and pregnancy all have increased.[1171] There are no indications that the initiation of sex has been delayed as a result of the program.

Other comparative research on the impact of abstinence and comprehensive sex education programmes on adolescent sexual behaviour has been conducted in the United States.[1172] Douglas Kirby, who has reviewed more than fifty educational programmes, concludes that about

---

1168 Marianne Cense, Marloes Martens, Sanna Maris, Ellis Janssen and Hanneke de Graaf, in opdracht van ZonMW, *Onderzoek naar determinanten van succesvolle implementatie van het leskatern relaties & seksualiteit in het basisonderwijs*. Utrecht, 2011.
1169 Ibid., pp. 15 and 25.
1170 Ine Vanwesenbeeck, Floor Bakker, Michelle van Fulpen, Theo Paulussen, Jos Poelman and Herman Schaalma, "Seks en seksuele risico's bij VMBO-scholieren anno 2002", *Tijdschrift voor Seksuologie*, 2003, 27, pp. 30-39.
1171 Ibid., p. 37.
1172 Douglas B. Kirby, "The Impact of Abstinence and Comprehensive Sex and STD/HIV Education Programs on Adolescent Sexual Behaviour", *Sexuality Research & Social Policy*, Vol. 5, No. 3, 2008, pp. 18-27.

two thirds of comprehensive programmes show strong evidence that they affect young people's sexual behaviour. Among the measured effects are a delayed initiation of sexual activity and also an increase of the use of condoms and other contraceptives. He found that so-called abstinence-only programmes did not delay initiation of sex and only three out of nine had any significant positive effect on any sexual behaviour.[1173] However, more recent research in the United States did find that abstinence education has an effect on the sexual behaviour of teenagers between 10 and 17, resulting in a later sexual initiation and a lower teenage birth rate.[1174]

A weakness of comparative research like Kirby's is to be found in the fact that it precisely assesses the impact on adolescents' sexual behaviour and that it does not take into account the adolescents' changing attitude towards marriage and the sexual expression of conjugal love. The long-lasting effects of these different types of sex education programmes remain unknown. As is the view of the British steering group, a sex education program for adolescents should not be limited to sexual behaviour, including its effects and risks, but should be more focussed on the meaning of relationships and on transmitting values. This brings us to the question on what the Church has to say on these matters.

As an illustration of what the Church's teaching could mean on a local, diocesan level, some fragments follow of a speech by the Archbishop of Westminster, Vincent Nichols, to an audience of foundation school governors.[1175] In his speech, Nichols is referring to the Government' point of view on the *Review of SRE in Schools*, by acknowledging the need for SRE in schools, as is already done in most Catholic schools. He also states that "we have been welcoming the fact that part of the purpose of this review is to make sure that more emphasis is given to the relationship aspect of this education and to the emotional content of our sexuality".[1176]

1173 Ibid., p. 18.
1174 Cf. John B. Jemmott, Loretta S. Jemmott and Geoffrey T. Fong, "Efficacy of a Theory-Based Abstinence-Only Intervention Over 24 Months. A Randomized Controlled Trial With Young Adolescents", *Archives of Pediatric Adolescent Medicine*, 2010, 164 (2), pp. 152-159; Colin Cannonier, "State abstinence education programs and teen birth rates in the US", *Review of Economics of the Household*, 2012, 10, pp. 53–75.
1175 Mgr. V. Nichols, at a diocesan conference in the diocese of Hexham and Newcastle for foundation school governors, 27 September 2008.
1176 Ibid.

On the other hand, Nichols insists that "in a Catholic school sex and relationship education will always be designed and delivered according to the teaching of the Church". He points out the right of governing bodies to determine the school's sex and relationship education programme. Therefore "we must strongly oppose any action or proposal that would sexualise children or be seen as in any way promoting sexual activity outside the context of married relationships. That is the principle of Catholic teaching which we must make clear and put forward over and over again. Insisting on this is not a matter simply of responding, or not, to public opinion or even to widespread behaviour. Rather it is a conviction of faith that here lies the correct use of the wonderful gift of human sexuality both as an expression of a conscious and faithful self-giving to another and as an action of such intimacy that it creates human life in partnership with the Creator of all."[1177]

Of course, SRE is just one aspect of Catholic education. To quote Nichols again: "A Catholic school expresses and explores this vision: of what it is to be a person; of what it is to live closely with others in both family and class; of what it is to contribute to a society; of what it is to have a vision of the origins and purpose of life which can shape and guide the life of a society; of what it is to know forgiveness and compassion; of what it is to live with the hope of eternal life and the fulfilment of all things in God."[1178]

7.3 Counselling and pastoral care in case of unintended pregnancy

In this part and the next, the focus will be on counselling and pastoral practices after the discovery of an unintended pregnancy. Preventive care and aftercare in the case of abortion is most often done by social workers, doctors and medical assistants and much less by priests, deacons or pastoral workers. However, it will be argued that moral and pastoral theology, as well as the study of spirituality, could offer insights which could be helpful for both counselling practices and pastoral care.

This part deals with counselling in general as well as with pastoral care to

---

1177 Ibid.
1178 Ibid.

pregnant women as this is provided by professionally educated members of the Catholic Church. This approach entails a limitation. Among members of other religious communities there might also be a need for counselling from a specific religious perspective, after the discovery of an unintended pregnancy. The other world religions are mainly dismissive of procured abortion, although in some cases exceptions are allowed.[1179]

7.3.1 Preventive counselling

Visser et al. show that during the decision making process on having an abortion or not, it rarely happens that a woman changes her mind after she has visited an abortion clinic for a first consultation. More than 90% of the interviewed Dutch women remained determined to have an abortion after the first consultation.[1180] However, there are reasons to think that the decision making process after the discovery of an unintended pregnancy does not always take place with the utmost care. It has already been shown that during the confrontation with an unintended pregnancy, men might show reactions of panic, denial, indifference or shame and guilt.[1181]

If the woman and/or her partner are believing persons, then the decision making process regarding the pregnancy needs to be seen in this light, too. A counsellor or any other person helping in the decision making process, should be attentive to the underlying emotions, expectations and convictions a pregnant woman has and he should not shy away from asking questions of an ethical nature.[1182] The outcome of each individual decision

---

1179 For an analysis of the different positions on abortions among members of the world religions, I refer to D.C. Maguire (ed.), *Sacred Rights. The case for contraception and abortion in world religions.* Oxford, 2003. Representatives of Islam in the U.K. have made their position clear on the value of embryonic life at recent consultations by the House of Lords. For instance, in 2002 the Islamic Medical Association writes in reaction to the House of Lords Select Committee on Stem Cell Research that "He/she should be fully respected from the moment of conception and the fertilised egg is a sacred being." Cf. House of Lords Select Committee on Stem Cell Research, *Report*, London 2002, par. 4.18. Ibrahim B. Syed, president of the Islamic Research Foundation International states that Islamic law only allows abortion when doctors declare with reasonable certainty that the continuation of pregnancy will endanger the woman's life. Cf. Ibrahim B. Syed, "Abortion in Islam", on the site www.islamawareness.net, accessed 14 December 2015.
1180 Visser, M.R.M. et al., op. cit., p. 81.
1181 Petersen, P., 1986, op. cit.; cf. part 3.3.2.3.
1182 Cf. parts 6.3 and 6.4.

making process regarding unintended pregnancy depends to a large extent on one's personal metaphysical prepositions, regardless whether they are expressed or not expressed. If these metaphysical prepositions are being kept under a 'veil of ignorance', to use the Rawlsian expression, this could have grave consequences for the spiritual life of the two begetters of the foetus.

It has been mentioned that the opinion and support of a partner have a great impact on pregnancy wantedness.[1183] Therefore, in prenatal care it is important that clinicians and social workers endeavour to include partners in order to enhance partner support during pregnancy. Similarly, if during a first consultation in an abortion clinic a woman expresses doubts on having an abortion, it can be crucial to include the partner in the decision making process. Once partners feel that they have input into the care of their unborn child, they may be more inclined to give positive support throughout the pregnancy.[1184]

A partner's input into the care of the unborn child can be further encouraged if there is a willingness to take part in the couple's prenatal consultation or a childbirth preparation class guided by a professional counsellor. Couples taking part in a prenatal treatment group showed higher scores in parent-child interaction after birth than couples who did not take part in such a group.[1185] Involvement of men could help women with doubts about having an abortion and it could help men to overcome attitudes of indifference or denial. It could also strengthen their self-confidence and thus reduce feelings of panic, shame or guilt after having conceived.

When a pregnant woman visits an abortion clinic or hospital in the Netherlands, in most cases the hospital pastor, the local parish priest or the imam in the case of a Muslim-woman are not involved in the decision-making process she is going through. According to Peter Deij and Jacolien Teekman, in the case of "persistent doubt" in a woman of faith, a conversation with a pastor, imam or other spiritual guide could provide some clarity in the matter.[1186] But the problem is, as has been shown, that women do not always show their doubts and in many cases mental health

---

1183 Kroelinger C.D. and Oths, K.S., op. cit.; cf. part 3.3.2.3.
1184 Ibid., p. 118.
1185 Audrey A. Bryan, "Enhancing Parent-Child Interaction With a Prenatal Couple Intervention", *The American Journal of Maternal/Child Nursing*, 2000, 25, 3, pp. 139-145.
1186 P. Deij, and J. Teekman, *Abortus, een levensbesluit*. Stade Fiom Utrecht, 2002, p. 44.

problems only become apparent after an abortion.[1187]

Jane Rzepka mentions the importance of a counsellor or pastor remaining faithful to his or her own convictions, while giving information or support to a pregnant woman who is considering an abortion. As regards the position of the pastoral or secular counsellor, she has the opinion that one cannot adequately counsel a woman who has a problem pregnancy unless one is willing to facilitate (to guide in her choosing) any of the three alternatives (adoption, abortion or keeping the baby) and help her become reconciled with herself after the decision has been carried through.[1188] However, it must be noted that the option of abortion is diametrically opposed to the other two options, since it regards a decision of life or death. Therefore, a transparent attitude in which the counsellor makes his or her objections to abortion known, could help the decision making process, as long as the counsellor fully respects the dignity of the person(s) involved in this decision and acknowledges their responsibility.

Although these two starting points differ, Rzepka has some helpful insights to offer in her treatment of pastoral problem pregnancy counselling. She considers the pastoral functions of "guidance" and "reconciling" as particularly relevant in this area.[1189] According to Rzepka, guidance consists of two components: informational and emotional.

7.3.2 Informational aspects of guidance

It is likely that when a pregnant woman wants to speak to a pastor about her dilemma, she has already spoken with others about her options. Only some 10% of the Dutch women who were interviewed by Visser et al. after having an abortion, did not tell anyone about their pregnancies.[1190] Maybe the woman has already gathered information from organisations which offer help in problem pregnancies. A first thing a pastor could do is to inquire if she has done so, and if not, provide information about other

---

[1187] In parts 3.3.1.2 and 3.1.3.
[1188] Jane R. Rzepka, *Counseling women who have unplanned pregnancies: a pastoral approach.* Berkeley (Ca.), 1982, p. 48.
[1189] Ibid., pp. 45-90; cf. William A. Clebsch and Charles R. Jaekle, *Pastoral care in historical perspective.* New York, 1975, pp. 32-67. As the four pastoral functions, Clebsch and Jaekle mention healing and sustaining besides guiding and reconciling.
[1190] Visser, M.R.M. et al., op. cit., p. 86.

organisations who are active in this area and to refer to these professional agencies.[1191] From the Dutch abortion practice it has been shown that discussing alternatives to abortion is far from obvious.[1192] We might expect that in a case where the woman shows her doubts on having an abortion, alternatives would be discussed in the clinic or hospital. Another problem with the current counselling practice is that many women do not mention their doubts to the consultant.[1193] It is therefore unlikely that in these cases the women discussed all the possibilities of support from others within their peer group, their partner in the first place, but also the possible help of other friends, of parents and grandparents. Outside her peer group, a woman might discover that professional and financial help is available to her while bringing up her child. In other situations, adoption or foster care might be discussed.

Nowadays, biological information regarding the growth of a human embryo is abundantly available on the internet, in libraries and elsewhere. Doctrinal information about abortion can also easily be found in today's media. However, sometimes it could be useful during a pastoral conversation to explain the principal teachings of the Church on abortion.[1194] In a pastoral conversation, alternatives to abortion could be further explored, with the help of other professionals or by referring to them. Further, a counsellor or pastor could try to involve members of the woman's peer group, as indicated by the woman herself, in order to enlarge the support of others before and after the birth of the child.

7.3.3 Emotional aspects of guidance

The guiding function of pastoral counselling also involves talking about emotional components of the woman's decision-making process

---

1191 Cf. part 7.1.
1192 Cf. part 1.2.1.
1193 Cf. part 3.3.1.2.
1194 Cf. Catechism of the Catholic Church, 1997, n. 2270 – 2275. There it says: "Human life must be respected and protected absolutely from the moment of conception. From the first moment of his existence, a human being must be recognized as having the rights of a person - among which is the inviolable right of every innocent being to life... Direct abortion, that is to say, abortion willed either as an end or a means, is gravely contrary to the moral law... Since it must be treated from conception as a person, the embryo must be defended in its integrity, cared for, and healed, as far as possible, like any other human being."

when she is confronted with an unintended pregnancy. The following emotional components of the decision may be important in the guiding process: reactions to the pregnancy, motivations for getting pregnant and the relationship with the partner, parents and/or friends.[1195]

As has been shown, it is not uncommon that women express ambivalence towards their pregnancy. Ambivalent feelings might have to do with the experience of a conflict in future plans and perspectives, with the reactions of her partner and significant others, and even with memories of the woman's own childhood.[1196] Emotions which might come along with the experiences of ambivalence are anxiety, fear, loneliness or anger. Especially during adolescence, the physiological and maturational changes which occur can lead to very strong emotional reactions.[1197] Anxiety might be felt because of uncertainties about one's future or one's capabilities in becoming a parent. If the woman's partner does not show empathy and responsibility during the decision making process, the woman might experience strong feelings of loneliness or emotional distress. In these situations, anger might be a logical reaction, anger at the partner or at oneself when recognizing one's own role in the pregnancy. In these situations, there is a risk that emotions are projected in an irrational way, towards the foetus. In such cases, guiding could be aimed at ordering the person's emotions and thoughts.

It has been mentioned above that memories of the woman's own childhood could play a role in the experience of a pregnancy. These memories could become relevant for the decision making process, even more so if they are not properly recognised by the woman herself or by her guide. It is known that avoidance of feelings negatively affects the process of resolution.[1198]

7.3.4 Spiritual aspects of guidance

Besides the informational and emotional aspects of guidance, also spiritual aspects need to be distinguished. Obviously, all three components of guidance are interrelated.

The confrontation with an unintended pregnancy could take place

---

1195 Rzepka, J.R., op. cit., p. 73.
1196 Cf. part 3.3.2.
1197 Rzepka, J.R., op. cit., pp. 74 and 194.
1198 Ibid., p. 77.

within a longer period of spiritual direction. According to William Barry and William Connolly, spiritual direction could be defined as help given by one Christian to another which enables that person to pay attention to God's personal communication to him or her, to respond to this personally communicating God, to grow in intimacy with this God, and to live out the consequences of the relationship.[1199] Spiritual guidance requires from the director both listening to the directee and to what God wants with this person.[1200]

Listening to what God wants can become particularly important when it comes to making a decision. Within the tradition of the Spiritual Exercises of Ignatius of Loyola, "a 'good and sound' decision requires two conditions, namely a previous disposition of availability to God's word, whatever that word might be, and the discernment of what is in fact more pleasing to God in my case."[1201] Ignatius underlines that an election should not go against the doctrine of the Church.[1202] In the case of guidance of a person who is confronted with an unintended pregnancy, this means that the guide must be attentive to ways which can be sought in order to safeguard the unborn life and which also serve the directee's spiritual and material well-being.

7.3.5 Several cases

When it comes to decision-making, every pregnant woman has her own story regarding the pregnancy and her request for an abortion. Deij and Teekman give many examples of stories they have heard from their clients. They provide one case in which the clinic (at first) refused the abortion because the woman acted under severe pressure from her husband.[1203] In two other cases the parents of a seventeen-year-old woman forced her to

---

1199 William A. Barry and William J. Connolly, *The practice of Spiritual Direction*. San Francisco, 1982., p. 8.
1200 Kees Waaijman, *Spiritualiteit. Vormen, Grondslagen, Methoden*. Kampen/Gent, 2000, p. 872.
1201 Michael Ivens S.J., *Understanding the Spiritual Exercises*. Leominster / New Malden, 1998, p. 128.
1202 Ignatius of Loyola, *The Spiritual Exercises*, n. 170. Translated with introductions and notes by Joseph A. Munitiz and Philip Endean, London, 1996. Michael Ivens S.J. comments on this line in the Spiritual Exercises: "Many of the choices made in the Exercises (e.g., choices of a state of life) are directly concerned with a person's role in the Church. But more widely all decisions are made in the Church and involve its holiness, witness or mission." In: Ivens S.J., M., op. cit., p. 134.
1203 Deij, P. and Teekman, J., op. cit., p. 58.

have the abortion.[1204] Both authors do not want to pass any moral judgment on these (or any of the) cases.[1205] Still, it is clear that in these latter cases the unborn is aborted against the woman's will and therefore illegally, due to a lack of care, both from the parents and from the medical and social profession, who should have prevented further proceedings.

Another case describes the situation of a family with three children, in which the coming of a fourth one would lead to many complications, both minor and serious. In this case the woman had had two extra consultations with a social worker, one together with her mother, the other one with her husband. He argued that he did not want another child and did not even want to talk about it. Again, this is an example in which true autonomy seems to be illusory. The woman admitted that she could have put aside all complications of having another baby, but that she had chosen for an abortion not because she wanted this, but out of consideration for her family.[1206] Although she describes her experiences of grief in a detailed way, no mention is made of any offer to the family to help in a professional or financial way. Yet again a relationship problem, this time because of a lack of real communication, lies at the bottom of the decision to have the abortion.

In these and other situations, one is confronted with a fundamental argument in the ethical and pastoral debate, namely that of freedom. There are situations, in which a pregnancy is hard to accept emotionally and psychologically, as can be the case after unwanted sexual contact, also within marriage, or when the mother has barely left behind her own childhood. In these situations, however, the question needs to be asked what solution could bring real freedom. One could argue with good reason that in the case of a married couple, it is precisely reciprocal responsibility that grants freedom and not a compelled abortion. An attempt could be made to confront the partner with this point of view. Or, in another situation, when two adolescents have been unwise in their sexual behaviour and are too young to bear the consequences, then this is rather an example of a lack of

---

1204 Ibid., pp. 55 and 57.
1205 At the time of writing their book, Deij and Teekman both worked as social workers for Stade-Fiom Utrecht. On p. 121 they state that social workers who workers who work for Fiom have a neutral vision on abortion. On Fiom, see also part 7.1.2.
1206 Deij, P. and Teekman, J., op. cit., p. 56.

freedom. Professional aid could be offered in order to find a solution which is life-giving both for the couple and for the child. Sometimes adoption or foster care needs to be considered.[1207] An even greater need of professional assistance exists in a situation of a woman who has been the victim of violence and subsequently feels compelled to terminate her pregnancy, also because society does not offer sufficient means to sustain her motherhood. Situations of violence are yet another example of a grave limitation of human autonomy.

In the U.K. and the Netherlands, the existing organizational structure, be it professional, or voluntary, or pastoral, is insufficient to offer concrete support in these and many other situations of women or families that can be real emergency situations.[1208] If there seem to be no real alternatives, one is compelled to speak of a situation which limits the woman's freedom of choice. If for example the British and Dutch situation is compared with another EU-country, Italy, one sees a strong civil pro-life network that in the period between 1975 and 2015 has offered concrete help to more than 170,000 pregnant women and young mothers, making use of voluntary means only.[1209] However strong or weak the organizational structures may be, pastoral care ought to aim at informing and accompanying the woman and her partner to the available possibilities to prevent abortion and to increase the quality of life of mother and child.

7.4 Counselling after prenatal diagnosis

What has been said in the previous part about counselling and pastoral care is equally relevant in cases in which a prenatal diagnosis points at a possible serious foetal anomaly. When such an anomaly has been diagnosed or suspected, parents often face difficult decisions regarding their child.[1210] The reality of such difficult decisions has been described by Diny Rozendal, based on her experience as a social worker in the Radboud Academic Hospital in Nijmegen.[1211] During one year, she accompanied 29 women

---

1207 Cf. part 7.1.3.
1208 Cf. parts 7.1.1 and 7.3.1.
1209 Movimento per la vita italiano, "22 maggio 1975 - 22 maggio 2015. Il movimento per la vita compie quarant'anni." Press announcement, Rome, 2015.
1210 Cf. parts 4.5 and 4.6.
1211 Diny Rozendal, "De praktijk...", *Annalen van het Thijmgenootschap*, 79, 2, 1991, pp. 81-91.

who came to her after prenatal diagnosis. In 12 of these cases a decision was taken to abort. In her role as a social worker, Rozendal primarily focused on the following questions:
- Do the parents understand the information, is it not all too technical?
- How do they cope with the information?
- How is the contact between both parents for discussing the problem?
- Are there any interfering factors, for example coming from the surroundings?
- Does the parents' religion or philosophy of life play a role?
- Is it a decision-making process with all due care, how are the arguments formulated, what are the deciding factors?[1212]

The reality of a decision-making process in the case of a diagnosed foetal abnormality is, of course, not simply rational. The possibility of a handicapped child can cause all kinds of emotional reactions from the parents, a state of shock, fear, grief, guilt or anger. At the same time an acceptance of the pregnancy could bring an enrichment of their lives, although mixed with many uncertainties. Counsellors then must reproduce the findings of the diagnosis in order to get a perspective as objective as possible, with all relevant information regarding the child and all the other consequences for the parents and their family. Depending on the parents' religion or philosophy of life, they might be advised to consult a hospital chaplain or representative for other faith and religions.

In chapter 5, it has been stated that the process of medicalization has had an influence on the way people look at pregnancy, especially if after prenatal diagnosis a certain anomaly has been discovered.[1213] This phenomenon could also implicitly have its repercussions on the counselling strategy after prenatal diagnosis.

Ethical objections can be raised in the case of a directive counselling strategy towards termination of pregnancy. According to the British Royal College of Physicians, the principle of non-directiveness in genetic counselling is embraced by all relevant professional bodies.[1214] The Dutch Association for Obstetrics and Gynaecology (NVOG) does not explicitly

---
1212 Ibid., p. 82.
1213 Cf. part 5.2.
1214 Royal College of Physicians: Prenatal Diagnosis and Genetic Screening. Community and Service Implications. London, 1989.

mention this principle, but states that the provider of prenatal screening needs to give clear information about all aspects of research, treatment, effects, risks and alternatives.[1215] The provider further needs to be aware of a possible shift in attention from the request made by the pregnant woman to the available tests being offered. The woman has a legal right 'not to know', if she explicitly indicates such a wish.[1216]

Still, a directive counselling style could be motivated by providers of prenatal screening on purely medical and legal arguments, but also on an unspoken fear for being held liable when an anomaly is discovered after the child's birth. The fear for a 'wrongful birth' or 'wrongful life' claim could result in an increase in referrals by G.P's, midwives or gynaecologists for advanced prenatal diagnostic tests, which carry an inherent risk of more miscarriages.[1217]

In order to know more about the extent to which geneticists agree with the principle of non-directiveness or incorporate it into their practice, Theresa Marteau et al. conducted a comparative study among geneticists in the U.K., Germany and Portugal.[1218] They found that among the 137 British geneticists who took part in the research, 70% used a non-directive counselling style after the diagnosis of Down's syndrome. This means that they tried to be "as neutral as possible, covering both positive and negative aspects of the diagnosis".[1219] 2% of the geneticists counselled directively in favour of continuing the pregnancy and 28% used a directive counselling style in favour of terminating the pregnancy. In Portugal, a directive counselling style towards pregnancy termination scored considerably higher (60%), whereas in Germany a directive counselling style towards pregnancy continuation scored higher than in both other countries (10%).

1215 Nederlandse Vereniging voor Obstetrie en Gynaecologie, *Kwaliteitsnorm Prenatale screening*, Utrecht, 2005, n. 3.3.
1216 Ibid. In the Netherlands, this right is based on the *Wet op de Geneeskundige Behandelingsovereenkomst* (WGBO), in: Civil Code, *Burgerlijk Wetboek*, Book 7, Title 7, Part 5, Art. 449.
1217 M.A.J.M. Buijssen, "Wrongful life: de zaak Kelly", *Pro Vita Humana*, 2003, 3-4, pp. 102-104. On the risks of prenatal diagnosis, see part 5.2.
1218 T. Marteau, H. Drake, M. Reid, M. Feijoo, M. Soares, I. Nippert, P. Nippert and M. Bobrow, "Counselling following Diagnosis of Fetal Abnormality: A comparison between German, Portuguese and UK Geneticists", *European Journal on Human Genetics*, 1994, 2, pp. 96-102
1219 Ibid., pp. 99-100.

Response rates in the three countries were between 53 and 61 percent. A disadvantage of this study is that the data relate to self-reports of geneticists about a counselling style which is considered as unacceptable by their own professional group. If they have a blind spot as regards their own directiveness, the logical consequence would be underreporting of this type of counselling.

For other conditions, such as open spina bifida or anencephaly, the non-directive counselling style among British geneticists scored considerably lower (respectively 47% and 36%), whereas for conditions like cleft lip or closed spina bifida, more geneticists counselled directively in favour of continuing the pregnancy (respectively 66% and 25%).[1220]

Clare Williams et at. point at certain difficulties practitioners encounter when they apply the principle of non-directiveness in their counselling strategy.[1221] Sometimes clients ask the practitioner directly what they would do if they were in the same situation. Still, as has been put forward by Angus Clarke, one of the reasons why the principle of non-directiveness is seen as important is precisely that it protects the professional against over-involvement.[1222] A more thorough discussion of the available options and ways of support would be a better approach than to give one's own opinion. In some cases, a client can demonstrate such an ambivalence about her or his coping with the option of an abortion, that the practitioner should be very clear that further diagnostic procedures have nothing to do with the option of abortion. When the ambivalence remains, the practitioner should rather be directive towards no further diagnostic procedures. However, in most cases the principle of non-directiveness remains to be applicable in counselling after prenatal diagnosis.

7.5 Spiritual and pastoral care after prenatal diagnosis

In relation to a non-directive counselling strategy towards expecting parents, it is important not to lose sight from the spiritual dimension of care.

1220 Ibid., p. 99.
1221 Clare Williams, Priscilla Alderson and Bobbie Farsides, "Is nondirectiveness possible within the context of antenatal screening and testing?", *Social Science & Medicine* 2002, 54, pp. 339–347.
1222 Ibid., p. 343; cf. A. Clarke, "The process of genetic counselling", in: P. Harper and A. Clarke (Eds.), *Genetics, society and clinical practice*. Oxford, 1997, pp. 179–200.

To illustrate this, let us first, by ways of comparison, look at the definition of palliative care, formulated by the World Health Organization (WHO):

"Palliative care is an approach that improves the quality of life of patients and their families facing the problem associated with life-threatening illness, through the prevention and relief of suffering by means of early identification and impeccable assessment and treatment of pain and other problems, physical, psychosocial and spiritual."[1223]

In this definition, a person asking for medical aid is considered as a person which can encounter physical, psychosocial *and spiritual* problems. According to the WHO, palliative care integrates the psychological and spiritual aspects of patient care.[1224] This principle of integrating all dimensions of care could similarly be applied in the case of counselling parents who are expecting a child with a certain anomaly.

In recent years, experience has also been gained with perinatal palliative care for infants with lethal anomalies.[1225] The hospital chaplaincy, together with nursing and social services, could provide spiritual and emotional support during the postpartum period of these young terminally ill patients, as well as bereavement support after the infant's death.

In 2010, the above mentioned definition of palliative care has been adopted by the Dutch association of integral cancer centres (VIKC) has adopted this definition in their national guideline on spiritual care, primarily meant for doctors and nurses.[1226] In the introduction of this guideline, the authors notice that people who have a life threatening illness, often ask themselves existential questions, such as: "For what did I deserve this?", "What have I done wrong?" or "What is the meaning of my life?" In order to deal with such questions, they view the relations between the spiritual, physical, psychological and social dimensions of the patient's existence as indicated in figure 11:

1223 Cf. World Health Organization on their website, accessed 14 December 2015.
1224 Ibid.
1225 D'Almeida, M. et al., op. cit., p. 53; cf. part 5.2.
1226 C. Leget, T. Staps, J. van der Geer, C. Mur-Arnoldi, M. Wulp and H. Jochemsen (Agorawerkgroep Richtlijn Spirituele Zorg), *Spirituele Zorg. Landelijke Richtlijn, Versie 1.0*. Utrecht, 2010.

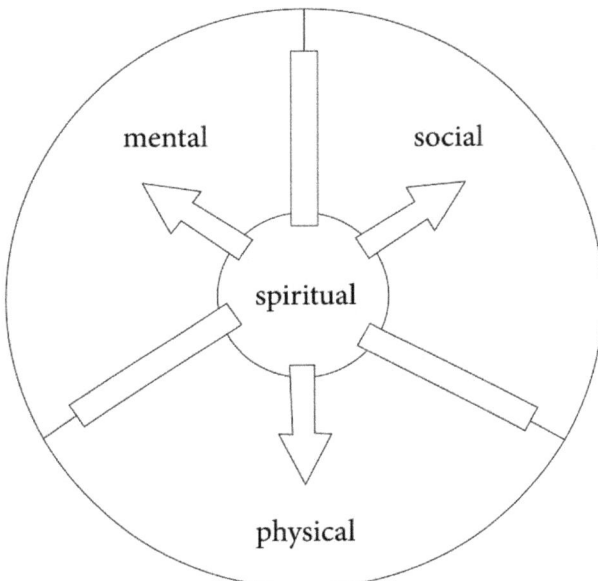

Figure 11: The position of spirituality in palliative care

Source: Leget., C. et al., 2010, op. cit., p. 3.

In this figure, the spiritual dimension is depicted as the most intimate and hidden dimension. This notion of the spiritual core, being the deepest centre of the person, where the person is open to the transcendent dimension and where the person experiences ultimate reality, corresponds with a phenomenological notion of spirituality.[1227] According to this approach, spirituality may or may not be linked to a system of religious beliefs, religious practices, or communities that support those practices and beliefs.[1228]

The authors of the Dutch guideline for spiritual care admit that the spiritual dimension is less measurable than the other three, but constantly in a reciprocally influencing relation with the other dimensions of the human

---

[1227] Cf. Peter H. van Ness (ed.), *Spirituality and the Secular Quest*, New York, 1996, p. XII; Waaijman, K., op. cit., p. 13.
[1228] Timothy P. Daaleman and Larry VandeCreek, "Placing Religion and Spirituality in End-of-Life Care", *Journal of the American Medical Association*, 2000, 284, 19, pp. 2514-2517.

person.[1229] In a similar way, Chris Gastmans et al. distinguish six dimensions in their view on nursing: good care involves the physical, relational, social, psychological, moral and spiritual dimension of the person who is taken care of.[1230] Considering nursing as moral practice, they state that "one must apply the criterion of the dignity of the human person, considered in all his or her dimensions."[1231]

The process of medicalization has led to an overemphasizing of the physical dimension of prenatal care. This could be illustrated by the choice for an abortion which could be offered to parents to prevent certain risks, for instance the risk of breast cancer which could be transmitted from the mother to her daughter.[1232] Such a one-sided emphasis on possible future risks leaves aside the relational, moral and spiritual dimensions of care, not only for the parents but even more so for the foetus.

The British Episcopate has authorised a document which offers a guideline for the decision making process after prenatal diagnosis.[1233] It presents a realistic approach to the dilemma with which a pregnant woman can be confronted when she is aware that the embryo which she carries might be handicapped. Such a situation can raise many difficult questions: Is it right to allow the birth of a disabled child? How much would the child suffer? And what about the suffering of its parents?

Examining these questions, the authors discuss the argument of aborting handicapped children because they would be a burden on other people: "They are said to be a burden on social resources and a burden on their families, especially on their parents. But it is an indignity to speak in this way, as if the only value of a human being were his or her utility. Even if a person is so extensively disabled that he or she cannot play a useful role in society, that in no way diminishes the essential worth and dignity of the

---

1229 Leget, C. et al., op. cit., p. 3.
1230 Chris Gastmans, Bernadette Dierckx de Casterle and Paul Schotsmans, "Nursing Considered as Moral Practice: A Philosophical-Ethical Interpretation of Nursing", *Kennedy Institute of Ethics Journal*, 1998, 8, 1, pp. 43-69.
1231 Ibid., p. 57.
1232 Cf. Slagboom, M., op. cit., pp. 51-52.
1233 Catholic Bishops of Great Britain, Joint Committee on Bioethical Issues, Antenatal Tests: What You Should Know. Answers to questions which face every pregnant mother. In: *Briefing*, 19:3 (3 Feb. 1989) 50-56; cf. *Medicina e Morale*, 40:1 (1990), 149-158.

person."[1234]

Diny Rozendal also points out the grim possibility of social pressure coming from the parents' surroundings to have the child aborted, which might even lead to reproaches in the case of a decision to accept the pregnancy. In every case, it is a decision under time constraints. It is therefore essential to accompany the parents in taking their time and making sure that they get all the support they need during and after the pregnancy. Should they wish to bring the pregnancy to term there obviously needs to be an offer of professional help.[1235]

As regards the quality of life of a handicapped person, the British Episcopal document on prenatal diagnosis makes a distinction between the 'subjective' and the objective value of life. "…a life which from a healthy person's point of view seems frustrating, miserable and unfulfilled, may be viewed very differently by the person whose life it is. It can be very hard for a healthy person to appreciate the quality (the 'subjective' value) of the joys and sorrows of a handicapped person…More important, every life has a value in itself. This is an objective value, to be respected even when defect, depression or decline prevent the person whose life it is from experiencing it as valuable. (…) Further, we should recognize that it is in and through the bodily life we have that God created us as persons. So the bodily life of human beings is not to be treated as disposable."[1236]

In summary, the British Episcopal document offers another perspective in the debate on the status of the human embryo, by pointing out the fundamental equality in dignity and rights of every human being, regardless of their handicap. Already during the pregnancy, this perspective could help parents in their - often difficult and painful - process of accepting the possibility of having a disabled child.

7.6 Abortion, counselling and virtue ethics

Virtue ethics can offer another approach, both in a secular and in a religious context, which can be helpful in the field of education and the

---

1234 Ibid., p. 151.
1235 Rozendal, D., op. cit., pp. 90-91.
1236 Catholic Bishops of Great Britain, Joint Committee on Bioethical Issues, 1990, pp. 151-152.

prevention of unintended pregnancies and abortions.[1237] As regards the education of virtues, the Church has a very long tradition. In particular, the example of Thomas Aquinas' virtue ethics is worth mentioning, because of his innovative influence in integrating normative ethics and virtue ethics, where the emphasis is on the latter.[1238] The whole teaching of Aquinas in the *Summa Theologica* is directed towards the way man is related with God, who offers communion with Himself in Jesus Christ and thus leads to the fulfilment of this communion in the beatific vision of God. One revolutionary aspect of Aquinas' virtue ethics is that he spoke in a positive way of the human passions, which need to be moderated by ways of the virtues. In particular, the virtues of prudence, temperance and of justice are meaningful when it comes to the prevention of abortion. The virtue of justice consists in the conformity of the will with the ordering of reason in relation to other human beings and to the community as a whole.[1239] By the act of abortion, not only the foetus is killed, but also the family and the community at large is deprived of one of its members.

The teaching of prudence is relevant in the area of education for responsible sexual behaviour, because it can teach "the knowledge of what to seek and what to avoid".[1240] Especially when young people are considering to engage themselves in a sexual relationship but do not feel themselves ready to become parents, they should be stimulated to apply the virtue of prudence. In a counselling situation, the three dimensions of responsible sexual behaviour could become addressed. First of all, the dignity of the own person is always involved in responsible or irresponsible sexual behaviour. When young people rush into a sexual relationship, then often mutual respect might later become an issue. Secondly, the seriousness and the sustainability of the relation itself could be an issue of conversation during counselling. Again, when young people start to become emotionally attached to someone they do not really love, this could create all sorts of tensions and problems. And thirdly, a counsellor could ask to reflect more deeply on the possible consequences of unsafe sexual behaviour and on

---

1237 See for instance Roger Crisp and Michael Slote (eds.), *Virtue Ethics*. Oxford, 1997.
1238 Cf. J.B.M. Wissink, in: H.W.M. Rikhof and F.J.H. Vosman (eds.), *De schittering van de waarheid. Theologische reflecties bij de encycliek Veritatis Splendor*. Zoetermeer, 1994, pp. 78-95, here p. 83.
1239 Th. Aquinas, *S.T.*, II, II, q. 58, a. 5c., also ad 2nd and ad 3rd.
1240 Th. Aquinas, *S.T.*, II, II, q. 47, a. 1c.

the willingness to accept the possible consequence of procreation. Thus, three values are central, values which are similarly central in the teaching of the Church: the value of one's own personality and dignity, then the value of the other person in the relationship and finally the value of human life itself, which could become apparent when conception takes place.

Closely connected to the virtue of prudence is that of temperance. According to Aquinas, temperance "does not withdraw man from pleasure, but only from those pleasures which are contrary to reason".[1241]

The integration of virtue ethics in today's counselling practices may not be as simple as it looks. Alasdair MacIntyre has pointed out that in our modern times, practising and educating virtues has become problematic because of the social and philosophical obstacles for seeing each human life as a whole, as a unity.[1242] "Social obstacles derive from the way in which modernity partitions each human life into a variety of segments, each with its own norms and modes of behaviour. So work is divided from leisure, private life from public, the corporate from the personal."[1243] He continues to observe that "equally, the unity of a human life becomes invisible when a sharp separation is made either between the individual and the roles that he or she plays [...] or between the different role – and quasi-role – enactments of an individual life so that life comes to appear as nothing but a series of unconnected episodes".[1244] He offers a different approach for what he considers as characteristics of Sartre's existentialism and Goffman's sociological theory about the liquidation of the self, which entails viewing "both conversations in particular and then human actions in general as enacted narratives".[1245] When a person is the subject of a narrative that runs from one's birth to one's death, then he or she is accountable for the actions and experiences which compose a life which could be narrated. And similarly, one can always ask the other for an account, which invites him or her to tell their life story.[1246]

MacIntyre's narrative approach could deepen a pastoral conversation or

---

1241 Th. Aquinas, *S.T.*, II, II, q. 141, 1 ad 1st.
1242 Alasdair MacIntyre, *After Virtue. A study in moral theory*. London, 1981.
1243 Ibid., p. 204.
1244 Ibid.
1245 Ibid., p. 211.
1246 Cf. Ibid., pp. 217-218.

a counselling session in which the above mentioned three dimensions of responsible sexual behaviour are addressed. Firstly, the counselee could be asked to reflect on the question to what extent he or she really knows the other person - and the narrative of his or her life - in the case an intimate relationship with this person is being considered. A further reflection could take place on the question of whether the expected short term pleasure of a sexual relationship fits in with what could be considered as valuable in the person's own life as a whole and whether the person sees these values being respected and cherished in the life of the other. And finally, the question could be raised if the counselee would be willing to assume responsibility for conceiving a new human life together with his or her partner.

An important characteristic of virtue ethics is its focus on moral agents and their lives. In particular if a woman is confronted with an unintended pregnancy, she might be inclined to focus on the obstacles which will arise in becoming a mother. By doing so, it could become extremely difficult to try to see things from the child's perspective or to reflect on the question in what way her life could be enriched as a mother.

In this regard, Rosalind Hursthouse argues that for mothers, bearing children is *morally* worthwhile and significant.[1247] Even without the theological motivation of the sanctity of life, children can be valued as 'good', in the sense that other things like health, knowledge, pleasure and virtue can be valued as 'good'. Just as every human being, every foetus has a future of value. Therefore, receiving a child could be thought of as something beautiful as such, but above that, the begetters of a child could consider the child as a new and beautiful creation *of them*. Hursthouse goes on to argue that if it can be established that children are 'good' (in the sense of being good; and insofar as one can establish such a thing), the begetter of a child could state that "if *our* or *my* child is a good in itself, then having *our* or *my* own child is intrinsically worthwhile. And although, for a man 'having our or my child' can only be playing his part in its generation and later on having it in his family, for a woman it is not only that but also the experience of bearing the child. So since for a woman bearing a child is in part constitutive of having a child, and since having one's own child is

---

[1247] Rosalind Hursthouse, *Beginning lives*. Oxford, 1987, p. 315.

intrinsically worthwhile, bearing a child is intrinsically worthwhile."[1248]

Hursthouse mentions other arguments in favour of bearing children which are worth mentioning: for instance that in bearing the child, the woman enriches her own life; that she gives her husband (or partner) the outcome of their union; that she gives her other (future) children a sibling; that she gives her and her partner's parents a grandchild and her friends or extended family a new member of their group.[1249] It could make sense that these points are discussed during a decision making process regarding unintended pregnancy. However, it must be admitted that the first argument in particular, that of the woman enriching her own life by giving birth, is not always experienced in this way by the woman while she is pregnant, nor by her partner. Sometimes it requires a lot of patience, endurance, courage and support from others to begin to value the pregnancy and the perspective of giving birth in a positive way.

7.7 Abortion prevention and the proof of fatherhood

Often, women mention problems within their relationship that make them decide in favour of abortion. It might be that the relationship was too short, or broken, or that the partner was unwilling to become a father.[1250] These kinds of situation might even form the basis for a legal conflict, especially when the mother wants to have the baby.

According to the Dutch legislation the father of the child has an obligation to contribute to the costs involved in rearing his child until it has reached the age of 21. Should he refuse or deny being the father then two possible juridical procedures exist to investigate his fatherhood.[1251] The first procedure only seeks to confirm his fatherhood, in order to make him contribute financially to the upbringing of the child. The second procedure creates, in the case of a positive outcome, a juridical bond between the father and the child, which has not only financial consequences, but also gives parental authority over the child, as well as the possibility for the child to bear the name of his father.

1248 Ibid., p. 312.
1249 Ibid., p. 315.
1250 Cf. figure 3, part 3.3.1.1.
1251 Cf. A.P. van der Linden, S.G.A. ten Siethoff and A.E.I.J. Zeijlstra-Rijpstra, *Jeugd en recht*, Houten, 2009, p. 45.

In both cases the man can prove that he is not the father of the child, by means of a blood or a DNA test or by proving that he could not have been the father at the moment of conception. If the fatherhood is uncertain, the examining magistrate can order that an inquiry be held. This can be done by a DNA test of the possible father and the child, and in some cases the mother as well. Fatherhood can normally be excluded with a 100% certainty, or proven with more than 99,9% probability. Another advantage is that this method is not physically damaging.[1252] If the man refuses to take part in the DNA test as has been directed by the magistrate, other material (like testimonies, photos, etc.) can be used to possibly confirm his fatherhood.[1253]

Despite the woman's wish to bring her pregnancy to term, she may, in some cases, fear the consequences of confronting the father and having to face the complications of the upbringing. In these cases it is all the more a responsibility of the doctor or the medical assistant to discuss with her the possibilities of material and personal support.

Finally, also in cases of sexual offence, DNA-research can be of great importance in order to gather evidence. In this regard, Makdoembaks pleads for a database of DNA-profiles from abortion tissue in case of teenage pregnancies. He argues that sometimes sexually abused minors can report this criminal offence only years later. In these cases, when there are no crime witnesses, a DNA-profile of the offender could be the only evidence.[1254]

As has been shown, legal measures can be taken in order to prove the fatherhood and also to make financial arrangements regarding the upbringing of the child. But this would not be necessary if the man were to accept his responsibility, and if the woman would allow him to do so.

7.8 Counselling and pastoral care after abortion

In chapter 3 the results of empirical psychological research have been pointed out indicating:

[1252] A. Heida, Vaderschapsprocedures en DNA-onderzoek, in *Tijdschrift voor familie- en jeugdrecht*, vol. 24, 2002, p. 123.
[1253] Ibid., p. 129 and F.B. Bakels, "Conclusie bij de uitspraak van de Hoge Raad d.d. 22-09-2000", *Rechtspraak van de Week: conclusies*, nr. 184, 2000, pp. 872-879. Hoge Raad is Dutch for Supreme Court.
[1254] Makdoembaks, N., op. cit., p. 218.

- the prevalence of guilt feelings or a conflict of conscience among more than 50% of both women and men after induced abortion;[1255]
- an increased risk (of circa 1.3) of a range of common mental health problems (major depression, anxiety disorders, self-harm, suicidal ideation, alcohol dependence and illicit drug dependence) after induced abortion;[1256]
- the prevalence of features of post-traumatic stress disorder and depression at a pathological level (of 8-15% of men and women), following induced abortion of a foetus with an anomaly.[1257]

If after induced abortion guilt feelings occur, counselling or pastoral care can be helpful. Further counselling could be aimed at the prevention of more abortions and at reconciliation with the unborn child, with the woman herself and with others. Pastoral care might be aimed at reconciliation with God and with the Church community.[1258]

In late modern times, talking about personal guilt has become uncommon. As a consequence, the responsibility of adult persons is implicitly denied. If on the other hand the person acknowledges his or her responsibility, one is not incapacitated but on the contrary, the possibility for personal growth is once more created.[1259] It is essential, in a counselling session or a pastoral conversation after induced abortion, not to have a judgmental attitude. Often, a personal tragedy lies behind the decision to have an abortion. Although the decision itself can be lamented, a person who has taken this decision does not lose her or his human dignity.

According to Peter Petersen, it requires an awareness of death in order to be mentally able to cope with an induced abortion.[1260] However, the coping process can be hindered by various destructive, defensive reactions against the awareness of death.[1261] Such a reaction might appear in one of the many forms of collective disguising of the true nature of an abortion.

1255 Kero, A. and Lalos, A., op. cit., cf. part 3.1.2.
1256 Fergusson, D.M. et al., 2008, op. cit.; also Gilchrist, A.C. et al., 1995, cf. part 3.1.3.1.
1257 Korenromp, M.J. et al., op. cit., cf. part 3.1.3.1.
1258 The next part enters into the possibilities of reconciliation with the Church community.
1259 Cf. Claudia Mariéle Wulf, *Schuld ins Wort gebracht*. Vallendar, 2008, p. 53.
1260 Petersen, P., 1986, op. cit., pp. 279-305; some of the results of his research have been analysed in part 3.1.3.2.
1261 Petersen, P., 1986, op. cit., pp. 279-305, in particular pp. 297-305.

A counsellor or pastor might encounter a counselee who denies that the dead embryo has been a living human being. With the available ultrasound techniques for prenatal diagnosis, such a denial becomes more and more improbable. Yet another form of denial has to do with the death itself of the embryo, caused by the abortion. This could be considered a reductionist view of reality, by considering death as the absolute end of human life.[1262] If on the other hand one sees death as the transition to a new life, as is the case in the monotheistic religions and in many other philosophies of life, this opens up a whole new perspective.[1263]

The counselee may also hide his or herself behind the legal possibility of induced abortion. Such an attitude might have been reinforced by the doctor or the staff at the clinic or in the hospital. By way of a legal justification, the doctor or other staff members cover up the awareness of death.[1264]

Besides these denying or legalistic reactions, Petersen mentions fear as the most common instrument to suppress the definitive character of abortion.[1265] Fear to harm one's own career by becoming a parent is often found among clients of abortion clinics, even more so when the woman is alone. The question is then how much time and effort is available from doctors and staff at the clinic or hospital and from other supporting organisations in order to help people after the discovery of an unintended pregnancy?

Perhaps the most subtle form of covering up the emotional and mental impact an abortion can have, has to do with a one-sided moral accusation of the persons involved. Unfortunately, this kind of one-sided accusation is also found among members of the Church or pro-life organisations. If a Church member or pro-life campaigner personally accuses a woman of having committed a severe crime by choosing abortion, but without offering her the possibility of clearing her mind about the question of guilt, or at

---

1262 Cf. part 3.1.3.2.
1263 Petersen, P., 1986, op. cit., p. 291; For a comparative scientific treatment of the world's religions and the different views on the afterlife I refer to Ninian Smart's *The World's Religions*, Cambridge, 1989. He distinguishes seven dimensions in the world's religions: the ritual, the experiential, the narrative, the doctrinal, the ethical, the social and the material dimension. All these dimensions play a role in one's ideas of the afterlife. Cf. Ninian Smart, 1989, pp. 11-22.
1264 Petersen, P., 1986, op. cit., p. 285.
1265 Ibid., pp. 286-288.

least refer her to persons who can help her to do so, then such a treatment irrefutably falls short.

Awareness of death brings along an acknowledgment of one's own responsibility in the decision to abort, as well as a process of bereavement, which might be characterised by phases of emotional disruption, emptiness and an approximation of the death experience.[1266] During this latter phase, it happens for instance that parents feel the need to give their unborn child a name or to express their feelings in a ritual, in music or in arts.

Sometimes, it happens that a pastor is confronted with a woman who has undergone an abortion and who comes to him for advice or support, either in the context of the sacrament of reconciliation or in a pastoral conversation. For instance, I recall a pastoral conversation with an older couple, married for more than fifty years. They said they had always been true to each other and they regularly went to Church. However, one thing they lamented enormously, they told me in tears, were the two abortions they had had forty years ago. They had prayed for God's forgiveness so often and they admitted that their lives would have been happier if they had not decided to abort. They had never told a priest what had happened, until that day. In the context of the sacrament of reconciliation, I could witness the relief they felt by letting this burden fall off their shoulders.

It is important that a pastor shows understanding for the emotional and psychological side of the bereavement process, without disguising the true nature of the act itself. The direct effect of an abortion is immediate and irreversible, but its psychological effects might appear years later.[1267] A pastor needs to know when he cannot resolve the problem by himself, but instead has to refer to a psychologist or a psychiatrist.

In many cases, women are convinced that they are following their conscience when taking the decision to abort. In this regard, as it comes to pastoral care, it is essential to note, that the Church "distinguishes between error, which always merits repudiation, and the person in error, who never loses the dignity of being a person even when he is flawed by false or inadequate religious notions. God alone is the judge and searcher of hearts, for that reason He forbids us to make judgments about the internal guilt of

---

1266 Ibid., pp. 298-305.
1267 Cf. part 3.1.3.3.

anyone. The teaching of Christ even requires that we forgive injuries…"[1268]

Because of the gravity of the object of every procured abortion, the killing of an unborn human being, the Church calls abortion an intrinsically evil act.[1269] It is important for a good understanding and a proper pastoral attitude to make a distinction between the term 'intrinsically evil act' and the term 'mortal sin'.[1270] "For a sin to be mortal, three conditions must be met: 'Mortal sin is sin whose object is grave matter and which is also committed with full knowledge and deliberate consent.'"[1271] Now, it cannot be presupposed that in every case a woman who takes a decision to abort, has full knowledge of embryonic development. Secondly, she might not be aware of the moral dimension of the decision. Neither is it guaranteed that possible alternatives to abortion are being taken into serious consideration. Finally it is not always the case that the decision is hers alone, and with her full consent.

The moral gravity of a sin changes when a person acts unknowingly or is forced by others. Committing a mortal sin necessitates a new initiative of God's mercy and a conversion of heart which is normally accomplished within the setting of the sacrament of reconciliation.[1272] Women who have had an abortion are encouraged to make use of this sacrament in order to receive God's forgiveness and peace.[1273] In situations in which the sacrament cannot be administered, a pastoral conversation might be helpful to relieve suffering and grief and to grow in trust in God's mercy.[1274]

Although the abortion practice in a clinic or hospital requires a consultation before the intervention, the truth is not always revealed during this conversation. There may, for instance, have been social pressure by the partner or the woman's parents which make her feel forced to have an abortion. In these cases the woman might feel forced to keep this pressure secret from the medical assistant. In this sense legalization can lead to more

---

1268 *Gaudium et Spes*, n. 28.
1269 John Paul II, 1993, n. 80, based on *Gaudium et Spes*, n. 27; cf. part 6.1.3.2.
1270 John Paul II, 1995, n. 99 on the sacrament of reconciliation.
1271 Catechism of the Catholic Church, 1997, n. 1857, referring to John Paul II, Postsynodal apostolic exhortation "*Reconciliatio et Paenitentia, to the bishops, clergy and faithful on reconciliation and penance in the mission of the Church today*", Vatican, 1985, n. 17.
1272 Catechism of the Catholic Church, 1997, n. 1856.
1273 Cf. Francis, 2015 (b), op. cit. and John Paul II, 1995, op. cit., n. 99.
1274 Cf. *Codex Iuris Canonici*, n. 844.

situations of grave injustice, since the impression is created that the choice is hers and that it is a 'normal' medical intervention. If, on the other hand the woman would receive proper pastoral care, or if intensive counselling would be offered, the hidden social pressure might be revealed and possibly, with involvement of the woman's partner or of significant others, be relieved.

Chapter 8

Preventing abortion

In chapter 6, the one Biblical passage which deals explicitly with abortion, Exodus 21, 22-25, was mentioned. The passage aims at protecting the rights of a husband regarding the unborn human life in his pregnant wife and sets a standard for retaliation. From the apostolic times, both Jewish and Christian authors have interpreted this passage as a normative statement against procured abortion in general, notwithstanding particular exceptions and an on-going discussion about the timing of ensoulment.

From the historical account throughout the centuries the conclusion must be drawn that the Catholic Church has always taken a position against procured abortion, independent of her stance regarding the ensoulment of the foetus. As we have seen, opinions regarding the ensoulment of the foetus differed considerably during the centuries. Consensus within the Church regarding immediate ensoulment at conception gradually came about after the discovery of the egg-cell by Karl Ernst von Baer in 1827.

The twentieth century is marked by resistance of the Church towards public support for procured abortion. The Second Vatican Council and later documents confirm that life must be protected from the moment of its conception. At the same time, in many Western countries procured abortion is legalised. In the 1990s this is followed by the allowance of experimentation on embryos. Since the Second Vatican Council, the Church has repeatedly called upon States to respect the rights of other innocent human beings and has urged politicians to ensure the protection of the unborn human life and to promote alternatives for abortion.

As regards prenatal diagnosis, the Magisterium takes a nuanced view, in the sense that it should be meant to promote the health of the embryo and the mother. Prenatal diagnosis is considered as illicit, when it is used in order to give the option of abortion.

The Church's vision on procured abortion does not stand alone, but has to be seen in the context of her view on natural law, on the formation of a personal conscience, on married love and on responsible parenthood. The principles of the natural law, of which the first is to do good and to avoid evil, are actively being discovered by man in the depth of his conscience. Because conscience is the fulfilment of practical reason, following ones conscience does not mean following a subjective, but an objective norm, insofar as this norm is known as objective. Therefore it is essential that one's personal conscience is formed by means of education. The application of virtue ethics could be a valuable instrument for the formation of young people.

The Second Vatican Council encourages human autonomy in earthly affairs, but if autonomy is looked at as a freedom from every hindrance or obligation, then there is a real risk that such a freedom without objective orientation becomes arbitrariness.[1275] In those cases, the claim of autonomy in relation to abortion does not do justice to the unborn human life.

In chapter 7 the services offered by care agencies in the U.K. and the Netherlands, which provide support for mothers and families who encounter difficulties raising their child(ren), was described. In the Netherlands their offer falls short of meeting the requests of women. In the U.K., the offer of rooms for young mothers is much more widespread, thanks to the network of LIFE-houses. Still, this type of care faces financial difficulties. Adoption is only rarely an alternative wished for by the biological parents. Foster care is more prevalent both in the U.K. as in the Netherlands, but this does not always lead to results hoped for.

Evaluation of the SRE-programs in schools in the U.K. and the Netherlands stresses the need of parental involvement in the provision of SRE, as well as the right of parents to withdraw their child from elements of SRE-programs. Earlier, a British review of the SRE practice concluded that more attention should be given to building and sustaining relationships and to the skills and values that young people need as they progress towards adulthood.

The focus of attention today with regard to professional help in pregnancy dilemmas, is on the woman. However, often her existential

---

1275 *Gaudium et Spes,* n. 36; cf. John Paul II, 1993, n. 38 and Wulf, C.M., 2009, op. cit., p. 71.

questions are not taken seriously. Although the legislator speaks of an autonomous choice, in reality this autonomy is often threatened because of the man's attitude towards her pregnancy, because of a lack of alternatives in available care, or because no serious effort has been undertaken to find available alternatives to abortion.

In many complex and often tragic cases, the man is hardly involved or not involved at all in the decision to terminate a pregnancy. The large number of cases in which financial reasons seem to be decisive for an abortion indicates that it is questionable whether in these cases there really is an emergency situation which could not be avoided, especially if more attention were to be given to underlying relational problems.[1276]

Often in the Netherlands, alternatives to abortion are not discussed during the intake conversation in a clinic or hospital, despite legal requirements.[1277] A counsellor or pastor could help to find ways to discuss alternatives to abortion with the couple and sometimes with other relatives or friends involved, in order to widen the decision making process. Alternative scenarios also need to be investigated, in collaboration with the medical staff, after the prenatal diagnosis of a severely handicapped child. Here, the equal rights of all persons and the possibilities for a loving upbringing are at stake.

In this research, suggestions have been made in order to reduce the number of abortions in the U.K. and the Netherlands, by avoiding inconsistencies between the abortion legislation and the current praxis, by enlarging possibilities for intensified, independent counselling and by promoting organizations which offer alternatives to abortion. It requires political willingness to do so. In the last two decades, few initiatives have been taken to change the abortion legislation in the U.K. and the Netherlands, to promote alternatives or to stimulate research to the possibilities of abortion prevention. Some of these parliamentary and civil initiatives could not count on governmental support.[1278]

1276 Cf. part 3.3.1.1.
1277 Cf. part 1.2.1.
1278 A recent plan developed by the British Department of Health to introduce independent counselling to women who visit an abortion clinic has been withdrawn by Health Minister Anna Soubry. Cf. Tim Ross, "Health minister Anna Soubry scraps abortion counselling plan", *Telegraph*, 31 October 2012.

Sociological research shows that the less restrictive abortion laws are, the more women are inclined to choose an abortion.[1279] In some situations it is necessary to make use of legal procedures in order to prove fatherhood and to establish a legal or financial bond between him and the mother and child. Promoting organizations which offer alternatives for abortions is another way to prevent abortions. In the U.K. and the Netherlands the establishment of organizations such as the LIFE and Siriz takes place in a secular context. Both British and Dutch organisations who supply care for women who want to bring their pregnancy to term, suffer from financial and capacity problems. It is highly desirable that the access to alternatives to abortion is expanded and promoted.

Because of all kinds of personal circumstances, the limited availability of alternatives such as material and personal support or adoption, or the complexity of finding the right help at the right moment, many women feel more or less forced to terminate their pregnancy. If they were helped in their own situation, if alternatives were available on a larger scale and if the right information were to be given to them, it is clear that many abortions could be prevented.

On the other hand, women are more likely to choose to have an abortion if the availability of abortion providers or the availability of the abortion pill increases.[1280] Likewise, proposed measures in the U.K. to make abortion more accessible by removing the requirement of two doctor's signatures or by allowing nurses to perform abortions, would more than likely lead to an increasing demand.[1281] Rather, it is necessary that education to teenagers, both boys and girls, is not limited to prevention of pregnancy only, but on the contrary is intended to make them more aware of their possible future role as parents, with all the beauty but also the responsibilities which result from this.

Every direct abortion deprives the foetus of a future like our own, which is potentially valuable.[1282] The future of value argument explains in a secular way the wrongness of the deliberate killing of human embryos. It is clear

---

1279 Cf. part 1.4.3.3.
1280 Ibid.
1281 Alan O'Dowd, "MPs want to drop second doctor's signature for abortion", *BMJ*, 2007, 335, 960.2.
1282 In part 5.1.4.

that in the current abortion legislation in the U.K. and the Netherlands, the future of value argument has not been given sufficient weight. I have pointed out the necessity to reopen the ethical debate on the status of the human embryo, as well as the urgency to diminish the long term negative mental health effects of abortion on women.

And last but certainly not least, it seems that the abortion praxis in the U.K. and the Netherlands largely ignores the role of the man and his responsibility as the begetter of the child. The Dutch evaluation report hardly talks about the man's role before an abortion. Based on the results of qualitative research on the man's attitude towards the unborn human life, it could be expected that if a serious effort were made by the counsellor to point out the man's responsibility, in many cases this might lead to a change in his attitude. The woman's judgment of the situation as an emergency could change as a result of this. It needs to be remarked that such an openness in the decision making process for the man's attitude would require a change in the abortion legislation. In the current situation, the members of staff in Dutch abortion clinics often do not feel obliged to undertake such an effort, because in their view, only the woman is responsible for taking the decision.[1283] For this reason, it might be preferable to introduce a regulation for intensified, independent counselling for couples who consider abortion.

One could think of situations in which it would be very awkward for a woman if a man were required to have a role in the decision-making process. In some cases, this would even be impossible. But there are also many situations in which it would make a big difference if a man makes it clear that he is willing to bear the consequences of his actions by taking responsibility for his child's future.

1283 Cf. part 3.3.1.2.

Summary in Dutch - Samenvatting in het Nederlands

Het doel van deze studie is een heroverweging van de abortuspraktijk in het Verenigd Koninkrijk (V.K.) en Nederland. Hiertoe wordt gebruik gemaakt van een filosofisch raamwerk zoals uiteen is gezet door Paul Ricoeur in zijn essay "Het probleem van de grondslagen van de moraal". Via deze benadering is het mogelijk om ethische en theologische vooronderstellingen te integreren met empirische gegevens en om concrete aanbevelingen te doen voor de huidige abortuspraktijk en voor toekomstig onderzoek.

Ricoeur gaat uit van vrijheid als principiële bron van ethiek die is gericht op het 'goede leven'. Maar deze vrijheid leidt pas werkelijk tot ethiek wanneer tevens de vrijheid in de tweede persoon, de vrijheid van de ander, wordt erkend. Bovendien dient als derde stap rekening gehouden worden met wat Ricoeur de bemiddeling van instituties noemt. Hierbij onderscheidt hij waarden, normen, geboden, wetten en natuurwetten. Bij waarden kan men bijvoorbeeld denken aan de waarde van het leven zelf, als ook aan fysieke en mentale gezondheid. Bij normen gaat het in het abortusvraagstuk met name om de status van het menselijk embryo. Geboden, ofwel imperatieven zoals Ricoeur ze noemt, betreffen in dit verband ofwel imperatieven die men zichzelf oplegt op grond van het geweten, ofwel die door een autoriteit worden opgelegd, zoals door de Staat, door ouders of familie, etc. Imperatieven door de Staat opgelegd worden verankerd in positieve wetgeving. In dit onderzoek wordt de abortuswetgeving in het V.K. en Nederland in twee casestudies nader geanalyseerd en beoordeeld op de mate van consistentie en tevens op de consequenties voor de betrokkenen.

Het concept van de wet voegt aan de noties van waarden, normen en imperatieven de mogelijkheid toe van universalisering. Wetten richten zich op universaliteit met het oog op de bescherming van bepaalde waarden. Evenals Kant in zijn theorie van maximes introduceert Ricoeur twee eenvoudige vragen die dienen als criterium voor universaliteit in besluitvormingsprocessen: "Zou ik kunnen verlangen dat iedereen op deze wijze zou handelen?" en "Kan mijn verlangen dienen als een universele wet?"

Tenslotte noemt Ricoeur het evangelisch perspectief in de ethische orde, hetgeen in dit onderzoek in de laatste hoofdstukken wordt uitgewerkt met betrekking tot het abortusvraagstuk. Na de oproep van het Tweede Vaticaans Concilie voor een openheid naar de wereld, heeft de integratie van resultaten van sociaalwetenschappelijk onderzoek geleid tot meer aandacht binnen de theologie voor de menselijke ervaring en de praktijk. Moraaltheologie als wetenschap laat zien dat de zoektocht naar de bescherming van universele waarden zoals leven en liefde existentiële vragen oproepen, die vaak niet op een bevredigende wijze worden beantwoord in de sociale ethiek.

In hoofdstuk 1 wordt het juridische raamwerk besproken voor de legalisering van abortus in het V.K. en Nederland. Zowel in het VK. als in Nederland is abortus onder bepaalde condities gelegaliseerd tot en met de vierentwintigste week van de zwangerschap. De Britse *Abortion Act*, die in 1967 door het Parlement werd aangenomen, kent een aantal gronden waarop een abortus legaal kan plaatsvinden. Verreweg het grootste aantal abortussen (97%) gebeurt onder grond C, hetgeen inhoudt dat de arts inschat dat het continueren van de zwangerschap, die niet verder dan 24 weken is gevorderd, grotere risico's met zich mee zou brengen voor de fysieke of mentale gezondheid van de vrouw dan het afbreken van de zwangerschap. Van risico's voor de fysieke gezondheid is slechts in minder dan een half procent van de gevallen sprake; het gaat dus bijna altijd om vermeende mentale gezondheidsrisico's. In 1990 werd in het V.K. de grens voor het legaal uitvoeren van een abortus verlaagd van 28 naar 24 weken. Andere amendementen faalden.

In Nederland werd na lange parlementaire debatten in 1981 de Wet Afbreking Zwangerschap aangenomen. In 2005 werd de werking van de wet geëvalueerd op basis van het onderzoek van Mechteld Visser et al., maar dit leidde niet tot principiële wetswijzigingen.

Een verschil tussen de wetgeving in beide landen is dat in het V.K. het aan meisjes beneden de 16 jaar is toegestaan een abortus te laten uitvoeren zonder de toestemming van de ouders. De in Nederland verplichte beraadtermijn van vijf dagen geldt in het V.K. niet, evenmin als een wettelijke verplichting om alternatieven voor abortus aan de orde te stellen in het consultatiegesprek. Sinds 2007 wordt in Nederland echoscopisch onderzoek (de 20 weken echo) aangeboden aan alle zwangere vrouwen; in het V.K. was dit al langer het geval.

In de laatste decennia heeft het denken over abortus een medicalisering ondergaan. In het V.K. is dit fenomeen zichtbaar doordat vrijwel alle abortussen worden uitgevoerd op grond van de veronderstelling dat voortzetting van de zwangerschap risico zou inhouden op aantasting van de mentale gezondheid van de vrouw.

Het probleem van het politieke debat zoals dat in het V.K. heeft plaatsgevonden is dat er geen ruimte is geboden voor het aan de orde stellen van de ethische en morele aspecten van abortus. Er heeft in opdracht van het Britse Parlement geen onderzoek plaatsgevonden naar de effectiviteit van de huidige abortuspraktijk, zoals in Nederland het geval is geweest. De bevindingen vanuit het Nederlandse onderzoek naar de abortuspraktijk bieden evenwel diverse waardevolle aanknopingspunten voor de Britse situatie.

In hoofdstuk 1 worden tevens de gevolgen gepresenteerd van de legalisering van abortus in het V.K. en Nederland. Sinds de jaren '70 van de vorige eeuw is in het V.K. het aantal abortussen meer dan verdubbeld. In Nederland vertoont het aantal abortussen sinds 1990 een vrijwel constante stijging, alleen in de laatste jaren is er sprake van stabilisatie. Uit de statistieken blijkt dat in het V.K. aanzienlijk meer abortussen worden gepleegd dan in Nederland; met name het aantal tienerzwangerschappen dat wordt gevolgd door een abortus, ligt beduidend hoger.

In beide landen is het percentage abortussen onder etnische groeperingen hoger dan onder de autochtone bevolking. Daarbij zijn er aanwijzingen dat jonge allochtone vrouwen een risicogroep vormen waarbij seksueel misbruik vaker voorkomt dan bij autochtone vrouwen. Tevens is er sprake van een toename van het aantal gevallen van seksueel overdraagbare aandoeningen, hetgeen risico's voor de gezondheid van het embryo met zich meebrengt.

De sociaalwetenschappelijke studie van Mark Levels toont een verband aan tussen restrictievere abortuswetgeving in diverse Europese landen en een verlaging van het aantal abortussen. Vergelijkbaar onderzoek uit de V.S. toont eveneens een verband aan tussen een strengere abortuswetgeving en een hogere prijs van abortus enerzijds en de aantallen tienerzwangerschappen en abortussen anderzijds.

Er is sprake van inconsistentie op een viertal punten tussen de voorschriften van de Nederlandse Wet Afbreking Zwangerschap en de huidige abortuspraktijk. Deze punten betreffen:

1) De criteria ontbreken om te bepalen wat een noodsituatie inhoudt, terwijl de wet aangeeft dat er sprake moet zijn van een noodsituatie om tot abortus over te gaan.

2) De juridische vereiste dat alternatieven voor abortus worden besproken tijdens het consultatiegesprek, wordt vaak niet nagevolgd.

3) De medische staf van de abortusklinieken en huisartsen verstrekken niet altijd voldoende en begrijpelijke informatie ten aanzien van de fysieke en mentale risico's en gevolgen van abortus. Een uitwisseling van ethische opinies is nog zeldzamer.

4) De medische staf van abortusklinieken is geneigd om zich te concentreren op de te volgen wettelijke procedure en de beslissing van de vrouw, in plaats van op de inhoud van de eigen afweging. De WAZ wijst er op dat twee autonome beslissingen genomen moeten worden, door de vrouw en door de arts.

In de analyse van de abortuswetgeving en –praktijk in het V.K. en Nederland wordt geconstateerd dat de huidige wetgeving in beide landen weliswaar de autonomie van de vrouw tracht te waarborgen, maar dat het ongeboren menselijk leven onvoldoende wordt beschermd ten opzichte van de oorspronkelijke intentie van de wetgever. Bij de huidige counselingpraktijk is er weinig aandacht voor alternatieven voor abortus. Tevens heeft de mannelijke verwekker geen enkele juridische status in het besluitvormingsproces.

In hoofdstuk 2 wordt een historische achtergrond geschetst van de legalisering van abortus in het V.K. en Nederland. De eerste feministische golf begon in het V.K. en Nederland in de tweede helft van de 19de eeuw. Invloedrijke vrouwen als Marie Stopes en Aletta Jacobs richtten zich met name op de emancipatie van vrouwen en op voorlichting inzake geboortebeperking, maar waren geen voorstander van abortus. Vertegenwoordigers van de tweede feministische golf in de jaren '60 en '70 van de vorige eeuw zagen legalisering van abortus als middel om emancipatie te bevorderen en tevens om het probleem van illegale abortussen tegen te gaan. In die jaren verschoof de publieke opinie in zowel het V.K. als in Nederland in dezelfde richting. Tijdens de derde feministische golf wordt door diverse auteurs gewezen op de beperkingen van het autonomie-ideaal en op de wens tot inclusiviteit van mannen bij het maken van reproductieve keuzes.

In dit hoofdstuk wordt de autonomiegedachte ter discussie gesteld in relatie tot de liberale abortuswetgeving zoals die vigeert in het V.K. en Nederland. Er wordt ingegaan op de vraag op welke manier ethische theorieën zoals ontwikkeld door Immanuel Kant, Martha Nussbaum en Judith Jarvis Thompson recht doen aan de balans tussen autonome keuze en respect voor het ongeboren menselijk leven.

In de recente literatuur wordt zelfbeschikking gezien als het bepalende kenmerk van autonomie. Volgens Kant "geeft" de autonome mens de universele wet aan zichzelf. Een ander uitgangspunt van Kant is dat de mens steeds als doel en nooit als middel dient te worden beschouwd. Toegepast op het abortusvraagstuk kan een Kantiaanse filosofie behulpzaam zijn indien de nadruk ligt op het vergroten van de menselijke capaciteiten. Daarentegen kan een autonomiebenadering die uitgaat van de beschikbare opties de vrouw in een nadelige onderhandelingspositie brengen ten opzichte van de man. De autonomie van de vrouw kan worden bedreigd wanneer de mannelijke verwekker negatief staat tegenover de zwangerschap. Onvoldoende aandacht van de zijde van de hulpverlening voor de mogelijkheden van de vrouw om de zwangerschap uit te dragen, kan eveneens haar autonomie belemmeren. Bovendien is het vanuit filosofisch oogpunt bezien onmogelijk om voor een ander menselijk wezen te beslissen of leven of niet leven de beste optie is.

Rosalind Dixon en Martha Nussbaum gaan in hun benadering weliswaar uit van de groei van menselijke vermogens, maar zij miskennen in de toepassing ervan een fundamenteel verschil tussen abortus en therapeutische ingrepen: abortus impliceert de dood van de foetus.

Paul Ricoeur wijst op de moeilijkheid van het toeschrijven van een bepaalde serie van gebeurtenissen aan één bepaalde handelende persoon, omdat de handelingen van ieder van ons zo sterk met elkaar verweven zijn. Wanneer we Ricoeurs fenomenologie toepassen op het abortusvraagstuk, dan wordt duidelijk dat de autonomie van de handelende persoon, in dit geval de zwangere vrouw, belemmerd kan worden door een afwerende houding van de mannelijke verwekker van het kind, ofwel door andere belangrijke personen in haar omgeving, zoals bijvoorbeeld de ouders.

Volgens Ricoeur kunnen waarden, normen, geboden, wetten en natuurwetten een bemiddelende rol spelen in het realisatieproces van vrijheid in intersubjectiviteit. In hoofdstuk 3 gaat het om de waarden van het leven en de gezondheid van de vrouw, in het bijzonder na het maken van een keuze voor abortus. In dit hoofdstuk wordt een overzicht gegeven van wetenschappelijk bewijsmateriaal ten aanzien van de psychologische, psychiatrische en fysieke risico's en effecten van abortus provocatus voor de vrouw, aan de hand van de internationale literatuur gepubliceerd tussen 1985 en 2015, waarbij enkele aanbevelingen worden gedaan voor nader onderzoek.

Hoewel de meerderheid van de ondervraagde Nederlandse vrouwen aangeeft tevreden te zijn na de ingreep in een abortuskliniek of ziekenhuis, kampt een gedeelte met psychologische en psychiatrische problemen, soms vele jaren nadien. Vergelijkbaar wetenschappelijk onderzoek toont aan dat elk jaar circa 42,000 Britse en 6,000 Nederlandse vrouwen lijden aan ernstige mentale gezondheidsproblemen na abortus.

Onderzoek hiernaar vertoont diverse methodologische moeilijkheden. Met name wordt het gebrek aan een goede controlegroep genoemd, waardoor mogelijke effecten van andere variabelen niet uitgesloten kunnen worden. Op grond van longitudinaal onderzoek verricht in Nieuw-Zeeland wordt geconcludeerd dat het ondergaan van een abortus voor vrouwen een verhoogd risico op mentale gezondheidsproblemen met zich meebrengt van circa 30%. Toekomstig interdisciplinair onderzoek naar mentale gezondheidseffecten van abortus zou zowel moeten kijken naar de psychologische consequenties als ook naar de ethische en morele overwegingen in het besluitvormingsproces. Daarbij zou gebruik gemaakt moeten worden van retrospectieve en prospectieve data, met behulp van kwalitatieve en kwantitatieve onderzoeksstrategieën.

Ten aanzien van fysieke risico's en gevolgen van abortus provocatus wijzen diverse internationale studies op het risico van vroegtijdige bevallingen bij zwangerschappen volgend op een abortus. Vroegtijdige geboorte wordt geassocieerd met een hogere prevalentie van ernstige afwijkingen bij de geboorte. Ander onderzoek wijst op de toegenomen risico's op een verergering van een bestaande chlamydia-infectie na abortus provocatus. Recentelijk heeft een aantal Aziatische studies een verband aangetoond tussen borstkanker en een abortusverleden. In verschillende Westerse studies werd een dergelijk onafhankelijk verband niet aangetoond. Dit verschil kan mogelijk worden verklaard uit de rol van samenhangende factoren zoals de hogere leeftijd van de eerste voltooide zwangerschap, vaker voorkomende kinderloosheid en het frequenter gebruik van orale anticonceptiva in Westerse landen. Tevens bemoeilijken methodologische problemen zoals het gebrek aan een voldoende lange tijdsduur dit epidemiologische onderzoek. Het is wel aangetoond dat het krijgen van kinderen en het geven van borstvoeding het risico op borstkanker verminderen.

Tenslotte concluderen verschillende studies dat er een verband bestaat tussen abortus enerzijds en het risico op zelfmoord, opname in de psychiatrie of zelfbeschadiging anderzijds.

Een analyse van de Nederlandse evaluatie van de abortuswetgeving uit 2005 biedt inzicht in de redenen voor abortus. Uit de evaluatie blijkt dat het totaal aan diverse relatieconflicten en –problemen vaker als reden worden genoemd om voor abortus te kiezen dan financiële redenen. Dit blijkt eveneens uit kwalitatief psychologisch onderzoek. De evaluatie geeft aan dat circa een kwart van de Nederlandse vrouwen twijfels heeft over abortus, zowel voor als na de ingreep. Vergelijkbaar internationaal onderzoek laat hogere percentages zien. Uit literatuurstudie blijkt tevens dat ambivalente gevoelens vaak voorkomen bij (ongewenste) zwangerschap. Het benoemen van dergelijke gevoelens is heel relevant voor de besluitvorming na ongewenste zwangerschap en voor de rol van de mannelijke verwekker hierbij. Meer aandacht dient daarbij uit te gaan naar situaties waarin huiselijk geweld zich heeft voorgedaan, alvorens een beslissing wordt genomen.

In hoofdstuk 4 is de aandacht gericht op de rechten en de waarde van het menselijk embryo. Het denkschema van Ricoeur volgend betreffende de grondslagen van de moraal, wordt in dit hoofdstuk de overgang gemaakt van waarden naar relevante normen met betrekking tot abortus.

Allereerst wordt een beschrijving gegeven van de normale ontwikkeling van het embryo. Een cruciaal argument in het abortusdebat is dat de conceptie een unieke gebeurtenis is waarbij nieuw menselijk leven ontstaat. Embryonale ontwikkeling wordt gekenmerkt door een intrinsieke finaliteit, geleid door de DNA-structuur in de celkern, die vanaf de conceptie aanwezig en actief is in een specifieke combinatie. Embryonale ontwikkeling verloopt geleidelijk, continu en gecoördineerd. Vandaar dat de vraag wordt gesteld naar de mate van juridische bescherming van het embryo. Een vergelijking met het internationaal recht toont aan dat de opvatting dat het leven beschermwaardig is vanaf de conceptie, het niet heeft gehaald in verdragen van de Verenigde Naties en de Europese Unie, noch in uitspraken van het Hooggerechtshof in diverse Europese landen. Onder juristen bestaat er vooralsnog geen internationale overeenstemming over de vraag wanneer het menselijk leven en het daarmee gepaard gaande recht op leven begint. Vanuit bio-ethisch standpunt bezien zou echter naast de toegeschreven waardigheid ook de intrinsieke waardigheid van het menselijk embryo onderscheiden en erkend moeten worden.

Een vergelijkende analyse met het Europese internationale recht laat zien dat, hoewel er enige erkenning is van de noodzaak tot de bescherming van de waardigheid van het menselijke embryo, dit niet heeft geleid tot een erkenning van het recht op leven in de zin van Artikel 2 van de Europese Conventie van de Mensenrechten.

De centrale en normatieve vraag in het abortusdebat betreft de status van het embryo als menselijk wezen en als persoon. Zowel in het V.K. als in Nederland zijn wetenschappelijke experimenten met embryo's toegestaan tot 14 dagen na de bevruchting. In het V.K. gebeurde dit op grond van aanbevelingen van de Warnock-commissie. Mary Warnock betoogde dat het embryo niet kan worden beschouwd als een menselijk wezen tot aan de vorming van de primitiefstreek na ca. 14 dagen, in verband met de mogelijkheid tot splitsing in een eeneiige tweeling. Echter, tot dusverre is niet waargenomen, hoe splitsing exact plaatsvindt. Bij dieren worden verschillen in ontwikkelingskenmerken al aangetoond bij blastomeren van 2 of 4 cellen; splitsing zou dus 'ingeprogrammeerd' kunnen zijn. Volgens Warnock en anderen is er sprake van een graduele ontwikkeling van het embryo. Dit roept de metafysische vraag op of de bezieling van het embryo vertraagd plaatsvindt, of onmiddellijk na de bevruchting. Volgens Rose Koch-Hershenov dient de vorming van een eeneiige tweeling beschouwd te worden als de scheiding van twee menselijke wezens, die een lichaam deelden (vgl. Siamese tweeling). Deze hylomorfische metafysica biedt een verklaring voor de regelmatige groei van het embryo vanaf de bevruchting. De mogelijkheid van eeneiige tweelingen is dan ook op zich geen houdbaar argument tegen de these van onmiddellijke bezieling.

Jeff McMahan, Ronald Dworkin, Hugo Tristram Engelhardt en anderen stellen dat het persoon zijn begint met het rationele vermogen of nog later. Een dergelijk standpunt leidt tot een dualisme tussen een menselijk wezen en een persoon. Er is immers geen aanwijsbaar moment van substantiële verandering in de ontwikkeling van het menselijk embryo.

Voor de stelling dat het menselijk embryo is te beschouwen als een persoon vanaf bevruchting, wordt als biologisch argument aangevoerd dat een zygote het begin vormt van een menselijk wezen met actieve potentialiteit. Als filosofisch argument voor deze stelling betoogt Robert Spaemann dat het onmogelijk is een potentieel persoon te zijn.

In hoofdstuk 5 worden filosofische achtergronden voor het besluitvormingsproces voor reproductieve keuzes overwogen. De fenomenologische benadering van Paul Ricoeur kan inzicht verschaffen in de ethische intentie en in de relatie tot de foetus. De tweede component van de ethische intentie van een goed leven is volgens Ricoeur gericht op de zorg met en voor anderen. De fenomenologische hermeneutiek van het zelf laat een dialectiek van het Zelf en de Ander zien die ervan getuigt dat de Ander niet alleen een tegenover is van het Zelf, maar tevens bepalend voor het eigen zelfbeeld. Wanneer het ethische doel van eigenwaarde opgesloten raakt in zichzelf, komt de reflectie op de openheid naar de ander in groot gevaar. Toegepast op het abortusdilemma wordt in dit verband gewezen op de mogelijkheid van vriendschap met het ongeboren kind.

Verder wijst Ricoeur er op dat de ethische intentie dient plaats te vinden via een rechtvaardige bemiddeling door instituties. Hij verwijst naar Hannah Arendt, die concludeert dat het recht van ieder individu om rechten te hebben nog fundamenteler is dan het streven naar gerechtigheid of naar vrijheid.

Tevens wordt betoogd dat de theorie van de rationele keuze met betrekking tot vruchtbaarheid ongeschikt is voor het funderen van een keuze voor abortus, omdat economische, sociale en morele kosten onvergelijkbaar zijn. Een dergelijke besluitvorming moet worden beschouwd als een onjuiste toepassing van het proportionaliteitsbeginsel, ook wel consequentialisme genoemd, omdat de toekomstige kwaliteiten van de foetus onbekend blijven en daarom niet vergeleken kunnen worden met eventuele voordelen van abortus.

Op grond van het argument dat door abortus provocatus een foetus wordt beroofd van zijn of haar toekomst zoals die van ons, een toekomst die potentieel waardevol is, betoogt Don Marquis dat abortus vrijwel altijd een immorele handeling is. Vanuit theologisch standpunt is de potentialiteit om uit te groeien tot een volwassen persoon al in het embryo aanwezig vanaf de conceptie. Echter, in de filosofische discussie wordt een dergelijk metafysisch begrip van potentialiteit bekritiseerd.

In dit verband wordt het concept van de menselijke waardigheid bediscussieerd in de bio-ethiek en in het internationaal recht. Daniel Sulmasy onderscheidt drie dimensies: toegeschreven waardigheid, intrinsieke waardigheid en opbloeiende waardigheid, waarbij de laatste betekenis een uitdrukking is van de intrinsieke waarde van de mens en verwijst naar het proces dat kan leiden tot menselijke uitmuntendheid. Het is duidelijk, dat personen met een bepaalde beperking delen in menselijke waardigheid. Net zozeer heeft ieder embryo een intrinsieke menselijke waardigheid, ook al moet die nog tot ontplooiing komen.

John Rawls kan worden beschouwd als een representant van de postmoderne liberale filosofie. Voor hem heeft zijn concept van rechtvaardigheid alleen betrekking op personen na hun geboorte. Hiermee maakt Rawls impliciet gebruik van een metafysisch concept van de menselijke persoon, dat de continuïteit van het menselijk bestaan en van de menselijke ontwikkeling voor en na de geboorte ontkent.

De gelijkwaardigheid van ieder individu sluit in dat steeds gekeken dient te worden naar ieder lid van de menselijke soort als een geheel en niet alleen naar een bepaalde afwijking of handicap, zoals vaak dreigt te gebeuren bij de ontdekking van een afwijking na prenatale diagnostiek.

Tenslotte wordt in dit hoofdstuk een ethisch standpunt geformuleerd over abortus provocatus, met behulp van het principe van handelingen met dubbel effect. Volgens dit principe, afkomstig uit de natuurwettheorie, kan een handeling moreel gerechtvaardigd worden wanneer aan vier voorwaarden tegelijkertijd wordt voldaan: 1) De handeling moet niet in zichzelf verkeerd zijn; 2) de intentie van de handelende persoon dient goed te zijn; 3) Het goede effect mag niet worden gerealiseerd door de negatieve bijwerking en 4) Er moet een verhoudingsgewijs voldoende ernstige reden zijn om een handeling met negatieve bijwerking te verrichten.

Er wordt geconcludeerd dat moreel gezien alleen in zeer specifieke medische gevallen een indirecte abortus kan worden uitgevoerd, waarbij de dood van de foetus wordt geaccepteerd om het leven van de moeder te redden. In deze uitzonderingssituaties wordt aan alle vier de voorwaarden van het principe van handelingen met dubbel effect voldaan. In alle andere gevallen zou abortus provocatus vermeden moeten worden, hetgeen niet alleen een verantwoordelijkheid is van de vrouw, maar ook van de partner, de direct betrokkenen en de maatschappij als geheel, die zou moeten zorg dragen voor alternatieven.

De verantwoordelijkheid van ouders en van de maatschappij geldt evenzeer bij een gezond kind als bij een kind waarvan de verwachting is dat het een bepaalde afwijking of beperking zal hebben. De tendens om zwangerschap te medicaliseren komt tot uiting komt bij de wijze waarop ouders en medische professionals omgaan met de resultaten van prenatale diagnostiek, met name wanneer het ongeboren kind een bepaalde afwijking blijkt te hebben. Medicalisering betekent hier dat de beslissing omtrent de voortzetting of afbreking van de zwangerschap vaak wordt gereduceerd tot de vraag hoe toekomstig lijden voorkomen kan worden.

Volgens Paul Ricoeur dient het idee van de wet aan de noties van waarde, norm en imperatief een vereiste van universaliteit toe te voegen. In hoofdstuk 6 wordt een analyse gemaakt van de historische zoektocht naar een universalisering van de ethiek van abortus. Betoogd wordt dat basiswaarden zoals autonomie, creativiteit, liefde en vriendschap en tenslotte het ontdekken en leven van de waarheid bedreigd kunnen worden vanwege misbruik van de vrijheid. Volgens Ricoeur is het probleem van de erkenning van de vrijheid van de ander het centrale thema van de ethiek. Terugkerend op de twee Kantiaanse vragen die werden gesteld als criterium voor universaliteit in besluitvormingsprocessen: "Zou ik kunnen verlangen dat iedereen op deze wijze zou handelen?" en "Kan mijn verlangen dienen als een universele wet?", dienen beide vragen ontkennend te worden beantwoord met betrekking tot de optie van abortus provocatus en de huidige legalisering, vanwege de dreigende aantasting van de vier basiswaarden en vanwege de schending van de waardigheid van de foetus.

In dit hoofdstuk wordt een historische analyse gemaakt van de moraaltheologische opvattingen omtrent abortus door de eeuwen heen, met name in de Rooms-katholieke traditie. In de Bijbel is één passage, namelijk Exodus 21: 22-25, die expliciet betrekking heeft op abortus, in dit geval een miskraam ten gevolge van een menselijk conflict. Deze passage moet in de context worden gezien van de tien geboden en met name het vijfde gebod, "Gij zult niet doden" (Exodus 20,13; Deuteronomium 5, 17). Jezus van Nazareth scherpt dit gebod aan vanuit de intentie om de vervulling te brengen van Wet en Profeten (cf. Mattheüs 5, 17-22).

De christenen namen vanuit de joodse traditie het respect over voor het menselijk leven in al zijn ontwikkelingsstadia, een houding die hen in conflict bracht met de omringende Romeinse cultuur. Vanaf de Didachè vindt men bij vele auteurs in het vroege Christendom en de Middeleeuwen een veroordeling van abortus, nog afgezien van de discussie over volledig gevormde en ongevormde foetussen. Deze discussie werd belemmerd vanwege het feit dat de eicel en de menselijke genetica nog onbekend waren.

Reflectie over de verhouding tussen lichaam en ziel door onder meer Thomas van Aquino leidden tot de bevestiging van de katholieke leer over de eenheid van lichaam en ziel en enkele decennia later tot het dogma van de onsterfelijkheid van de ziel. Tijdens de Renaissance en de Verlichting wordt de kerkelijke leer inzake abortus opgenomen in het kerkelijk recht. Tevens wordt de leer omtrent uitzonderingssituaties van indirecte abortus nader uitgewerkt. In de 19[e] eeuw, na de ontdekking van de eicel door Karl Ernst von Baer in 1827, groeide onder theologen de internationale consensus over de onmiddellijke bezieling van het bevruchte embryo.

In de 20[ste] eeuw wordt de kerkelijke leer van de gelijke waarde van het leven van de moeder en het ongeboren menselijk leven bekrachtigd. Het katholieke standpunt gaat uit van de beschermwaardigheid van het leven vanaf het moment van conceptie, waarbij het embryo gerespecteerd en behandeld dient te worden als een persoon. De Kerk verzet zich tegen overheidssteun voor directe abortus. De zorg van religieuzen voor jonge moeders en kinderen breidt zich aanvankelijk sterk uit, maar zal in de loop van de 20ᵉ eeuw in West-Europa geleidelijk verdwijnen. De publicatie van de encycliek *Humanae Vitae* in 1968, enkele jaren na het Tweede Vaticaanse Concilie, leidt tot een controverse over autonomie in relatie tot anticonceptie. Vanaf de jaren '80 breidt het verzet van de Kerk tegen abortus zich uit naar de kritiek op wetenschappelijke experimenten met embryo's. De Kerk is niet principieel tegen prenatale diagnostiek, maar wel indien dit als voorbode van abortus wordt beschouwd. Beslissingen die tegen het leven zelf ingaan kunnen redelijkerwijs niet worden gevraagd van een ander mens. Als theologische reden voor dit standpunt betoogt Mariéle Wulf dat een vrije, morele beslissing rekening dient te houden met de grotere mogelijkheid, het grotere leven.

Middels de theologie van het lichaam heeft paus Johannes Paulus II een bijdrage geleverd aan pastorale en morele aanwijzingen voor verantwoord ouderschap. In hun pastorale optreden dienen de leden van de Kerk altijd een onderscheid te maken tussen een onrechtmatige handeling en de persoon die de handeling verricht en die niet zijn of haar waardigheid verliest. Afhankelijk van de omstandigheden is er al dan niet sprake van schuld in geval van abortus, zoals ook het kerkelijk recht laat zien.

Met betrekking tot de christelijke interpretatie van het menselijk geweten en gewetensvorming, bevestigt de Kerk de authentieke vrijheid van de mens en de autonomie inzake aardse aangelegenheden, zolang als deze autonomie het respect voor de menselijke persoon niet schendt en niet gekant is tegen het leven zelf. Het onderscheid zoals dit in de moraaltheologie wordt gehanteerd tussen *synderesis* (oergeweten) en *conscience* (het feilbare geweten) is nog altijd behulpzaam voor een begrip van de relatie tussen het menselijk geweten en menselijke autonomie.

In de hoofdstukken 7 en 8 wordt aandacht besteed aan de vraag hoe abortus voorkomen kan worden. De belangrijkste beschikbare alternatieven voor abortus in het V.K. en Nederland worden behandeld, zoals professionele, vrijwillige of financiële assistentie bij de opvoeding door jonge ouders, adoptie en pleegzorg. Er wordt eveneens gekeken naar de organisatiestructuur waarin deze alternatieven zijn ingebed. Geconcludeerd wordt dat de bestaande organisatiestructuur in het V.K. en Nederland om alternatieven voor abortus aan te bieden, onvoldoende mogelijkheden biedt om de preventie van abortus te bevorderen.

Vervolgens wordt de relatie tussen onderwijs, abortus en anticonceptie besproken. In het hulpverleningscircuit wordt door velen betoogd dat anticonceptie een middel is ter voorkoming van abortus. Daarentegen gaat het kerkelijk leergezag uit van het standpunt dat seksualiteit als een authentieke liefdesdaad tevens openheid voor nieuw leven omvat. De kennis op het gebied van seks- en relaties-educatie (SRE) zoals die op Nederlandse scholen wordt overgedragen, wordt sterk beïnvloed door de mogelijke risico's van onveilig seksueel gedrag. Onderzoek naar SRE in het V.K. beveelt aan dat in het onderwijs meer nadruk wordt gelegd op het opbouwen en onderhouden van relaties. Evaluatie van SRE-programma's in scholen in het V.K. en Nederland benadrukt het belang van betrokkenheid van ouders bij het SRE-aanbod, als ook het recht om kinderen niet te laten deelnemen aan elementen van het SRE-programma.

Aanbevelingen worden geformuleerd ten aanzien van de betrokkenheid van de partner bij de besluitvorming ten aanzien van ongewenste zwangerschap, als ook ten aanzien van informationele, emotionele en spirituele aspecten van begeleiding tijdens het besluitvormingsproces.

Vanuit de deugdenethiek kan naast een theologische eveneers een seculiere bijdrage worden geleverd aan een prudentere houding van man en vrouw ten aanzien van de kwaliteit van hun relatie en tevens aan een zorgvuldiger besluitvormingsproces bij ongewenste zwangerschap.

Vervolgens wordt ingegaan op de vraag hoe moet worden omgegaan met gegevens voortkomend uit prenatale diagnostiek, met name wanneer het ongeboren kind een bepaalde afwijking blijkt te hebben. Voortschrijdende mogelijkheden zoals bij de 20-weken echoscopie roepen de principiële vraag op of er in de samenleving sprake is van een toenemende druk op ouders om bij de verwachting van een gehandicapt kind tot abortus over te gaan. Het principe van integratie van alle dimensies van zorgverlening, inclusief de spirituele dimensie, dient te worden toegepast in de counsellingpraktijk van ouders die een kind verwachten met een bepaalde afwijking.

Een recente ontwikkeling ten aanzien van de rol van de man en diens verantwoordelijkheid als verwekker van het embryo is de toepassing van DNA-onderzoek als wettelijk middel om het vaderschap te bewijzen. Dit kan bijdragen tot een uitspraak om actief ofwel passief (middels een financiële bijdrage) aan de opvoeding van het kind bij te dragen.

Pastorale nazorg tenslotte (nadat een abortus heeft plaatsgevonden), zou zich moeten richten op zelfacceptatie, gepast berouw en het zich openstellen voor Gods vergeving en vrede.

In de professionele hulpverlening in relatie tot zwangerschapsdilemma's ligt de aandacht te eenzijdig bij de vrouw. Meer aandacht voor de onderliggende relatieproblematiek en voor alternatieven voor abortus zou wenselijk zijn, ter bescherming van het ongeboren kind en tevens om fysieke, psychologische and spirituele problemen bij de vrouw op korte en lange termijn te voorkomen. Via counseling of pastorale zorg zouden alternatieven voor abortus besproken moeten worden. Dit geldt tevens indien na prenatale diagnostiek een bepaalde afwijking bij het kind wordt geconstateerd of vermoed. Om al deze redenen dient het politieke en ethische debat over de preventie van abortus in het V.K. en Nederland te worden heropend.

Bibliography

Aar, F. van, Koedijk F.D.H., Broek I.V.F. van den, Op de Coul, E.L.M., Soetens, L.C., Woestenberg, P.J., Heijne, J.C.M., Sighem, A.I. van, Nielen, M.M.J. and Benthem, B.H.B. van, *Sexually transmitted infections, including HIV, in the Netherlands in 2013*. National Institute for Public Health and the Environment, Bilthoven, 2014.
Abbà, Giuseppe, *Quale impostazione per la filosofia morale? Ricerche di filosofia morale – 1*, Rome, 1996.
Abelard, Petrus, *Scito te ipsum seu Ethica*, XIV. In the German translation by Philipp Steger, *Erkenne dich selbst*, Hamburg, 2006.
Abram, Anna, "Sexual and Relationship Education in Great Britain: Problems and Opportunities for Faith Schools with Special Reference to the Roman Catholic Context." In: Glombik, Konrad (ed.), *Wychowanie Seksualne w Rodzinie i w Szkole*. Opole, 2010, pp. 11-24.
Akerlof, George A., Yellen, Janet L. and Katz, Michael L., "An Analysis of Out-of-Wedlock Childbearing in the United States", *Quarterly Journal of Economics*, 1996, 111, pp. 277-317.
Almli, C. Robert, Ball, Robert H. and Wheeler, Mark E., "Human Fetal and Neonatal Movement Patterns: Gender Differences and Fetal-to-Neonatal Continuity", *Developmental Psychobiology*, 2001, 38, pp. 252-273.
American College of Obstetricians and Gynecologists (ACOG), Committee on Ethics, *The Limits of Conscientious Refusal in Reproductive Medicine: Opinion 385*. Washington DC, 2007, reaffirmed 2010.
American Psychiatric Association, "Factsheet on Posttraumatic Stress Disorder", Washington DC, 2013.
American Psychological Association, Task Force on Mental Health and Abortion. *Report of the Task Force on Mental Health and Abortion*, Washington DC, 2008.
Amery, Fran, "Social Questions, Medical Answers. Contesting British Abortion Law", *Social Politics*, 2014, 21 (1), pp. 26-49.
Ananth, Cande V., Smulian, John C. and Vintzileos, Anthony M., "The effect of placenta previa on neonatal mortality: A population-based study in the United States, 1989 through 1997", *American Journal of Obstetrics and Gynecology*, 2003, 188, 5, 1299-1304.
Ancel, Pierre-Yves, Lelong, Nathalie, Papiernik, Emiel, Saurel-Cubizolles, Marie-Josèphe and Kaminski, Monique, "History of induced abortion as a risk factor for preterm birth in European countries: results of the EUROPOP survey", *Human Reproduction*, 2004, 19, 3, pp. 734-740.
Andorno, Roberto, "Human Dignity and Human Rights as a Common Ground for a Global Bioethics", *Journal of Medicine and Philosophy*, 2009, 34, pp. 223-240.
Anonymus, "De animatione foetus", in: *Nouvelle revue théologique*, 1879, 11, pp. 163-186.
Antoninus of Florence, *Confessionale Anthonini*, Paris, 1517.
Aquinas, Thomas, *Questiones disputatae De veritate*, 16 and 17, translated into German by Edith

Stein, *Übersetzung Des Hl. Thomas von Aquino Untersuchungen über die Wahrheit, I, Eingeführt und bearbeitet von Andreas Speer und Francesco Valerio Tommasi*. Edith Stein Gesamtausgabe, 23, Freiburg 2008.

Aquinas, Thomas, *Scriptum super Sententiis Petri Lombardi*, 3, d.3, q.5, a.2 ad responsio. Edited by M.F. Moos, OP, Paris, 1956.

Aquinas, Thomas, *Summa Theologica*. Edition in Latin, Ottawa, 1953, or in the English Benziger Bros. edition, 1947, translated by Fathers of the English Dominican Province.

Aquinas, Thomas, *Super secundam epistolam S. Pauli ad Corinthios Lectura*. Translated into French by Jean-Eric Stroobant de Saint-Éloy O.S.B., *Commentaire de la deuxième épître aux Corinthiens*, Paris, 2005.

Arendt, Hannah, *Essays in Understanding 1930-1954*. Edited by Jerome Kohn, New York, 1994.

Arendt, Hannah, *The Origins of Totalitarianism*, New York, 1966.

Aristotle, *De Anima*. Translated into English by R.D. Hicks, Amsterdam, 1965.

Aristotle, *Historia Animalium*, Translated into English by J.A. Smith and W.D. Ross (eds.), The Works of Aristotle, Vol. IV, Oxford, 1956.

Aristotle, *De Generatione Animalium*. Translated into English by Jonathan Barnes (ed.), The Complete Works of Aristotle, Vol. I, Princeton, 1985.

Aristotle, *Metaphysics*. Edited and translated into English by J. Warrington, London, 1956.

Aristotle, *Nicomachean Ethics*. Translation, introduction and commentary by Sarah Broadie and Christopher Rowe, Oxford, 2002.

Ashcroft, Richard, Dawson, Angus, Draper, Heather and McMillan, John, *Principles of Health Care Ethics*. Second Edition, Chichester, 2007.

Ashley OP, Benedict and O'Rourke OP, Kevin, *Healthcare Ethics. A Theological Analysis*. Third edition, St. Louis, MO., 1989.

Athanagoras, *Embassy for the Christians*, 35. Transl. and annotated by Joseph Crehan S.J., Westminster, Mar., 1956.

Augustine, *Civitate Dei*, transl. by W.M. Green, *City of God*, Vol. VII in: Henderson, J., (ed.), The Loeb Classical Library no. 417, Cambridge/London, 1972.

Augustine, *Contra Iulianum*, transl. and annotated by Roland Teske S.J., *Answer to the Pelagians, II: Answer to Julian*, in: John Rotelle O.S.A., The works of Saint Augustine. A Translation for the 21st Century, Part I, Vol. 24, New York, 1998.

Augustine, *De nuptiis et concupiscentiis*, transl. and annotated by Roland Teske S.J., *Answer to the Pelagians, II: Marriage and Desire*, in: John Rotelle O.S.A. (ed.), The works of Saint Augustine. A Translation for the 21st Century, Part I, Vol. 24, New York, 1998.

Augustine, *De Genesi ad litteram*, transl. and annotated by Edmund Hill O.P., *On Genesis: The Literal Meaning of Genesis* in: John Rotelle O.S.A. (ed.), The works of Saint Augustine. A Translation for the 21st Century, Part I, Vol. 13, New York, 2002.

Augustine, *De vera religione*. Translated in German by Josef Lössl, Augustinus, *Die wahre Religion*, in Ibid., Opera – Werke, Vol. 68, Paderborn, 2007.

Augustine, *Enchiridion de fide, spe et caritate*, 86, transl. by B.M. Peebles, *Faith, hope and charity*, in: The Fathers of the Church, Vol. 2, New York, 1947.

Augustine, *Quaestionum in heptateuchum, libri VII*, in: Corpus Scriptorum Ecclesiasticorum Latinorum, vol. 28, 80, New York, 1895.

Bates, Claire, "Revealed: The thousands of pregnancies aborted for 'abnormalities' including

cleft palates and Down's syndrome", *Daily Mail*, 5 July 2011.
Bhadoria, A.S., Kapil, U., Sareen, N. and Singh, P., "Reproductive factors and breast cancer: A case-control study in tertiary care hospital of North India", *Indian Journal of Cancer*, 2013, 50, (4), pp. 316-321.
Bagchus, Lotje, Martens, Marloes and Sluis, Maria van der, *Relationele en seksuele vorming in het basisonderwijs. Een effect- en procesevaluatie van de lespakketten 'Relaties en seksualiteit' en 'Lekker in je vel'*, Amsterdam, 2010.
Bakels, F.B., "Conclusie bij de uitspraak van de Hoge Raad d.d. 22-09-2000", *Rechtspraak van de Week: conclusies*, nr. 184, 2000, pp. 872-879.
Bacchus, Loraine, Mezey, Gill and Bewley, Susan, "Domestic violence: prevalence in pregnant women and associations with physical and psychological health", *European Journal of Obstetrics & Gynecology and Reproductive Biology*, 2004, 113, pp. 6-11.
Bankole, Akinrinola, Singh, Susheela and Haas, Taylor, "Reasons why women have induced abortions: evidence from 27 countries", *International Family Planning Perspectives*, 1998, 24, pp. 117-127.
Banks, Olive, *Becoming a Feminist. The Social Origins of 'First Wave' Feminism*, Sussex, 1986.
Barnabas, the Epistle of, translated by James A. Kleist S.J., Westminster, Mar., 1948.
Baroncini, Basti, *Man en abortus. Over de keuze, de ingreep en de verwerking*, Amsterdam, 2010.
Barry, William A. and Connolly, William J., *The practice of Spiritual Direction*, San Francisco, 1982.
Basil the Great, *Epistle nr. 188, to Amphilochius*, in: Migne, J.P., Patrologia Graeca, Vol. 32, Turnhout, 1961.
Beal, John P., Coriden, James A. and Green, Thomas J. (eds.), *The New Commentary on the Code of Canon Law* / Commissioned by the Canon Law Society of America, Mahwah, N.J., 2000.
Becker, G.S. and Barro, R.J., "A Reformulation of the Economic Theory of Fertility", *The Quarterly Journal of Economics*, 1988, 103, 1, pp. 1-25.
Becker, Lawrence C. and Becker, Charlotte B., *Encyclopedia of Ethics*. Second edition, Vol. II, New York and London, 2001.
Becker, Marcel, Stokkom, Bas van, Tongeren, Paul van and Wils, Jean-Pierre (eds.), *Lexicon van de ethiek*, Assen, 2007.
Beers, Britta C. van, *Persoon en lichaam in het recht. Menselijke waardigheid en zelfbeschikking in het tijdperk van medische biotechnologie*, dissertation, Amsterdam, 2009.
Bellieni, Carlo V. and Buonocore, Giuseppe, "Abortion and subsequent mental health: Review of the literature", *Psychiatry and Clinical Neurosciences*, 2013, 67, pp. 301–310.
Bellivier, Florence and Egea, Pierre, "Les chemins de la liberté (petite leçon de biopolitique)", *Recueil Dalloz*, 2004, 10, pp. 647-652.
Benagiano, Giuseppe and Pera, Alessandra, "Decreasing the need for abortion: challenges and constraints", *International Journal of Gynecology and Obstetrics*, 70 (2000), pp. 35-48.
Benedict XVI, "Address to the Fathers of the General Congregation of the Society of Jesus", 21 February 2008.
Benso, Silvia, "The Gift of the Other: Levinas and the Politics of Reproduction. Book review", *Dialogue*, 2007, 46, 2, pp. 409-411.
Berg, Matthijs van den, Timmermans, Daniëlle R.M., Kate, Leo P. ten, Vugt, John M.G. and Wal, Gerrit van der, "Informed decision making in the context of prenatal screening",

Patient Education and Counseling, 2006, 63, pp. 110-117.
Bernard of Clairvaux, *De diligendo Deo*, translated in German by Gerhard B. Winkler, *Bernhard von Clairvaux. Sämtliche Werke lateinisch/deutsch*, Innsbruck 1990, I, XIII, pp. 136-137.
Beyleveld, Deryck and Brownsword, Roger, *Human Dignity in Bioethics and Biolaw*, Oxford, 2001.
Bhattacharya, Siladytia, Lowit, Alison, Bhattacharya, Sohinee, Raja, Edwin, Lee, Amanda, Mahmood, Tahir and Templeton, Allan, "Reproductive outcomes following induced abortion: a national registerbased cohort study in Scotland", *British Medical Journal Open*, 2012, 2, 4, pp. 1-12.
Bianchi-Demicheli, Francesco, Kulier, Regina, Perrin, Eliane and Campana, Aldo, "Induced abortion and psychosexuality", *Journal of Psychosomatic Obstetrics and Gynecology*, 2000, 21, pp. 213-217.
Bianchi-Demicheli, Francesco, Perrin, Eliane, Lüdicke, Frank, Bianchi, Patrizia, Chatton, Dominique and Campana, Aldo, "Termination of pregnancy and women's sexuality", *Gynecological and Obstetrical Investigation*, 2002, 53, pp. 48-53.
Biemans, W.J.A., "Procured Abortion", in: Eijk, W.J. et al. (eds.), 2014, pp. 163-174.
Bijma, Hilmar H., Heide, Agnes van der, and Wildschut, Hajo I.J., "Decision-Making after Ultrasound Diagnosis of Fetal Abnormality", *Reproductive Health Matters*, 2008, 16 (31 Supplement), pp. 82-89.
Birmingham, Peg, *Hannah Arendt & Human Rights. The Predicament of Common Responsibility*, Bloomington, In., 2006.
Bishops' Conference of England and Wales, *Statement concerning moral questions*, London, 1970.
Bisschoppen van Nederland, *Bisschoppelijke verklaring over abortus arte provocatus*, Utrecht, 1974.
Blier Blaymore, J.A., Liebling, J., Morales, Y. and Carlucci, M., "Parents' and Pediatricians' Views of Individuals with Meningomyelocile", *Clinical Pediatrics*, 1996, 35, 3, pp. 113-117.
Böckle, Franz, *Grundbegriffe der Moral. Gewissen und Gewissensbildung*, Würzburg, 1966.
Boonin, David, *A Defense of Abortion*, Cambridge, 2003.
Borland, Sophie, "'Backstreet abortion' pills being illegally sold on the internet for just £15", on: Mail Online, 5 March 2011.
Bos, Pien, Reysoo, Fenneke and Werdmuller, Astrid, *'In één klap moeder, en ook weer niet.' Onderzoek naar demografische en sociaal-economische kenmerken en motieven van vrouwen die tussen 1998-2007 in Nederland hun kind ter adoptie hebben afgestaan*, Den Bosch, 2011.
Bourassa, Dominique and Bérubé, Joselyn, "The prevalence of intimate partner violence among women and teenagers seeking abortion compared with those continuing pregnancy", *Journal of Obstetrics and Gynaecology Canada*, 2007, 29, 5, pp. 415-423.
Bowen-Moore, Patricia, *Hannah Arendt's Philosophy of Natality*, New York, 1989.
Bradshaw, Zoë and Slade, Pauline, "The effects of induced abortion on emotional experiences and relationships: A critical review of the literature", *Clinical Psychology Review*, 2003, 23, pp. 929-958.
Brannen, Julia and Nilsen, Ann, "Individualisation, choice and structure: a discussion of current trends in sociological analysis", *The Sociological Review*, 2005, 53, 3, pp. 412-428.
Breeze, A.C.G., Lees C.C., Kumar A., Missfelder-Lobos H.H. and Murdoch E.M., "Palliative care for prenatally diagnosed lethal fetal abnormality", *Archives of Disease in Childhood.*

Fetal and Neonatal edition, 2007, 92, pp. F56-F58.
Brewster, David H., Stockton, Diane L., Dobbie, Richard, Bull, Diana and Beral, Valerie, "Risk of breast cancer after miscarriage or induced abortion: a Scottish record linkage case-control study", *Journal of Epidemiology and Community Health,* 2005, 59, pp. 283-287.
Brind, Joel, "Breast cancer in relation to abortion: results from the EPIC-study. Letter to the editor.", *International Journal of Cancer,* 2008, 122, pp. 960-961.
Brind, Joel, "Induced Abortion as an Independent Risk Factor for Breast Cancer: A Critical Review of Recent Studies Based on Prospective Data", *Journal of American Physicians and Surgeons,* 2005 (a), 10, 4, pp. 105-110.
Brind, Joel., "Methodological concerns re: abortion and breast cancer in Scotland", *Journal of Epidemiology, Community and Health,* electronic letter published on 13 June 2005 (b).
Brind, Joel, "The abortion – breast cancer connection", *National Catholic Bioethics Quarterly,* 2005 (c), pp. 303-329.
Brind, Joel, Chinchilli, Vernon M., Severs, Walter B., Summu-Long, Joan, "Induced abortion as an independent risk factor for breast cancer: a comprehensive review and meta-analysis", *Journal of Epidemiology and Community Health,* 1996, 50, 481-496.
British Medical Association, *The law and ethics of abortion,* London, 2007.
Britt, Kara, Ashworth, Alan and Smalley, Matthew, "Pregnancy and the risk of breast cancer", *Endocrine-Related Cancer,* 2007, 14, pp. 907-933.
Brody, Baruch, *Abortion and the Sanctity of Human Life: A Philosophical View,* Cambridge, Ma., 1975.
Broek, Angela van den, Kleijnen, Ellen and Keuzenkamp, Saskia, *Naar Hollands gebruik? Verschillen in gebruik van hulp bij opvoeding, onderwijs en gezondheid tussen autochtonen en migranten,* Sociaal en Cultureel Planbureau, Den Haag, 2010.
Broen, Anne N., Moum, Torbjørn., Bødtker, Anne S. and Ekeberg, Øivind, "Psychological Impact on Women of Miscarriage Versus Induced Abortion: A 2-Year Follow-up Study", *Psychosomatic Medicine,* 2004, 66, pp. 265-271.
Broen, Anne N., Moum, Torbjørn., Bødtker, Anne S. and Ekeberg, Øivind, "The course of mental health after miscarriage and induced abortion: a longitudinal, five-year follow-up study", *BMC Medicine,* 2005, 3, 18.
Bron, Klazien and Kruidenier, Eelco, *20-weken echo en spina bifida,* Utrecht, 2011.
Brooke, Stephen, "Abortion Law Reform 1929 – 1968", in: Kandiah, Michael D. and Staerck, Gillian (eds.), *The Abortion Act 1967*: Institute of Contemporary British History Witness Seminar, London, 2002, pp. 15-20. 22-5.
Brooke, Stephen, "A New World for Women? Abortion Law Reform in Britain during the 1930s", *American Historical Review,* 106, 2001, pp. 431-459.
Brown, Callum G., *Religion and Society in Twentieth-Century Britain,* Harlow, 2006.
Bruijn, Jan de, *Geschiedenis van de abortus in Nederland. Een analyse van opvattingen en discussies 1600-1979,* Amsterdam, 1979.
Bryan, Audrey A., "Enhancing Parent-Child Interaction With a Prenatal Couple Intervention", *The American Journal of Maternal/Child Nursing,* 2000, 25, 3, pp. 139-145.
Budgeon, Shelley., *Third-Wave Feminism and the Politics of Gender in Late Modernity,* New York, 2011.
Buijssen, M.A.J.M., "De rechtspositie van gewetensbezwaarden in de gezondheidszorg", in: *Pro Vita Humana,* 2003, nr.3-4, pp. 98-101.

Buijssen, M.A.J.M., "Wrongful life: de zaak Kelly", *Pro Vita Humana*, 2003, 3-4, pp. 102-104.
Bultmann, Rudolf, *Theology of the New Testament*. Translated into English by K. Grobel, Waco, Texas, 2007.
Calhoun, Byron C., Napolitano, Peter, Terry Melissa, Bussey, Carie, Hoeldtke, Nathan J., "Perinatal hospice. Comprehensive Care for the Family of the Fetus with a Lethal Condition", *Journal of Reproductive Medicine*, 2003, 48, pp. 343-348.
Calhoun, Byron C., Thorp, John M. and Carroll, Patrick S., "Maternal and Neonatal Health and Abortion: 40-Year Trends in Great Britain and Ireland", *Journal of American Physicians and Surgeons*, 2013, 18, (2), pp. 42-46.
Callahan, Daniel, *Abortion: Law, Choice and Morality*, London, 1970.
Cannonier, Colin, "State abstinence education programs and teen birth rates in the US", *Review of Economics of the Household*, 2012, 10, pp. 53–75.
Carroll, Patrick, "The Breast Cancer Epidemic: Modeling and Forecasts based on Abortion and Other Risk Factors", *Journal of American Physicians and Surgeons*, 2007, 12, 3, pp. 72-78.
Carroll, Patrick, "Legally Induced Abortion: The Demographic Profile and Hazards to the Health of Women", *Studies on Ethno-Medicin*, 2011, 5 (1), pp. 1-10.
Cataldo, Peter J. and Moraczewski, Albert S., *The Fetal Tissue Issue: Medical and Ethical Aspects*, Braintree, MA, 1994.
Catholic Archbishops of Great Britain, *Abortion and the right to live*, London, 1980.
Catholic Bishops' Conference of England and Wales, *Cherishing Life*, London, 2004.
Catholic Bishops of Great Britain, Joint Committee on Bioethical Issues: Antenatal Tests: What You Should Know. Answers to questions which face every pregnant mother, in *Briefing*, 19:3 (3 Feb. 1989) 50-56; cf. *Medicina e Morale*, 40:1 (1990), 149-158.
Caygill, Howard, *A Kant Dictionary*, Oxford, 1995.
Ceder, Don, "De grens van het leven", *Pro Vita Humana*, 2014, 21 (2), p. 1.
Cense, Marianne, Martens, Marloes, Maris, Sanna, Janssen, Ellis and Graaf, Hanneke de, in opdracht van ZonMW, *Onderzoek naar determinanten van succesvolle implementatie van het leskatern relaties & seksualiteit in het basisonderwijs*, Utrecht, 2011.
Centraal Bureau voor de Statistiek, *Onderzoek Gezinsvorming* 1982, Den Haag, 1984.
Centraal Bureau voor de Statistiek, *Relatie en gezin aan het begin van de 21ste eeuw*, Den Haag/ Heerlen, 2009.
Church Assembly Board for Social Responsibility, Church of England, *Abortion. An Ethical Discussion*. Oxford, 1965.
Clebsch, William A. and Jaekle, Charles R., *Pastoral care in historical perspective*, New York, 1975.
Clarke, A., "The process of genetic counselling", in: P. Harper and A. Clarke (Eds.), *Genetics, society and clinical practice*. Oxford, 1997, pp. 179–200.
Clement of Alexandria, *Der Erzieher*. Transl. into German by O. Stählin, München, 1934.
Coker, Ann L., "Does physical intimate partner violence affect sexual health? A systematic review", *Trauma, Violence, & Abuse*, 2007, 8(2), pp. 149–177.
Coleman, Priscilla K., Reardon, David C., Strahan, Thomas and Cougle, Jesse R., "The psychology of abortion: A review and suggestions for future research", *Psychology & Health*, 2005, 20, 2, pp. 237-271.

Coleman, Priscilla K., Rue, Vincent M. and Coyle, Catherine T., "Induced Abortion and intimate relationship quality in the Chicago Health and Social Life Survey", *Public Health*, 2009, 123, pp. 331-338.
Collaborative Group on Hormonal Factors in Breast Cancer (Beral, V., Bull, D., Doll, R., Peto, R., Reeves, G.), "Breast cancer and abortion: collaborative reanalysis of data from 53 epidemiological studies, including 83,000 women with breast cancer from 16 countries", *The Lancet*, 2004, Mar. 27; 363, pp. 1007-1016.
Collaborative Group on Hormonal Factors in Breast Cancer (Beral, V. et al.), "Breast Cancer and breastfeeding: collaborative reanalysis of individual data from 47 epidemiological studies in 30 countries, including 50302 women with breast cancer and 96973 women without the disease", *The Lancet*, 2002, 360, pp. 187-195.
College voor Zorgverzekeringen, *Financieel verslag uitvoeringstaken CVZ 2012*, Diemen, 2013.
Combes, Philippe, Gaillard, Marie-Cécile, Pellet, Jacques and Demongeot, Jacques, "A score for measurement of the role of social vulnerability in decisions on abortion", *European Journal of Obstetrics & Gynecology and Reproductive Biology*, 2004, 117, pp. 93-101.
CommunicateResearch, "Choose Life Poll", London, 2006.
Compagnoni, Francesco, Piara, Giannino and Privitera, Salvatore, *Nuovo dizionario della teologia morale*, Cinisello Balsamo (Milano), 1990.
ComRes, "Christian Institute Abortion Poll", London, 2014.
Concilium Ancyranum (Council of Ancyra), in: Mansi, Johannes, *Sacrorum conciliorum nova et amplissima collectio*, Vol II, ab anno CCCV usque ad annum CCCXLVI, orig. ed. Florence, 1759, reprod. Paris, 1901.
Concilium Eliberitanum (Council of Elvira), in: Mansi, Johannes, *Sacrorum conciliorum nova et amplissima collectio*, Vol II, ab anno CCCV usque ad annum CCCXLVI, orig. ed. Florence, 1759, reprod. Paris, 1901.
Concilium Trullanum (Quinisextum), (Council of Trulla), in: Mansi, Johannes, *Sacrorum conciliorum nova et amplissima collectio*, Vol. XI, ab anno DCLIII usque ad annum DCLXXXVII, orig. ed. Florence, 1765, reprod. Paris, 1901.
Concilium Wormatiense (Council of Worms), in: Mansi, Johannes, *Sacrorum conciliorum nova et amplissima collectio*, Vol. XV, ab anno DCCCLV usque ad annum CDDDLXVIII, orig. ed. Florence, 1765, reprod. Paris, 1901.
Conklin, Mary P., O'Connor, Brian P., "Beliefs about the fetus as a moderator of post-abortion psychological well-being", *Journal of social and clinical psychology*, 1995, 14, 1, pp. 76-95.
Congregation for the Doctrine of the Faith, Declaration *De abortu procurato*, Vatican, 1974.
Congregation for the Doctrine of the Faith, Instruction *Donum Vitae*, Vatican, 1987.
Congregation for the Doctrine of the Faith, Instruction *Dignitas personae*, Vatican, 2008.
Connery S.J., John, *Abortion: The development of the Roman Catholic Perspectives*. Loyola University Press, 1977.
Conrad, Peter, "Medicalization and Social Control", *Annual Review of Sociology*, 1992, 18, pp. 209-232.
Cooper, Joel, *Cognitive Dissonance. Fifty Years of a Classic Theory*, London, 2007.
Costeloe, Kate L., Hennessy, Enid M., Haider, Sadia, Stacey, Fiona, Marlow, Neil and Draper, Elizabeth S., "Short term outcomes after extreme preterm birth in England: comparison of two birth cohorts in 1995 and 2006 (the EPICure studies)", *BMJ* 2012; 345: e7976 doi: 10.1136/bmj.e7976.

Cour de cassation (Chambre criminelle) de la France (French Court of Cassation), 2 December 2003, in: *La Semaine Juridique*, 2004, 15, p. 682.
Coyle, Catherine T. and Rue, Vincent M., "Men's Perceptions Concerning Disclosure of a Partner's Abortion: Implications for Counseling", *European Journal of Counselling Psychology*, 2015, 3 (2), pp. 159–173.
Crisp, Roger and Slote, Michael (eds.), *Virtue Ethics*, Oxford, 1997.
Curley, Maureen and Johnston, Celeste, "The Characteristics and Severity of Psychological Distress After Abortion Among University Students", *Journal of Behavioral Health Services & Research*, 2013, pp. 279–293.
Curran, Charles E., *The Moral Theology of Pope John Paul II*, Washington D.C., 2005.
D'Almeida, Michelle, Hume, Roderick F., Lathrop, Anthony, Njoku, Adaku and Calhoun, Byron C., "Perinatal Hospice: Family-Centered Care of the Fetus with a Lethal Condition", *Journal of American Physicians and Surgeons*, 2006, 11, 2, pp. 52-55.
Daaleman, Timothy P. and VandeCreek, Larry, "Placing Religion and Spirituality in End-of-Life Care", *Journal of the American Medical Association*, 2000, 284, 19, pp. 2514-2517.
Daling, Janet R., Malone, Kathleen E., Voigt, Lynda F., White, Emily and Weiss, Noel S., "Risk of Breast Cancer Among Young Women: Relationship to Induced Abortion", *Journal of the National Cancer Institute*, 1994, 86, pp. 1584-1592.
Deetman, Wim, Draijer, Nel, Kalbfleisch, Pieter, Merckelbach, Harald, Monteiro, Marit and Vries, Gerard de, *Seksueel misbruik van minderjarigen in de Rooms-katholieke Kerk*, Amsterdam, 2011.
Deetman, W.J., et al., *Seksueel misbruik van en geweld tegen meisjes in de Rooms-katholieke Kerk. Een vervolgonderzoek*, Amsterdam, 2013.
Dekker, Jeroen, Amsing, Mariette, Bij, Ingrid van der, Dekker, Marieke, Grietens, Hans, Harder, Annemiek, Koedijk, P.C.M., Parlevliet, Sanne, Schreuder, Pauline, Talhout, Mandy en Timmerman M.C., *Jeugdzorg in Nederland, 1945-2010. Resultaten van deelonderzoek 1 van de commissie-Samson: Historische schets van de institutionele ontwikkeling van de jeugdsector vanuit het perspectief van het kind en de aan hem/haar verleende zorg*, Groningen, 2012.
Demmer, Klaus, *Moraltheologische Methodenlehre*, Freiburg, 1989.
Demmer, Klaus, *Deuten und handeln. Grundlagen und Grundfragen der Fundamentalmoral*, Freiburg, 1985, or the Italian version *Interpretare e agire. Fondamenti della morale cristiana*, Torino, 1989.
Denbow, Jennifer, "Abortion: When Choice and Autonomy Conflict", *Berkeley Journal of Gender, Law and Justice*, 2005, pp. 216-228.
Denzinger, Heinrich, *Enchiridion symbolorum definitionum et declarationum de rebus fidei et morum. / Kompendium der Glaubensbekenntnisse und kirchlichen Lehrentscheidungen*, Freiburg, 2005.
Department for Children, Schools and Families (DCSF) and Department of Health (DH), *Teenage Pregnancy Strategy: Beyond 2010*, London, 2010.
Department for Children, Schools and Families (DCSF): *Review of Sex and Relationships Education (SRE) in Schools. A report by the External Steering Group*, London, 2008.
Department of Health, *Abortion Statistics England and Wales: 2006*, London, 2007.
Department of Health: *Abortion Statistics, England and Wales: 2013*, London, 2014.
De Souza, E., Alberman, E. and Morris, J.K., "Down's syndrome: screening and antenatal diagnosis regionally in England and Wales 1989-2008", *Journal of Medical Screening*, 2010, 17, 4, pp. 170-175.
Didachê, the, or the teaching of the twelve apostles; transl. by James A. Kleist S.J.,

Westminster, Mar., 1948.
Di Nucci, Ezio, "On how to interpret the role of the future within the abortion debate", *Journal of Medical Ethics*, 2009, 35, pp. 651-652.
Dixon, Rosalind and Nussbaum, Martha C., "Abortion, Dignity and a Capabilities Approach", *Chicago Public Law and Legal Theory Working Paper*, No. 345, Chicago 2011, pp. 1-17.
Does de Willebois, Alexander E.M. van der, *Het vaderloze tijdperk*, Brugge, 1984.
Donagan, Alan, "Conscience", in: Becker, Lawrence C. and Becker, Charlotte B. (eds.), *Encyclopedia of Ethics. Second Edition*, Vol. I. New York and London, 2001, pp. 297-299.
Dubuc, Sylvie and Coleman, David, "An increase in the sex ratio of births to India-born mothers in England and Wales: Evidence for sex-selective abortion", *Population and Development Review*, 2007, 33, pp. 383-400
Dupré, Catherine, "Dignity, Democracy, Civilisation", *Liverpool Law Review*, 2012, 33, pp. 263-280.
Dupré, Catherine, "Human Dignity in Europe: A Foundational Constitutional Principle", *European Public Law*, 2013, 19, 2, pp. 319-340.
Dworkin, Ronald, *Life's Dominion: an Argument about Abortion and Euthanasia*, London, 1993.
Easton, Scott, Coohey, Carol, O'leary, Patrick, Zhang, Ying and Hua, Lei, "The Effect of Childhood Sexual Abuse on Psychosexual Functioning During Adulthood", *Journal of Family Violence*, 2011, 26, pp. 41-50.
Eeden, R. van, *Abortus in Engeland*, Den Haag, 1975.
Eggink, Alex J., "Foetale therapie voor spina bifida", *Nederlands Tijdschrift voor Geneeskunde*, 2012, 156: A4924.
Eijk, W.J., Hendriks, L.M., Raymakers, J.A. and Fleming, J.I. (eds.), *Manual of Catholic Manual Ethics. Responsible Healthcare from a Catholic Perspective*. Ballarat, 2014; Dutch edition: Eijk, W.J., Hendriks, L.M. and Raymakers, J.A., *Handboek Katholieke Medische Ethiek. Verantwoorde gezondheidszorg vanuit katholiek perspectief*, Almere, 2010.
Eijt, José, *We waren er altijd. Zusters in zorg en verpleging. Franciscanessen van de H. Elisabeth 1880-2009*, Rotterdam, 2009.
Eijt, José and Hautvast, Suzanne, *Een missie in de marge. Dochters van Onze Lieve Vrouw van het Heilig Hart in Nederland en Indonesië 1911-2000*, Hilversum, 2002.
Emmerik, Arnold A.P. van, Kamphuis, Jan H. and Emmelkamp, Paul, "Prevalence and Prediction of Re-Experiencing and Avoidance after Elective Surgical Abortion: A Prospective Study", *Clinical Psychology and Psychotherapy*, 2008, 15, pp. 378-385.
Epstein, Isidore (Ed.), *Hebrew-English edition of the Babylonian Talmud*, translated into English by H. Freedman, London etc., 1972.
Engelhardt, H. Tristram, "The Ontology of Abortion", *Ethics*, 1974, 84, pp. 217-284.
Engelhardt, H. Tristram, *Manuale di bioetica*, Milano, 1999.
Erwin, Alan, "Northern Ireland abortion law can be challenged, court rules.", *Irish Times*, 2 February 2015.
European Commission, *Communication on the European Citizens' Initiative 'One of us'*, Brussels, 28 May 2014.
European Court of Human Rights, Case of Vo versus France. Application No. 53924/00, 8 July 2004. In: *Report of Judgments and Decisions*, no. VIII, 2004.
European Parliament, Press release "European Parliament hearing on 'One of Us' European Citizens' Initiative", 9 April 2014.

Eynikel, Erik, Noort, Ed, Baarda, Tjitze and Denaux, Adelbert (eds.), *Internationaal Commentaar op de Bijbel*, Kampen, 2001.
Family Planning Association, Factsheet "Abortion Practice and Provision in Northern Ireland", Belfast, 2014.
Family Planning Association, Factsheet "Sexually Transmitted Infections", London, 2010
Fensham, Frank C., *Exodus*, Nijkerk, 1970.
Ferguson, Philip M., Gartner, Alan, and Lipsky, Dorothy K., "The Experience of Disability in Families: A Synthesis of Research and Parent Narratives", in: Parens, Erik and Asch, Adrienne, *Prenatal Genetic Testing*, Garrison, New York, 2000.
Fergusson, D.M., Horwood, L.J. and Boden, J.M., "Abortion and mental health disorders: evidence from a 30-year longitudinal study", *British Journal of Psychiatry*, 2008, 193, pp. 444-451.
Fergusson, D.M., Horwood, L.J. and Boden, J.M., "Does abortion reduce the mental health risks or unwanted or unintended pregnancy? A reappraisal of the evidence", *Australian and New Zealand Journal of Psychiatry*, 2013, 47 (9), pp. 819-827.
Fergusson, David M., Horwood, L. John and Ridder, Elizabeth M., "Abortion in young women and subsequent mental health", *Journal of Child Psychology and Psychiatry*, 2006, 47 (1), pp. 16-24.
Festinger, Leon, *A theory of cognitive dissonance*, Evanston, Il., 1957.
Fichte, Johann, "System der Sittenlehre", in: Fichte, J, *Johann Gottlieb Fichte's Nachgelassene Werke*, vol. III, Bonn, 1835.
Fienus, Thomas, *De formatrice foetus*, Louvain, 1624.
Finnis, John, *Natural Law and Natural Rights*. Second Edition, Oxford, 2011.
FIOM, Smulders, Maaike and Heuvel, Monique van den, (red.), *Choice. Jaarmagazine 2013*, Den Bosch, 2014.
FIOM, Brenninkmeijer, M. and Oude Lenferink-Groeneveld, P. (red.), *Leuk om jong moeder te zijn? Praktische informatie voor jong zwangeren en jonge moeders*, Den Bosch, 2005.
Fischer, Aart A. et al., Rapport Abortus-vraagstuk van Commissie van de Nederlandse Vereniging voor Psychiatrie en Neurologie, in: *Medisch Contact*, 1970, 25, pp. 143-154.
Flake, Alan, "Fetal Therapy. Medical and Surgical Approaches", Creasy, Robert, Resnik, Robert, and Iams, Jay, (Eds.), *Maternal-fetal Medicine. Principles and Practice*. Fifth Edition, Philadelphia, Pennsylvania 2004, pp. 483-494.
Flannery S.J., Kevin, "Applying Aristotle in contemporary embryology", *The Thomist*, 2003, 67, pp. 249-278.
Flavius Josephus, *Antiquitates*. English translation and commentary by Louis H. Feldman, *Judean Antiquities, 1-4*. In: Mason, Steve (ed.), *Flavius Josephus. Translation and Commentary*. Vol. 3, Leiden, 2000.
Flavius Josephus, *Contra Apionem*. English translation and commentary by John M.G. Barclay, *Against Apion*. In: Mason, Steve (ed.), *Flavius Josephus. Translation and Commentary*. Vol. 10, Leiden, 2007.
Ford, Norman, "The Moral Significance of the Human Foetus", in: Ashcroft, Richard et al., 2007, pp. 387-392.
Ford, SDB, Norman, *The Prenatal Person. Ethics from Conception to Birth*, Malden, MA., 2002.
Forouzanfar, Mohammad H., Foreman, Kyle J., Delossantos, Allyne M., Lozano, Rafael, Lopez, Alan D., Murray, Christopher J.L. and Naghavi, Mohsen, "Breast and cervical

cancer in 187 countries between 1980 and 2010: a systematic analysis", *The Lancet*, 2011, 378, pp. 1461–84.
Fostering Network, "Head, Heart, Hands. Introducing social pedagogy into foster care", London, 2013, p. 4.
Francis, Apostolic exhortation *Evangelii Gaudium*, Vatican, 2013.
Francis, Encyclical letter *Laudato Si'*, on care for our common home, Vatican, 2015 (a).
Francis, "Letter of his Holiness Pope Francis according to which an indulgence is granted to the faithful on the occasion of the extraordinary Jubilee of Mercy", Vatican, 2015 (b).
Francome, Colin, *Abortion in the USA and the UK*, Hants, 2004.
Fukuyama, Francis, *The Great Disruption. Human Nature and the Reconstitution of Social Order*. New York, 1999.
Furedi, Ann and Hume, Michael (eds.), *Abortion Law Reformers. Pioneers of Change*, Stratford-upon-Avon, 2007, originally published in 1997.
Galvão, Pedro, "Boonin on the future-like-ours argument against abortion", *Bioethics*, 2007, 21 (6), pp. 324-328.
Gastmans, Chris, Dierckx de Casterle, Bernadette and Schotsmans, Paul, "Nursing Considered as Moral Practice: A Philosophical-Ethical Interpretation of Nursing", *Kennedy Institute of Ethics Journal*, 1998, 8, 1, pp. 43-69.
General Congregation n. 35 of the Society of Jesus, decree 1, "With renewed vigor and zeal. The Society of Jesus responds to the invitation of the Holy Father", Rome, 2008.
Giannakoulopoulos, Xenophon, Teixeira, Jerónima, Fisk, Nicholas and Glover, Vivette, "Human fetal and maternal noradrenaline responses to invasive procedures", *Pediatric Research*, 1999, 45, pp. 494-499.
Gilbert, R.E., Augood, C., Gupta, R., Ades, A.E., Logan, S., Sculpher, M. and van der Meulen, J.H.P., "Screening for Down's syndrome: effects, safety, and cost effectiveness of first and second trimester strategies", *BMJ*, 2001, 323, pp. 1-6.
Gilchrist, A.C., Hannaford, P.C., Frank, P. and Kay, C.R., Termination of pregnancy and psychiatric morbidity. In: *British Journal of Psychiatry*, 1995, 167, pp. 243-248.
Girma, Sourafel and Paton, David, "Is education the best contraception: the case of teenage pregnancy in England?", *Social Science & Medicine*, 2015, 131, pp. 1-9.
Gissler, Mika, Berg, Cynthia, Bouvier-Colle, Marie-Hélène and Buekens, Pierre, "Pregnancy-associated mortality after birth, spontaneous abortion, or induced abortion in Finland, 1987-2000", *American Journal of Obstetrics and Gynecology*, 2004, 190, pp. 422-427.
Gissler, Mika, Hemminki, Elina, Lonnqvist, Jouko, "Suicides after pregnancy in Finland, 1987-94: Register linkage study", *British Medical Journal*, 1996, 313, pp. 1431-1434.
Glendon, Mary Ann, *Abortion and Divorce in Western Law: American Failures, European Challenges*, Cambrigde (Ma.), 1987.
Goenee, Maaike, Picavet, Charles and Wijsen, Ciel, *Factsheet Landelijke abortus registratie 2011*, Rutgers WPF, Utrecht, 2013.
Goldacre, M.J., Kurina, L.M., Seagroatt, V. and Yeates, D., "Abortion and Breast Cancer: A Case-Control Record Linkage Study", *Journal of Epidemiology and Community Health* 55.5 (May 2001), pp. 336–337.
Government of Ireland, "Protection of Life During Pregnancy Act", in: *Irish Statute Book*, nr. 35 of 2013.
Graaf, Arie de, "Gezinnen in beweging", in Bucx, F. (ed.), *Gezinsrapport*, Sociaal Cultureel

Planbureau, Den Haag, 2011, p. 82-96.

Green, J.M., Hewison, J., Bekker, H.L., Bryant, L.D. and Cuckle, H.S., "Psycho-social aspects of genetic screening of pregnant women and newborns: a systematic review", *Health Technology Assessment*, 2004, 8, pp. 1-124.

Gregory IX, "Decretales", in: Friedberg, E.A. and Richter, A.L. (eds.), *Corpus Iuris Canonici. Editio Lipsiensis Secunda*, Leipzig 1879.

Gregory XIV, "Sedes apostolica pia mater", in: Ferraris, F.L.: *Bibliotheca canonica iuridica moralis theologica*, 1885, pp. 39-40.

Grisez, Germain, *Abortion. The Myths, the Realities and the Arguments*, New York and Cleveland, 1970.

Grisez, Germain, *The Way of the Lord Jesus, Vol. I, Christian Moral Principles*, Chicago, 1983.

Grisez, Germain, *The Way of the Lord Jesus, Vol. II, Living a Christian Life*, Quincy, Ill., 1993.

Grundy, Trevor, "Gender-Based Abortions Spark Outrage In England As Sex Selection Becomes An Option", *The Huffington Post*, 10 October 2013.

Guenther, Lisa, *The Gift of the Other: Lévinas and the Politics of Reproduction*, New York, 2006.

Haakonssen, Knud, "Natural Law", in: Becker, Lawrence C. and Becker, Charlotte B., *Encyclopedia of Ethics*. Second edition, Vol. II, New York and Londen, 2001, pp. 1205-1212.

Habermas, Jürgen, *The Future of Human Nature*, translated from German by Hella Beister and William Rehg, Cambridge, U.K., 2003, or the original edition: Habermas, Jürgen, *Die Zukunft der menschlichen Natur. Auf dem Weg zu einer liberalen Eugenik?*, Frankfurt, 2005.

Hajian-Tilaki, K.O. and Kaveh-Ahangar, T., "Reproductive factors associated with breast cancer risk in northern Iran", *Medical Oncology*, June 2011, 28 (2), pp. 441-446.

Haldane, John and Lee, Patrick, "Aquinas on Human Ensoulment, Abortion and the Value of Life", *Philosophy*, 2003, 78, pp. 255-278.

Hamama, Lydia, Rauch, Sheila A.M., Sperlich, Mickey, Defever Erin and Seng, Julia S., "Previous experience of spontaneous or elective abortion and risk for posttraumatic stress and depression during subsequent pregnancy", *Depression and Anxiety*, 2010, August 27(8), pp. 699–707.

Hanna, D.R., "The Lived Experience of Moral Distress: Nurses Who Assisted With Elective Abortions", *Research and Theory for Nursing Practice*, 2005, 19, 1, pp. 95-124.

Harré, R. and Lamb, R. (Eds.), "Superego" In: Ibid., *The Encyclopedic Dictionary of Psychology*. Oxford, 1983, pp. 619-620.

Hart, R. and McMahon, C.A., "Mood state and psychological adjustment to pregnancy", *Archives of Women's Mental Health*, 2006, 9, pp. 329-337.

Haviland, M.G., Sonne, J.L. and Woods, L.R., "Beyond posttraumatic stress disorder: Object relations and reality testing disturbances in physically and sexually abused adolescents", *Journal of American Academy of Child and Adolescent Psychiatry*, 1995, 34, pp. 1054-1059.

Health Council of the Netherlands, *Screening for Chlamydia,* publication no. 2004/07, The Hague, 2004.

Hegel, Georg W.F., "Grundlinien der Philosophie des Rechts" [1821], in: Hegel, Georg W.F., *Werke 7*, Frankfurt am Main, 1970.

Heida, A., "Vaderschapsprocedures en DNA-onderzoek", *Tijdschrift voor familie- en jeugdrecht*, vol. 24, 2002, pp. 122-129.

Heijst, Annelies van, Derks, Marjet and Monteiro, Marit, *Ex Caritate. Kloosterleven, apostolaat*

en nieuwe spirit van actieve vrouwelijke religieuzen in Nederland in de 19^e en 20^e eeuw, Hilversum, 2010.
Heijst, Annelies van, *Liefdewerk. Een herwaardering van de caritas bij de Arme Zusters van het Goddelijk Kind, sinds 1852*, Hilversum, 2002.
Henderson, Katherine DeLellis, Sullivan-Halley, Jane, Reynolds, Peggy, Horn Ross, Pamela L., Clarke, Christina A., Chang, Ellen T., Neuhausen, Susan, Ursin, Giske and Bernstein, Leslie, "Incomplete pregnancy is not associated with breast cancer risk: the California Teacher Study", *Contraception*, 2008, 77, 6, pp. 391-396.
Henriet, Laurence and Kaminski, Monique, "Impact of induced abortions on subsequent pregnancy outcome: the 1995 French national perinatal survey", *British Journal of Obstetrics and Gynaecology*, 2001, 108, pp. 1036-1042.
Henshaw, Richard, Naji, Simon, Russell, Ian and Templeton, Allan, "Psychological responses following medical abortion (using mifepristone and gemeprost) and surgical vacuum aspiration. A patient-centered, partially randomised prospective study", *Acta Obstetrica et Gynecologica Scandinavica*, 1994, 73, pp. 812-818.
Hermans, Chris A.M., "When theology goes 'practical'. From applied to empirical theology", in: Hermans, Chris A.M. and Moore, Mary E. (Eds.), *Hermeneutics and empirical research in practical theology. The Contribution of Empirical Theology by Johannes A. van der Ven*. Leiden/Boston, 2004, pp. 21-51.
Hertz, Anselm et al., *Handbuch der Christlichen Ethik, Band 2,* Freiburg, 1978.
Hess, Rosanna, "Dimensions of Women's Long-Term Post-abortion Experience", *The American Journal of Maternal/Child Nursing*, 2004, 29, 3, pp. 193-198.
Hilhorst, Marieke, *Instellingen voor onderwijs en opvoeding aan meisjes van zustercongregaties. Historische achtergronden en ontwikkelingen tot 1970*. In: Deetman, W.J., et al., 2013, pp. 283-304.
Hill, Clifford, *Sex under sixteen? Young People Comment on the Social and Educational Influences on Their Behaviour*, London, 2000.
Hill, Thomas, "Autonomy of moral agents", in: Becker, Lawrence C. and Becker Charlotte B. (eds.), *Encyclopedia of Ethics. Second edition.* Vol. I, New York / London, 2001, pp. 111-115.
Hoekstra, R.E., Ferrara, T.B., Couser, R.J., Payne, N.R. and Connett, J.E., "Survival and Long-Term Neurodevelopmental Outcome of Extremely Premature Infants Born at 23–26 Weeks' Gestational Age at a Tertiary Centre", *Pediatrics*, 2004, 113, pp. e1–e6.
Hoften, Carlijn van, Burger, Huibert, Peeters, Petra H.M., Grobbee, Diederik E., Noord, Paul A.H. van and Leufkens, Hubert G.M., "Long-term oral contraceptive use increases breast cancer risk in women over 55 years of age: the DOM cohort", *International Journal of Cancer*, 2000, 87, pp. 591-594.
Holland, Alison T., *Simone de Beauvoir and the Women's Movement*, Northumbria, 2002.
Home Office, *Domestic Violence, A National Report*, London, 2005.
Home Office, *Safety and justice: sharing personal information in the context of domestic violence – an overview*, London, 2004.
Honein, M.A., Kirby, R.S., Meyer, R.E., Xing, J., Skerrette, N.I., Yuskiv, N., Marengo, L. Petrini, J.R., Davidoff, M.J., Mai, C.T., Druschel, Ch. M., Viner-Brown, S. and Sever, L.E., "The Association Between Major Birth Defects and Preterm Birth", *Maternal and Child Health Journal*, 2009, 13, pp. 164-175.

Honnefelder, Ludger, "Praktische Vernunft und Gewissen", in: Hertz, Anselm et al., *Handbuch der Christlichen Ethik*, Bd. 3, Freiburg, 1982.

House of Commons Education Committee, *Life lessons: PSHE and SRE in schools. Fifth Report of Session 2014-2015*, London 2015.

House of Commons Science and Technology Committee, *Human Reproductive Technologies and the Law. Fifth Report of Session 2004-2005, Volume I*, London, 2005.

House of Commons Science and Technology Committee, *Human Reproductive Technologies and the Law. Fifth Report of Session 2004-2005, Volume II, Oral and written evidence*, London, 2005.

House of Commons Science and Technology Committee, *Scientific Developments Relating to the Abortion Act 1967. Twelfth Report of Session 2006/2007, Volume I*, London, 2007 (a).

House of Commons Science and Development Committee: *Scientific Developments Relating to the Abortion Act 1967. Twelfth Report of Session 2006/2007, List of Evidence*, London 2007 (b).

House of Lords Select Committee on Stem Cell Research, *Report*, London 2002.

Houston, Helen and Jacobson, Lionel, "Overdose and termination of pregnancy: an important association?", *British Journal of General Practice*, 1996, 46, pp. 737-738.

Howe, Holly L., Senie, Ruby T., Bzduch, Helen and Herzfeld, Peter, "Early Abortion and Breast Cancer Risk Among Women Under Age 40", *International Journal of Epidemiology*, 1989, 18, 300-304.

Huang, Yubei, Zhang, Xiaoling, Li, Weiqin, Song, Fengju, Dai, Hongji, Wang, Jing, Gao, Ying, Liu, Xueou, Chen, Chuan, Yan, Ye, Wang, Yaogang and Chen, Kexin, "A meta-analysis of the association between induced abortion and breast cancer risk among Chinese females", in: *Cancer Causes Control*, 2014, 25, pp. 227–236.

Human Fertilisation and Embryology Act 1990, in: *United Kingdom Public General Acts*, London, 1990, chapter 37.

Human Fertilisation and Embryology Act 2008, in: *United Kingdom Public General Acts*, London, 2008, chapter 22.

Hursthouse, Rosalind, *Beginning lives*, Oxford, 1987.

Husfeldt, Charlotte, Kierstein-Hansen, Susanne, Lyngberg, Ann, Nøddebo, Merete and Petersson, Birgit, "Ambivalence among women applying for abortion", in: *Acta Obstetricia et Gynecologica Scandinavica*, 1995, Nov., 74, 10, pp. 813-817.

Husserl, Edmund, *Cartesian Meditations. An introduction to phenomenology*. Translated by Dorion Cairns. The Hague, 1960.

Huxtable, Richard, "Get out of jail free? The doctrine of double effect in English law", in: *Palliative Medicine*, 2004, 18, pp. 62-68.

Ignatius of Loyola, *The Spiritual Exercises*. Translated with introductions and notes by Joseph A. Munitiz and Philip Endean, London, 1996.

Information Services Division Scotland, *Abortion Statistics 2013*, Edinburgh, 2014.

Innocentius III, "Letter to a Carthusian prior as of Oct. 4, 1211", in: Potthast, A., (ed.) *Regesta Pontificum Romanorum*, Berlin, 1874, p. 372, nr. 4312.

Inspectie voor de Gezondheidszorg (Healthcare Inspectorate), *Jaarrapportage 2013 van de Wet Afbreking Zwangerschap*, Utrecht, 2014.

Inspectie voor de Gezondheidszorg, (Healthcare Inspectorate) *Verantwoorde zorg in abortusklinieken, met ruimte voor verbetering*, Utrecht, 2013.

International Theological Commission, *The hope of salvation for infants who die without being baptised*, Vatican, 2007.
Ivens S.J., Michael, *Understanding the Spiritual Exercises*, Leominster / New Malden, 1998.
Jabeen, Suraiya, Haque, Musarrat, Islam, Johirul, Hossain, Mohammad Z., Begum, Atiya. and Kashem, Abul, "Breast Cancer and Some Epidemiological Factors: a Hospital Based Study", *Journal of Dhaka Medical College*, 2013, 22 (1), pp. 61-66.
Jacob-Hargot, Thérèse, *Pour une libération sexuelle véritable*, Langres – Saint Geosmes, 2010.
James, Montague, *The Apocryphal New Testament*, Londen, 1975.
Jarvis Thomson, Judith, "A Defense of Abortion", *Philosophy & Public Affairs*, Vol. 1, n. 1, 1971, pp. 47-66.
Jemmott, John B., Jemmott, Loretta S. and Fong, Geoffrey T., "Efficacy of a Theory-Based Abstinence-Only Intervention Over 24 Months. A Randomized Controlled Trial With Young Adolescents", *Archives of Pediatric Adolescent Medicine*, 2010, 164 (2), pp. 152-159.
Jerome, *Letter 121 Ad Algasiam*, in: Saint Jérôme, *Correspondance*, Vol. VII, Transl. in French by J. Labourt, Paris, 2003.
John Paul II, *Address to the participants of the International Paul VI Award ceremony*, Vatican, 2003.
John Paul II, Encyclical *Veritatis Splendor*, Vatican, 1993.
John Paul II, Encyclical *Evangelium Vitae, on the value and inviolability of human life*, Vatican, 1995.
John Paul II, *General Audience, 20 February 1980. Man Enters the World As a Subject of Truth and Love*, Vatican, 1980.
John Paul II, General Audience of Wednesday 1 August 1984 on Responsible Parenthood, in: *L'Osservatore Romano, Weekly Edition in English*, 6 August 1984, p. 1.
John Paul II, General Audience of Wednesday, 22 August 1984 on the Church's Position on Transmission of Life, in: *L'Osservatore Romano, Weekly Edition in English*, 27 August 1984, p. 7.
John Paul II, Postsynodal apostolic exhortation *Familiaris Consortio. On the role of the Christian family in the modern world*. Vatican, 1981.
John Paul II, Postsynodal apostolic exhortation *Reconciliatio et paenitentia. To the bishops, clergy and faithful on reconciliation and penance in the mission of the Church today*. Vatican, 1985.
Jones, David, *The Soul of the Embryo*, London, 2004.
Jones C.SS.R., Frederick M., *Alphonsus de Liguori. Selected writings*, New York, 1999.
Kaczor, Christopher, *The Ethics of Abortion. Women's Rights, Human Life, and the Question of Justice*, New York and London, 2011.
Kandiah, Michael D. and Staerck, Gillian, *The Abortion Act 1967*, ICBH Witness Seminar Programme, Institute of Contemporary British History, London, 2002.
Kant, Immanuel, *Beobachtungen über das Gefühl des Schönen und Erhabenen*. [1764], Leipzig, ca. 1913.
Kant, Immanuel, *Critique of Pure Reason*. Translated and edited by Paul Guyer and Allen W. Wood, Cambridge, 1998.
Kant, Immanuel, *Grundlegung zur Metaphysik der Sitten* [1785], in: Weischedel, W. (Ed.), *Immanuel Kant, Werke in sechs Banden*, 2005, IV.
Katzive, Laura and Rahman, Anika, *Central and Eastern Europe: an examination of abortion laws in the global context*. Presented by K.H. Martinez at the Schweitzer Conference on

Improving Quality of Reproductive Health Services: Focus on Abortion Care, Prague, January 24-26, 2001.

Kelly, David F., *Contemporary Catholic Health Care Ethics*, Washington D.C., 2004.

Keown, John, *Abortion, doctors and the law. Some aspects of the legal regulation of abortion in England from 1803 to 1982*, Cambridge, 1988.

Kero, Anneli, Högberg, Ulf, Lalos, Ann, "Wellbeing and mental growth – long-term effects of legal abortion", *Social Science & Medicine*, 2004, 58, pp. 2559-2569.

Kero, Anneli, Lalos, Ann, "Ambivalence – a logical response to legal abortion: a prospective study among women and men", *Journal of Psychosomatic Obstetrics and Gynecology*, 2000, 21, pp. 81-91.

Ketting, E. and Visser, A.P., "Contraception in the Netherlands: the low abortion rate explained", *Patient Education and Counseling*, 1994, 23, pp. 161-171.

Kirby, Douglas B., "The Impact of Abstinence and Comprehensive Sex and STD/HIV Education Programs on Adolescent Sexual Behaviour", *Sexuality Research & Social Policy*, Vol. 5, No. 3, 2008.

Kirkman, Maggie, Rowe, Heather, Hardiman, Annarella, Mallet, Shelley and Rosenthal, Doreen, "Reasons women give for abortion: a review of the literature", *Archives of Women's Mental Health*, 2009, 12, pp. 365-378.

Klemetti, R., Gissler, M., Niinimäki, M. and Hemminki, E., "Birth outcomes after induced abortion: a nationwide register-based study of first births in Finland", *Human Reproduction*, 2012, Nov., 27 (11), pp. 3315-3320.

Koch-Hershenov, Rose, "Totipotency, Twinning, and Ensoulment at Fertilization", *Journal of Medicine and Philosophy*, 31, 2006, pp. 139-164.

Komonchak, Joseph, "*Humanae Vitae* and Its Reception: Ecclesiological Reflections", *Theological Studies*, 39, 1978, pp. 221-257.

Kooten, Maartje van, Berloo, Willy van and Vanwesenbeeck, Ine, *Psychosociale gevolgen van abortus. Een overzicht van de literatuur*, RutgersNissogroep, Delft, 2004.

Korenromp, Marijke J., *Parental adaptation to termination of pregnancy for fetal anomalies*. Doctoral thesis, Utrecht University, 2006.

Korenromp, Marijke J., Page-Christiaens, Godelieve C.M.L., Bout, J. van den, Mulder, Eduard J.H., Hunfeld, Joke and Bilardo, Caterina M., "Psychological consequences of termination of pregnancy for fetal anomaly: similarities and differences between partners", *Prenatal Diagnosis*, 2005, 25, pp. 1226-1233.

Koster, E., Rademakers, J., Jansen-Van Hees, A.C. and Willems, F., *Medicamenteuze abortus als alternatief voor de zuigcurettage: eerste ervaringen met de abortuspil in Nederland*, Utrecht, Nisso, 2001.

Kraaykamp, Gerbert, "Trends and Countertrends in Sexual Permissiveness: Three Decades of Attitude Change in The Netherlands 1965–1995", *Journal of Marriage and Family*, 2002, 64, pp. 225–239.

Kroelinger, Charlan D. and Oths, Kathryn S., "Partner Support and Pregnancy Wantedness", *Birth*, 2000, 27, 2, pp. 112-119.

Laar-Jochemsen, T.W. van, Zijp-Zuidema, C.E. and Jochemsen, H., *Psychische problematiek bij vrouwen na abortus provocatus en de rol van de huisarts*, Prof. dr. G.A. Lindeboom Instituut, Ede, 2006.

LaFollette, Hugh, *Personal Relationships: Love, Identity, and Morality*, Oxford, 1996.
Lanfranchi, Angela, "Normal Breast Physiology: the Reasons Hormonal Contraceptives and Induced Abortion Increase Breast-Cancer Risk", *Issues in Law & Medicine*, 2014, 29, 1, pp. 135-146.
Larsen, William J., *Human Embryology*, 3rd ed., Philadelphia, 2001.
Larsson, Margareta, Aneblom, Gunilla, Odlind, Viveka and Tydén, Tanja, "Reasons for pregnancy termination, contraceptive habits and contraceptive failure among Swedish women requesting an early pregnancy termination", *Acta Obstetricia et Gynecologica Scandinavica*, 2002, 81, pp. 64-71.
Lauzon, Pierre, Roger-Achim, Diane, Achim, André and Boyer, Richard, "Emotional distress among couples involved in first-trimester induces abortions", *Canadian Family Physician*, 2000, 46, pp. 2033-2040.
Lederman, Regina and Weis, Karen, *Psychosocial Adaptation to Pregnancy. Seven Dimensions of Maternal Role Development*. Third edition, New York, 2009.
Lee, Ellie, Clements, Steve, Ingham, Roger and Stone, Nicole, *A matter of choice. Explaining national variation in teenage abortion and motherhood*, Southampton, 2004.
Lee, Ellie, *Abortion, Motherhood and Mental Health. Medicalizing Reproduction in the United States and Great Britain*, New York, 2003 (a).
Lee, Ellie, "Tensions in the Regulation of Abortion in Britain", *Journal of Law and Society*, 2003 (b), 30, 4, pp. 532-553.
Lee, Patrick, *Abortion & Unborn Human Life*, 2nd ed., Washington DC, 2010.
Leget, Carlo, "Analyzing dignity: a perspective from the ethics of care", *Medical Health Care and Philosophy*, published online 12 July 2012.
Leget, C., Staps, T., Geer, J. van der, Mur-Arnoldi, C., Wulp, M. and Jochemsen, H. (Agorawerkgroep Richtlijn Spirituele Zorg), *Spirituele Zorg. Landelijke Richtlijn, Versie 1.0*, Utrecht, 2010.
Lekkerkerker, A.F.N., *De brief van Paulus aan de Romeinen*, vol. I, Nijkerk, 1971.
Levels, Mark, *Abortion laws in Europe between 1960 and 2010. Legislative developments and their consequences for women's reproductive decision-making*. Dissertation, Nijmegen, 2011.
Levinas, Emmanuel, *Alterity & transcendence*. Translated into English by Michael B. Smith, New York, 1999.
Levinas, Emmanuel, *Totality and Infinity. An essay on exteriority*. Translated into English by Alphonso Lingis, The Hague, 1979.
Levine, Phillip B., "Parental involvement laws and fertility behavior", *Journal of Health Economics*, 2003, 22, pp. 861-878.
Life, *Annual Review 2010/11*, Lemington Spa, 2012.
Liguori, Alphonsus de, *Theologia Moralis*. Edited by J. Aertnys, C.SS.R., and C.A. Damen, C.SS.R., Torino, 1947.
Linden, A.P. van der, Siethoff, S.G.A. ten and Zeijlstra-Rijpstra, A.E.I.J., *Jeugd en recht*, Houten, 2009.
Lipp, Allyson and Fothergill, Anne, "Nurses in abortion care: Identifying and managing stress", *Contemporary Nurse*, 2009, 31, pp. 108-120.
Lonergan, Bernard, *Method in theology*, Toronto/London, 1971.
Loon, Joost van, *Deconstructing the Dutch Utopia. Sex education and teenage pregnancy in the*

Netherlands. London, 2003.
Lowery, Curtis L., Hardman, Mary P., Manning, Nirvana, Clancy, Barbara, Whit Hall, R. and Anand, K.J.S., "Neurodevelopmental Changes of Fetal Pain", *Seminars in Perinatology*, 2007, 31, pp. 275-282.
Lugo S.J., Joannis De, *Disputationes scholasticae et morales*, vol. VI, *De Iustitia et Iure*, Paris, 1869, disp. 10, sect. 5.
Lynch, Ami, "Abortion", in: Heywood, Leslie L., *The Women's Movement Today. An Encyclopedia of Third-Wave Feminism*, Westport (CT.) and London, 2006, Vol. 1, pp. 1-4.
MacIntyre, Alasdair, *After Virtue. A study in moral theory*, London, 1981.
MacIntyre, Alasdair, *Dependent Rational Animals. Why Human Beings Need the Virtues*, London, 1999.
Major, Brenda, Cozzarelli, Catherine, Cooper, M. Lynne, Zubek, Josephine, Richards, Caroline, Wilhite, Michael and Gramzow, Richard H., "Psychological Responses of Women After First-Trimester Abortion", *Archives of General Psychiatry*, 2000, 57, pp. 777-784.
Makdoembaks, Nizaar, *Geheime abortus maskeert kindermisbruik. Hoge embryosterfte door falend soa-beleid*, Amsterdam, 2008.
Marquis, Don, "Strong's objections to the future of value account", *Journal of Medical Ethics*, 2011, 37, pp. 384-388.
Marquis, Don, "Why abortion is immoral", *Journal of Philosophy*, 1989, 86, 4, pp. 183-202.
Marquis, Don, "Why Most Abortions are Immoral", in: Edwards, R. B. and Bittar, E. (Eds.), *Advances in Bioethics. Bioethics for medical education*. Volume 5, 1999, pp. 215-244.
Marteau, T., Drake, H., Reid, M., Feijoo, M., Soares, M., Nippert, I., Nippert, P. and Bobrow, M., Counselling following Diagnosis of Fetal Abnormality: A comparison between German, Portuguese and UK Geneticists, in: *European Journal on Human Genetics*, 1994, 2, pp. 96-102.
Maude, Aylmer, *Marie Stopes: Her Work and Play*, London, 1933.
Maughan, B., Collishaw, S. and Pickles, A., "School Achievement and Adult Qualifications among Adoptees: A Longitudinal Study", *Journal of Child Psychology and Psychiatry and Allied Disciplines*, 1998, 39, 5, pp. 669-685.
McClellan, Jon, Adams, Julie, Douglas, Donna, McCurry, Chris and Storck, Mick, "Clinical characteristics related to severity of sexual abuse: A study of seriously mentally ill youth", *Child Abuse and Neglect*, 1995, 19, pp. 1245-1254.
McClellan, Jon, McCurry, Chris, Ronnei, Marylin, Adams, Julie., Eisner, Andrea and Storck, Mick, "Age of Onset of Sexual Abuse: Relationship to Sexually Inappropriate Behaviors", *Journal of the American Academy of Child and Adolescent Psychiatry*, 1996, 34, 10, pp. 1375-1383.
McLeod, Hugh, *Religion and Society in England 1850-1914*, Basingstoke, 1996.
McLeod, Hugh, *The Religious Crisis of the 1960s*, Oxford, 2007.
McLeod, Hugh, "The Sixties: Writing the Religious History of a Crucial Decade", *Kirchliche Zeitgeschichte*, 2001, 14, pp. 36-48.
McMahan, Jeff, "Cloning, killing, and identity", *Journal of Medical Ethics*, 1999, 25, pp. 77-86.
McMahan, Jeff, *The Ethics of Killing. Problems at the Margins of Life*, Oxford, 2002.
Mealey, Ann Marie, *The Identity of Christian Morality*, Farnham, 2009.

Medoff, Marshall, "Abortion costs, sexual behavior, and pregnancy rates", *The Social Science Journal*, 2008, 45, pp. 156-172.

Melina, Livio, Noriega, José and Pérez-Soba, Juan José, *Camminare nella Luce dell'Amore. I fondamenti della morale cristiana*, Siena, 2008.

Michels, Karin B., Xue, Fei, Colditz, Graham A. and Willet, Walter C., "Induced and Spontaneous Abortion and Incidence of Breast Cancer among Young Women. A Prospective Cohort Study", *Arch Intern Med*, 2007, 167, pp. 814-820.

Miller F.S.E., Paula Jean, "The Theology of the Body. A New Look at *Humanæ Vitae*.", *Theology Today*, 57, 2001, 4, pp. 501-508.

Ministerie van Volksgezondheid, Welzijn en Sport, *Verslag 'Behandelgrens pasgeborenen en grens abortushulpverlening'*, bijlage bij Kamerstuk 30371, nr. 21, Den Haag, 2011.

Ministry of Foreign Affairs, *Q&A Abortion in the Netherlands*, The Hague, 2011.

Mirrlees-Black, Catriona, *Domestic violence: findings from a new British Crime Survey self-completion questionnaire*. Home Office Research Study 191, London, 1999.

Modi, N. and Glover, V., "Fetal pain and stress", in: Anand, K.J.S, Stevens, B.J. and McGrath, P.J., *Pain in Neonates, 2nd Revised and Enlarged Edition*. Pain Research and Clinical Management, Vol. 10, Amsterdam, 2000, pp. 217-227.

Mohangoo, A.D. and Buitendijk, S.E., *Aangeboren afwijkingen in Nederland 1997-2007. Gebaseerd op de landelijke verloskunde en neonatologie registraties*, TNO KvL/P&Z 2009/112, Leiden, 2009.

Mommsen, Theodor, Krueger, Paul and Watson, Alan, (eds.), *The Digest of Justinian*, Philadelphia, Pennsylvania, 1985.

Moore, Keith L. and Persaud, T.V.N., *The Developing Human. Clinically oriented embryology*, 7th ed., Philadelphia, 2003.

Moreau, Caroline, Kaminski, Monique, Ancel, Pierre-Yves, Bouyer, Jean, Escande, Benoit, Thiriez, Gérard, Boulot, Pierre, Fresson, Jeanne, Arnaud, Catherine, Subtil, Damien, Marpeau, Loic, Rozé, Jean-Christophe, Maillard, Françoise and Larroque, Béatrice, "Previous induced abortions and the risk of very preterm delivery: results of the EPIPAGE study", *British Journal of Obstetrics and Gynaecology*, 2005, 112, pp. 430-437.

Morrissey, R.O., *The Canonical Effects of Abortion in the 1983 Code of Canon Law. Dissertatio ad lauream in Facultate Iuris Canonici apud Pontificiam Universitatem S. Thomae in Urbe*, Rome, 1995.

Movimento per la vita italiano, "22 maggio 1975 - 22 maggio 2015. Il movimento per la vita compie quarant'anni", Press announcement, Rome, 2015.

Mühlemann, K., Germain, M. and Krohn, M., "Does an Abortion Increase the Risk of Intrapartum Infection in the Following Pregnancy?", *Epidemiology*, 1996, 7, 2, pp. 194-198.

Nakamura, Katrina, Sheps, Sam and Arck, Petra Clara, "Stress and reproductive failure: past notions, present insights and future directions", *Journal of assisted reproduction and genetics*, 2008, 25, pp. 47-62.

National Collaborating Centre for Mental Health, *Induced Abortion and Mental Health. A systematic review of the mental health outcomes of induced abortion, including their prevalence and associated factors*, London, 2011.

National Conference of State Legislatures, "Fetal homicide laws", on their website, accessed 23 December 2015.

Nationale Raad voor Liturgie, *Liturgie van de sacramenten en andere kerkelijke vieringen. Het doopsel van kinderen*, Zeist, 1993.

Nederlands Genootschap van Abortusartsen, *Beroepscode Abortusartsen*, Utrecht, 2012.

Nederlands Genootschap van Abortusartsen, *Guideline for counselling women considering termination of pregnancy*. Translated by Joop Hoekstra. Original title: Richtlijn begeleiding van vrouwen die een zwangerschapsafbreking overwegen. Utrecht, 2011.

Nederlandse Vereniging voor Obstetrie en Gynaecologie, *Kwaliteitsnorm Prenatale screening*, Utrecht, 2005.

Nietzsche, Friedrich, *Beyond Good and Evil. Prelude to a Philosophy of the Future*. Translated and edited by Marion Faber, Oxford/New York, 1998.

Noonan, John T., Jr., *Contraception. A History of Its Treatment by the Catholic Theologians and Canonists*. Enlarged Edition, Cambridge (Ma.) and London, 1986.

Noonan, John, T., Jr., *The morality of abortion. Legal and historical perspectives*, Harvard U.P., 1970.

Nussbaum, Martha C., *Women and Human Development: The Capabilities Approach*, Cambridge, U.K., 2000.

O'Dowd, Adrian, "MPs want to drop second doctor's signature for abortion", *BMJ*, 2007, 335, 960.2.

Oepkes, D., Wieringa, J., "Recht op prenatale kennis", *Medisch contact*, 2008, 63, 31-32, pp. 1296-1298.

Office for National Statistics, *2011 Census Analysis: How do Living Arrangements, Family Type and Family Size Vary in England and Wales?* London, 2014.

Office for National Statistics, *Ethnicity and National Identity in England and Wales 2011*, Titchfield, 2012.

Office for National Statistics, *Marriage, Divorce and Adoption Statistics, Series FM2 2006*. Newport, 2009.

Office for Standards in Education, Children's Services and Skills, *Not yet good enough: personal, social, health and economic education in schools*, Manchester, 2013.

O'Reilly, Monica, "Careful counsel: Management of unintended pregnancy", *Journal of the American Academy of Nurse Practitioners*, 2009, 21, pp. 596–602.

Parens, Erik and Asch, Adrienne (Eds.), *Prenatal Testing and Disability Rights*, Washington, 2000.

Parens, Erik and Asch, Adrienne, "The Disability Rights Critique of Prenatal Genetic Testing. Reflections and Recommendations", *The Hastings Center Report*, 1999, 29, 5, pp. S1-S22.

Paton, David, "Random behaviour or rational choice? Family planning, teenage pregnancy and sexually transmitted infections", *Sex Education*, 2007, 6, (3), pp. 281-308.

Paton, David, "The economics of family planning and underage conceptions", *Journal of Health Economics*, 2002, 21, pp. 207–225.

Paul VI, Encyclical letter *Humanae Vitae*, Vatican, 1968.

Petersen, Peter, *Schwangerschaftsabbruch – unser Bewußtsein vom Tod im Leben. Tiefenpsychologische und anthropologische Aspekte der Verarbeitung*, Stuttgart, 1986.

Petersen, Peter, "Awareness of death and interpersonal relations after induced abortion", *Zeitschrift für Geburtshilfe und Perinatologie*, 1987, 191, 2, pp. 47-54.

Philo of Alexandria, *De specialibus legibus*. German translation by L. Cohn, I. Heinemann, M. Adler and W. Theiler, *Über die Einzelgesetze*, Berlin, 1962.

Picavet, Charles and Vlugt, Ineke van der, *Factsheet Tienerzwangerschappen in Nederland*, Rutgers

WPF, Utrecht, 2014.
Piotrowska-Nitsche, Karolina, Perea-Gomez, Aitana, Haraguchi, Seiki and Zernicka-Goetz, Magdalena, "Four-cell stage mouse blastomeres have different developmental properties", *Development*, 132, 3 (2004), pp. 479-490.
Pius XI, encyclical *Casti Connubii*, Vatican, 1930.
Pius XII, *Discorsi e Radiomessaggi di Sua Santità Pio XII*, Vatican, 1939-1958, esp. 1944 and 1951.
Plusa, Berenika, Hadjantonakis, Anna-Katerina., Gray, Dionne, Piotrowska-Nitsche, Karolina, Jedrusik, Agnieszka, Papaioannu, Virginia, Glover, David M. and Zernicka-Goetz, Magdalena, "The first cleavage of the mouse zygote predicts the blastocyst axis", *Nature*, 434 (2005), pp. 391-395.
Pradel, Jean, "La seconde mort de l'enfant conçu (à propos de l'arrêt d'Assemblée plénière du 29 juin 2001)", *Recueil Dalloz*, 2001, 36, pp. 2907-2913.
Quinn, Warren, "Abortion: Identity and Loss", *Philosophy and Public Affairs*, 1984, 13, pp. 24-54.
Rager, Günther, *Die Person. Wege zu ihrem Verständnis*, Fribourg, 2006.
Rawls, John, *Political Liberalism*, New York, 1993.
Reading, A.E., Cox, D.N., Sledmere, C.M. and Campbell, S., "Psychological Changes Over the Course of Pregnancy: A Study of Attitudes Toward the Fetus/Neonate", *Health Psychology*, 1984, 3, pp. 211-221.
Reagan, Charles E., *Paul Ricoeur. His Life and His Work*, Chicago, 1996.
Reardon, David C., *The after effects of abortion*, Elliot Institute, Springfield (Il.), 1990.
Reardon, David C., *Limitations on post-abortion research: why we know so little*, Elliot Institute, Springfield (Il.), 1997.
Reardon, David C., Ney, Philip G., Scheuren, Fritz J., Cougle, Jesse T., Coleman, Priscilla K. and Strahan, Thomas W., "Deaths Associated With Pregnancy Outcome: A Record Linkage Study of Low Income Women", *Southern Medical Journal*, 2002, 95, 8, pp. 834-841.
Reardon, David C., Cougle, Jesse R., Rue, Vincent M., Shuping, Martha W., Coleman, Priscilla K. and Ney, Philip G., "Psychiatric admissions of low-income women following abortion and childbirth", *Canadian Medical Association Journal*, 2003, 168 (10), pp. 1253-1256.
Reath, Andrews, "Autonomy, ethical", in: Craig, Edward (Ed.), *Routledge Encyclopedia of Philosophy*, vol. I, London, 1998, pp. 586-592.
Rebeyka, Ivan, "Fetal cardiac surgery", Allan, Lindsey, Hornberger, Lisa and Sharland, Gurleen, (Eds.), *Textbook of Fetal Cardiology*, London, 2000, pp. 525-533.
Reeves, Gillian, "Reply to: Breast cancer in relation to abortion: Results from the EPIC-study", *International Journal of Cancer*, 2008, 122, p. 962.
Reeves, Gillian K., Kan, Sau-Wan, Key, Tim, Tjønneland, Anne, Olsen, Anja, Overvad, Kim, Peeters, Petra, Clavel-Chapelon, Françoise, Paoletti, Xavier, Berrino, Franco, Krogh, Vittorio, Palli, Domenico, Tumino, Rosario, Panico, Salvatore, Vineis, Paulo, Gonzalez, Carlos A., Ardanaz, Eva, Martinez, Carmen, Amiano, Pilar, Quiros, José R., Tormo, Maria, Khaw, Kai-Thee, Trichopoulou, Antonia, Psaltopoulou, Theodora, Kalapothaki, Victoria, Nagel, Gabriele, Chang-Claude, Jenny, Boeing, Heiner, Lahmann, Petra H., Wirfält, Elisabeth, Kaaks, Rudolf and Riboli, Elio, "Breast cancer risk in relation to abortion: Results from the EPIC-study", International *Journal of Cancer*, 2006, 119, pp. 1741-1745.

Reichlin, Massimo, "The argument from potential: a reappraisal", *Bioethics*, 1997, 11, 1, pp. 1-23.
Rhonheimer, Martin, *Natural Law and Practical Reason. A Thomist View of Moral Autonomy*. Translated from the German by German Malsbary, New York, 2000.
Ricoeur, Paul, "Action, story and history: on re reading *The Human Condition*", in: Williams, Garrath (Ed.), *Hannah Arendt. Critical Assessments of Leading Political Philosophers. Vol. III. The Human Condition*, Abingdon, 2006.
Ricoeur, Paul, *Oneself as another*. Originally published as *Soi-même comme un autre* [1990], translated into English by Kathleen Blamey, Chicago, 1992.
Ricoeur, Paul, "The problem of the foundation of moral philosophy", Originally published as *Le problème du fondement de la morale*, in: *Sapienza. Rivista internazionale di filosofia e di teologia*, 1975, 28, 3, pp. 313-337, translated into English by David Pellauer in: *Philosophy Today*, 1978, 22, 3, pp. 175-192; translated into Dutch by Hendrik Opdebeeck, *Het probleem van de grondslagen van de moraal*, Kampen, 1995.
Ricoeur, Paul, "The Three Levels of Medical Judgment", in: Idem, *Reflections on The Just*. Translated by David Pellauer, Chicago, 2007, pp. 198-212.
Rikhof, H.W.M. and Vosman, F.J.H. (eds.), *De schittering van de waarheid. Theologische reflecties bij de encycliek Veritatis Splendor*, Zoetermeer, 1994.
RIVM, *Informatie over de screening op Downsyndroom*, brochure, Bilthoven, 2011.
Rodriguez, Ned, Vande Kemp, Hendrika and Foy, David W., "Posttraumatic Stress Disorder in Survivors of Childhood Sexual and Physical Abuse: A Critical Review of the Empirical Research", *Journal of Child Sexual Abuse*, 1998, 7, 2, pp. 17-45.
Ross, Tim, "Health minister Anna Soubry scraps abortion counselling plan", *Telegraph*, 31 October 2012.
Rothhaar, Markus, "Human dignity and human rights in bioethics: the Kantian approach", *Medical Health Care and Philosophy*, 2010, 13, pp. 251-257.
Rousseau, Jean-Jacques, *Émile, ou, de l'éducation*. Translated in Dutch by Anneke Brassinga, Meppel, 1980.
Royal College of Obstetricians and Gynaecologists, *Fetal Awareness. Review of Research and Recommendations for Practice. Report of a working party*, London, 2010.
Royal College of Obstetricians and Gynaecologists, *The Care of Women Requesting Induced Abortion. Evidence-based Clinical Guideline Number 7*, London, 2011.
Rozendal, Diny, "De praktijk...", *Annalen van het Thijmgenootschap*, 79, 2, 1991, pp. 81-91.
Rzepka, Jane R., *Counseling women who have unplanned pregnancies: a pastoral approach*, Berkeley (Ca.), 1982.
Sahn, D.J. and Mack, G., "Fetal cardiology/past and future", in: Allan, Linsey., Hornberger, Lisa and Sharland, Gurleen, *Textbook of Fetal Cardiology*, London, 2000.
Saunders, Peter, "Income Support for Families and the Living Standards for Children", in: Kamerman, Sheila, Phipps, Shelley and Ben-Arieh, Asher (Eds.), *From Child Welfare to Child Well-Being. An International Perspective on Knowledge in the Service of Policy Making*, Dordrecht, etc. 2010, pp. 275-292.
Savulescu, Julian, "Abortion, embryo destruction and the future of value argument", in: *Journal of Medical Ethics*, 2002, 28, 3, pp. 133-136.
Savulescu, Julian, "Is current practice around late termination of pregnancy eugenic and discriminatory? Maternal interests and abortion", in: *Journal of Medical Ethics*, 2001, 27,

1, pp. 165-171.
Scheler, Max, *The Human Place in the Cosmos*. Translated from the German by Manfred S. Frings, Illinois, 2009.
Schinkel, Anders, *Conscience and Conscious Objections*, dissertation, Amsterdam, 2006.
Schockenhoff, Eberhard, *Wie gewiss ist das Gewissen? Eine ethische Orientierung*, Freiburg, 2003.
Second Vatican Council, *Declaration on Religious Freedom Dignitatis Humanae*, Vatican, 1965.
Second Vatican Council, Pastoral Constitution on the Church and the Modern World *Gaudium et Spes*, Vatican, 1965.
Sedgmen, B., McMahon, C., Cairns, D., Benzie, R.J. and Woodfield, R.L., "The impact of two-dimensional versus three-dimensional ultrasound exposure on maternal–fetal attachment and maternal health behavior in pregnancy", *Ultrasound Obstetrics and Gynecology*, 2006, 27, pp. 245-251.
Shah, P.S. and Zao, J. on behalf of Knowledge Synthesis Group of Determinants of preterm/LBW births. "Induced termination of pregnancy and low birthweight and preterm birth: a systematic review and meta-analyses", *British Journal of Obstetrics and Gynaecology*, 2009, 116, pp. 1425-1442.
Siddiqui, A., Hägglöf, B. and Eisemann, M., "Own memories of upbringing as a determinant of prenatal attachment in expectant women", *Journal of Reproductive and Infant Psychology*, 2000, 18, 67-74.
Simmonds, Katherine E. and Likis, Frances E., "Providing Options Counseling for Women With Unintended Pregnancies", *Journal of Obstetric, Gynecologic, and Neonatal Nursing*, 2005, 34 (3), pp. 373-379.
Singer, Peter, *Rethinking Life & Death: The Collapse of Our Traditional Ethics*, New York, 1994.
Siriz, *Jaarverslag 2010*, Amersfoort, 2011.
Siriz, *Jaarverslag 2012*, Amersfoort, 2013.
Siriz, *Ontwikkeling en groei. Jaarverslag 2013*, Amersfoort, 2014.
Sixtus V, Effrenatam. In: Ferraris, F.L.: *Bibliotheca canonica iuridica moralis theologica*, 1885, pp. 36-38.
Skorupski, John, "Autonomy and impartiality", in: Timmermann, Jens, (Ed.), *Kant's Groundwork of the Metaphysics of Morals. A Critical Guide*. Cambridge, 2009, pp. 159-175.
Slade, P., Heke, S., Fletcher, J. and Stewart, P., "A comparison of medical and surgical termination of pregnancy: choice, emotional impact and satisfaction with care", *British Journal of Obstetrics and Gynaecology*, 1998, 105, pp. 1288-1295.
Slagboom, Maarten, *Echo. Prenataal onderzoek en keuzevrijheid*, Amsterdam, 2011.
Smart, Ninian, *The World's Religions*, Cambridge, 1989.
Smit, Joke, "Het onbehagen bij de vrouw", *De Gids,* 130, nr. 9-10, 1967, pp. 267-281.
Smith, Barry and Brogaard, Berit, "Sixteen Days", *Journal of Medicine and Philosophy*, 2003, 28, 1, pp. 45-78.
Smith, Janet E., *Humanae Vitae a generation later*, Washington D.C., 1991.
Smits, Pieter, *The right to life of the unborn child in international documents, decisions and opinions*, doctoral thesis University of Leiden, 1992.
Sociaal en Cultureel Planbureau, *In het zicht van de toekomst. Sociaal en cultureel rapport 2004*, Den Haag, 2004.
Söderberg, Hanna, Janzon, Lars and Sjöberg, Nils-Otto, "Emotional distress following induced abortion. A study of its incidence and determinants among abortees in Malmö,

Sweden", *European Journal of Obstetrics & Gynecology and Reproductive Biology*, 1998, 79, pp. 173-178.
Spaemann, Robert, *Persons*. Translated from the German by Oliver O'Donovan, Oxford, 2006.
Speckhard, Anne and Rue, Vincent M., "Complicated Mourning: Dynamics of Impacted Post Abortion Grief", *Journal of Prenatal and Perinatal Psychological Health*, 1993, 8, 1, pp. 5-32.
Spitz, Irving M., Bardin, Wayne, Benton, Laurie and Robbins, Ann, "Early pregnancy termination with mifepristone and misoprostol in the United States", *New England Journal of Medicine*, 1998, 338, pp. 1241-1247.
Steinberg, Julia R. and Russo, Nancy F., "Abortion and anxiety: what's the relationship?", *Social Science and Medicine*, 2008, 67, pp. 238-252.
Steinbock, Bonny, Why most abortions are not wrong. In: Edwards, R. B. and Bittar, E. (Eds.), *Advances in Bioethics. Bioethics for medical education*. Volume 5, 1999, pp. 245-267.
Stichting Samenwerkende Abortusklinieken/ Centra voor Seksuele Gezondheid Nederland (StiSAN), C. Rijneveld (red.) '*Als het moet, doe het goed*', Heemstede, 2002.
Stopes, Marie, *Contraception (Birth control), its theory, history and practice. A Manual for the Medical and Legal Professions*. London, 1927.
Stopes, Marie, *Married Love*. London, 1918, Dutch translation: *Hij en zij in het huwelijk. Nieuwe bijdrage tot de oplossing van het sexueele vraagstuk*, Amsterdam, 1931.
Stopes, Marie, *Radiant Motherhood*. London, 1920, Dutch translation: *Hij en zij en hun kind. Een boek voor jonge echtgenooten en voor allen, die de toekomst moeten maken*, Amsterdam, 1925.
Stovall, T.G., "Early Pregnancy Loss and Ectopic Pregnancy", in: Berek, J.S., Adashi, E.Y. and Hillard, P.A., (eds.), *Novak's Gynecology*, thirteenth edition, Philadelphia (etc.), 2002, pp. 507-542.
Strong, Carson, "A critique of 'the best secular argument against abortion'", *Journal of Medical Ethics*, 2008, 34, pp. 727-731.
Stubblefield, Phillip G., "First and Second Trimester Abortion", in: Nichols, David H. and Clarke-Pearson, Daniel L. (Eds.), *Gynecologic, Obstetric, and Related Surgery*, Second Edition, St. Louis, 2000.
Stump, Eleonore, *Aquinas*, London, 2003.
Sulmasy, OFM, Daniel P., "Dignity and Bioethics: History, Theory and Selected Applications", in: President's Council on Bioethics, *Human Dignity and Bioethics. Essays Commissioned by the President's Council on Bioethics*. Washington D.C., 2008, pp. 469-501.
Sumner, L.W., *Abortion and Moral Theory*, Princeton, 2014.
Tang, Mei-Zu C., Weiss, Noel S., Daling, Janet R. and Malone, Kathleen E., "Case-Control Differences in the Reliability of Reporting a History of Induced Abortion", *American Journal of Epidemiology* 151.12 (June 15, 2000): pp. 1139–1143.
Taylor, Charles, *The Ethics of Authenticity*, Cambridge, Ma. and London, 1992.
Tertullian, *Apologeticum*. Transl. into Dutch and commented by Chr. Mohrmann, Utrecht, 1951.
Tertullian, *Über die Seele (De Anima)*, 37, 5. Transl. into German by J.H. Waszink, Zürich, 1980.
Thorp, John M., Hartmann, Katherine E., Shadigian, Elisabeth, "Long-Term Physical and Psychological Health Consequences of Induced Abortion: Review of the Evidence",

Obstetrical and Gynecological Survey, 2002, 58, 1, pp. 67-79.
Tillich, Paul, *Dynamics of faith*, London, 1957.
Torres-Padilla, Marie-Elena, Parfitt, David-Emlyn, Kouzarides, Tony and Zernicka-Goetz, Magdalena, "Histone arginine methylation regulates pluripotency in the early mouse embryo", *Nature*, 445 (2007), pp. 214-218.
Tymstra, T., Bosboom, J. and Bouman, K., "Prenatal diagnosis of Down's Syndrome: Experiences of women who decided to continue with the pregnancy", *International Journal of Risk & Safety in Medicine*, 2004, 16, pp. 91-96.
UNICEF, *An overview of child well-being in rich countries. A comprehensive assessment of the lives and well-being of children and adolescents in the economically advanced nations*. Report card 7, Florence, 2007.
United Nations Department of Economic and Social Affairs, Population Division: *Abortion Policies. A Global Review. Volume I, Afghanistan to France; Volume II, Gabon to Norway and Volume III, Oman to Zimbabwe*, New York, 2002.
United Nations Educational, Social and Cultural Organization, *Declaration on Bioethics and Human Rights*, Paris, 2006.
United States Conference of Catholic Bishops. *Ethical and religious directives for Catholic Health Care Services*, Washington DC, 2009.
Van Ness, Peter H. (ed.), *Spirituality and the Secular Quest*, New York, 1996.
Vanwesenbeeck, Ine, Bakker, Floor, Fulpen, Michelle van, Paulussen, Theo, Poelman, Jos and Schaalma, Herman, "Seks en seksuele risico's bij VMBO-scholieren anno 2002", *Tijdschrift voor Seksuologie*, 2003, 27, pp. 30-39.
VBOK, *Jaarverslag 2008*, Amersfoort, 2009.
VBOK, *Omzien in verwachting*, Amersfoort, 1996.
VBOK/Siriz, *Peiling 20-weken echo*, Amsterdam, 2010.
Veen, H.C.J. van der, Bogaerts, S., *Huiselijk geweld in Nederland. Overkoepelend syntheserapport van het vangst-hervangst-, slachtoffer- en daderonderzoek 2007-2010*, Meppel, 2010, pp. 67-59.
Veenhoven, Ruut, "Alternatieven voor abortus", in: *Politiek Perspectief*, 1 nr. 5, Sept./Okt. 1972, pp. 27-31.
Velleman, J. David, "Against the Right to Die", originally published in: *Journal of Medicine & Philosophy*, 1992, 17, 6, pp. 665-681, revised in 2004.
Ven, Johannes A. van der, *Practical Theology: An Empirical Approach*, Kampen, 1993.
Vermeulen, Ben P., *De vrijheid van geweten, een fundamenteel rechtsprobleem*, Arnhem, 1989.
Verpleegkundigen en Verzorgenden Nederland (V&VN), Commissie Ethiek, "Omgaan met gewetensbezwaren, wie moet de gevolgen dragen?", 2008.
Visser, M.R.M., Janssen, A.J.G.M. Janssen, Enschedé, M., Willems, A.F.M.N., Braake, Th.A.M. te, Harmsen, K., Smets, E.M.A., Haes, J.C.J.M. de and Gevers, J.K.M., as commissioned by ZonMw consultancy: *Evaluatie Wet afbreking zwangerschap*, Amsterdam, 2005.
Waaijman, Kees, *Spiritualiteit. Vormen, Grondslagen, Methoden*, Kampen/Gent, 2000.
Wade S.J., Francis, "Potentiality in the abortion discussion", *Review of Metaphysics*, 1975, 29, pp. 239-255.
Wald, N.J., Huttly, W.J., Hennessy, C.F., "Down's syndrome screening in the UK in 1998", in: *The Lancet*, 1999, 354, p. 1264.
Waldstein, Wolfgang, *Das Menschenrecht zum Leben. Beiträge zu Fragen des Schutzes menschlichen*

Lebens. Berlin, 1982.
Walker, Rebecca, "Becoming the Third Wave", in: Heywood, Leslie L. (ed.), *The Women's Movement Today. An Encyclopedia of Third-Wave Feminism*, Westport, 2006, vol. 2, pp. 3-5.
Wallin Lundell, Inger, Sundström Poromaa, Inger, Frans, Örjan, Helström, Lotti, Högberg, Ulf, Moby, Lena, Nyberg, Sigrid, Sydsjö, Gunilla, Georgsson Öhman, Susanne, Östlund, Ingrid and Skoog Svanberg, Agneta, "The prevalence of posttraumatic stress among women requesting induced abortion", *The European Journal of Contraception and Reproductive Health Care*, 2013, 18, pp. 480–488.
Walser, Robyn D. and Kern, Jeffrey M., "Relationships Among Childhood Sexual Abuse, Sex Guilt, and Sexual Behavior in Adult Clinical Samples", *The Journal of Sex Research*, 1996, 33, 4, pp. 321-326.
Warnock, Mary, "Do Human Cells Have Rights?", *Bioethics*, 1987, 1, 1, pp. 1-14.
Warnock, Mary (ed.), *A Question of Life. The Warnock report on Human Fertilisation and Embryology*, Oxford, 1985.
Watt, Helen, "Preimplantation Genetic Diagnosis: Choosing the 'Good Enough' Child", *Health Care Analysis*, 2004, 12, 1, pp. 51-60.
Watt, Holly and Newell, Claire, "Law 'does not prohibit' sex-selection abortions, DPP warns", *Daily Telegraph*, 7 October 2013.
Weber, Max, *Wirtschaft und Gesellschaft. Grundrisse der verstehende Soziologie*, Tübingen, 1976.
Webber, Michelle and Bezanson, Kate (Eds.), *Rethinking Society in the 21st Century: Critical Readings in Sociology*, Toronto, 2008.
Wellings, Kaye and Kane, Roslyn, "Trends in teenage pregnancy in England and Wales: how can we explain them?", *Journal of the Royal Society of Medicine*, 1999, 92, pp. 277-282.
Wet Afbreking Zwangerschap (WAZ or Wafz), as of May 1st, 1981, in: *Staatsblad van het Koninkrijk der Nederlanden*, Den Haag, 1981, nr. 257.
Wet van 20 juni 2002, houdende regels inzake handelingen met geslachtscellen en embryo's (Embryowet), in: *Staatsblad van het Koninkrijk der Nederlanden*, Den Haag, 2002, nr. 338.
Wiebe, Ellen, Najafi, Roya, Soheil, Naghma and Kamani, Alya, "Muslim women having abortions in Canada. Attitudes, beliefs, and experiences", *Canadian Family Physician*, 2011, 57, April, e134-e138.
Wilkinson, Paul, French, Rebecca, Kane, Roslyn, Lachowycz, Kate, Stephenson, Judith and Grundy, Chris, "Teenage conceptions, abortions, and births in England, 1994-2003, and the national teenage pregnancy strategy", *The Lancet*, 2006, 25, 1879-1886.
Williams, Clare, Alderson, Priscilla and Farsides, Bobbie, "Is nondirectiveness possible within the context of antenatal screening and testing?", *Social Science & Medicine*, 2002, 54, pp. 339–347.
Wils, Jean-Pierre, "*Naturrecht*", in: Wils, Jean-Pierre and Hübenthal, Chris, *Lexikon der Ethik*, Paderborn, 2006, pp. 273-275.
Wils, Jean-Pierre, *Versuche über Ethik. Studien zur theologischen Ethik*, Freiburg, 2005.
Wool, Charlotte, "Systematic Review of the Literature. Parental Outcomes After Diagnosis of Fetal Anomaly", *Advances in Neonatal Care*, 2011, 11, 3, pp. 182-192.
Wulf, Claudia Mariéle, *Der Mensch – ein Phänomen. Eine phänomenologische, theologische und ethische Anthropologie*, Vallendar, 2011.
Wulf, Mariéle, *Een antropologie van de christelijke ethiek. Beschuldigd, bevrijd, bemind. Handboek Moraaltheologie, deel 1. Inleiding in de moraaltheologie*, Almere, 2013 (a).

Wulf, Mariéle, *Morele denkpatronen. Wetten, waarheid, waardigheid. Handboek moraaltheologie, deel 2. Geschiedenis en methoden van de moraaltheologie*, Almere, 2013 (b).

Wulf, Mariéle, "Psychotrauma en het concept van het leven", *Minor geloof en cultuur, collegereeks 2011-2012 Christelijke ethiek in een postchristelijke cultuur*, Unpublished manuscript.

Wulf, Claudia Mariéle, *Schuld ins Wort gebracht*, Vallendar, 2008.

Wulf, Claudia Mariéle, *Was ist gut? Eidetische Phänomenologie als Impuls zur moraltheologischen Erkenntnistheorie*, Vallendar, 2010.

Wyldes, M.P. and Tonks, A.M., "Termination of pregnancy for fetal anomaly: a population-based study 1995 to 2004", *British Journal of Obstetrics and Gynaecology*, 2007, 114, pp. 639-642.

Zolese, G. and Blacker, C.V.R., "The psychological consequences of therapeutic abortion", *British Journal of Psychiatry*, 1992, 160, pp. 742-749.

Zuccaro, Cataldo, *Bioetica e valori nel postmoderno. In dialogo con la cultura liberale*, Brescia, 2003.

Index

Abbà, Giuseppe 96
Abelard, Petrus 112
abortion pill 47-48, 65, 284, 340
abortion rate 51-54, 61-64, 68
Abortion Recovery Care & Helpline 301
adoption 40, 50, 75-76, 97, 158, 201, 248, 276, 304-306, 313-314, 338, 340
Alton, David 72
ambivalence and pregnancy 123, 127, 137-138, 154, 162-166, 170, 315, 321-322,
American Psychological Association, Task Force on Mental Health and Abortion (APA TFMHA) 116-117, 119, 130, 136
Amery, Fran 80
Ancel, Pierre-Yves 142
Andorno, Roberto 188
Antoninus of Florence 270
Aquinas, Thomas 96, 208, 269, 290, 295, 326-327
Arendt, Hannah 223-224
Aristotle 102-104, 203, 205-207, 212, 220-221, 259, 269
Ashley, Benedict 207-208, 215
Augustine 112, 223, 265-267
authenticity 170, 218, 236, 238, 247

Baer, Karl Ernst von 206, 337
Bagchus, Lotje 307
Bankole, Akinrinola, 159
baptism 266-267, 293
Barnabas 263
Baroncini, Basti 169-170
Barry, William 316
Basil of Caesarea 267
Beauvoir, Simone de 84, 91, 345
Beers, Brigitta van 196
Bellieni, Carlo 116, 127
Benagiano, Giuseppe 44
Benedict XVI 25, 267
Benso, Sylvia 238
Berg, Matthijs van den 241
Bernard of Clairvaux 112
Bérubé, Jocelyn 172

Bhadoria, Ajeet 150
Bhattacharya, Siladytia 141, 143
Bianchi-Demicheli, Francesco 172-173
Birmingham, Peg 223
Bisschoppen van Nederland 280-281
Blier Blaymore, Jo Ann 225
Böckle, Franz 106, 180
Boonin, David 229-230
Bos, Pien 305
Bourassa, Dominique 172
Bradshaw, Zoë 173
Brannen, Julia 192
Breeze, Andrew 244
breast cancer and abortion 144-151, 324
Brewster, David 147-148
Brind, Joel 144, 146-147
Brody, Baruch 179
Broek, Angela van den 59
Broen, Anne 121
Brooke, Stephen 85
Bruce, Fiona 29, 73
Budgeon, Shelley 91
Buonocore, Giuseppe 116, 127
Burrowes, David 73

Calhoun, Byron 244
Callahan, Daniel 107, 285
Carroll, Patrick 148-149
categorical imperative 94, 98
Catholic Archbishops of Great Britain 286
Catholic Bishops' Conference of England and Wales 280, 282
Catholic Bishops of Great Britain, Joint Committee on Bioethical Issues 287, 324-325
Ceder, Don 41
Cense, Marianne 307
chlamydia and other STI's 68, 153, 176, 307-308
clandestine abortions 47-48, 71
Clement of Alexandria 263
Coker, Ann 131
Coleman, Priscilla 117, 121, 123, 140, 172

conjoined twins 208
Congregation for the Doctrine of the Faith 279, 281-283, 287
Connolly, William 316
Conrad, Peter 15
conscience 21, 83, 109-114, 123, 131, 161, 251, 256, 281, 294-297, 331, 334, 338
conscientious objections 33, 38, 43, 50, 76, 113-114
consequentialism 22, 217, 228, 247, 283
conversion 135, 170, 236, 334
Corethics 72, 301
Council of Ancyra 264, 268
Council of Trulla 268
Council of Worms 268
Cour de cassation de la France 195-196
Curran, Charles 290-291

Daling, Janet 145
decision-making process 16, 20-23, 34, 41-45, 48-49, 74, 79-81, 83, 97-98, 102, 105, 111, 139, 162, 166, 170, 173-174, 176, 217-252, 254, 305, 311-313, 315, 317, 319, 324, 329, 339, 341
Deetman, Wim 275
Dekker, Jeroen, 275
Denbow, Jennifer 18, 98-99
Department of Health 33, 61-62, 67, 120, 302, 307, 339
Didachê, the 262-263
dignity, human 22, 25, 95-96, 99-100, 187-189, 197-199, 211, 231-233, 237, 245, 249-251, 255, 277, 282-283, 287-288, 324-326
dignity and human conscience 113, 294, 296, 313, 327, 332, 334
Di Nucci, Ezio 245
divorce rate 21, 54, 58, 288
Dixon, Rosalind 94, 100-101
Dorries, Nadine 38-39
double effect, principle of acts with, 34-35, 217, 231, 238-239, 249, 271
doubts and abortion 44, 76-77, 93, 99, 154-155, 160-162, 165, 167, 174, 247, 299, 312-314
Down's syndrome 55-56, 60, 76, 240-241, 243, 302, 321
Dworkin, Ronald 200, 210-211, 218

ectopic pregnancy 141, 151, 153, 209, 239, 251
Eeden, R. van 46
Eggink, Alex 243
Eijk, Willem 35, 187, 203, 205-207, 212
embryology 31, 36, 93, 167, 180-187, 193, 200-202, 204
emergency situation 32, 41-43, 71, 73-75, 162, 168, 174-176, 251, 286, 318, 339, 341
Emmerik, Arnold van 125
empiricism 105-107, 133, 179
Engelhardt, H. Tristram, 200, 210, 212
ensoulment 22, 200, 203, 205-209, 215, 269, 272, 281, 337
equality argument 223-226, 245-246, 326
ethical intention 14, 16, 24, 219-226
ethnicity and abortion 55, 59, 67-68, 70, 306
European Commission 199
European Commission of Human Rights 190, 192-194
European Court of Human Rights, 187, 194-197
European Parliament 199, 301

family planning 52-53, 63-66, 85, 109, 277, 279-280, 307
Family Planning Association 66
fatherhood 11, 33, 42, 44, 92, 102-103, 105-106, 137-139, 154, 157-158, 161, 167-170, 220-221, 300, 329-331, 340
feminism 17-18, 81, 83-86, 90-92, 175
Ferguson, Philip 225
Fergusson, David 123, 128-130, 140, 176
fertilisation 93, 182, 200-202, 205-208, 214, 237, 272
Festinger, Leon 161
Fichte, Johann 111-112
Fienus, Thomas 271-272
Finnis, John 23, 25, 115, 217, 228, 231, 235, 237-238
FIOM 303, 305

Fischer, Aart 89
Flake, Alan 243
Flannery, Kevin 204
Flavius Josephus 260-261
foetal pain 38, 185-187, 222
foetal viability 41, 101, 180-182, 185, 189, 249
Ford, Norman 216
foster care 76, 97, 201, 276, 304-306, 314, 318, 338
Fostering Network 305
Francis 25, 285-286, 292
Francome, Colin 52
freedom 16-17, 19-21, 24, 26, 77, 90-91, 95-96, 104, 110-111, 115, 175-176, 209, 219, 223-224, 233, 250, 253-254, 279, 288, 303, 317-318, 338
Friedan, Betty 85-86
friendship 26, 220-221, 235, 238, 254
Fukuyama, Francis 21, 288
future of value argument 214, 217, 228-231, 237, 245, 286, 328, 340-341

Galvão, Pedro 229-230
Gastmans, Chris 324
General Congregation n. 35 of the Society of Jesus 25
general practitioner, role of 33, 44-45, 68, 78, 80, 155, 165, 172
Giannakoulopoulos, Xenophon 185-186
Gilchrist, Anne 127
Girma, Sourafel 63-64
Gissler, Mika 151
Goldacre, Ben 147
Green, Josephine 242
Gregory IX 268
Gregory XIV 270
Grisez, Germain 23-24, 217, 227, 237-238, 256, 271
Guenther, Lisa 237

Habermas, Jürgen 244-245
Hajian-Tilaki, K.O. 150
Hamama, Lydia 125
Hanna, D.R. 136
Harries, Richard 269

Haviland, M.G 164
Health Care Inspectorate 48, 56, 59, 77
heart, Biblical meaning of 294-295
Hegel, Georg W.F. 21
Heijst, Annelies van 275-276
Henderson, Katherine DeLellis 148-149
Henshaw, Richard 122
Hermans, Chris 26
hermeneutics 21, 26, 107, 219, 297
Hess, Rosanna 126, 134, 136-137
Hilhorst, Marieke 275
Hill, Clifford 54
Hill, Thomas 94
Hoekstra, R.E. 38
Honein, Margaret 140
House of Commons 36, 39, 73, 80, 202
House of Commons Education Committee 307
House of Commons Science and Technology Committee 36-38, 72, 185
House of Lords 31, 34-35, 38, 72, 272, 311
House of Lords Select Committee on Stem Cell Research 311
Houston, Helen 152
Howe, Earl 72
Howe, Holly 146
Huang, Yubei 150
Hursthouse, Rosalind 328-329
Husfeldt, Charlotte 161
Husserl, Edmund 19

Ignatius of Loyola 316
infertility 36, 45, 151, 200, 202
interdisciplinary research 14, 26, 29, 139
International Theological Commission 267
In vitro fertilisation 202, 207
Islam and abortion 124, 311
Ivens, Michael 316

Jabeen, Suraiya 150
Jacob-Hargot, Thérèse 291
Jacobs, Aletta 84, 91, 345
Jarvis Thompson, Judith 18, 85, 94, 107-108, 285
Jerome 264-265
John Paul II 14, 24, 257, 279, 283-285, 288-

290
Jones, David 268, 269, 272
justice 20, 22, 90, 100, 220-221, 223-226, 233-235, 237-238, 251, 279, 326, 338

Kaczor, Christopher 101, 114, 180, 182, 185-186
Kant, Immanuel 16, 18, 22, 83, 94-100, 104, 232
Keown, John 80
Kero, Anneli 123, 131-133, 161
Ketting, E. 44-45
Kirby, Douglas 308-309
Kirkman, Maggie 159
Klemetti, Reija 141-143
Koch-Hershenov, Rose 207-208, 215
Komonchak, Joseph 280
Kooten, Maartje van 120
Korenromp, Marijke 126, 246
Kraaykamp, Gerbert 87
Kroelinger, Charlan 168

Laar-Jochemsen, Tirza van 78, 119
LaFollette, Hugh 248
Lanfranchi, Angela 144
Lauzon, Pierre 138
Lederman, Regina 154
Lee, Ellie 53, 72, 79
Lee, Patrick 109, 183
Leget, Carlo 232, 323
Levels, Mark 68-69, 226-227, 344
Levinas, Emmanuel 219, 221, 235-237
Levine, Phillip 69-70
LIFE 300-301, 306, 338, 340
Liguori, Alphonsus de 296
Lipp, Allyson 136
Lonergan, Bernard 105, 134, 170, 179
Lugo, Joannis De 271
Lynch, Ami 90-91

MacIntyre, Alasdair 248, 327-328
Major, Brenda 116, 121, 136
Makdoembaks, Nizaar 68, 330-331
Marquis, Don 211, 217, 228-230, 245
marriage rate 21, 54-55, 58, 63, 288
Marteau, Theresa 320

maternal mortality 151-153
Maughan, Barbara 304
McClellan, Jon 164
McLeod, Hugh 274
McMahan, Jeff 200, 210, 214
Mealey, Ann Marie 218-219
medicalization 15, 17, 30, 79-81, 239-245, 319, 324
Medoff, Marshall 69
Melina, Livio 111, 295
mental health problems after abortion 115-117, 124-130, 136-140, 172, 176, 313, 331, 341
metaphysical concept of personality 22, 182, 199-200, 208, 215, 234-235, 237, 312
Michels, Karin 148
Miller, Paula Jean 289
Ministry of Foreign Affairs 65
Modi, Neena 185
Mohangoo, A. 60
monozygotic twinning 22, 182, 200, 203-205, 207-208, 215-216
moral theology 11, 24-26, 110, 112, 252-253, 256, 271
Movimento per la vita italiano 318
Mühlemann, Kathrin 143

Nakamura, Katrina 209
National Collaborating Centre for Mental Health 116, 120
National Conference of State Legislatures 249
National Health Service 33, 39, 66, 136, 212
Nationale Raad voor Liturgie 293
natural family planning 201, 277, 291
natural law 15, 20, 23-25, 34, 228, 231, 238, 277-278, 291, 338
Nichols, Vincent 309-310
Nietzsche, Friedrich 3
non-directive counselling 76-77, 320-322
Noonan, John 256-257, 260, 262, 290-291
nursing and abortion 33, 38, 43, 47, 50, 76, 113, 136, 160, 292-293, 322-324, 340
Nussbaum, Martha 18, 83, 94, 99-101

Office for Standards in Education, Children's Services and Skills 306
'One of us' federation 199
O'Reilly, Monica 76

palliative care 239-240, 244, 322-323
Parens, Erik 225, 246
parental consent 42, 64, 74
pastoral care and abortion 44, 289, 293, 311-315, 318-319, 328, 331-335, 339
Paton, David 12, 63-64, 307
Paul VI 277-281, 289-290
Petersen, Peter 133, 139, 160, 167-168, 332
phenomenology 19, 22, 110, 134, 136, 208-209, 217, 219-226, 323-324
Philo of Alexandria 260-261
Pius IX 271
Pius XI 273
Pius XII 273
post-traumatic stress disorder 125-126, 136, 164, 174, 331
potentiality argument 101, 181, 195, 200, 203, 212-214, 237
prenatal care 31, 189, 243, 312, 324
prenatal diagnosis 17, 42, 50-51, 55, 59, 76, 225, 239-245, 247, 286-288, 319-326, 332, 337, 339
preterm birth 37, 140-143, 176, 243
ProLife Alliance 72, 302
pro-life organizations 12, 25, 29, 36, 40, 72, 120, 135, 302-306, 318, 333
psychiatric indication and abortion 127-128, 138-139, 152, 176
public opinion and abortion 49-50, 74, 83, 87-88

Rager, Günther 181
rape and abortion 31, 131, 286
Rawls, John 22, 217, 233-235, 237, 312
reconciliation 12, 134, 136, 166, 267, 291-292, 331, 333-334
Reardon, David 127-128, 152
Reeves, Gillian 148
Reichlin, Massimo 212-214
relationship problems after abortion 15, 172-174

relationship problems before abortion 15, 18, 153, 157-160, 172-173
Rhonheimer, Martin 96
Ricoeur, Paul 13-17, 19-24, 102-104, 115, 177-179, 217-224, 226, 245, 251, 253-256
right to life 22, 187-199, 212, 229-230, 251, 284-285
Rodriguez, Ned 164
Rothhaar, Markus 231
Rousseau, Jean-Jacques 111-112
Royal College of Obstetricians and Gynaecologists 13, 33, 114, 150, 185
Rozendal, Diny 319, 325
Rzepka, Jane 313, 315

Savulescu, Julian 179, 182
Schinkel, Anders 113-114
Second Vatican Council 25, 256, 276-277, 283, 296, 337-338
sex and relationships education 306-310, 338
sex-selective abortion 73, 75, 279-280
sexual abuse 68, 70, 76, 91, 164-165, 174, 275, 330
Siddiqui, Anver 163-164
Silence No More Awareness 301-302
Singer, Peter 182
Siriz 302-303, 306, 340
Sixtus V 270
Slade, Pauline 122, 124, 173
Slagboom, Maarten 247
Smart, Ninian 332
Smit, Joke 86, 91
Smith, Barry 208
Smith, Janet 280
Smits, Pieter 188-193
Society for the Protection of the Unborn Child 301
Söderberg, Hanna 137
Spaemann, Robert 200, 215-216, 237, 250, 285
Speckhard, Anne 137-138
spina bifida 60, 241, 243, 321
spontaneous abortion 18, 125, 145, 148, 151, 200, 203, 209-210

Steel, David 71, 74, 80, 88
Steinberg, Julia 130-131
Steinbock, Bonny 210-211
Stirezo Pro Life 303
Stopes, Marie 84, 91
Strong, Carson 230, 245
Stubblefield, Phillip 46
suicidal ideation and abortion 127, 129, 144, 151-152, 176
Sulmasy, Daniel 231-233
Sumner, L. 186

Tang, Mei-Zu 146
Taylor, Charles 218, 236-237
teenage pregnancy 34, 49, 53, 55, 58, 63-64, 69-70, 91, 97, 300, 304, 306-307, 309, 330, 340
Tertullian 263-265
theology of the body 289-290
Thorp, John 116, 129, 143-144
Tillich, Paul 113
Timon 304

ultrasound scan 60, 70, 163, 185, 228, 240-241
UNICEF 61-62
United Nations Educational, Social and Cultural Organization 188-189
United States Conference of Catholic Bishops 286
Universal Declaration of Human Rights 187-189, 273
Universal Declaration on Bioethics and Human Rights 188-189
universality 21-23, 251, 253, 255

Vanwesenbeeck, Ine 308
Veenhoven, Ruut 87
Velleman, David 18, 98
Ven, Johannes van der 26
Vermeulen, Ben 113
Verpleegkundigen en Verzorgenden Nederland, Commissie Ethiek 43
virtue ethics 326-328, 338
Visser, Mechteld 40, 46, 48-49, 59, 68, 77, 79, 122-123, 155-162, 166, 311, 313, 343
violence and abortion 44, 131, 151-152, 171-172, 174, 262, 305, 318

Wade, Francis 212-213
Walker, Rebecca 90
Wallin Lundell, Inger 126
Walser, Robyn 165
Warnock, Mary 200-203, 212-213
Weber, Max 21
Wellings, Kaye 55, 63
Wiebe, Ellen 124
Wilkinson, Paul 64
Williams, Clare 321
Wils, Jean-Pierre 96
'wrongful birth' claims 245, 320
Wulf, Mariéle 20, 111, 213, 250, 254, 282, 354

Wyldes, Mike 56